Founding Fathers

Founding Fathers

The Puritans in England and America

John Adair

BAKER BOOK HOUSE

Grand Rapids, Michigan 49506

PHOTOLITHOPRINTED BY CUSHING - MALLOY, INC.
ANN ARBOR, MICHIGAN, UNITED STATES OF AMERICA

Contents

List of Illustrations   ix
Foreword   xi
Prelude: A Voyage to America   1

 1 To the Fountains   24
 2 Some Early English Protestants   57
 3 The Fatal Storm   75
 4 Elizabethan Puritans   84
 5 God's Pathfinders   105
 6 'This Wanton Heart of Ours'   127
 7 The Prelude   141
 8 America: Land of Promise   163
 9 This War Without an Enemy   180
10 A Confusion Called a Commonwealth   207
11 Dear New England, Dearest Land To Me!   239
12 The Puritan Within Us   265

Suggestions for further reading   286
Index   299

72373

For Thea, Katharine and James

List of Illustrations

Between pages 148–9

1   Sir Richard Saltonstall [Peabody Museum, Salem, Massachusetts]
2   The burning of Master Laurence Saunders [Mansell Collection, London]
3   Puritans in New England [BBC Hulton Picture Library]
4   An Indian brave [Mansell Collection, London]
5   Sir John Eliot [By kind permission of the Lord Eliot]
6   Sir William Waller [By kind permission of Mrs C Gascoigne, Stanton Harcourt, Oxon]
7   John Winthrop [American Antiquarian Society, Worcester, Massachusetts]
8   John Winthrop the Younger [Photograph courtesy of the Massachusetts Historical Society, Boston, Massachusetts. Copy Photographer: Stephen J Kovacik]
9   The Chapel of Littlecote House, Berkshire [By permission of Mr D S Wills]
10 A Puritan schoolboy [The Simon Carter Gallery, Woodbridge, Suffolk]
11 Edward Winslow [Pilgrim Society, Plymouth, Massachusetts]
12 William Pynchon [Courtesy of the Essex Institute, Salem, Massachusetts]
13 Hugh Peter [By permission of the President and Fellows of Queens' College, Cambridge. All rights reserved]

Foreword

Anyone seeking to understand the Puritans has to free his mind at the outset from two popular misconceptions. One is the assumption that the Puritans were primarily strict and dour moralists, kill-joys and even hypocrites. This is one modern sense of the word, but to read it back into history is an error. In fact 'Puritan' was originally one of several names applied by contemporary critics and enemies to 'the hotter sort of Protestants'. Hence the other misconception – that a body of distinctive Puritan doctrines existed which distinguishes them from other Protestants – is equally fallacious. 'Puritanism' covers a spectrum of beliefs which stems from Luther and the Reformation.

My primary purpose in this book is to tell the story of the Puritans from the beginning to the end. As it develops, that story becomes an epic, with the foundation of New England and the English Civil War as the double climax. Then come the years of dissension and decline. Only by grasping the beginnings of Puritanism clearly can we understand this end. For the seeds of its future lay in the ground long before men coined the name 'Puritan'.

Over the sweep of two centuries several broad themes have emerged. One concerns the complex relationship of the Renaissance and Reformation. These two young parents gave birth to the English Puritans among their other progeny. Over the years they developed and spread their wings in such ways as to put intolerable strains on their marriage and their children. Another theme concerns the relation of the Puritans to the English nation as a whole. It seeks to answer the question why the Puritans both succeeded and failed in the spiritual, intellectual, social and political leadership they felt called by God to provide to England's people, both at home and beyond the Atlantic.

There has been a natural tendency in historians to emphasize the uniqueness of the Puritans in order to guard us against making them in our own image. But this distancing of people from us in history can be overdone. After all, the Puritans also lived in a tumultuous century. They faced the same human crises as we do: birth, marriage, illness and misfortune, success and prosperity, partings and bereavements, old age and death. Indeed, the human predicament today has more in common with the Puritan understanding of it than at any other time in the last three centuries. How can man live by the lights of conscience and humanity in a world which is governed in part by stark determinism? How can he preserve his freedom in a world in which nations are divided into two hostile blocs, with a future that threatens an Armageddon more frightful than a millenarian imagination could ever paint? In this context, the Puritan view of man and the grounds of his hope may strike us as both deeper and more realistic than the facile optimism of recent generations.

The Puritan ladies, who excelled at needlework, made the most exquisite patchwork quilts to keep their beds warm in the long, cold New England winters. Although this book may seem to be no more than a loosely connected patchwork of individual stories within the framework of a general narrative, I hope that the reader will discern the unifying theme of the growth of the Puritan pattern of values in relation to their beliefs. For in a sense the book is about us all. For those values, cut off by the mysterious processes of secularization from their religious roots, became the moral framework of northern European and American civilization. Thus we are all, in varying degrees, heirs to the Puritan tradition. The Puritans in these pages – or at least their digested values – still live inside us. In that sense the book is about ourselves, our present and our future as a civilization.

PRELUDE

A Voyage to America

On Saturday, 22 March 1630, John Winthrop awoke early in his lodgings at Southampton. For a week or more he had awaited impatiently the arrival of the ships that would take him and his company of Puritan emigrants to New England. That morning Winthrop wrote in haste to his eldest son with the welcome news that 'we are now going to the ship, under the comfort of the Lord's gracious protection and good providence'.

Later that day, after his ship the *Arbella* had come down river, crossed the Solent and anchored off Cowes on the Isle of Wight, he added to the same letter that they were preparing to set sail for America that very night. 'The Lord in mercy send us a prosperous voyage. Farewell, my dear son. The Lord bless you and all my children and friends. Commend me to them all, as if I named them; for I am in great straits of leisure.' In another letter to his wife Margaret, at home with the younger children at Groton Manor in Suffolk, he exhorted her to 'be comfortable and trust in the Lord, my dear wife, pray, pray. He is our God and Father; we are in covenant with him, and he will not cast us off. So, this once more, I kiss and embrace you and all my children'.

The *Arbella* was the flagship of a fleet of eleven ships chartered by the Massachusetts Bay Company to sail from Southampton to New England that spring. About 700 emigrants crowded into the passenger ships, while 240 cows and 60 horses stood tethered below decks on the two transports. Two more ships, with another 220 settlers, would sail independently from Plymouth and Bristol. By contrast, ten years earlier, the *Mayflower* had carried a mere hundred or so landsmen. By the end of 1630 a total of seventeen ships would have crossed the Atlantic to the new colony of Massachusetts Bay, carrying the largest migration that England had yet seen in one year.

As Winthrop said, he was extremely busy throughout that Saturday in March and indeed for many days previously. For the shareholders of the Massachusetts Bay Company had elected him

1

their Governor in the previous October. They chose Winthrop, a man of 'integrity and sufficiency', because they judged him 'as being one every way well fitted and accomplished for the place of Governor'. Yet the 'extraordinary great commendations' upon which their choice of this new recruit was largely based must have been from friends who sensed his potential. For Winthrop, aged about forty-one, was untried as a leader. He had held no military or naval command. He had gained some experience running a small estate in Suffolk, and he had served as a justice of the peace in that county and had had some legal training. He possessed a measure of natural authority from his social rank as a gentleman. But above all, he was sustained by a sense that God had called him to be the Governor. Moreover the Company's Charter, the legal source of his authority, travelled with him in the *Arbella*. Like the Ark of the Covenant to the ancient Israelites it symbolized for the Puritan emigrants to the Bay Colony that the powers of government were moving with them from London to New England. They could create a nation.

The Charter placed the government of the new colony in the hands of the Governor, his Deputy and a group of other magistrates known as Assistants, who were also elected annually by the freemen of the Company meeting in General Court. Three other men had been nominated for the office of Governor at the time of Winthrop's election: John Humphrey, Isaac Johnson and Sir Richard Saltonstall. Humphrey became Deputy Governor and the other two were chosen to be Assistants. As Humphrey later decided not to go to New England, Thomas Dudley was chosen in his place. Dudley, Johnson and Saltonstall all sailed on the *Arbella*. Indeed the ship had been renamed in honour of Johnson's wife, the Lady Arbella, a sister of the Earl of Lincoln. With considerable courage she had resolved to accompany her husband. Saltonstall, a widower, had five of his six children on board with him: Richard 19 years of age, Rosamund 17, Samuel 15, Robert 12 and Grace 8. He left 10-year-old Henry at home, possibly because he was sickly. Winthrop had three sons aboard with him. Henry, the eldest, was Winthrop's second son by his first wife. He had proved to be something of a 'ne'er-do-well' and embarked with his father to begin a new life in America, leaving a pregnant wife at home with his mother at Groton. Alas, tragedy awaited him at the end of the voyage.

Hopes that the ship would sail that Saturday night were dashed as the wind shifted to another direction. For a week the *Arbella* tossed at anchor off Cowes. For the children it was an exciting time as they explored the ship, a large one of 350 tons, and made the acquaintance of the more friendly sailors among the crew of 52 men. They explained the rigging aloft and told the boys about the working of the 28 brass cannon on the gun deck. Winthrop could calm Margaret's natural anxieties by assuring her in a letter that her sons Stephen and Adam 'are well and cheerful, and have no mind for home. They lie both with me, and sleep as soundly in a rug (for we use no sheets here) as ever they did at Groton; and so I do myself (I praise God)'.

Winthrop and his companions would have known what to expect in their life on board ship, for they would undoubtedly have read the published account of Francis Higginson, a minister from Leicester, who had made the voyage in the *Talbot* the previous year. Three editions of his *True Relation of the Last Voyage to New England* appeared in 1630, the first in time for Winthrop to buy it at the Sign of the Blue Bible in Green Arbor, London. Higginson painted some graphic pictures of the storms and hazards that lay ahead of them on the 'tossing waves of the western sea'. But the winds that caused the *Talbot* to dance in the spring of 1629 were strangely absent a year later. Day followed day as the *Arbella* swung at anchor.

They were waiting for a west wind, but on Monday 29 March the wind at last shifted and blew from the north, which was sufficient to set them on their way. The seamen heaved at the windlass pulling up the heavy anchor, singing a shanty as they tramped around, and then swarmed aloft like monkeys to break out the sails. Similar preparations could be seen on board the *Ambrose*, *Jewel* and *Talbot*, which had come down from Southampton to join them. Again Winthrop felt that the awful hour of separation from home was upon him. In the privacy of his cabin he finished a long and loving letter to Elizabeth, reminding her of their agreement to meet 'in spirit' on Mondays and Fridays at five o'clock in the evening. Yet the blustering wind carried them only as far as Yarmouth, some ten miles west along the coast of the Isle of Wight, before Captain Milborne ordered the sails to be furled again and the anchor dropped. Two Dutch ships which ventured beyond the Needles into the open sea were battered by storm waves and forced to put back.

Winthrop wrote again to Margaret with this news. Far from complaining, he saw in these events the need to praise, for the hand of providence could be seen at work. Like all Puritans, Winthrop believed that God was in control of nature and history, and that all things are working together for the good of those who love Him. Ten days of inaction, cooped up together on board ship, may have frayed the tempers of less religious people. Yet Winthrop could report to his wife that the two sabbaths aboard had passed 'very comfortably (God be praised) and we are daily more and more encouraged to look for the Lord's presence to go along with us'. A child or two on the *Talbot* had been taken sick with measles, but nothing worse had befallen the company.

On Saturday 3 April, a fortnight after coming aboard the *Arbella*, Winthrop wrote again to Margaret while opportunity still presented itself, for 'if the wind turn we shall soon be gone'. With little to do now that everyone was in their ship and all the stores roped down in the holds, Winthrop felt marvellously free. Moreover, the sea air had improved the physical health of the passengers. 'As for me,' he assured her, 'I was never more at liberty of body and mind these many years.'

His burden as leader of the small community had been much eased by the helpful and sympathetic attitude of the ship's master, Captain Peter Milborne. The relationship between Puritan emigrants and the crews of their ships could be troublesome. The sailors swore oaths and behaved in ways which offended the Puritans' consciences while their officers could often place their own commercial advantage or safety above the interests of the passengers. Thus Winthrop found it cause to thank God for bringing Captain Milborne's heart 'to afford us all good respect and to join with us in every good action. Yesterday he caused his seamen to keep a fast with us, wherein the Lord assisted us and our minister very comfortably; and when five of the clock came,' he told his wife, 'I had respite to remember you in spirit before the Lord.'

Not all of the company aboard the *Arbella* and its sister ships were Puritans. Many of the farmers, yeoman, tradesmen and servants were drawn to America for worldly reasons, though they had accepted the government of the Massachusetts Bay Company. They ensured that Winthrop and his colleagues would not lack work as magistrates. After supper at the end of that Friday's fast they discovered 'some notorious lewd persons' who had seized the opportunity, while almost everyone else sat listening to the addresses of Mr Phillips, or kneeling in common prayer, to commit theft and other villanies, 'for which we caused them to be severely punished'. The Governor and Assistants intended to establish strict discipline from the start.

Next Tuesday morning a long boat brought Captain Burleigh to the side of the *Arbella*. Winthrop had just begun to keep a daily journal and he recorded the visit of this 'grave, comely gentleman of great age' who now served as Captain of Yarmouth Castle. In the days of Queen Elizabeth, when Sir Francis Drake and Sir Walter Raleigh had sailed the Atlantic, Burleigh had been a sea captain. He had many stories to tell his courteous listeners as they entertained him to a meal. The Spaniards had once captured him at sea and held him in prison for three years. Four ships in Sir Thomas Roe's expedition to explore the coast of Guiana in 1610 had been commanded by Burleigh and his three sons, he proudly told them. Winthrop had been born in Armada Year, when Burleigh had doubtless fought in the English fleet, and he must have been fascinated by the tales of this old man of the sea, a living link with the heroic days of the voyages of discovery and the war with Spain.

During Wednesday night a light breeze began to come from the east and north, and after dawn the white sails were let down on the topsail, top gallant and royal square yards, the spars slung horizontally across the three masts. Four hours later the *Arbella* slipped by the Needles, barely moving on a sea as still as a village pond. With lanterns glowing on the poop as navigational lights for the other vessels, the *Arbella* sailed in a freshening breeze and passed Portland Bill at dawn. The great adventure had at last begun.

*   *   *

'Sail astern! Sail astern!' shouted the lookout man, perched in the crow's nest high on the mainsail mast. As the morning sun arose he made out eight sails in the distance. England stood at war with Spain and these ships could be privateers from Dunkirk, a port in the Spanish Netherlands. As Captain Burleigh may have warned them, these lean sea-wolves had heard about the fleet bound for New England and had gathered to lurk as near the shipping lanes as their respect for the warships of King Charles would allow. Milborne gave orders to clear the *Arbella* for action. Sailors began taking down hammocks, stowing gear, loading and running out the cannon and filling the powder chests from the magazine. The landsmen were stationed among the seamen with swords and pistols at the ready, while 25 men with muskets took up their battle stations.

As the eight ships drew closer Milborne and his fellow captains aboard the *Ambrose*, *Jewel* and *Talbot* studied them carefully through their brass telescopes. The previous year the *Eagle* (as the *Arbella* was then named) had served as flagship to Sir Kenelm Digby's privateering fleet in the Mediterranean, and so Milborne was no stranger to warfare at sea. Not liking the silent menace of this unknown squadron they made ready for the worst contingency. Sailors dismantled some deck-huts, probably chicken and pig houses, which blocked the fields of fire. Anything inflammable, such as straw from mattresses, was thrown overboard. The captain took a cross bow and shot a ball of wild-fire a long way into the sea to test it. The women and children were ushered down below decks. None panicked. 'Our trust was in the Lord of Hosts; and the courage of our captain, and his care and diligence, did much encourage us,' wrote Winthrop. Milborne tacked about and stood to meet the supposed adversaries, only to discover that they were friends. As the ships passed they saluted each other with cannon and musket, 'and so (God be praised) our fear and danger was turned into mirth and friendly entertainment'. To complete this good day they saw two boats fishing in the channel and sent skiffs to buy their catch of fresh fish.

Beyond the Scilly Isles Winthrop in the *Arbella* caught sight of a Protestant Dutch privateer escorting home a Spanish prize taken off Brazil. Shortly afterwards the *Jewel* and *Ambrose* collided. Though neither ship was badly damaged the *Ambrose* dropped out of sight on the rest of the voyage. It was Sunday, but seasickness 'put us all out of order'; even Mr Phillips felt too ill to preach. Those well enough, under Winthrop's leadership, fetched out the children and others who lay groaning in the cabins. Having stretched a rope from the steerage along the deck to the mainmast 'we made them stand, some on one side and some on the other, and sway it up and down till they were warm, and by this means they soon grew well and merry'.

Late next day the Puritans experienced their first storm at sea. Higginson had written that such sea-storms were ordinary events in the Atlantic and, providing the captain had sufficient sea-room, there was little danger. But his confident words could hardly reassure the inexperienced landsmen huddled below decks as the waves began to pound against the oak plank ship sides only a few inches thick. As the wind howled and the rain lashed their faces, the seamen for their part went aloft to take in the topsail. They lowered the mainsail but the wind whipped the foresail to pieces. Waves dashed over the reeling deck, washing overboard the tub with the last of the fish catch. Black clouds obscured the full moon. Each ship took it in turn to set a lantern on the poop so they should not part company at night, and the *Jewel* carried the light now. But so great was the danger of losing or going foul of one another that Milborne hung out a light in his mizzen. Even so, before midnight the *Talbot* was lost to sight in the mountainous seas. Under these trying conditions the *Arbella* soon proved her sailing capacities by running before the wind with bare masts, save for a mainsail to give her steerage.

For three days and nights the storm raged. Captain Milborne, who had been below decks checking for leaks, was aghast when he saw the slovenly condition of the gun deck where the landsmen lodged. Many of the passengers had not gone up the steps into the fresh air for days, and the deck was foul with vomit, rotten victuals and excrement. Such 'beastliness', Milborne informed Winthrop, would endanger the health of the ship. Having prayed about the matter the Puritan leaders gave orders for four men to clean the deck for three days, and then four others to succeed them on a roster.

After the storm abated Captain Milborne again showed his practical understanding of human nature. Realizing that his passengers needed some relief he invited the masters of the two consort ships aboard for dinner by the signs of hanging out his flag and lowering his topsails. The white flag with its red cross would have reminded everyone that it was 23 April, the day of England's patron saint, St George.

As May Day approached the three Bay Company ships exchanged salutes with two English vessels bound for Canada, a small break in the monotony as one grey day at sea followed another. Boredom led to trouble. Two young men fought each other, flouting the rules of conduct for the voyage that Winthrop and the Assistants had published at Southampton. They received the mild punishment of walking on deck until night with their hands bound behind them. Another man, 'for using contemptuous speeches in our presence', was laid in iron fetters until he promised open confession of his offence.

As the days passed Winthrop and his fellow magistrates found themselves called upon to deal with similar offences, which they did with firmness and humanity. Milborne could not have been more helpful. When complaint was made to him of some injury that one of the under officers of the ship had done to one of the landsmen, the captain commanded the culprit to be tied up by the hands and a weight to be hanged about his neck. Winthrop interceded on the man's behalf and with some difficulty persuaded the captain to remit the punishment.

Sometimes providence supplied the appropriate punishment. A sailor, 'a most prophane fellow', died in the *Jewel*. On Higginson's voyage another mariner, a notoriously wicked fellow who had boasted of getting a wench with child before leaving England, caused a nuisance by swearing, mocking the fast-days, as well as 'railing and jesting against Puritans'. He fell sick of smallpox died. A maid servant in the *Arbella*, being seasick, drank so much rum that she was senseless and almost died. 'We observed it a common fault in our young people', noted Winthrop, 'that they gave themselves to drink hot waters very immoderately.' It is interesting that the Puritan leaders do not seem to have tried to add further punishment in this case of excessive drinking, although drunkenness was abhorrent to their religion.

Winthrop had leisure to observe natural phenomena. He knew some astronomy, for he wrote about the Pole Star's different 'declination', a technical term for its angular distance north or south from the celestial equator. The new moon, when it first appeared, was much smaller than at any time he had seen it in England. Although several hundred miles from land they saw birds on the Atlantic waves. Whichever way the wind blew it was definitely colder: the sun did not give out as much heat as in England. On Saturday 8 May they saw their first whale.

The previous year Higginson, while 'sitting at my study on the ship's poop', had observed bonito fish and porpoises, great jelly-fish and a grampus fish, a blowing, spouting dolphin-like creature. He also saw 'a mountain of ice, shining as white as snow'. Sights of Biblical monsters such as the leviathan whales who inhabited 'the greatest sea in the world' seemed to Higginson to be one of the rewards of travel. 'Those that love their own chimney-corner and dare not go beyond their own town's end, shall never have the honour to see these wonderful works of Almighty God.'

The sea around the *Arbella* and her consorts sometimes appeared to the landsmen like a flat meadow, while at others it wore a terrible countenance, breaking into high white-crested hills and deep valleys. For storms again assailed the three ships, now about half way across the Atlantic. During the worst night the sail attached to a yard under the bowsprit was ripped to shreds. It was 'a great mercy of God' that it did split, for otherwise it would have endangered the breaking of the bowsprit and topmasts, which in the absence of an east wind would have meant returning to England.

*   *   *

In mid-voyage Winthrop delivered a lay sermon in which he shared his vision for New England with his fellow passengers. It bears the title 'Christian Charity: A Model Hereof'. Winthrop began with a spiritual and rational defence of the fact that 'God Almighty in his most holy and wise providence has so disposed of the condition of mankind as in all times some must be rich, some poor, some high and eminent in power and dignity, others mean and in subjection.' God is glorified by the variety and difference of his creatures. Such an order allows more opportunity for manifesting complementary spiritual qualities. Lastly, it means that every man has need of another, so 'they might be all knit more nearly together in the bond of brotherly affection'.

It was the spirit of Christ, the spirit of love, which would knit together a truly Christian society. But if they neglected to observe the articles of their covenant with God then they would certainly incur divine wrath. 'Now the only way to avoid this shipwreck and to provide for our posterity is to follow the counsel of Micah: to do justly, to love mercy, to walk humbly with our God,' said Winthrop.

> For this end we must be knit together in this work as one man; we must entertain each other in brotherly affection; we must be willing to abridge ourselves of our superfluities for the supply of others' necessities; we must uphold a familiar commerce together in all meekness, gentleness, patience, and liberality; we must delight in each other, make others' conditions our own, rejoice together, mourn together, labor and suffer together always having before our eyes our commission and community in the work, our community as members of the same body, so shall we keep the unity of the spirit in the bond of peace.

As the *Arbella* sailed on Winthrop looked to the future. If only they could prove faithful in their venture, he said, then men would exclaim of succeeding plantations, 'The Lord make it like that of New England!' Surely their 'special overruling providence' had been given to them for this great purpose. 'For we must consider that we shall be as a city upon a hill, the eyes of all people are upon us; so that if we shall deal falsely with our God in this work we have

9

undertaken and so cause Him to withdraw His present help from us, we shall be made a story and a byword through the world.' Thus a choice faced them – between life or death, good or evil. 'Therefore let us choose life,' Winthrop said in conclusion, 'that we and our seed may live by obeying His voice, and cleaving to Him, for He is our life and our prosperity.'

*   *   *

Early in June the three ships sailed into more thick fogs. In the great cabin Winthrop and his fellow Puritans held a fast on Friday and a thanksgiving on Saturday for they now knew they were near land. On Tuesday 8 June they sighted Mount Desert Island, which lies off the rocky coast of Maine. It was a pleasant, sunny day, and from the shore came the scents of an English garden. Higginson had seen 'yellow gilliflowers' amid the rockweed on the waves. He could also make out fields which were a carpet of flowers. Such sights had 'made us desirous to see our new paradise of New England' and doubtless Winthrop's company on the *Arbella* were seized by a similar excitement. A wild pigeon perched on the rigging of their ship. Sailing southwards they saw Cape Ann and hailed an English shallop putting out to fish on the Isle of Shoals. As the ship threaded its way through the islands towards their anchorage at Cape Ann they caught sight of the *Lion* and saluted her with two cannon. The *Lion* was one of the two ships that had sailed from the West Country ports.

Captain Milborne sent a skiff for the *Lion*'s master, Captain William Peirce. He then went ashore and sometime later returned with Captain Endecott, the Governor sent out by the Massachusetts Bay Company in September 1628 to start the colony. A Puritan contemporary described Endecott as a man of 'courage, undaunted, yet sociable, and of a cheerful spirit, loving and austere': in short, he was 'a fit instrument to begin this wilderness-work'. That afternoon Endecott led his successor ashore to the settlement he had established on a neck of land within a fine natural harbour. They still used the Indian name of *Nahumkeck* for this place, but later the Puritans called it Salem. About 350 colonists had arrived during the previous two years, joining the sparse population of planters, traders and fishermen already in the Bay, some of whom had withdrawn from the Puritan colony of New Plymouth in its southern corner. More than 200 of these settlers were in Salem and the remainder were at work establishing the town of Charlestown.

In July 1629 Salem consisted of ten wooden houses and some incomplete ones along a street leading up from the jetty to the higher ground of the peninsular. Here the great guns of the colony were placed, probably in a defensive work pointing inland to the menace of the dense forest inhabited by savage Indians. Besides the heavy ordnance, wrote Higginson, they had the additional safeguard of 'true religion and the ordinances of Almighty God taught among us' by plenty of preaching and diligent catechizing. Endecott had built himself a fair house and here he entertained the salt-stained travellers to a feast of venison and beer. Meanwhile the landsmen and their families on the *Arbella* went ashore and gorged themselves on the wild strawberries and gooseberries that grew in profusion on Cape Ann. At nightfall all the passengers, except a few ladies who remained in Salem, had boarded the ship again.

Next morning an Indian – a sagamore or chief of a clan of the Agawam tribe – and one of his men came aboard the *Arbella* and stayed all day. The landsmen must have crowded the ship's side as the pair paddled their canoe alongside. Higginson had described the members of this tribe as tall and strong, their tawny bodies naked but for deerskin cloaks over one shoulder and aprons before their 'privities'. Their black hair was cut in front like a gentleman's, with one lock longer than the rest, the origin, he thought, of a fashion he had observed in London. He believed they worshipped two gods: a good one called *Tantum* and an evil spirit *Squantum*. We neither fear them nor trust them, he had told his readers in England, for 40 musketeers will drive 500 Indians out of the field, but 'we use them kindly'. From the first Winthrop followed that simple policy.

That afternoon the *Jewel* arrived and anchored nearby. Next morning the sailors warped in the *Arbella* down a channel so narrow it could not tack to and fro. Against the wind the mariners manoeuvred the ship by attaching rope hawsers to bollards on land and pulling them in on their capstan. Eventually they came to anchor in the inner harbour. Winthrop and the other passengers disembarked while ropes and pulleys drew up their chests of possessions from the hold and deposited them into the waiting boats. As they looked back at the *Arbella* they saw the crew run out five cannon and fire a salute. Captain Milborne had paid his respects in the language of the sea to John Winthrop and his colleagues, whom he had come to admire and love.

*   *   *

There is a gap in Winthrop's journal until 17 June, for he was probably too busy to keep up his diary. That day Winthrop recorded that he went with a party southwards by boat from Salem to the Mystic River and sailed up it for about six miles searching for a suitable place for 'our sitting down'.

Thomas Dudley, the Deputy Governor, explains both Winthrop's silence and the expedition in a letter he wrote the following year to the Countess of Lincoln, whose husband the Earl he had once served as steward. Upon landing, he wrote, they found the colony in a 'sad and unexpected condition'. Since Higginson had penned his rosy account the previous summer some 80 people had died during the severe winter, out of a population only about 200 strong; many of the survivors were weak and sick, and little corn or bread remained for their hungry mouths. Salem 'pleased us not', but Dudley does not give their reasons. Hence their journey to the wide estuary where the Mystic and Charles rivers flowed into the Bay amid a confusing map of headlands and islands. Probably they favoured this area because it was more central in the lands granted them by charter.

Meanwhile the other ten ships that had set out from Southampton in the wake of the *Arbella* arrived off the New England coast. When Winthrop and his party returned to Salem they saw the *Ambrose* already at anchor there. On 1 July the *Mayflower* and *Whale* sailed into the harbour at Charlestown, their passengers in good health but most of the livestock dead, including a mare and stallion belonging to Winthrop. The *Talbot*, which reached them next day, had lost fourteen passengers. The *Hopewell*, *William and Francis*, *Trial* and *Success* straggled into haven during the next few days, with those on board reduced to near-starvation by the long passage. On Thursday 8 July the Puritans in the plantations kept a day of thanksgiving for their safe voyage across the great Atlantic sea.

*   *   *

Among those who had landed on the previous Thursday was Henry Winthrop, John's second son by his first wife. This 'sprightly and hopeful young gentleman' had intended to travel with his father in the *Arbella* but, with characteristic irresponsibility, he went ashore on the Isle of Wight and missed the boat back. The day after his arrival at Salem he went swimming in a small creek and was drowned. A week later, with a ship making ready for the voyage home, Winthrop wrote his first letter from America to Margaret. Together with Winthrop's daughter-in-law—'my dear daughter'—she was anxiously awaiting news at Groton Manor:

My dear Wife,
Blessed by the Lord, our good God and merciful Father, that yet has preserved me in life and health to salute you, and to comfort your longing heart with the joyful news of my welfare, and the welfare of your beloved children. We had a long and troublesome passage, but the Lord made it safe and easy to us; and though we have met with many and great troubles (as this bearer can certify thee) yet he has pleased to uphold us, and to give us hope of a happy issue. I am so overpressed with business, as I have no time for these or other mine own private occasions. I only write now, that you may know, that yet I live and am mindful of you in all my affairs. The larger discourse of all things you shalt receive from my brother Downing, which I must send by some of the last ships.

We have met with many sad and discomfortable things, as you shall hear after; and the Lord's hand hath been heavy upon myself in some very near to me. My son Henry! my son Henry! ah, poor child! Yet it grieves me much more for my dear daughter. The Lord strengthen and comfort her heart, to bear this cross patiently. I know you will not be wanting to her in this distress. Yet, for all these things (I praise my God) I am not discouraged; nor do I see cause to repent or despair of those good days here, which will make amends for all.

I shall expect you next summer (if the Lord please), and by that time I hope to be provided for your comfortable entertainment. My most sweet wife, be not disheartened; trust in the Lord, and you shall see his faithfulness. Commend me heartily to all our kind friends at Castleins, Groton Hall, Mr Leigh and his wife, my neighbour Cole, and all the rest of my neighbours and their wives, both rich and poor. Remember me to them at Assington Hall, and Codenham Hall, Mr Brand, Mr Alston, Mr Mott, and their wives, goodman Pond, Charles Neale, &c. The good Lord be with you and bless you and all our children and servants. Commend my love to them all. I kiss and embrace you, my dear wife, and all my children, and leave you in his arms, who is able to preserve you all, and to fulfil our joy in our happy meeting in his good time. Amen.
Your faithful husband,
JO. WINTHROP.
I shall write to my son John by London.

Writing to his eldest son a week later Winthrop dealt largely with business and family matters for John was acting as his agent and the needs of the colony pressed hard. Yet the tragic death of Henry was still upon his mind. 'It is like you shall hear (before this come to you) how the Lord hath disposed of your brother Henry. The Lord teach you and the rest by it to remember your Creator in the days of your youth, and to improve your time to his service while it lasts.' He closed the long letter with some reassuring words about their new country. Winthrop could discern little difference between it and England. Only two days had been hotter than those in Suffolk during the summer. 'Here is as good land as I have seen there, but none so bad as there. Here is sweet air, fair rivers and plenty of springs, and the water is better than England. Here can be no want of anything to those who bring means to raise out of the earth and sea. But people must come well provided and not in too large a number at any one time.'

'The Lord's hand had been very heavy upon our people in these parts,' wrote Winthrop to his son in August, but he accepted the calamities in a Christian spirit. A Puritan distinguished between secondary causes – the natural or historical reasons why things happened – and primary causes, which belonged to the spiritual realm dominated by God's will, often inscrutable but ever-to-be-trusted. Thus Winthrop can blame the infectious and mortal sickness in the colony upon the poor diet on board ship during the long crossing. 'Remember to bring juice of lemons to sea with you, for you and your company to eat with your meat as sauce,' he would remind Margaret before she sailed to join him. But the Lord's hand was also at work behind the scenes, chastising, purifying and pointing them unerringly to the sole purpose of their pilgrimage upon earth. On 9 September, in a letter heavy with more losses, John assured Margaret that he did not regret the decision to come to America:

> My dear Wife,
> The blessing of God all-sufficient be upon you and all my dear ones with you forever.
>   I praise the good Lord, though we see much mortality, sickness and trouble, yet (such is his mercy) myself and children, with most of my family, are yet living, and in health, and enjoy prosperity enough, if the afflictions of our brethren did not hold under the comfort of it. The Lady Arbella is dead, and good Mr Higginson, my servant, old Waters of Neyland, and many others. Thus the Lord is pleased still to humble us; yet he mixes so many mercies with his corrections, as we are persuaded he will not cast us off,

14

but, in his due time, will do us good, according to the measure of our afflictions. He stays but till he has purged our corruptions, and healed the hardness and error of our hearts, and stripped us of our vain confidence in this arm of flesh, that he may have us rely wholly upon himself.

The French ship, so long expected, and given for lost, is now come safe to us, about a fortnight since, having been twelve weeks at sea; and yet her passengers (being but few) all safe and well but one, and her goats but six living of eighteen. So as now we are somewhat refreshed with such goods and provisions as she brought, though much thereof has received damage by wet.

I praise God, we have many occasions of comfort here, and do hope that our days of affliction will soon have an end, and that the Lord will do us more good in the end than we could have expected, that will abundantly recompense for all the trouble we have endured. Yet we may not look at great things here. It is enough that we shall have heaven, though we should pass through hell to it. We here enjoy God and Jesus Christ. Is not this enough? What would we have more? I thank God, I like so well to be here, as I do not repent my coming; and if I were to come again, I would not have altered my course, though I had foreseen all these afflictions. I never fared better in my life, never slept better, never had more content of mind, which comes merely of the Lord's good hand; for we have not the like means of these comforts here, which we had in England. But the Lord is all-sufficient, blessed by his holy name. If he please, he can still uphold us in this estate; but, if he shall see good to make us partakers with others in more affliction, his will be done. He is our God, and may dispose of us as he sees good.

I am sorry to part with you so soon, seeing we meet so seldom, and my much business had made me too oft forget Mondays and Fridays. I long for the time when I may see your sweet face again, and the faces of my dear children. But I must break off, and desire you to commend me kindly to all my good friends, and excuse my not writing at this time. If God please once to settle me, I shall make amends. I will name now but such as are nearest to you, my broth. and sister Gostlin, Mr Leigh, etc. Castleins, my neighbour Cole and his good wife, with the rest of my good neighbours, tenants and servants. The good Lord bless you and all our children and family. So I kiss my sweet wife and my dear children, and rest

Thy faithful husband,

J. WINTHROP.

I would have written to Maplested, if I had time. You must excuse me, and remember me kindly to them all.

This is the third letter I have written to you from New England.

15

The servant who rode with this letter to the waiting ship would have seen the burnished leaves of autumn. For Winthrop and his company it was the first fall they had experienced in New England: the brilliant colours of the forest maples and beeches stood out among the sombre unchanging colours of the evergreens. Soon, though, the weather grew distinctly colder, and when Winthrop wrote again to Margaret in November he reported that death so far had claimed no less than twelve of his own 'family': Waters, his wife and two of his children; a kinsman, Mr Gager, and his man Smith of the village of Buxhall in Suffolk, together with his wife and two children, the wife of Taylor of Haverill, a market town in the same county, and their child; and 'my son H. makes the twelve'. In addition Jeffrey Ruggle of Sudbury and about twenty others from that town had died. Moreover, 'the Lord had stripped us of some principal persons', such as Mrs Phillips, whose husband had ministered to them so ably on the *Arbella*, Mr Rossiter and Mr Johnson.

Of the second of these two Assistants, Isaac Johnson, who died about a month after his wife Arbella, Winthrop wrote in his journal an epitaph which praises both his virtue and public spirit: 'He was a holy man, and wise, and died in sweet peace, leaving a good part of his substance to the colony.' Winthrop, however, at some later date scored out the word 'good' and substituted 'some': perhaps Johnson's will had not been as generous as his dying words had promised. Dudley, who may have been present at his deathbed, bears out Winthrop's testimony. Isaac Johnson, he wrote, was 'a prime man among us, having the best estate of any, zealous for religion and the greatest furtherer of this plantation. He made a mostly godly end, dying willingly, professing his life better spent promoting this plantation than it could have been any other way.' He was only twenty-nine.

The one thousand or more people who had arrived in the Company's fleet that year soon dispersed and set about building their homes in a handful of settlements in Massachusetts Bay. Winthrop and many others had already moved to Charlestown, a cluster of houses begun the year before on the north bank of the Charles River in the vicinity of a pallisaded and thatched house belonging to a blacksmith, Thomas Walford. Across the river they could see the three hilltops of the plateau on another peninsula which the Indians called Shawmut. A minister named William Blackstone lived like a hermit in a cottage with a garden and orchard on the southern slopes of this plateau. There is a solid tradition that

Isaac Johnson visited him there early that summer and first heard from him about 'an excellent spring there', a conversation which led to the founding of a town which in turn burgeoned into the great city of Boston.

Once over the river and in Blackstone's parlour, Johnson would have much to discuss with his host in what must have been an exciting reunion. For they had first met as freshmen in that great nursery of Puritans in the University of Cambridge, Emmanuel College. They had taken their degrees in the same year and received their ordination as deacons and ministers in the same diocese. Johnson had married Lady Arbella in 1623, thus uniting himself to the Puritan family that had founded the school where Blackstone had been educated and the scholarship which had provided for his education. Johnson may have told his friend of their fears in Charlestown that the poor water supply there had contributed to the sickness which still ravaged the small population. Perhaps he pressed Blackstone to come back with him and tell Winthrop about the spring and running fresh water on Shawmut. Certainly by early August a decision had been taken to found a town there, which they called first Trimountaine and then Boston. On 30 September, as he lay dying, Johnson asked to be buried in the lot he had chosen in Boston, adjacent to the land of his friend Blackstone. His corpse was the first to be interred in what is now the old King's Chapel burying ground.

Meanwhile other settlements had been founded in the vicinity of Boston harbour. About four miles from Charlestown, on the north bank of the Charles river, Sir Richard Saltonstall and his servants established Watertown, so called because of the profusion of springs and streams there. Another Assistant or magistrate, William Pynchon, founded Roxbury on a tributary of the Charles, about two miles south-west of Boston. Pynchon came from East Anglia and was one of the original 'undertakers' or patentees. For his portrait, which hangs today in Salem, he wore a close-fitting, black skull-cap, a wide, white collar and a long, black coat studded with silver buttons. Other settlers built the first houses at Medford on the Mystic river and at Lynn, midway between Boston and Salem just north of the Saugus river. The men from the western counties of England built Dorchester, four miles south of Boston, in a bay where the Neponset river flows into the sea.

'This dispersion troubled some of us', wrote Thomas Dudley, not least because rumours of an impending French attack had reached their ears. In December Winthrop and most of the Assistants met at Roxbury and there agreed to build a fortified town upon the neck of land between there and Boston, but that idea fell through, not least because the proposed site lacked running water. A fortnight later they talked again at Watertown and inspected a place a mile down river and agreed that it would be a fit site for their fortified town. Eventually they decided to start building Newtown there next spring. Some years later they would change the name to Cambridge.

*   *   *

'He is desirous to come, but saith he cannot be absent two hours.' So Winthrop replied to an invitation from Dr Samuel Fuller to visit Plymouth. Endecott had already established good relations with the 'Plymotheans'. When infectious fever and scurvy had hit the Salem settlement in the winter of 1629 Governor William Bradford of Plymouth had sent their physician – his brother-in-law Fuller – to let blood and prescribe medicines. Looking to first causes he saw it as essential 'to pacify the Lord's wrath'. After getting to know Endecott the Puritan physician could describe him to Bradford simply as 'my dear friend and a friend to us all'. Perhaps Fuller's spiritual conversation helped Endecott in his hour of bereavement, for his wife succumbed that winter to the raging illness. Like many Puritans, however, Endecott had no relish for the single state. Within a year he had married again.

The two friends had discussed in full the vexed and central question of how the church should be ordered in Massachusetts Bay. Officially the leaders of the colonizing enterprise there still denied being separatists or 'Brownists', so named after one of the early advocates of the view that Puritans should tarry no longer for the Church of England to complete its reformation but set up their own independent congregations. The Leyden congregation of John Robinson, which had supplied the Puritan core of the *Mayflower*'s passengers in 1620, was such a group. Winthrop and company remained in nominal wedlock with the English Church 'by law established', although in reality the relation had become threadbare. The bonds which held them were fashioned more of sentiment than conviction. They had no intention of establishing bishoprics in New England or allowing the rites and ceremonies of the Book of Common Prayer in the plantations. Indeed Endecott soon shipped home two lawyers, the brothers Browne, who had innocently begun holding services according to Queen Elizabeth's Prayer Book while protesting against the 'rash innovations' they saw in the Salem church. Endecott had seen eye-to-eye with the Plymouth brethren on such matters. 'I acknowledge myself much bound to you for your kind love and care', he wrote to Governor Bradford, 'in sending Mr Fuller amongst us, and rejoice much that I am by him satisfied, touching your judgement, of the outward form of God's worship. It is (as far as I can gather) no other than is warranted by the evidence of truth, and the same which I have professed and maintained ever since the Lord in mercy revealed himself to me.' Endecott felt that he and Bradford were 'servants of one master'. Consequently, he continued, 'where this is, there can be no discord, nay, here must needs be sweet harmony; and the same request (with you) I make unto the Lord, that we may, as Christian brethren, be united by an heavenly and unfeigned love . . . I propose to see your face shortly.'

John Winthrop soon built upon this sure foundation of common values. On 28 June the following year, only a fortnight after he had disembarked from the *Arbella*, Fuller could write thus to Bradford: 'The Governor is a godly, wise and humble gentleman, and very discreet, and of a fine and good temper. The Governor has had conference with me, both in private and before sundry others.' Fuller also reported a conversation that he had with William Coddington, one of the Assistants, a close friend and former parishioner of John Cotton at Boston in England. Cotton had charged them as they left Southampton that 'they should take advice of them at Plymouth and should do nothing to offend them'.

Resolved 'to pacify the Lord's wrath', the first cause of the fatal sickness among them, Winthrop and his fellows consulted the three Plymotheans then in Salem: Dr Fuller, Isaac Allerton, who acted as business agent for Plymouth, and Edward Winslow, Assistant Governor of the colony. Winslow had sailed across on the *Mayflower* and soon proved his worth as a leader. Besides becoming Governor of Plymouth in 1635 he would serve the Puritan colonies in the Bay virtually as 'foreign secretary' during the years when his friend Oliver Cromwell came to power and ruled in England. They concluded that 'the Lord was to be sought in righteousness' and the last Friday in July was set aside as a day of solemn prayer and fasting, so 'that they may humble themselves before God and seek him in their ordinances . . . and they earnestly entreated that the church at Plymouth would set apart the same day, for the same ends, beseeching God as to withdraw his hand of correction'.

At Charlestown during the fast day a month later Winthrop, Dudley, Isaac Johnson and others had followed the example of the Plymouth and Salem churches and established an independent congregation. As the separatist brethren had always done they each signed a covenant 'to unite ourselves unto one congregation or church . . . and bind ourselves to walk in all our ways according to the rule of the Gospel . . . so near as God shall give us grace'. A friend of Winthrop's called Mr Wilson was formally chosen as minister, although he had been serving them in that capacity since early July. Winthrop carefully adds that the imposition of hands upon Mr Wilson's head was used as a sign of election and confirmation, not with the intent that the minister should renounce the holy orders he had received in England. For hostile voices at home were already labelling the colonists of the Bay Company as Brownists and ill-affected to the parent state of England. In the early days of August most of Wilson's congregation moved across the Charles river to Boston.

The stipend of Mr Wilson was fixed at twenty pounds a year until his wife came over from England. Mrs Wilson, however, proved most unwilling to leave her native shores, especially when she heard of the fate of Mrs Phillips and other ladies in New England. Her husband went to the pains of sailing the Atlantic again in 1631 to persuade her, but to no avail. 'I marvel what mettle she is made of,' wrote Margaret Winthrop in disapproval to her son. 'Sure she will yield at last, or else we shall want him exceedingly in New England.' Wilson's departure back to America alone 'very much affected' her, but she was soon 'well pacified'. It took Wilson another journey home before his wife would accompany him back to America, a reluctant pilgrim to a strange land.

As the colonists rushed to complete their houses before the onset of winter the building trades found themselves much in demand. Therefore they raised the price of their labour. The Puritans, however, held firmly to the medieval Christian doctrine of the just wage. There was a right reward for doing a particular job. It was unchristian, they held, to take advantage of a neighbour's need. At the General Court that August, Winthrop and his fellow magistrates passed a law that carpenters, joiners, bricklayers, sawyers and thatchers should take no more than two shillings a day, under pain of a ten shillings fine. Next spring these legal rates were lifted but two years later they had to be re-imposed, presumably to curb a further outbreak of profiteering.

Until Christmas Eve the weather was cold but sunny, with mild frosts at night. But that day a searing north-west wind chilled them to the bone. It was so icy that some had frost-bitten fingers they were in danger of losing. The wind drove a shallop ashore on Noddle's Island and three of Winthrop's servants spent a night without fire or food huddled among the rocks, before reaching Boston the following day. Two days later, on Sunday, the rivers had frozen up, so that the people of Charlestown could not come to the sermon at Boston until the afternoon at highwater.

That bitter north-west wind also caught Richard Garrett, a shoemaker of Boston, and his party in their shallop as they sailed southwards to Plymouth. The boat took in much water through a cracked stern which immediately frozen hard; their efforts to free her with numb and bleeding hands were desperate but unavailing. 'So they gave themselves for lost,' wrote Winthrop, 'and, commending themselves to God, they disposed themselves to die.' Then one of the company sighted some land near Cape Cod through the freezing rain. They hoisted up part of the torn sail and, 'by God's special providence, were carried through the rocks to the shore'. The party struggled through white gripping ice to land. Lacking an axe they could not get a good fire going and were forced to lie in the open air all night. Next day they resolved to send two men to fetch help from Plymouth, supposing it lay seven or eight miles away, though it was nearer fifty. Fortunately the pair met two Indian squaws, who told their husbands about the Englishmen. One of these Indians found the shivering party, then built a wigwam and cut firewood for them. When Garrett died two days later the Indian hewed a hole in the frozen ground with his hatchet and covered the grave with a great heap of wood to keep the corpse from the wolves.

Meanwhile the other Indian had guided two of the party to Plymouth, nearly fifty miles away, and Governor Bradford sent out a boat to fetch them. Both Englishmen died from frostbite, as did one of their fellows after reaching the safety of Plymouth. Garrett's young daughter survived. Harwood, the only other survivor, and like Garrett a godly member of the Boston congregation, lay long under the surgeon's hands before he recovered.

In February the ice broke up. Snow showers and sharp frosts still came, but the continuous chilling cold of the New England winter had begun to ease. The 'poorer sort of people' who lived in tents or ramshackle wooden huts, had suffered much. Until a ship arrived with a store of lemon juice many died of scurvy. It was a common observation, Winthrop reports, that those who 'fell into discontent and lingered after their former conditions in England' were most vulnerable to this disease.

The ship which brought the life-saving lemons was the *Lion*, which had sailed from Bristol on 1 December and consequently endured a very tempestuous passage. The son of a Dorchester man called Way clambered out along the spritsail yard in a storm, probably seeking a thrill as the ship rode the waves. He fell off and could not be rescued, 'though he kept in sight near a quarter of an hour'. On 8 February Winthrop went aboard the *Lion*, riding at anchor off Long Island. William Peirce, the master, would have reported that a swarm of fourteen Dunkirkers had attacked three of the ships returning the previous year with the loss of a dozen or more men. The *Charles*, one of the two English men o' war that engaged the enemy, was so knocked about that not much of her was left above the water. Next day the *Lion* sailed up to Boston, where she rode very well at anchor despite the great drifts of white ice in the bay.

Early next month, as William Peirce made ready his vessel for a voyage to England, Dudley and Winthrop made haste to finish their letters home. Dudley told the Countess of Lincoln that his long letter outlining the history of events since the colony began was written on his knee by the fireside that sharp winter, with many interruptions from his family. Outside he could hear wolves howling in the forest. He ended the catalogue of deaths and illnesses by declaring that they were not discouraged, 'bearing God's corrections with humility and trusting in his mercies, considering how at a low ebb he had raised up our neighbours at New Plymouth'.

Winthrop wrote to his wife and son on 28 March, a day or two before the *Lion* sailed. They would be his last letters, or so he hoped, for he expected them both to come out soon, preferably with William Peirce 'because of his skill and care of his passengers', even if they had to wait two or three months for his ship to be ready.

Among the passengers who returned to England on board the *Lion* was Sir Richard Saltonstall, together with his two daughters. His son Richard and the younger boys remained in Watertown. The departure home of this leading 'undertaker' is rather a mystery. Dudley wrote that Sir Richard intended to return, but we know that he never set foot in New England again. Perhaps he had become disillusioned with Massachusetts Bay that winter. He had been reprimanded by the Court of Assistants for non-attendance on one occasion. Most probably, as a widower, he sought another wife for himself and suitable husbands for his daughters. He may also have wanted to resume his career as a merchant, having acquired some 600 acres of land in Watertown for his sons.

By early April the prevailing westerlies were driving the *Lion* homewards, her bows cutting a path through the dangerous vastness of the Atlantic seas. Four or five weeks of solitude stretched before Sir Richard Saltonstall like a blank diary. His sea-chest may have contained some works by Erasmus, Luther or Calvin, as well as Foxe's *Book of Martyrs* and various collections of sermons by English Puritan divines. Such books would serve to remind him of the birth and early struggles of the Puritan movement.

1

To the Fountains

One spring day in 1512, two men reined in their horses near the lazar-house on Harbledown hill and looked down upon the walled city of Canterbury. One of them, the Dutch scholar Desiderius Erasmus, remembered later their vision of the great cathedral, which 'rises so majestically into the air as to strike even the distant beholder with religious awe. Two vast towers seem to greet the pilgrim as he approaches, while the pealing of their bells echoes far and wide over the country.' As these same bells saluted them Erasmus and his companion John Colet, Dean of St Paul's, rode down the narrow lane and entered the city.

Next morning a monk took the two pilgrims into the Cathedral, the scene in 1180 of the martyrdom of St Thomas Becket. At the wooden Altar of the Sword's Point they received in their hands a piece of one of the murderous Norman knights' blades – 'the sacred rust of this iron, in love of the martyr we religiously kiss'. Descending to the crypt they were shown the skull of St Dunstan set in silver, the forehead smoothed by pilgrims' kisses. In the gloom Erasmus could see the hair shirt once worn by Becket to mortify his flesh – 'the very aspect of which made us shudder, such a reproach were they to our luxurious softness,' wrote Erasmus. Having returned to the choir their guides unlocked various cupboards full of ivory, silver and gilt boxes of relics: one inventory lists over four hundred items, including two teeth of St Alban, a cutting from St Cuthbert's beard, eleven holy arms and three hands, pieces from the manger and sepulchre, and part of the column which supported Jesus when he was scourged. The monks produced a selection from the repository, 'all which we adoringly kissed'. Yet Colet, a fastidious man, visibly recoiled in disgust when he was invited to kiss the arm of St George, a grisly bone with bleeding flesh still clinging to it.

'After this,' continued Erasmus, 'we viewed the altar-table and its ornaments, and then the objects which had been stored up beneath the altar. All were so rich, that you could call Midas and

Croesus beggars by comparison if you had beheld that quantity of gold and silver.'

For most pilgrims the sight caused religious awe at the earthly glory won by the miracle-working fame of St Thomas. Yet this display of material wealth began to weary and then anger the irrascible Colet, 'a learned and pious man, but less well-disposed than I could have wished to this department of religion,' noted Erasmus. 'Is it true, good father, what I hear, that Thomas in his life time was very good to the poor?' an unsmiling Colet asked the guide. 'Most true,' replied the monk, listing many instances of his bounty to those in need. 'Then, I do not suppose his disposition has changed, unless for the better?' The guide nodded in agreement. Colet then demanded to know if he thought Thomas would mind if some poor woman with starving children at home, or a husband laid up with sickness, were to take some small part of these great riches as a gift or a loan. The monk in charge of the golden head made no reply. With his usual impetuosity Colet said in a loud voice, 'I for my part am quite confident that the saint would even rejoice to be the means, in death as in life, of relieving by his riches the destitution of the poor.' Erasmus watched with wry amusement as indignation chased unbelief from the face of the custodian. A few conciliatory words from Erasmus and some shillings pushed into the collection box soon soothed his feelings.

Having inspected the treasures of the shrine itself they were led back to the sacristry by Prior Goldstone. A black leather case was produced and opened while all present knelt. Inside were some soiled and torn pieces of linen cloth, apparently parts of a handkerchief once used by Becket 'to wipe the perspiration from his face or his neck, the runnings from his nose, or such other superfluities from which the human frame is not free'. Goldstone offered to present Colet with one of the pieces, supposing that nothing could be a more acceptable gift. Colet gingerly took hold of a piece at arm's length and then with a look of repugnance dropped it back into the box.

After a glass of wine the two scholars bade their farewells and set out for London. At Harbledown they were ambushed by the inmates of the lazar-house. Colet was riding on the left of Erasmus and thus nearer to the almshouse. He was sprinkled with a shower of holy water, and bore it as best he might. But when the upper leather of Becket's shoe, bound with a rim of brass, was held out for him to kiss, his temper flared. 'What!' he exclaimed, 'do these asses

25

imagine that we must kiss every good man's shoe? Why, by the same rule, they might as well offer us his spittle or dung to be kissed.'

*   *   *

The pilgrimage of Erasmus and Colet to Canterbury illustrates in a nutshell the growing tension of values in Europe. For us the two scholars symbolize the new or more modern values of the Renaissance while the guardians of the shrine of St Thomas seem to be tending the debased values of the Middle Ages. The Renaissance, as we call it, was a mysterious process which escapes definition. We know that about the year 1500 the study of classical antiquity intensified as more scholars acquired knowledge of Greek, and that the invention of the printing press added a new dimension to the story. But men of the Renaissance were not antiquaries merely unearthing values from the past. The fresh impact of the classical authors in the better texts provided by such scholars as Erasmus only stimulated values that were already present in a latent form within the mind of European man.

We can imagine European civilization about 1500 as a river. It was fed by three major tributaries. One descended from the hills of Hebrew experience by way of Christianity and the Bible. The second tributary stemmed from the fountains of Greece and Rome. The third stream arose in the mist-shrouded tribal cultures which existed in Europe before the coming of the Roman legions or the Christian missions. These cultures were rooted in nature and stocked with pagan, animistic and magical values. Over the centuries the waters had become a single river and no one thought of attempting to distinguish between them. Moreover, in the medieval synthesis they had achieved a kind of balance. It was this harmony which the Renaissance would both shatter on one level and renew on another.

In its narrower sense the Renaissance consisted of an exploration down one of these streams until men reached in their imaginations the very springs that fed it. There they tasted, so they believed, the values which had made Greece and Rome great. In the literature and history of antiquity they glimpsed the sovereign value which the best classical authors placed upon man. The idea of freedom – the belief that man is an autonomous being responsible for his own actions – was perhaps the supreme expression of the Greek mind. The Greeks saw man as godlike in nature. He is gifted

26

with reason and inclined towards virtue. Man can make whatever he will of himself. Such a vision of man born again into late medieval Europe gave a springtime freshness to the world. A few generations later Miranda's speech in *The Tempest* captured the mood as it spread greenly across the century:

> O wonder!
> How many goodly creatures are there here!
> How beauteous mankind is! O brave new world,
> That has such people in it!

Thus the superior smile of Erasmus and the irritation of Colet as they surveyed the bogus relics at Canterbury reflected a new framework of values in the making. Such gross superstition was beneath the dignity of man.

Italy was the homeland of the Renaissance. Both Erasmus and Colet made the pilgrimage there to drink at the fountain of purer learning. Florence, Rome and Venice in turn provided leadership for the movement. In Rome the new vision of man's godlike potential formed the centrepiece of perhaps the most remarkable Renaissance picture of all, Michelangelo's frescoes in the Sistine Chapel of St Peter's Cathedral. On the ceiling he painted a reclining Adam, naked as a Greek god. The outstretched forefingers of God and Adam are almost touching. The invisible spark of creativity, the gift of godlike reason, seems to be passing from the fingertip of God to man made in His own image.

No words appear on the sublime picture, but if a caption is needed a contemporary fellow-Florentine named Pico della Mirandola had supplied it in his discourse *On the Dignity of Man*, which Michelangelo would have read. 'As God says to Adam, "You shall have the power to degenerate into the lower forms of life, which are brutish. You shall have the power, out of your soul's judgement, to be reborn into the higher forms, which are divine."'

The fusion between Christian and Greek ideals led Erasmus to emphasize the universal rather than the national, peace rather than war. For himself he claimed to be a citizen of the world, making his own the words of his blessed 'Saint Socrates': 'I am not an Athenian or Greek, but a citizen of the world.' But even Socrates had donned armour and limped into battle for Athens. That subtle Greek mind could distinguish between nationalism and patriotism, the proper love of one's homeland. 'Day by day fix your eyes on the greatness of Athens,' said Pericles to his countrymen, 'until you are filled with the love of her; and when you are impressed by the spectacle of her glory, reflect that this empire has been acquired by men who knew their duty and had the courage to do it.' But not all Greeks shared the lofty patriotism of Pericles. In reality the citizens of Athens could be as superior to foreigners as the Florentines, and as violent towards strangers as the Londoners of Tudor England.

The universal and peaceful spirit of Erasmus abhorred both the nationalism that was rending Christendom and also the Church's willingness to condone it. Neither he nor Colet could fully accept that any war could be called just. 'War is sweet to those who know it not,' the title of his popular treatise on the subject, sums up the Erasmian view. He castigated the preachers at the courts of Europe. According to these 'animals in black and white vestments' it is always a holy war, 'for in France they say God is on the French side and they can never be overcome that have God for their protector; in England and Spain the cry is, the war is not the King's but God's.'

Perhaps it is not fanciful to see in the national feeling stirring in Europe at the time another rebirth. Tribalism reborn was breaking through the veneer of Christendom. Men wished to return to one of the sources of their society: the primitive kinship group that set them apart, made them different. The burgeoning interest in national history and language were both expressions of this new corporate self-consciousness and means to creating it. It was individualism on a national scale.

The relation of the Renaissance proper to this other renewal was ambivalent. Take language as an example. Although scholars wanted to spread knowledge of Greek and Latin as universal languages yet their emphasis on good style and their scorn of the impure medieval Latin spoken by clerics actually hastened the day when the 'classics' would become an academic study. Moreover, when Renaissance authors chose to write in their native languages they imported this concern for excellence in style and vocabulary, so that in their hands they revealed a new potential. Thus the vernacular languages of Europe, the linguistic symbols of national identity, came to be seen as possible vehicles for the expression of truth, beauty and goodness.

Undoubtedly the most important book in the hands of the translators was the Greek New Testament. Although Colet was perhaps not the first to turn the thoughts of Erasmus to applying his considerable linguistic abilities and consummate scholarship to the New Testament, he certainly urged his friend to join him in Oxford and lecture either on Latin poetry or the Old Testament. In 1516, about four years after that visit to Canterbury, Erasmus produced his most celebrated and most revolutionary work: the New Testament in the original Greek. 'Sir, we would see Jesus,' some Greeks had implored the disciples in St John's Gospel. The main motive of Erasmus was to answer this cry by the common man. As the scholar made clear in his preface, he saw the Greek text and its accompanying Latin version as the basis for translations into the vernacular, so ordinary people could see Jesus and become like him: 'I would have the weakest woman read the Gospels and the Epistles of St Paul . . . I would have those words translated into all languages, so that not only Scots and Irishmen, but Turks and Saracens might read them. I long for the ploughman to sing them to the traveller to beguile with them the dullness of his journey. . . . These sacred words give you the very image of Christ speaking, healing, dying, rising again, and make him so present, that were he before your very eyes you would not more truly see him.'

While Erasmus worked on his translation of the New Testament in Cambridge, a Florentine civil servant and diplomat named Niccolo Machiavelli was finishing a manuscript in Italian which was far removed from the spirit of the simple carpenter of Nazareth. Machiavelli loved Florence better than his own soul and Italy after her. In this treatise on statecraft entitled *The Prince* he created a realistic picture of the kind of ruler who would expel all foreign usurpers from Italy and unite the land. He taught that the lessons of the past, especially of Roman history, should be applied to the present. In the military field, for example, the Prince should dismiss his mercenaries and rely upon native militia like the Greeks and Romans in the best ages. Provided the Prince ruled with reason and justice, these citizen soldiers would not let him down.

Above all Machiavelli was an acute observer of the present. He was interested in reality, in what worked and what did not. In him the new spirit of natural inquiry turned towards politics and statecraft, searching for a science. Foreshadowing the development of secular society he distinguished the art of government as an autonomous area guided by its own principles. These had much to do with human nature but nothing in common with the erroneous and superstitious laws of Christianity. Christian morality may be a useful social convention but it should have no place in the counsels of the Prince. The Prince as an individual may or may not possess such private virtues as truthfulness, mercy and affability. But the only concern of the Prince as ruler was to preserve the state. Nothing was a virtue which brought failure; nothing a vice which promoted success. If the prince feels endangered by the popularity or unpopularity of a faithful adviser, for example, he should sacrifice him ruthlessly in his own interest. Had not Machiavelli's model, Cesare Borgia, executed Ramiro d'Orco, the general who conquered Romagna for him, and left his corpse in the Piazza at Cesaria to appease the people? Success is the redeeming virtue of princes, and expediency the means to it. Men are ungrateful, fickle, false, cowardly and covetous, yet 'as long as you succeed they are yours entirely'.

For the great Florentine, who elsewhere advocated the republican method, the mere form of government mattered little compared to the importance of maintaining absolute power. But to his contemporaries, especially the English, his views seemed to endorse the tendency towards absolute monarchy. Although the first published translation of *The Prince* did not appear until 1640 manuscripts of it in English had circulated much earlier. Cardinal Pole remembered a conversation he had in his youth with Thomas Cromwell, then chief minister to Henry VIII. Cromwell poured scorn on the *Republic* of Plato, which he said led to nothing. He offered to lend Pole a much better book which he possessed in manuscript, *The Prince* of Machiavelli.

There were other ways in which the Renaissance served in the short term to enhance the new monarchies and national glory. The Renaissance principle that 'man is the measure of all things' was applied to royal architecture with spectacular effect. In his *De Architectura Libri Decem*, written about 50 BC, the Roman architect and engineer Marcus Pollio Vitruvius had urged the necessity for symmetry and proportion in building, which should reflect the human form. In about 1515 Vitruvius was translated into Italian. His ideas accorded perfectly with the main direction of Renaissance thought. As man is made in the image of God so are his human proportions. In architecture such proportions must be regarded as divine in origin. With such an authority as its basis architecture could be regarded as a science. As a building came to be seen as a system, like the human body, so the architect saw himself as an artist responsible for the whole, from conception and design to the surrounding gardens and details of interior embellishment.

Renaissance monarchs such as Henry VIII, grown rich upon the spoil of the monasteries, could afford to build the 'cloud topp'd towers, the gorgeous palaces' of their reigns to their own greater glory. Such medieval manors as Eltham Palace, where as a boy King Henry had met Erasmus, were no longer grand enough. They were replaced by such splendid creations as Nonsuch and Greenwich, Whitehall and Hampton Court. 'More like unto a paradise than any earthly habitation,' wrote one contemporary upon seeing Hampton Court for the first time.

To men such as Leonardo da Vinci architecture seemed to hold limitless possibilities. Machiavelli had met Leonardo in 1502 while he was serving as an ambassador with Borgia. Leonardo, about fifty years old at the time, was already widely known as an example of *l'uomo universale*, that universal man of action and thought which Renaissance men aspired to be. Borgia was employing Leonardo as a military engineer, but he was ceaselessly at work during campaigning season filling one notebook after another with detailed drawings of human and natural phenomena. With boundless curiosity, matched by powers of observation and skills as a draughtsman, he kept at work penetrating into the reality of things. To these attributes of a scientist he joined a creative mind which fathered ideas for inventions. Many of these, such as his drawings of flight machines, were not feasible in his day, but they were the seeds of things to come.

Leonardo's notebooks revealed how the spirit of rational inquiry, grounded in the philosophy of Greece and Rome, could lead such lonely explorers of truth into conflict with the intellectual orthodoxy of their day. In fact Leonardo's attitude to Christianity seems to have been ambiguous: outwardly conventional but inwardly questioning. Vasari, whose *Lives of the Painters, Sculptors and Architects* appeared about thirty years after Leonardo's death, had done some thorough research among those who knew the artist. According to him, Leonardo had such a heretical frame of mind that he did not adhere to any kind of religion, believing that it was better to be a philosopher than a Christian. Yet Leonardo carefully stipulated the number of masses that were to be sung for the repose of his soul.

Although Leonardo shared most medieval assumptions about the natural world, he was certainly prepared to follow reason when it conflicted with the authority of the Bible. He divined correctly, for example, the significance of the marine fossils he found in the mountains of Italy. Contrary to the teachings of the Church, that God had separated land and sea on the third day of creation, Italy

31

must once have been under the primeval ocean. In his notebooks Leonardo considered and discarded a compromise solution – that the fossils were formed during the Deluge, for the remains were found, he argued, in different geological layers. The whole concept of a Flood seemed irrational because no one could say how the water departed. Thus Leonardo conceived a doubt which would flower into the scepticism of Darwin three centuries later.

'One must treat these people of extraordinary genius as if they were celestial spirits and not like beasts of burden,' wrote Cosimo de' Medici with Fra Lippo Lippi in mind. This sense of being special or unique developed among artists the significance of individuality. Erasmus, an artist in words, personified this new value placed upon the creative individual. Like the painters and potters of ancient Greece, artists such as Albrecht Dürer took to signing their names or monograms, saying in effect 'I, Dürer, made this.'

A few people, foreshadowing Montaigne's *Essays*, began to be conscious of themselves as unique individuals; they became interested in studying themselves. Both Leonardo da Vinci and Dürer painted self-portraits. Benvenuto Cellini, the Florentine goldsmith, wrote an *Autobiography* in which he described his rather obnoxious personality with obvious relish.

Like his fellow Italian artists Leonardo prized what he called 'the chief gift of nature, which is freedom'. Unlike the English humanists he did not esteem the society of friends, for their presence detracted from his complete, dedicated, solitary, single-minded path. 'If you are alone you belong entirely to yourself,' he wrote. 'If you are accompanied by even one companion you belong only half to yourself, or even less, in proportion to the thoughtlessness of his conduct; and if you have more than one companion you will fall more deeply into the same plight.' The age of the individual had dawned.

Values such as man, freedom, reason and individuality had to compete against other values for living room. Apart from the thrusting value placed by individual nations on themselves, a tribal renaissance which effectively checked the universal brotherhood and golden age of peace propounded by Erasmus, the humanist ideals nurtured by classical studies struggled against the growing affluence of the age. For there was more gold and silver around in 1500 than at any time previously. The sight and prospect of riches excited men's greed. Thus material values with their focus in wealth marched forwards to lay siege to the heart of Europe.

Leonardo da Vinci illustrates the confusion as men were both attracted and repelled by the imminence of greater wealth than their fathers or grandfathers could have imagined. 'If you want money in abundance,' wrote Leonardo to himself, 'you will end up by not enjoying it.' About 1500 he penned a prophetic drawing of implements – rakes, musical instruments, pincers, spectacles – raining down from the sky: 'Oh human misery; of how many things you make yourself a slave for money.' Yet with such a genius at his command Leonardo himself could not resist the temptation to try to make his fortune. He conceived a machine for grinding needles at a prodigious speed, using revolving leather belts and an abrasive wheel, an invention which he believed would make him rich. While in the service of Venice he sketched some submarines for an attack on the besieging Turkish fleet. The completeness of his imagination led him towards the climax of the story even before the designs had dried upon the page: he positively revelled in the thought of the Turkish booty that would be given him. Neither the fortune from the needle-making machine nor the treasure from the galleys materialized, but they reveal that money could sway even such a superior mind as Leonardo possessed.

Erasmus, who was not adverse to money himself, could see clearly that material values had secured an especially corrupting influence on the Church. He saw the amassed wealth of the Church and its worldliness in sharp contrast to the teaching of Christ and those saints who approached him nearest in spirit. His friend, Sir Thomas More, saw the same cancer of covetousness at work in the body politic. The rich sought to become richer, and they did so at the expense of the poor. In *Utopia* he wrote:

> When I consider and turn over in my mind the state of all commonwealths flourishing anywhere today, so help me God, I see nothing else than a kind of conspiracy of the rich who are aiming at their own interests under the name and title of commonwealth. They invest and devise all ways and means by which they first may keep, without fear of loss, all that they have amassed by evil practices and secondly they then purchase as cheaply as possible and abuse the toil and labour of the poor. These devices became law as soon as the rich have once decreed their observance in the name of the public, that is of the poor also!

The discovery of America opened up a new vista of wealth for Europe. Indeed More's *Utopia*, 'The Island of Nowhere', had been stimulated in part by the discoveries by European seamen of primitive societies living in the New World. Raphael Hythlodaye, the *raconteur* of this traveller's tale, was a real person. More had met him in Antwerp. He had sailed on three voyages with Amerigo Vespucci, the Florentine explorer of the coasts of South America. The new continent would be named after Amerigo in the erroneous belief that he had reached the mainland first. Love of money, that motive which More and the English Christian humanists so despised, was the mainspring of these voyages of discovery. The wealth which Venice and Genoa had garnered from the East, aroused deep envy among nations beyond the Alps. They hired mercenary seamen such as Vespucci to search for a sea route by sailing not east through the Mediterranean but west across the Atlantic. The Spanish king employed a Genoese sea captain named Christopher Columbus, whose services had been turned down by France and England. In his path Columbus found the Bahamas, Cuba and Haiti. In three later voyages searching for the passage through to the East, he found central America and the West Indies.

After Columbus returned from his first voyage Cesare Borgia's father, the Spanish-born Pope Alexander VI, Rodrigo Borgia, had divided the New World between Spain and Portugal. Spain was now the rising star in the Catholic world. That same year, after the union of the kingdoms of Aragon and Castile and the complete expulsion of the Moors, Alexander conferred the title of 'Catholic Majesty' upon the King of Spain. When Columbus died in 1506 Spain had already planted colonies in the lands he had discovered, seeds of a Catholic empire. Moreover, in the fabulous kingdoms of those parts there was gold and silver enough to make Spain the most influential nation on earth. Under the Emperor Charles V, who was also King of Spain from 1519 to 1555, the power of the country would reach its zenith.

Meanwhile the English conceived hopes of securing an empire in the New World to rival those of Spain and Portugal. A sea captain from Genoa and Venice had settled in Bristol under the anglicized name of John Cabot. In 1497, together with his son, he sailed west to discover the same passage to India and China sought by Columbus. Crossing the Atlantic they made their landfall near the present Cape Breton, sailed down the coast of Nova Scotia and sighted Newfoundland. They had reached the shores of America on 24 June 1497, a year before Columbus who was then still occupied in the West Indies. Next year they sailed southwards down the American coast, possibly as far as Chesapeake Bay. As England would never be tired of repeating with national pride, their man had reached the mainland of north America first. England, which had been remote from the centre of things, now found herself exceptionally well placed. But had England the men to take advantage of this turn of fortune?

* * *

In 1505, the year Colet became Dean of St Paul's, his father died. Sir Henry Colet was a prosperous mercer who had risen to be Lord Mayor of London. He also acquired extensive lands, including some 2000 acres in Buckinghamshire. As the eldest of Sir Henry's 22 children, and the only survivor, John Colet inherited all his fathers wealth. He resolved to found a new school in the shadow of St Paul's Cathedral for the study of good literature, both Latin and Greek. 'For my intent is by this school especially to increase knowledge and worshipping of God and our Lord Jesus Christ, and good Christian life and manners in the children.' It was the first school in England to be refounded completely upon Renaissance lines. Colet opened it to 'the children of all nations'. The funds were sufficient to educate 153 young scholars (the number of the miraculous draught of fish), which made St Paul's larger than Eton, Winchester or Westminster.

By 1512 the handsome stone building stood ready. Those boys who had paid their entrance fee of four pence (the rest of their education was free) took their seats in the long, high school room divided into four sections by curtains. They were left in no doubt about why they were there. One of the windows bore the legend *Doce aut Disce aut Discede* – 'Teach or Learn or Leave.'

The statutes which Colet drew up for St Paul's School were widely influential. Manchester Grammar School, founded fifteen years later, still has a High Master and an Eighth Form (rather than the more common Sixth Form), both on the Pauline model. Merchant Taylors' School, the great but shortlived school which Wolsey founded at Ipswich, and many other grammar schools – such as Guildford in Surrey – also based themselves on the statutes of Colet.

Besides Latin the boys in these new modelled schools would learn Greek, a language previously not taught in England. Even at the universities only a handful of scholars studied it. Few attended the lectures on Greek that Erasmus gave at Cambridge. By chance a list of over 2000 books sold by an Oxford bookseller, John Dorne, at about this time has survived, and there are only two works in Greek among them. Colet secured an accomplished Greek scholar, William

35

Lilly, as the first High Master. Lilly had learnt his Greek on the island of Rhodes. The Greek Grammar he wrote for St Paul's School became a standard textbook for many English schools. Shakespeare, who doubtless pored over it while he was a boy at Stratford Grammar School, mentioned it twice in his plays.

Good literature in Colet's eyes meant authors who combined wisdom with pure, chaste language. He clearly preferred explicitly Christian wisdom. After learning the catechism in English the children were to proceed to the *Institutum Christiani Hominis*, 'which that learned Erasmus made at my request', and that same author's *Copia Verborum*. Colet then listed some suitable Christian authors who wrote good Latin. He made it clear that neither pagan and immoral content nor corrupt medieval style would be tolerated. 'I say that filthiness and all such abusion which the later blind world brought in, which more rather may be called blotterature than literature, I utterly banish and exclude out of this school.' The school motto, *Fide et Literis* – 'In faith and in letters' – perfectly summed up the founder's intention.

Such an education, training both the mind in reasoning and the character in virtue, would prepare both lay men and clerics for service to God and their country. The Puritan poet John Milton – the greatest product of St Paul's School – expressed this Renaissance ideal in his own day when he wrote that the best education is 'that which fits a man to perform justly, skilfully and magnanimously all the offices, both private and public, of peace and war'.

Hence the emphasis placed at St Paul's School from the first upon skill in rhetoric. The ancients believed that eloquence as a speaker was essential if a man was to be effective in public life. Boys at St Paul's were taught from an early age to stand up and recite in public, either alone or in company with others in Latin or Greek plays. But technique alone was not the aim. Cicero had defined an orator as 'a good man, skilled in speaking'. Richard Pace, who wrote a book in Latin restating that doctrine, extolled Colet for founding his school and encouraging boys to practice public speaking. He also praised William Lilly, who delivered orations before such distinguished people as the Emperor Charles V and Queen Anne Boleyn, for being such a splendid example to his charges.

Not all shared the unqualified approval of the King's Secretary for Colet's influence on education. The Bishop of London, an old man of medieval cast of mind, spoke for many who feared and detested the new learning. As Colet informed Erasmus in a letter, the prelate has been 'blaspheming our school before a large concourse of people, declaring that I have erected what is a useless thing, yea a mischievous thing – yea more (to give his own words) a temple of idolatry'. Colet could 'laugh heartily' at such a charge. Sir Thomas More also treated the critics lightly. 'I am not surprised,' he wrote to Colet, 'if some are bursting with envy at your famous school. For they see that just as the Greeks came forth from the Trojan horse, and destroyed barbarian Troy, so there are coming forth scholars from your school who expose and overthrow their ignorance.'

In the light of such criticism it is not surprising that Colet entrusted the oversight of St Paul's School not to the church authorities in London but to the 'honourable Company of Mercers' in London. According to Erasmus, he did so because he found the least corruption of his day among married citizens of established reputation, a biting indictment of his fellow clergymen. Significantly Colet specifically allowed the High Master of St Paul's School to be a 'wedded man', thus furthering the establishment of a teaching profession distinct from the celibate clergy. William Lilly was a married man and father of fifteen children. As the value of man and his experience in this world began to rise so the values of marriage and the lay state moved upwards in their train.

The relation between the sexes, especially in marriage, was bound to be affected when Renaissance education was slowly extended from boys to girls. Thomas More was a pioneer in this respect. Like William Lilly he had lived in the Charterhouse for a time. Although he chose not to be a Carthusian he retained always a preference for the disciplined life of a monk. The desire to avoid concupiscence led him to marry. That negative reason as the prime motive for marriage was essentially medieval and also deep-rooted: it would surface again in the Book of Common Prayer. Having inspected the three daughters of an Essex gentleman – their father obligingly pulled back the covers as they lay naked in bed – More chose the second 'fairest and best favoured' one. Yet when he considered the feelings of the eldest daughter at seeing her sister married first, he changed his mind and out of pity 'framed his fancy' towards her. When Jane died after bearing him three daughters and a son, he married again. His second wife was Alice Middleton, widow of a mercer, 'aged, blunt and rude'. More evidently loved Dame Alice, although he once described her ungallantly as 'neither a pearl nor a girl'. She possessed the English characteristic of always speaking her mind. Towards the end of one of his visits Erasmus wrote to a friend, 'I am tired of England and More's wife is tired of me.'

More's efforts at educating Jane, who was seventeen when they married, proved to be a fruitless exercise. He tried to interest her in books and music. He asked her to repeat the substance of the sermons they heard together, so they could discuss them. Jane did nothing but cry, and wish she was dead. 'Use your rights,' said his father-in-law when they visited him, 'and give her a good beating.' 'I know what my rights are,' replied More, 'but I would rather you used your authority.' But when John Colt lost his temper with Jane she fell at More's feet in penitential tears. Erasmus speaks warmly of Jane's kindness and the happiness she brought to More's household, but she was no scholar.

More fared better as a teacher with his daughters. 'Erudition in women,' he wrote, 'is a new thing and a reproach to the sloth of man.' His house in London, with its library, chapel and garden, was like a small Oxford college. Over the years his four children and eleven grandchildren, as well as various adopted children and wards, learnt their Latin and Greek in the hall. Their tutors ate at More's table. John Clements, one of Lilly's first pupils at St Paul's School, and a future President of the Royal College of Physicians, taught Margaret More and later married one of her adopted sisters. Visiting scholars, such as the German astronomer Nicholas Kratzer, often stayed there and taught the girls. With his penchant for flowery praise Erasmus compared More's household in Chelsea to Plato's Academy. The wit and humour which so delighted Erasmus also made More a marvellous father. He always found time to play with his children. Indeed, as they grew up he often advised them 'to take virtue and learning for their meat, and play for their sauce'.

Eventually education would unlock for women the door into the private garden of friendship. For friendship is based upon common values and interests. Following the example of the ancients, the scholars of the Renaissance esteemed this relationship perhaps more highly than natural kinship. Erasmus said he could never read Tully's treatise *On Friendship* without kissing the book. The English humanists formed a close-knit coterie of friends. More wrote of William Lilly as 'my dearest friend'. His beloved Colet was also his *vitae magister*, or confessor. Erasmus addressed letters to More, 'the sweetest of all my friends, with whom I am always pleased to join in any enjoyment grave or gay'. Thomas Linacre, whom More would meet often at court, was another friend after his own heart. Linacre helped him to translate the biography of Pico della Mirandola. Linacre's personal motto was *Ad Fontes*, 'To the Fountains' – perhaps the one phrase which sums up the direction and spirit of the Renaissance. He developed a deep interest in medical science and became one of the founders of the Royal College of Physicians. If Erasmus tended to exaggerate the virtues of his friends there can be no doubt that the quality of these English scholars deeply impressed him. It seemed to him as if their common labours would bring to birth the golden age.

* * *

Darkness over Saxony. As the first approach of dawn edged black night in the small town of Wittenberg, an Augustinian friar found his place among the crowded benches of the lecture room. Himmel barely had time to light his wax candle and open his notebook when the professor walked in and began his lecture. As morning light filled the room the candles were snuffed out. Himmel could see more clearly the lecturer, a fellow Augustinian named Dr Martin Luther: a man of 33 or 34 years in monk's habit beneath his academic gown. But it was Luther's voice and the clarity of his lecture on Galatians which most impressed Himmel:

> He was a man of middling height, with a voice both sharp and gentle: it was soft in tone, sharp in the enunciation of syllables, words and sentences. He spoke neither too rapidly nor too slowly, but evenly and without hesitation, as well as very clearly, and so logically that each part flowed naturally out of what went before. He did not get lost in a maze of language, but first expounded the individual words, then the sentences, so that one could see how the content of the exposition arose, and flowed out of the text itself. For it all hung together in order, word, matter, natural and moral philosophy.

Those who heard Luther deliver these lectures in the autumn of 1516 could not have guessed at the story of spiritual turmoil which lay behind his words. As a boy Martin Luther was brought up in the town of Mansfield. From grammar school he went on to the University of Erfurt, where he worked hard, played the lute well and talked in such a way that his fellow undergraduates called him 'the philosopher'. In 1505 he became a Master of Arts. 'What grandeur and splendour there was,' he later recalled 'when one received the master's degree! They came with flaming torches and presented them. I think that no earthly joy could be compared to it.'

Then Luther abruptly executed a decision which must have been shaping in his mind for some time: he entered the monastery of Augustinian Hermits or Friars in Erfurt as a novice. Three years later he began to lecture at a new university which the Elector of Saxony had founded at Wittenberg, a place of less than 3000 inhabitants. After a brief return to Erfurt he went back to Wittenberg to become a professor and stayed there for the rest of his life.

It was there that Luther became a fledgling biblical scholar. In his first year at Wittenberg he began to learn Greek and Hebrew, and studied the writings of the early Church Fathers, especially St Augustine. He read and wrote incessantly. 'Before I was married,' he remembered later, 'the bed was not made for a whole year and became foul with sweat. But I worked so hard and was so weary I tumbled in without noticing it.'

Already Luther showed a combative temperament. A humanist scholar, for example, who criticized the Augustinians could be abused as an 'aged and distracted scarecrow'. But such skirmishes probably offered no more than light relief from the serious purpose in hand. What mattered most to Luther was to become a master of 'that theology which extracts the nut from the shell, the grain from the husk, the marrow from the bone'.

Thus for Luther theology was never an academic subject. His elusive quarry was the essence of the Gospel, and he pursued it relentlessly by seeking to establish the meaning of each word and each verse before him. But as Luther proceeded in this methodical manner, step-by-step further into the hinterland of the Bible, in another and as yet unconnected part of his life he felt a growing sense of utter separation from the ultimate subject of his studies. After a honeymoon period in the novitiate, Luther succumbed to the doubts and fears that beset him: his persistent state of sin and the sentence of damnation carried with it became an intolerable weight on his shoulders. Neither years of mortifying the body, accompanied by repeated confessions and further penances, nor the spiritual direction of his superiors, could ease this weight in the soul of the young monk.

'In this state,' Luther wrote later, 'hope despairs and despair hopes; and nothing seems alive but that inward groaning that cannot be uttered in which the Spirit ascends, moving upon the face of these waters veiled in darkness . . . no one can understand these things but he who has them.' When Luther came to describe this spiritual wasteland to great congregations, or expound the geography of despair in lecture rooms to such students as Himmel, his hearers could certainly understand what he meant. Thousands upon thousands of Protestants, including those called Puritans in old and New England, would also recognize this dreadful state. 'Art not thou the Man that I found crying without the walls of the City of Destruction?' asks Bunyan's Evangelist. 'Yes, dear Sir, I am the Man,' replies Christian.

For many people today there is still a basic pattern of experience that enables us to identify ourselves with Luther. At the age of about seventeen or eighteen years the self emerges much more strongly, together with an acute self-consciousness. As if to emphasize the disharmony of a world out of tune, moral values awaken in the mind: goodness and evil are felt as living, throbbing realities. The new ability to think in abstractions, joined to these values, weave ideals for the future. Yet the attempt to reform oneself – to be less self-centred or selfish – proves ineffectual. Moral rules, taken from the Bible or written out for oneself, cannot solve the problem. If we keep them the soul becomes puffed up with conceit or pride, the most deadly form of self-regard. Failure leads to despair, and despair to self-pity or self-hatred.

For Luther, who possessed no such sketchmap of moral development, the unexpected experience was made even more alarming by his unique combination of characteristics. Self made itself felt in him with singular intensity. Like many creative people he was a virile and sexual man, or, as he put it, 'full of fire'. He inherited not only great energy but also a volcanic tendency to anger and aggressiveness. These strong emotional endowments co-existed within the mental framework of late medieval Christianity, the village religion of his peasant family in Thuringia. That religion, with the moral codes of Moses and Christ, he had accepted with his immense capacity for faith. So the concept of hell, for example, assumed a terrifying reality for him. He worked in the strong primary colours of his day, painting for himself in his own imagination the height, length, depth and inescapable end of his state. For what he now experienced was utter alienation from God. He projected his vast inner anger against God onto the face of the world and society about him. 'In addition to being alarmed and terrified by God's wrath, man can find consolation in no creature

41

and whatever he looks at appears opposed to him. For the whole creation acts with its creator: and especially when a man's conscience is against God; and as a result everything appears angry; everything adds to his wretchedness: all things around are enemies.'

In the autumn of 1515 Luther worked late into the night in his study, a room in the square tower of the Augustinian house in Wittenberg, preparing a new course of lectures on the Epistle to the Romans. On his table stood the edition of St Paul's Epistles published recently by the French humanist scholar Lefèvre, whose commentary on the Psalms he had already used on his course the year before. Before the lectures were complete he was able to consult the edition of the Greek New Testament by Erasmus. Not unlike Colet before him, Luther concentrated on clarifying first the literal meaning, using all the lexicons, commentaries and critical editions to that end. 'Languages,' he wrote later, 'do not make a theologian: they are only a help. Before a man can speak on anything, he must first know and understand his subject.'

In his studies on Romans that autumn Luther's mind was arrested by the phrase 'the just shall live by faith', which he could not understand. He wrestled with it, meditating 'day and night on the interconnection of the words', like a man attempting to break a cypher or to crack the meaning of an ancient inscription in an unknown language. What shifted in his creative unconscious first was the meaning of 'just'. Besides signifying justice, in the usual sense of a moral balance between actions and reactions ('an eye for an eye'), it is related to the justification, 'to make just'. This phrase translates a Greek word in the Bible usually rendered into English as 'to pronounce righteous' or 'to make righteous'. Luther restructured the atoms of this key sentence. The way in which God makes man just or righteous (when he is standing, so to speak, guilty in the dock) is by the free gift of faith! 'This straightway made me feel as though reborn, and as though I had entered through open gates into paradise itself. From then on, the whole face of scripture appeared different.'

As Luther put it himself, 'I had broken through'. What he had done, although it probably took him some months to realize it, was to understand the principle which explained how the limitless power of God actually worked in the life of man. The relation of two apparently opposed terms – 'justice' and 'faith' – had fallen into place, not unlike Einstein's resolution of concepts in 'matter is frozen energy'.

The simplicity of this central idea of justification by faith astounded and delighted Luther. Through a forest of complexities, tangles which in every field detain inferior minds, he had broken through to the clear, simple fountain of God's mercy. We can imagine his exultation as he sat back in his chair one night and contemplated what, through God's mercy, he had achieved by his perseverance. He would never forget that this day-star had shone in the darkest watch of his spiritual night.

Luther knew that he now faced the immense task of re-interpreting the Bible and the Church's doctrine in the light of this new principle. His vocation as theologian, preacher and teacher came together as an integrated whole. He would be plunged back into the complexities of language as he tried to express the new wine of the Gospel in the old wineskins of the theological concepts available to him. But throughout his life Luther held firmly to that original principle. He fought to guard its hallmarks of simplicity and clarity against all the tendencies of clever men to make it more complicated or to allow it to be diluted into traditional teachings. In his translation of the Bible, for example, Luther inserted the word 'alone' into the sentence 'the just shall live by faith', claiming that the German idiom required it, although St Paul did not have it. So *sola fide*, 'by faith alone', became the watchword of the Reformation.

In 1541, after a conference of three Catholic theologians (headed by Luther's old foe Professor Johann Eck) and three Reformed ones, which the Emperor Charles V had convened at Ratisbon, had produced a statement setting out the points upon which they agreed and those where they differed, Luther would have none of the compromise committee formula. In a letter to the Elector of Saxony he declared: 'We hold that man is justified by faith without the works of the law; this is our formula, and to this we adhere. It is short and clear. Let the devil and Eck, and whoever will, storm against it.'

Faith then is a gift, given freely by a gracious and merciful God; it is never deserved or merited by man. It is the garment with which God clothes the naked; it is the wealth which he bestows upon the poor out of his boundless treasure. For the person so gifted, the eyes of the soul are henceforth fixed resolutely upon God and not upon self or its 'good works'. In this God-centred life the Christian shared in the present and living Christ, who is active in the soul. 'It is faith in Christ which makes him live in me and move in me and act in me: in the same way as a healing ointment acts on a sick body and we are hereby not only made one flesh and body with Christ, but have an intimate, ineffable exchange of our sins for his righteousness.'

Luther accepted that the natural and inevitable fruit of such faith is good works, but these actions had nothing to do with the fundamental issue of salvation. He did not see the Christian as necessarily becoming a better person in the eyes of the world. Faith was always needed. Man remains a sinner, prey to doubt, fear and dread. 'Always a sinner, always a penitent, always right (*justus*) with God', he once proclaimed. He had striven and failed to become a saint in the Church's definition of the word, namely one who leads a life of exceptional holiness and thus obtains an exalted station in heaven and the entitlement of the veneration of the faithful on earth. Now he knew that 'God wants sinners only . . . God has nothing to do with holy men.' Anything which smacked of such meritorious sanctity Luther abhorred. He was a religious genius, not a saint.

* * *

On All Saints Day in October 1517 Luther nailed his celebrated 95 Theses to the door of the Castle Church in Wittenberg, giving notice that he would defend publicly these articles criticizing the practice of selling indulgences (remissions of time in purgatory granted to pilgrims out of the treasury of merit filled up by Christ and the saints). As Pope Leo X had granted these particular indulgences to help finance the renovation of St Peter's in Rome the papacy could not ignore this challenge to its authority, especially as the news of Luther's act had spread around Germany in a fortnight. At a disputation held with Eck in Leipzig in 1519 Luther denied both the primacy of the Pope and the infallibility of general councils.

With his black-and-white mind Luther moved rapidly to the conclusion that the Church of Rome, in his eyes the champion of salvation by good works, must be none other than the Antichrist mentioned in the Book of Revelation. Thus he added to his division between faith and works yet another great dichotomy. His movement would find its identity as a 'protest' against Rome. The name 'Protestant' actually derives from the 'Protestatio' of six princes and fourteen cities, advocates of the Reformation among the members of the Diet of Speyer in 1529. They were protesting against the decision of the Catholic majority to end all toleration of Lutherans in their districts.

In 1520 Luther completed the break with Rome by publishing

three famous reformation treatises. Condemned as heretical, Luther burned the papal document announcing that sentence. Duly excommunicated and summoned to appear before the Emperor Charles V at the Diet of Worms in 1521, he determined to go 'even if there were as many devils there as tiles on the roofs'. Having stood at Worms in the midst of his enemies, like Christ before the High Priest he later mused, Luther would not recant, 'since it is hard, unprofitable and dangerous to act against one's conscience'. Then, pausing, he added in German 'God help me, Amen'. Dismissed from the hall, he made his way back to his lodgings through the crowds who thronged to see him. On the steps of the inn he raised high his hand with fingers outstretched in a gesture of victory used by German soldiers. By his courage in coming to Worms he had thrust the Reformation onto the stage of history.

Fearful for his safety the Elector of Saxony (with Luther's connivance) arranged for him to be abducted to the Castle of the Wartburg, a fortress set upon a crag in the wooded hills of Thuringia – 'in the region of the birds,' wrote Luther, 'who sing beautifully on the trees, praising God night and day with all their might.' He stayed here for some ten months. The warden included him once in a hunting party. But he hated killing. 'There is some point in tracking down bears, wolves, boars and foxes,' he reflected, 'but why should one pursue a harmless creature like a rabbit?' A hare ran under his gown but the dogs bit through the cloth and killed it. 'Just as the Pope and the Devil treat us,' wrote Luther, for whom nature was a book of spiritual analogies.

In his castle refuge Luther wrestled with his doubts. 'How often my heart wavered and punished me and reproached me with its strongest argument: are you the only one who's clever? Can you really say that all the others are wrong and have been wrong for such a long time?' He thought and wrote incessantly, producing notably a fine translation of the New Testament in German from the original Greek based upon the text of Erasmus.

While Luther lived in seclusion at the Wartburg Castle his ideas spread rapidly through the country. With a growing popular religious enthusiasm went the abandonment of those religious practices which Luther had criticized. Priests married, monks and nuns left their monasteries. In Wittenberg itself the reforming movement galloped so far ahead that it created chaos. Luther received a summons to return and restore some sort of order. A fellow professor of his at the University, Andreas Carlstadt, had shown himself to be a man of violent and uncompromising temper in the prosecution of his reformed beliefs, and was seizing the religious leadership of the town from Luther's more moderate lieutenants, such as Philip Malanchton.

A group of Anabaptists or 're-baptizers' had recently settled in Wittenberg under the leadership of Thomas Münzer. They claimed to be inspired directly by the Holy Spirit. True believers should be re-baptised, they held, for infant baptism was a meaningless medieval charade. Andreas Carlstadt and this group, fellow extremists, set about destroying all altars, images and crucifixes. After Luther's return, Carlstadt went into voluntary exile. Luther resumed the leadership; he lectured at the University again, and as a minister to the main congregation in the town, he succeeded in abolishing such popish practices as private masses, confessions and fasts.

Thomas Münzer did not share the pacifist views of such Anabaptist leaders as Menno Simons. In 1525 he ardently supported the German peasants when they rose in revolt. The origin of the troubles lay in economic and social grievances, but prophets like Münzer whipped up the fury of the peasants with violent, apocalyptic sermons and pamphlets. The peasants supported by some townsfolk, a number of German knights and apostate priests, produced a manifesto for freedom. Besides the abolition of certain taxes and also the state of serfdom, they demanded the right to elect their own pastors. Mob violence broke out. Devoid of proper leadership, bands of peasants burnt down castles and monasteries in a blind swipe against all authority. At first Luther attempted to mediate between landlords and peasants. Then disgust at the brutality of the peasants overcame him and he urged the secular sword to take action. The armies of the Protestant princes ruthlessly supressed the rising. After the defeat of the peasants at the battle of Frankenhausen (1525) Münzer was captured and executed.

*   *   *

To describe the lay Christian's relation to the world about him Luther introduced the great concept of a calling or vocation. Unlike the monk, who separates himself from other people, the Christian has a calling which throws him together with others. Luther dismissed any spiritual distinctions between Christians: all stood equal and alone before the throne of God; none could win any advantage by his state of life or good works. Daily work is transformed when the love of God flows through a Christian towards his neighbour. Even the tackle and gear of the tradesman's shop preached the message of brotherly love, as Luther once said:

> To use a rough example: If you are a craftsman you will find the Bible placed in your workshop, in your hands, in your hearts; it teaches and preaches how you ought to treat your neighbour. Only look at your tools, your needle, your thimble, your beer barrel, your articles of trade, your scales, your measures, and . . . they shout this to your face, 'My dear, use me towards your neighbour as you would want him to act toward you with that which is his.'

Unlike the monks, who made prayer their priority, Luther placed his emphasis upon work first and prayer second. Petitionary prayer must only be resorted to when all other possibilities had been tried and found incapable of helping. Only the man who has worked as hard as possible can pray with power, for he alone has a good conscience. 'We serve here in an inn,' Luther wrote, 'where the Devil is master and the world keeps house, and where the servants are every conceivable sort of vice and all of them are enemies of the Gospel.' Yet 'God is not sleeping or snoring.' In such a lodging house the Christian needs to ask for daily strength from this watchful God. For all around him Luther sees that God 'does everything, acts, punishes and makes, is mighty present and fulfils everything powerfully in all creatures'. The Christian is called to co-operate in vocation and prayer with this never-sleeping providence of God as the energetic vision of the divine purpose becomes ever more apparent.

Luther did not minimize the sufferings involved in work, rather in the tradition of St Paul he boasted of them. For he saw vocation and marriage as places where the Christian shared crucifixion with his Master. Unruly subjects, shabby clothes, the dirt of toil, the contempt of the proud: all these were examples he gave of the cross in vocation. They could only be avoided by escaping like a fugitive into the cloister.

Family life is especially demanding. It is a school of character, where husband and wife can learn fortitude, patience, charity and humility. The husband has the lifelong responsibility of earning the daily bread. The wife has the bearing of children, with all the trials of pregnancy as well as the mortal danger of childbirth. The new babies brought fresh trials to their parents, such as keeping them awake by crying all night. Yet all these troubles were as nothing compared to the value of marriage as now restored by God. Thus, wrote Luther, when the neighbours pull the leg of a father hanging out the nappies to help his wife, he can say to himself 'Let them laugh. God and the angels smile in heaven.'

About marriage Luther could speak from experience. In 1525, when he was forty-two, Katherine von Bora arrived in Wittenberg. She was one of a group of nuns who had abandoned their convents. To a reformed minister she expressed her willingness to marry him or Martin Luther. Hearing of it Luther wrote, 'I am ready. I believe in marriage and I intend to get married before I die.' Luther's parents came to the wedding. The Elector of Saxony gave them an empty monastery in Wittenberg as a present.

In this home Katherine, sixteen years younger than Luther, bore him five children. Luther found time to work on his vegetable patch in the cloister farm, while Katharine tended an orchard and their hens, ducks, pigs and cows. In later years they owned a small farm at Zulsdorf. Luther's warm and humorous affection for 'my Katie' grew over the years. 'I give more credit to Katharine than to Christ, who has done so much more for me,' he wrote. She 'is in all things so obliging and pleasing to me,' he said after a year of marriage, 'that I could not exchange my poverty for the riches of Croesus.' Once, when she fell ill, he wrote to her: 'Oh Katie, do not die and leave me.'

Yet Luther's marriage had its feet in the medieval world of his youth. Man was naturally the superior partner. 'Women,' he declared, 'were created with large hips so that they should stay at home and sit on them!' Wives owed love and obedience to their husbands; children must obey their parents. Once Katie interrupted his flow of talk at the dinner table to say, 'Doctor, why don't you stop talking and eat.' 'I wish,' snapped Luther, 'that women would repeat the Lord's Prayer before opening their mouths.' He attempted to educate Katharine so that she might share more fully in the life of his mind and spirit. Ten years after their wedding, Luther reported to a friend: 'My Lord, Katie greets you, she plants our fields, pastures and sells cows. . . . In between she has started to read the Bible. I have promised her 50 gulden if she finishes by Easter. She is hard at it and is at the end of the fifth book of Moses.'

Luther knew also the cross which lies at the heart of Christian marriage. Their six children gave them broken nights of sleep and later their ceaseless chatter got on his nerves. 'Christ said we must become as little children to enter the kingdom. Dear God, this is too much. Have we got to become such fools?' Of course he loved them and expressed it in countless ways, just as he loved Katharine, but he was never sentimental about marriage. Preoccupied by his calling, overburdened with work and naturally of irascible temper, Luther could not have been an easy man to live with. Doubtless Katharine quarrelled violently with him on occasions, 'Good God,' wrote Luther 'what a lot of vexation there is in marriage! Adam has made a muck of our nature. Think of all the rows Adam and Eve must have had in the course of their 900 years. Eve would say "You ate the apple," and Adam would reply, "You gave it to me."'

The poverty of early married life led him to take in student boarders, who recorded his table talk for posterity. There are 6,596 entries in the *Table Talk*, which at least confirms that Luther was a prolific talker. Some are remarks upon familiar anti-papal and anti-monastic themes – 'The monks are the fleas on God Almighty's fur coat.' But one conversation reveals that the reformer also experienced that rising sense of the reality and value of this world, which left the other world of after-life somehow unreal and uninviting. 'I cannot think what we shall find to do in heaven' mused Luther, 'No change, no work, no eating, no drinking, nothing to do. I suppose there will be plenty to see.' 'Yes' quoted Melanchton, who was at the table, 'Lord, show us the Father and it suffices us.' 'Why, of course,' responded Luther 'that sight will give us quite enough to do.' Yet he must have known the textbook answer before he raised the question.

The arguments in the heated controversy between Erasmus and Luther revolved around the issue of human freedom. For many centuries Christian theologians had argued about the relation of grace – God's action for and in man – and human freedom. Under the influence of St Augustine Christian orthodoxy placed more emphasis upon grace. It had stressed the sinfulness of man in Adam's descent and his powerlessness to help himself. God's choice determined who should be saved, and therefore some were predestined to that end. Theologians then had to face the questions which these central beliefs posed to the intelligent religious mind. In what sense had Christ died for all men? How did Baptism and the Eucharist fit in to this scheme of things? Was human freedom towards God an illusion or a reality? In their attempts to accommodate God's sovereignty over all creation with man's experience of at least a measure of freedom and moral responsibility in relation to him the theologians had analysed grace into several different categories.

In sailing upon this much-frequented if dangerous inland sea,

neither Luther nor Erasmus ran upon the rocks of heterodoxy.
Luther took a Pauline and Augustinian view while Erasmus
meticulously placed in the scale of freedom the subdued but
significant case for more freedom than Augustine had allowed. Man
cannot merit grace in the first place, but can earn by his strivings
the increase of grace. This essentially Thomist view rested upon the
fundamental principle that 'grace does not destroy nature but
perfects it'. Thus Erasmus could preserve and present in moderate
terms his humanist belief in the dignity and high destiny of man. As
always he took what he conceived to be the middle way, urging
toleration upon those to the right and left of him.

So both the protagonists agreed that reason could not solve the
enigma. Luther kept reiterating the great principle that God justifies
men by grace, and that all else, such as the workings of predestination (which both St Paul and St Augustine taught), is a
mystery to be accepted in adoring trust. Erasmus, characteristically
recalling that there were some sacred groves or gardens in Greece
barred to men, wanted to eschew needless metaphysical specu-
lation. For him true religion lay in following the simple example of
Christ as found in the Scriptures. There are only a few dogmas on
which the Gospels give us clear directions; the remaining questions
can be left unsolved without detriment to our salvation. Erasmus
and Luther seem to us to be so close. Apart from temperament, what
really divided them?

Long before becoming involved in the dust and heat of public
controversy, with its need to score debating points and not to lose
face, Luther had shown a remarkably clear and calm awareness of
the conflict of values which divided him from Erasmus. In 1517 he
informed a friend that he was reading some works by Erasmus. He
admired the way that the author constantly exposed the evils of the
Church, especially by learnedly accusing not only monks but also
priests of lazy, deep-rooted ignorance. Erasmus had performed the
task to which he was called. 'Only I fear he does not spread Christ
and God's grace sufficiently abroad, of which he knows very little.'
What Erasmus and such writers as Pico della Mirandola did
proclaim was a pagan faith in the reason, power and divinity of man.
'The human is to him of more importance than the divine,' wrote
Luther perceptively of his future adversary. The saving simplicity
of the Gospel is hidden to the questing mind of reason. God reveals
the secret to the heart of man, not his clever intelligence. 'Erasmus,
who does not go beyond the light of nature,' said Luther, 'may like

Moses die in the plains of Moab without entering into the promised land of those higher studies that belong to godliness.'

The literature of the classics does not of itself produce virtue. 'Everyone who is a good Hebrew and Greek scholar is not a true Christian,' he wrote. 'Even Dr Hieronymus with his five languages cannot approach Augustine with his one tongue.' That saint, and still more Christ, is exalted far above Cicero. Yet classical studies are necessary. The new learning, especially the rising influence of Plato, had helped to dethrone Aristotle and discredit the whole medieval scholastic system. Latin, Greek and Hebrew literature remained a necessary proving ground for serious students of the Bible. 'Do not give way to your apprehension,' he wrote in 1523 to Eobanus Hessus who had expressed his alarm at the apparent contempt for learning shown by the reformer, 'lest we Germans become more barbarous than ever we were because of the decline of letters through our theology. I am persuaded that, without a skilled training in literary studies, no true theology can establish and maintain itself.'

Just as Luther, like Colet, saw classical literature as ancillary to the study of Christianity, so he placed reason firmly in a subordinate position to faith. When a man's life was truly centred upon God, all his human qualities found their proper function. Even reason, 'the Devil's whore' when seducing men from putting their whole trust in God, became an honest bondwoman in the believing Christian. Looking upwards, it was faith, always faith, that man needed. As man looked downwards and outwards from God, the natural reason – a gift from God – stood ready to serve him in his dealings with the world.

Erasmus never ceased to deplore 'these odious dissensions' with Luther. He called the Reformation 'this stupid and pernicious tragedy', though at the news of Luther's marriage he added with a sly smile, 'Perhaps one should call it a comedy, since it ends with wedding bells.' At least the two great men agreed on one humanist principle: they deplored executing men and women for their religious opinions. In 1528, when the Parisian authorities burnt Louis de Berguia for heresy, the Dutch scholar exclaimed: 'The idea of burning a man because he is wrong! I wonder where they got it from.'

Having demolished the pretensions of the Papacy, Luther entrusted the headship of his churches to the secular rulers who would accept the Reformation. Yet these men were contemporaries of Cesare Borgia. Luther had no illusions about them: 'the biggest fools and most arrant knaves upon earth'. So spiritually dangerous was their station in life, he thought, that a prince is 'a rare beast in heaven'. A Christian ruler, educated well and guided by faithful pastors in his spiritual responsibilities, would look upon the office as a vocation. He would eschew using his power to make money for himself, but rather unsheath his sword only to punish evil. Thus he would seek justice, which is love in impersonal social relations. An unselfish love of neighbour would be his inspiration rather than his own glory. He would not act merely 'for the sake of his beautiful yellow hair'.

As the true Church was the invisible communion of all faithful Christians, Luther made no attempt to separate the true Christians from those who seemed to be so. He contented himself with the guiding thought that the Church existed where the Word of God is preached and the sacraments properly celebrated. He hated the reformed congregations being called 'Lutheran'. He was relaxed and apparently casual about external practices, which already caused heat among lesser men. He did not care about the wearing or not of surplices, or the elevation of the elements at mass. He also set his face against sacerdotalism in any form. Supposing, he wrote, a little group of pious laymen captured and marooned in some wilderness had no priest among them consecrated by a bishop. They could elect or call one of their number to preach and give them the sacraments. He would be as truly a priest as though popes and bishops had consecrated him. Herein lay the seed of the congregational practice that would one day flower in the American wilderness.

Besides the German Bible Luther endowed the churches with his sermons, catechisms and service books, together with a hymnal containing many of his own compositions. 'I have no use for cranks who despise music, because it is a gift of God,' he wrote. Next to the Word of God only music deserves to be extolled as 'mistress and governess of the feelings of the human heart'. Meanwhile, in neighbouring Switzerland, music was being driven out of church in the name of the Reformation.

Ulrich Zwingli was born in Switzerland a year later than Luther. As a young man he devoted himself to humanistic studies. He taught himself Greek and Hebrew, learnt St Paul's Epistles by heart and read the Fathers. Already a priest he served as chaplain to Swiss mercenaries in the papal service. Later he reacted against pilgrimages to a famous shrine in his parish. His lectures on the New Testament in Zurich in 1519 sparked off the Reformation in Switzerland. He subsequently invited Erasmus to Zurich to receive the freedom of the city, an offer the scholar declined. Zwingli always tried to minimize his debt to Luther, though his annotated Bible (1522) shows that he had read him. Yet he felt jealous of the German's reputation as the author and supreme leader of the Reformation. For Zwingli always remained a fervent Swiss patriot. In translating the Twenty-third Psalm, he rendered the second verse: 'He maketh me to lie down in an Alpine meadow.'

When the two men met at Marburg in 1529 a deep difference revealed itself on the nature of the Eucharist. Luther, already put off by Zwingli's strange dialect, took even greater exception to his sacramental theology. Zwingli regarded the communion service as a straightforward memorial, a vivid metaphor rather than a miracle. Martin Bucer, a former Dominican who had corresponded with Luther in 1518 after hearing him speak in an early public disputation, had hoped to mediate between the two positions. For he was a German yet he had come in Zwingli's party. Luther's obduracy, however, left no room for manoeuvre. At the first plenary session Luther lifted up the velvet cloth on the table and wrote in chalk: *Hoc est meum corpum.* 'They can leave that saying as it is whether they like it or not', he declared.

Oecolampadius, one of Zwingli's party, insisted that these words must be metaphorical, because the flesh profits nothing and the body of Christ has ascended into heaven. Luther asked why the ascension should not also be regarded as a metaphor. Zwingli argued that in the Aramaic language the copulative verb was omitted, so Jesus actually said 'This – my body.' So the Lord may have meant 'This *represents* my body' rather than the traditional translation.

This argument over sacramental theology disclosed a far deeper divide, one of considerable significance for the English Puritans in following generations. Zwingli had selected for emphasis the Pauline text, 'The letter killeth, but the spirit giveth life', which he coupled with Johannine verse, 'The flesh profiteth nothing.' His discovery that flesh and spirit are incompatible had led him to abandon art and music (although he himself could play six instruments). Here Zwingli was the dichotomizer, not Luther. At Marburg he advanced his apparent dichotomy to prove his view of the sacrament. Luther held in reply that flesh and spirit could be joined, and that the spiritual does not exclude the physical. Luther showed here his grasp of Biblical truth, for the division of flesh and spirit is more Greek than Hebrew. But Zwingli's dichotomy, shared by Calvin, and other reformers, was to have a baleful influence on the later history of the Puritans.

In fact the gap between the positions was not as wide as it seemed. It could have been bridged there and then. But Melanchton, a natural ecumenist, feared that agreement with Zwingli would jeopardize a possible reunion with the Catholics, which was still a possibility. Luther soon recovered from his temporary affection for Zwingli. He left Marburg regarding the Swiss theologian and his fellow 'sacramentalizers' as 'wanton enemies of God'. When Zwingli met his death in 1531 (killed holding the banner of the Zürich forces under attack from the five forest cantons), Luther made no pretence at grief. A minister of the Word who wielded a sword had brought such a fate upon his own head.

Martin Bucer assumed the leadership of the reformed Church in Switzerland and south Germany, but already another star had appeared in the sky. John Calvin, who was twenty-two when Zwingli died, came from north-west France, the son of a clerical lawyer. An able and industrious scholar he became one of the more learned reformers, his first published work being a commentary on Seneca's *De Clementia*. In 1536 Calvin brought out the first edition of his *Institutes of the Christian Religion*, a clear and systematic statement of reformed theology. The French reformer never met Luther but he admired him from afar. He saw himself as continuing rather than supplanting his work. Indeed Luther's published sermons and Erasmus' Greek New Testament were the primary influences on the mind of the young Calvin. Luther, for his part, thought well of Calvin. After reading Calvin's tract on *The Supper of the Lord*, in which the author set out a doctrine somewhat between the two extremes of Marburg, Luther commented to his Wittenberg bookseller, 'He is certainly a learned and pious man . . . if Oecolampadius and Zwingli had expressed themselves in this way at the beginning, we should never have been involved in so long a controversy.'

In 1545, the year when Calvin published this work on the sacrament, he had already established himself in Geneva. He would remain in that city until his death in 1564, growing each year in influence. There he evolved his system of church government. Each congregation was ruled by pastors and teachers, elders and deacons. Over them all sat an elected consistory of ministers and laymen. The consistory worked together with the town council – the secular arm – to tighten up social morality. Prohibited activities included adultery, gambling, swearing, dancing, drunkenness, drama, witchcraft, charging inflated prices for goods or services, sleeping during sermons and any practice conceivably described as Roman Catholic. Those who opposed the regime were harried out of the city. The philogist Castellio, schoolmaster in Geneva, had to resign because he described the *Song of Solomon* as a love-song, not a Christian allegory, and because he criticized Calvin's interpretation of the Apostle's Creed. Belsec was imprisoned and banished for questioning Calvin's doctrine of predestination. Michael Servetus, a Spanish physician condemned by the Inquisition for doubting the full divinity of Christ, who for some unaccountable reason fled to Geneva, was burnt at the stake on 27 October 1553.

In Calvinist theory Church and State were distinct. The Church had authority over religion, the realm of the 'soul or the inner man'. The State complemented it by the 'setting up of civil and external justice of morals'. The State must not interfere in the Church but help it in all possible ways. In practice, however, Calvin dominated both. An austere and intellectual man, without charm though personally kind, he possessed the kind of burning faith that commanded respect rather than love. Under him Geneva became very much like a Bible theocracy with Calvin as the prophet of the Lord.

In spiritual terms Calvin contributed nothing original to the Reformation, but he had a genius for clarifying thought and ordering society. Of all those who attempted to produce a systematic reformed theology and church polity he was by far the most successful. Calvin crystallized the Reformation. But he represents that second stage in all human enterprises, when the 'organizers' take over from the 'pioneers' and say 'You cannot do that' or 'We have made a rule now to deal with that situation.'

Doubtless good organization, epitomized by Calvin's Geneva, made it possible for the Reformation to advance. But the journey led away from that spring of original Christianity which Luther had disclosed to his contemporaries. In Calvinism those extraordinary notes of freedom and joy, rising like a descant above the common hymn of faith, are somehow missing. Untidy though his theology may have been, slipshod and ramshackle though his church polity remained, Luther could still communicate the sparkling clarity and depth of that original water. Doubtless Protestantism needed the ships, the navigational instruments and charts which Calvin supplied. But Luther belonged to a different order. 'They are trying to make me into a fixed star,' said Luther. 'I am an irregular planet.'

In 1545 Luther presented a different picture to the young clear-eyed professor whom Himmel had admired at the lecture rostrum some thirty years earlier. To the daily burden of business and 'the toil of scribbling', other weights now dragged down his spirits: the roll of drums over Germany summoning recruits for the Imperial regiments enlisting against him, the voices of Protestant radicals shouting him down with arrogant confidence that they alone understood the Bible, and the memory of his beloved daughter Magdalena who had died three years ago.

Luther had accepted an invitation to act as arbitrator between the two counts of Mansfeld in Eisleben, his birthplace some 70 miles from Wittenberg. Once there Luther's spirits seem to have revived. To Katie, whom he called playfully a 'self-tormentor' because she was worrying so much about him, he wrote to say the beer was very good there. During the next few days he preached to full churches and negotiated a satisfactory settlement. After the reconciliation he sat down to a hearty dinner and enjoyed the good company. Later that same evening, however, he suffered a series of heart attacks and died in the early hours of 17 February 1546. 'O God,' Albrecht Dürer had once exclaimed when the supposed news of the reformer's death reached him, 'if Luther is dead who will expound the holy Gospel so clearly to us?'

2

Some Early English Protestants

The Puritans of Elizabethan and Stuart times, both in England and America, shared a common history. In company with all English Protestants they looked back with pride to the founding fathers of their faith. An Elizabethan Puritan divine named John Foxe wrote what was for them the definitive history modelled on Eusebius and entitled 'Acts and Monuments of these latter and perilous days, wherein are comprehended and described the great persecutions and horrible troubles that have been wrought and practised by the Romish prelates, specially in this realm of England and Scotland, from the year of our Lord 1000 unto the time now present.' A printer's addition on one page gave it a shorter and more popular title: Foxe's *Book of Martyrs*.

Foxe's history came second only to the English Bible in influence upon the Puritan spirit, as John Bunyan testified. All the Puritans read it, imbibing the values of the author as spiritual mother's milk. After the English translation of Foxe's Latin original appeared in 1563, a volume of some 1800 folio pages, the Convocation of Canterbury ordered copies to be placed along side the Bible in cathedrals and churches. A second edition followed seven years later, expanded to 2314 pages. In 1577, on his voyage around the world, Sir Francis Drake, a friend of its author, would occasionally amuse himself after dinner by colouring the 170 or so woodcut pictures. The sixth edition in English came out in 1610, and the seventh in 1632. The Lord Mayor of London directed that city orphanages and the halls of city companies should all have copies available for public reading.

Foxe's book is interesting today because it gives us in outline the Puritan interpretation of history. It also supplies us with some colourful details about the early English Protestants, especially those destined for martyrdom, as well as some vignettes of English sovereigns and statesmen. Apart from the fact that it was written in Latin and modelled upon a Greek author the *Book of Martyrs* reflects the Renaissance in its approach to history. For Foxe employed the historical method of consulting first-hand accounts as employed by Greek historians such as Herodotus, attempting first to discover with accuracy what actually happened. Translated into Tudor English, often verbose but sometimes vivid and arresting, his history seemed to contemporaries to possess an unimpeachable authority. They received it as gospel truth – an English supplement to the Acts of the Apostles.

'We will begin our history with the story of John Wyclif our countryman . . .' With these words Foxe struck a characteristically nationalist note for his readers: his book was going to be about England and how the English – under God's providence – had been leaders in the work of Reformation from the start. The Church of Rome had soon obscured the risen sun of the Gospel by its man-made clouds of ignorance. In that black medieval night Wycliffe had shone briefly like a candle, but the Devil's instruments in England had silenced him and ruthlessly extinguished many of his followers. Shortly after the burning of Huss, a disciple afar of our English Wycliffe, 'it pleased God to open to man the art of printing'. Then such scholars as Erasmus and Colet, Pico della Mirandola and Grocyn, prepared the ground for the Reformation by discerning truth from error, religion from superstition. After their learned writings had opened a 'window of light unto the world' there immediately followed Martin Luther, 'shining in the Church as bright daylight after a long and dark night'.

Into this Puritan sketch of five centuries of medieval history, Foxe set the story of England's first Protestant martyrs, the Lollards. The name 'Lollard' (like the later term, 'Puritan') was originally a nickname foisted on the followers of Wycliffe by their enemies. Foreshadowing their nonconformist successors, the Lollards met together in houses or barns to read Wycliffe's translation of the New Testament into English and to sing psalms – 'lollen' means to sing in Dutch. Despite some determined attempts to stamp out Lollardry – the first Lollard was burnt in 1401 – it survived as a clandestine network of small congregations, strong in London, the home counties and East Anglia. Many people shared the views of Lollards on certain issues, such as pilgrimages, without adopting their general radical position. Writing about Colet during his account of their visit to Canterbury, Erasmus had noted 'he was not a Wycliffite, though I should imagine he had read Wycliffe's books; where he got them from I cannot tell'. Certainly Lollards travelled long distances to hear Colet preach, and one compared him to

Gamaliel in the Acts. Colet's superior, the Bishop of London, took a hard line against the Lollards, compelling 22 to abjure and burning at least two others. As Colet wrote to Erasmus, the bishop 'never ceased to harass me'.

Further study of the Bishops' Registers which Foxe consulted confirms the broad lines of the picture he painted. Diocesan heresy trials give us some glimpses of these Wycliffites. Fifty-one men and nine women, for instance, stood trial in Norwich in 1428. Apart from four priests and a propertied man, they were all servants or artisans, such as shoemakers, tailors, skinners, glovers, a miller and a parchment maker. Between them they held in an unsophisticated way a wide variety of Lollard beliefs, including the priesthood of all believers, the invisible nature of the Church and a refusal to swear oaths. Several were accused of hostility to the ringing of church bells. One suspect had called them 'Antichrist's horns'. The main motive for ringing them, they claimed, was to enable the priest to collect money. Some Lollards spoke against the practices of fasting and abstinence. Margery Baxter disliked not eating meat on Fridays for a good housekeeping reason that it made much better sense to eat the scraps left over from the preceding day than to go to the market and buy fish. The Lollards, like Luther much later, expressed their beliefs in homely language. As the death penalty was reserved for relapsed heretics, none of these Norwich folk incurred punishments more painful than floggings, imprisonment and public penances done barefooted with candle in hand.

Support for these proto-martyrs providentially appeared in the Renaissance scholars, who, wrote Foxe, 'began the first push to be given against the ignorant faction of the Pope's pretended church'. After they had sapped and mined under the walls of Rome there 'immediately followed Martin Luther, with others after him; by whose ministry it pleased God to make a more full reformation of his Church'. From 1518 onwards the writings of Luther were shipped illegally into the country. As English printers imported barrel-loads of paper from the continent, smugglers found it easy to interleave some printed but uncut sheets among the blanks. A colony of alien German merchants living in London probably acted as a bridgehead for the reception of Luther's ideas. Lollard congregations also eagerly devoured Luther's message. Some became Lutheran; others retained their identity for a time before losing it in the stream of Elizabethan nonconformity.

Unlike Wycliffe's teachings, Luther's ideas soon attracted

interest among the nobility and gentry. Writing to Luther in May 1519 Erasmus mentioned that some 'among the greatest' in England approved of his writings. Wycliffe had not grasped the simple idea of justification by faith. That was the key which unlocked hearts in all classes and intellects. For it gave to biblical religion a centre or core. It was Luther, wrote Foxe, who first 'showed that sins are freely remitted for the love of the Son of God, and that we ought faithfully to embrace this bountiful gift'.

This central doctrine had certainly become the topic of hot theological discussion in the two Universities at an early date. In 1520 the ledger of John Dorne shows that he sold a dozen books by Luther in the town of Oxford. Doubtless his counterpart at Cambridge had sold even more copies, for a group of scholars began to meet each week to discuss the new theology. Their meeting place, a tavern called the 'White Horse', soon became known as 'Little Germany'. Most leaders of the later English Reformation were Cambridge men. Foxe would immortalize their names: Thomas Bilney, George Joy, William Roy, Robert Barnes, Miles Coverdale, John Frith, John Lambert, Hugh Ridley, Thomas Cranmer, Rowland Taylor, Thomas Arthur and Matthew Parker.

In 1520 Bilney, a Norfolk man by birth, was a member of Trinity Hall, a college founded by a bishop of Norwich after the Black Death to produce priests for the Church. The founder's coat-of-arms – a silver crescent upon a black field – still adorns the old red-brick Tudor library. Bilney failed to dispel his guilty anxiety by a regime of fastings, masses and penances. About this time he read the Latin parallel version of the Greek New Testament. 'At the first reading (as I well remember) I chanced upon this sentence of St Paul (O most sweet and comfortable sentence to my soul!) in 1 Tim. i, "It is a true saying, and worthy of all men to be embraced, that Christ Jesus came into the world to save sinners; of whom I am the chief and principal." This one sentence, through God's instruction and inward working, which I did not then perceive, did so exhilarate my heart, being before wounded with the guilt of my sins, and being almost in despair, that even immediately I seemed unto myself inwardly to feel a marvellous and quietness, insomuch that my bruised bones leaped for joy.' Many later Puritans would record much the same experience.

Hugh Latimer was ten years older than Bilney, a senior and respected man in the University. Not long after Bilney's conversion he delivered a speech in public that was violently hostile to the writings of Philip Melanchton, Luther's lieutenant-general of theology. Bilney heard the address and next day called upon Latimer in his room in the neighbouring college of Clare Hall to reason with him. 'By his confession,' wrote Latimer, 'I learned more than in many years before. So from that time forward I began to smell the word of God, and forsook the school-doctors and such fooleries.' The two men became firm friends. They walked daily together on Castle Hill, which their enemies re-named 'Heretics' Hill' in their honour. Doubtless they looked forwards to receiving William Tyndale's new translation of the Bible, for they both knew that Oxford man and the labour he was engaged upon.

Among the great treatises Luther published in 1520, the probable year of Bilney's rebirth, the *Freedom of the Christian Man* sought to explain the relation between faith and works. For the Christian, wrote Luther, works are expressions of faith, not instruments to win God's favour.

> When God in his sheer mercy and without any merit of mine has given me such unspeakable riches, shall I not then freely, joyously, wholeheartedly, unprompted do everything that I know will please him? I will give myself as another Christ to my neighbour as God gave himself for me. I must even take to myself the sins of others as Christ took mine to himself. Thus we see that the Christian man lives not to himself but to Christ and his neighbour through love. By faith he rises above himself to God and from God goes below himself in love and remains always in God and in love.

Inspired by this new motive, Bilney and Latimer visited and comforted the sick in the town lazar-house. They also acted as pastors to the prisoners in Cambridge Castle, ministering with tenderness to those awaiting execution in the condemned cells.

Bilney practised abstinence and self-denial. He slept as little as possible so that he wasted no time through sloth. He contented himself with one meal a day so that he could distribute the rest of his commons to the needy. 'He could abide,' wrote Foxe, 'neither singing nor swearing.' The 'dainty singing' of the greater churches, such as King's College Chapel, was to him 'mocking against God', and whenever an undergraduate called Thomas Thirlby (a future bishop of Catholic persuasion) played upon a recorder in his rooms immediately below Bilney he 'would resort straight to his prayers'. Latimer, however, remained always enthusiastic about the simplicity, unworldliness and sincerity of 'little Bilney' or 'Saint Bilney' as he affectionately called his friend. In Latimer's eyes he was 'meek and charitable, a simple good soul not fit for this world'.

Meanwhile more hostile acquaintances had come to share the view that Bilney was not fit for this world. In 1525 a clerical diplomat in Wolsey's service named Stephen Gardiner became Master of Trinity Hall. Gardiner shared in the new emphasis upon Greek studies but in matters of doctrine he stood firmly entrenched in the conservative tradition of Linacre and Grocyn. He attended some of the discussions at the White Horse but probably only in order to spot potential heretics. Two years after Gardiner's appointment Bilney was arrested for preaching heresy during a visit to his home county. He escaped the stake by recanting.

Back in Cambridge again Bilney's conscience began to torment him. Latimer feared that if he left his friend alone he would commit suicide. Late one night in a room in Trinity Hall Bilney bade farewell to his friends, saying that on the morrow 'he would go forth to Jerusalem'. He went back to Norwich. After preaching in the fields near the city he was arrested and condemned to death. On 19 August 1531 he was burnt outside the city wall in a low valley known as 'Lollard's Pit'. In London, Sir Thomas More awaited eagerly to hear if he had recanted: whether he did so or not is a matter for dispute. Among the spectators who saw Bilney die stood a Norwich man who was a Fellow of Corpus Christi College at Cambridge. His name was Matthew Parker and he would serve as Queen Elizabeth's second Archbishop of Canterbury until she sacked him for being too soft towards the Puritan heirs of Bilney.

*   *   *

After his fateful divorce from Catherine of Aragon and the break with Rome during the 1520s King Henry VIII needed new friends in Europe to replace her traditional Catholic allies. Following the advice of Wolsey's successor, Thomas Cromwell, Henry courted Luther, the key to an alliance with the German Protestant states. Both parties viewed each other with suspicion tinged with dislike. Luther could not forget that Henry had once penned a tract defending the seven sacraments against him, winning from the pope the proud title *Defender of the Faith* which is still stamped on British coins. Luther for his part, impolitic as always, had not countenanced Henry's divorce. Yet to all intents the two men shared the common Catholic doctrine of the eucharist. Armed with gifts the English ambassador arrived in Wittenberg to persuade Luther to despatch Melanchton to London for theological talks. But the

Elector of Saxony, fearing for Melanchton's life, would not allow him to go to London, nor to accept an invitation from Francis I to speak in Paris. Had the Elector agreed to these requests the course of European religious history might have taken a significantly different course.

At first all seemed to go well. The English ambassadors made no haste. In 1536 Luther wrote to a friend that he was hoping to get rid of the English embassy soon, but they showed no intention of leaving. With characteristic breadth of mind he advised the German negotiators of the treaty not to worry about 'ceremonials', for these matters would sort themselves out in time. A treaty with a league of German reformed princes was signed. Henry also married the daughter of a Lutheran prince, Anne of Cleves. Yet within months Henry repudiated his plain bride, abandoned the league and executed Cromwell. Even before the alliance was concluded Henry had issued the conservative Six Articles of 1539, 'a whip of six tails'. They upheld those traditional Catholic beliefs and practices which centred upon the conservative doctrine of the mass. Hugh Latimer, now Bishop of Worcester, resigned his see in protest. Henceforth the policy for the rest of the reign, which ended in 1547, was grimly conservative in matters of doctrine.

In this prevailing mood during the winter of Henry's reign those who preached Lutheran views openly ran the dangers of being executed under the laws against heresy. At the same time Henry's ministers harried those who denied the new political orthodoxy. The old friends of Catherine of Aragon, Sir Thomas More and John Fisher, Bishop of Rochester, both lost their heads in 1535 for not accepting the royal supremacy. In their steps came other Catholic martyrs. Three years later Bishop Hugh Latimer preached a sermon to a Franciscan friar called Forrest, one of Catherine of Aragon's confessors. He bravely endured a horrible death by being slowly roasted in chains. In 1540 the even-handed cruelty of the King's policy was vividly displayed when three Protestants were burnt for heresy at Smithfield at the same time as three obdurate Catholics were being hanged, drawn and quartered for treason.

Robert Barnes, one of those burnt that day, was another Cambridge convert. A Norfolk man by birth, he became a novice at the Augustinian house in Cambridge during the time when Erasmus was lecturing on Greek in the university. He studied abroad and may have heard Luther explaining himself to the general chapter of the Augustinians held in 1518 at Heidelberg. He returned to Cambridge, apparently as prior, and lectured on the Latin authors.

Miles Coverdale sat at his feet. Stephen Gardiner also met him about this time, and described Barnes as 'one of a merry scoffing wit, friar-like and as a good fellow in company well beloved of many'. Tried for heresy in 1526, Barnes abjured and did his public penance at St Paul's Cathedral with four German merchants of the Steelyard, who were condemned for propagating Lutheran views. In 1528, still in danger, he feigned suicide by leaving his clothes and a note near a river and then made his way to Antwerp. Under an assumed name he wandered about Europe, making an especially favourable impression upon the King of Denmark. For a time he studied with Luther in Wittenberg. Cromwell summoned Barnes home and then sent him back to Germany as an ambassador. In 1539 the former friar took part in a conference with German theologians in London, supporting them against the English conservatives. After Cromwell's fall Gardiner, now Bishop of Winchester, secured his condemnation to death without even the pretence of a trial. Thus died the one person who had known both Henry VIII and Martin Luther and thought it possible that they could yet agree. As Luther said of him, 'he always wished to help England'.

Nor did refuge on the continent spell security to those who fell foul of King Henry's religious policy, as the case of William Tyndale illustrates. Tyndale had failed to win the support of Tunstall, the successor of Colet's bishop, for his proposed translation of the Hebrew Old Testament and Greek New Testament into English, and so he had gone abroad. In Hamburg and later in Antwerp, assisted by a series of gifted collaborators of whom the most notable proved to be Coverdale, he laboured at translating the Bible. Favourably disposed English merchants in London and Antwerp provided Tyndale with both funds and hospitality, and doubtless their ships carried back into the country the first of some forty editions of Tyndale's *New Testament*, when it came off the presses of Cologne and Worms in 1525. The following year Tunstall joined Archbishop Warham and Sir Thomas More in a bitter attack upon the work, not least the blatant Lutheran doctrine in Tyndale's preface and notes. Whether the agents of Henry VIII or some English Catholics on the continent secured his arrest when he unwisely strayed beyond the liberties of Antwerp is not clear. But Tyndale was burnt at the stake in 1536, uttering as his memorable last words: 'Lord, open the King of England's eyes.'

*   *   *

Under King Henry's successor, the boy king Edward VI, the leading English divines turned their attention from Wittenberg to Geneva and Zürich. The Duke of Somerset himself corresponded with Calvin. Archbishop Cranmer invited several stars of the Reformation to England to serve as consultants to the English reformers. In 1549 Martin Bucer, then 56 years old, became Regius Professor of Divinity at Cambridge. The other chair at Oxford went to Bucer's friend Peter Martyr, the English name of Pietro Martire Vermiglio. This Florentine, a former Augustinian monk, had taught the new theology at Strassbourg.

Bucer found much to encourage him in the land of his exile. He could tell a correspondent that 'all the services in the churches are read and sung in the vernacular tongue, that the doctrine of justification is purely and soundly taught, and the Eucharist administered according to Christ's ordinance.' He objected to certain things in the new Prayer Book, such as making the sign of the cross in the consecration prayer, anointing in baptism, prayers for the dead and the blessing of water for the font. In the tradition of Luther, however, he did not object to vestments, delivering his opinion to Cranmer that they are things indifferent, neither prescribed nor proscribed in the Bible. If the lawful authority ordered them they should be worn. Later, in Elizabeth's reign Archbishop Whitgift, who was a young undergraduate in Cambridge when Bucer taught there, would quote the great man's authority for the practice of the Church of England. Bucer died in March 1551 and some 3000 mourners attended his funeral in Great St Mary's Church. In his brief time Bucer had seen the Reformation take root in England.

How did these momentous changes in religion affect the ordinary lay men and women? The correspondence of one English family helps us to answer this question. The Johnsons were merchants and their letters deal mostly with the prosaic matters of trade. But they shared the new Protestant beliefs and attitudes to the full. They were Puritans in the making.

Calais is the main setting of their story. This well-fortified city with its fine harbour had been in English hands for generations. Above the walls arose the tower of St Nicholas, the mariners' saint, and the tall spire of Our Lady Church, where merchants of the Staple would attend mass in their fur-trimmed robes. In Calais at Christmas 1534 young John Johnson sat doing his accounts in a gabled merchant's house, looking out on the cobbled market square. According to the purser of a visiting Italian ship, *The Salvator of Venice*, the lad had the good looks, fair complexion and reddish-gold hair which foreigners noted so often among the English. As a bound apprentice John wore plain fustian doublet and breeches, with white linen: the richer satin and silk clothes and embroidered lace shirts of the day were strictly forbidden to inferior social orders. With his goose-quill pen John inscribed in the ledger in his small but fine writing the state of his account at the threshold of his career: 'John Johnson ought to have that which is owing to me per my master, Anthony Cave, merchant of the Staple here in Calais, which is my father's bequest, Richard Johnson, Jesu rest his soul, being the sum of £54.10s.0d. mere sterling.' Apart from £5 in cash that was all that he was worth in money.

John Johnson would have received a good basic education, for English merchants such as Anthony Cave believed passionately in the new Renaissance learning. In the steps of the Mercers other great London companies either founded or refounded schools. Cave himself, a merchant of considerable wealth, founded a grammar school at Lathbury, a mile north of Newport Pagnell. Although John acquired some knowledge of Latin his education followed his practical bent and equipped him for a career as a merchant. He could certainly speak and write fluently in French and Flemish, the languages of the wool trade. He also mastered arithmetic in both roman and arabic numerals, as well as the art of keeping single and double entry accounts.

Not all of Anthony Cave's wealth came from the backs of English sheep. Through Cromwell's influence his father became High Sheriff of Northamptonshire. At the dissolution of the monasteries Cave secured some fine abbey buildings and lands for his sons. As his inheritance Anthony received Tickford Priory, just inside the boundary of neighbouring Buckinghamshire and close to the market town of Newport Pagnell. Many of the Puritan families in the next generation, such as the Winthrops in Suffolk, owed their fortunes to their share of monastic lands. No single act did more to unite the English gentry to the Tudor monarchy and the Protestant religion. 'Butter the rooks' nests,' Sir Thomas Wyatt said to Henry VIII, worried at the danger of revolt, 'and they will never trouble you.'

At Tickford Priory one summer day John Johnson first met his future wife, a girl with the pure Renaissance name of Sabine. She was Cave's niece and the sister of Ambrose Saunders, one of his other apprentices. She came from a large family of six brothers and six sisters. After her father's death her mother married again, and it is most probable that Sabine joined Cave's household, where she would be ruled by a condition in his will that his daughters were not to marry for money or gain, but 'as God disposes, and on the advice of their kin'. Given that John was an acceptable suitor to the family the match depended upon whether or not God would dispose Sabine to accept him.

Sabine was a vivacious and spirited girl with a mind of her own. She kept John on tenterhooks for a year or two. During 1538, when John was abroad, he plied his 'entirely beloved' with gifts: a basket full of black French cherries, some coloured silk ribbons, 'a neck-kerchief for my mistress' and delicately-worked lace from Antwerp. No longer an apprentice, he could exchange his 'work-day gown' for a wardrobe of white lawn shirts, doublets of striped and russet satin, Spanish cloaks and surcoats bright with gold and silver lace. He had a fur collar added to his best gown, and bought new gloves and 'a hat dressed with laces' off one of his friends. He even purchased a bottle or two of perfume for himself. Sabine could no longer resist him, and they became formally betrothed. As Cave was against his own daughters marrying before the age of twenty John had to wait until the autumn of 1541 for their wedding in Tickford Church.

John was now a fully-fledged merchant of the staple, exporting England's principal commodity of sacks of wool and fleeces to market in Calais. He also dealt in other goods, such as bales of linen and fine woollen cloth, barrels of herring, Norfolk grain and French wines. He traded in partnership with his younger brothers Otwell and Richard, and also in close liaison with a Flemish merchant firm. As he prospered he leased a country house from Sir Thomas Brudenell at Glapthorn, a hamlet close to Oundle in Northampton-shire. While he was abroad – mainly in Calais – Sabine stayed at home and ran the farm. From the first days of their marriage they hated being apart. When John left her not long after their wedding her cousin Thomas Saxby wrote from Calais to tell her that her 'bed-fellow at the making hereof was in good health and merry, with all our loving friends here'. He was hoping that the Hollanders would soon buy his wool, 'and then you shall have him the sooner with you, for I assure you he thinks only to be at home with you, as you would have him with you'.

If something displeased Sabine she made sure that John knew

about it. When, for example, business delayed him in plague-ridden Calais beyond the summer months of 1545 she wrote sharply to him: 'You do write that you be weary of London, but my trust is that you be not weary of your own house, nor of nobody in it . . .', signing herself 'Your loving and obedient wife that will be!' She sent him cheeses, chickens and pigeon pies, and begged him to avoid the crowded streets, 'desiring you most heartily to keep yourself well till you come home to me, and then I will keep you so well as God will give me grace'.

John replied from Calais on 8 November, promising to be home before Christmas. 'The death is here not very sore; howbeit, we be all in God's hands: as it pleaseth him, sobeit. I will keep myself for your sake as well as I can, and at my coming home I am content that you have the keeping of me. Howbeit, I may not be no more shrewdly spoken to, nor yet curstly looked on!' After some business matters he added, 'As the Lord knoweth, to whom I commit you in haste, going to my bed at ten of the clock at night – and would you were in my bed to tarry me! I bid you Goodnight, good wife sometimes!' Sabine replied, 'I am glad to hear that I did please you so well at your last being at home, praying to the Lord to give me grace that I may do always so; and whereas you do wish yourself at home (I would no less), and desiring you most heartily to come home so soon as you can, and keep yourself well, good husband . . .'

Behind these playful words lay the fear of sudden death engendered by the resurgence of the plague, which scythed down men, women and children by the hundred. John countered his wife's anxiety with a Luther's faith in the providence of God. 'I am in the hands of God, whom it may please to dispose me according to his godly will, and he it is that knows what is best for us. If it will please the same God to send me life (as your prayer is), then I shall help the bringing up of my children the best I can, and so provide for them and you as nigh as God will give me grace. But if God will otherwise dispose me, you must be content to receive it thankfully at the Lord's hands.'

John's sense of humour soon invaded this serious letter. Supposing Sabine's wish was granted, and he alone among men survived. Then 'you were like to lose me, your husband. For if there were in this town no more men left but I, the women of this town would keep me perforce from you, and then you were never the better! By Saint Mary! I should have much ado to please so many women! God save me from being troubled with many women, for I have much ado to please you alone, as you know! I pray you, keep yourself well that I may find you merry at my coming home, for here be many fair widows would have me, if you would not be angry therewith'. In reply Sabine wished all those widows two husbands apiece rather 'than you should be troubled with them'. She added delightfully, 'when it shall please God to send you home, I put no doubts but that we shall agree very well these cold nights . . .'

In November the following year, when Sabine heard that John lay sick in Calais with the ague, a fever akin to malaria, she rode at once to London on her little black mare, accompanied by Thomas, the groom. Brushing Otwell aside she took the first ship to Calais. 'Your wife's unbelieving of your amendment', he wrote to his brother from their Lime Street office, 'is grown into such desperation, in a manner, that no manner of persuasion could stay her from coming over unto you at this instant – which, if it be as discreetly done as rashly or woman-like, I refer to your judgement.' After Sabine had landed she went to John's lodgings, nursed him back to full health and then accompanied him home to Glapthorn for Christmas.

The Johnsons represent the first generation of Englishmen to accept the reformed faith. Their friend Parson Smith, chaplain to the Staple in Calais, had to answer to Cardinal Wolsey in person for possessing Luther's books. Above all the English Bible, with Tyndale's Lutheran preface to unlock its secrets, was never far from their sides. 'Your Bible I will send you,' wrote Richard Johnson to John, 'but I pray you let me have another.' The English merchant community resident on the continent had served as Tyndale's patrons as he laboured to produce his translation. Richard, writing from Calais, mentioned with excitement to his brothers that Miles Coverdale was coming to preach in the town. They were all avid listeners to sermons. Otwell could end one letter by explaining he was 'in much haste, going to a good sermon'. Yet the black-and-white mental framework of the miracle play, the great cosmic war between God and Satan as they tugged at man's soul, remained as real to the Johnsons as it did to their contemporary Martin Luther. Otwell enclosed with one letter a song upon 'the great benefits and works of God' which the Earl of Suffolk's players sang after performing their drama about 'the battle betwixt the Spirit, the Soul and the Flesh'.

For one member of the family the struggle resulted in a radical change of career. Sabine's brother Laurence, a former student at

Eton and King's College in Cambridge, took out indentures with a distant relative, an eminent London merchant named Sir William Chester. As Foxe related in the *Book of Martyrs*, Laurence could not settle down like his brothers-in-law to life in the counting-house. When he should have been perched on his stool filling in the great ledgers Saunders retreated to a private corner where he lamented his sins and prayed earnestly. For 'the Lord so wrought in his heart that he could find no liking in that vocation'. Eventually Chester set Laurence free and he returned to Cambridge. There he learnt both Hebrew and Greek so that he could read the Bible in the original languages. Then Laurence offered himself for ordination so that he could fulfill his calling as a Protestant preacher.

To most contemporary country clergymen in Henry VIII's reign the ardour with which Laurence approached the work of preaching seemed remarkable. The incumbent of Chicheley, a parish near Newport Pagnell in the gift of Sir Anthony Cave, was no exception. John Johnson acted as Cave's agent in the parish and he reported as much to Laurence. From Fotheringay, where he was ministering to the 'Lack-Latins' of a collegiate church, Laurence spoke in his reply for future generations of Puritan preachers: 'There be, I say, of them that think it an high point of divinity to use seldom preaching, thereby to make it as a dainty dish – as a dish of strawberries which come but once in the year; but I take God's Word to be that necessary, quotidian, ghostly food to feed the soul withal, even as the body hath need of daily bodily food. The Lord give us eyes to see what appertaineth unto our duties, and to study to do the same, and not to lie sweating on the to-side, like sluggish, reckless stewards!'

If the preacher waged war against the Devil so did the armies of the Protestant princes. Like Luther, the Johnsons interpreted the struggles convulsing the Holy Roman Empire in terms of the eternal war of God and the Devil, good versus evil. For Otwell, when the Palsgrave of the Rhine and other princes threw in their lot with the Protestant cause it simply meant that they had turned 'from the Devil to God'. A gentle man by nature, Otwell could break into a veritable passion when he wrote about 'the great Antichrist of Rome and his synagogue'. In July 1545 he informed John that the Emperor was still at Worms and drawing no nearer to agreement with the Protestants 'by reason of the devilish suggestion of the great and abominable harlot of Babylon and daily feeding of him and his papistical prelates with great abundance of exportioned Romish ducats . . .'

The year 1545 seemed to herald the beginning of an apocalyptic civil war in Europe. As the Emperor summoned the Council of Trent to meet that December to serve as the spearhead of the powerful energies of the Catholic reaction, so Imperial regiments mustered to take the field against the German champions. The Johnsons shared to the full the same confidence of ultimate victory as did ailing Luther in Wittenberg. On 26 October John wrote to Anthony Cave, 'I trust God will so work that the devil and his angels shall not prevail against the faithful in Christ.' As for the Pope, they shared a faith that 'Christ's own Word shall tread him underfoot'. After victory God will 'send us universal peace and a reformation of Popish errors'. This vehement Protestantism would continue to characterize English merchants resident on the continent. The Company of Merchant Adventurers, who dealt in cloth rather than wool, maintained a factory at Delft, the embarkation port of the Pilgrim Fathers. Its scattered groups of merchants in the Dutch cities would entertain such famous Puritan ministers as Robert Brown, Thomas Cartwright, John Robinson and William Ames. As the Johnson correspondence shows, the Puritan tradition was deep rooted in this community.

Waves of pestilence rather than war brought death into the circle of the Johnson family and friends. They longed for a remission of these scourges. 'I pray God send quietness,' wrote Sir Anthony Cave to John in November 1544, 'for we have deaths, pests and wars to know God.' But worse befell them. A year later Otwell concluded a letter from London to John with the sad words 'it has pleased God this day to take Henry Johnson, my boy, from me by death'. His son had died in his arms. But faith rose to the challenge, and the bereaved father added: 'Our Lord have his soul and all Christian souls, and keep you in health.' To escape infection Otwell moved to his brother-in-law's house, only to report a few days later: 'God Almighty has still his scourge for me in his hands, for on Wednesday last he struck William, my brother Gery's lad, with the plague as we suppose, for he complains much under his arm and is become very sick.' William died within a day or two.

The face of death ever before their eyes certainly deepened the faith of these early English Protestants. It cast them on their knees in humble supplication and loving trust. 'Let God do his pleasure with me,' wrote Otwell. God alone knew the time of a person's death, which happened 'at the Lord's pleasure, who be our guide thereunto'. There is no hint of theological controversy in the Johnson letters, for the laity in those days as now left all that largely to the clergy. What they desperately needed was a faith strong enough to hold a dead son in its arms. That is what the Reformation gave them.

Sometimes the prayers in their letters have the music of Cranmer's collects, which the Archbishop was writing for the first Book of Common Prayer (1549). The widow, Mrs Margaret Baynham, with whom John Johnson lodged in Calais, had already lost two husbands and two brothers-in-law; the plague which broke out in the spring of 1545 decimated her remaining relatives and friends in the town. 'I beseech his almighty goodness, even as he daily reneweth my sorrow and heaviness, so mercifully to send me patience in all my trouble and adversity, and to obtain the same the better, I desire you and good Master Cave to pray for me.' She added a postscript: 'This being written in the morning, John Grant and Margery my sister's daughter departed this world about eleven of the clock before dinner. Now is our lamentation and mourning greater than ever it was before, Almighty God be our comfort.'

God's hand did not rest heavy on the Johnson brothers for long. On 22 May 1548 Otwell could joyfully remind John that their wives were both pregnant by ending a letter 'with hearty commendations to my sister your wife's belly from Mary my boss her belly, and all our friends here, fare you well in Christ Jesus.' In June, Mary bore him a daughter. They called her Abigail, for as Otwell said, it meant in English 'my father has rejoiced'. For his part John called his son Evangelist, an early example of the widespread Puritan practice of bestowing names inspired by the English Bible.

For several years the brothers enjoyed their family life in peace. Meanwhile under Edward VI the Church of England began to assume a distinctly Protestant aspect wholly congenial to the brothers. Sabine wrote to John in Calais in June 1551: 'This next week and God send fair weather, I will shear sheep. My parlour is well nigh trimmed. I trust it will be ready against your coming home: if it be 14 days before Midsummer, it will please me very well. So the Lord knoweth, He send us of his grace and merry meeting. Amen.' Yet even as she wrote these words, unbeknown to her a dark cloud had gathered on the horizon.

Nobody knows the origin of the terrible disease known as sweating sickness or the 'sweat'. It surfaced first in London in 1485, a month after the battle of Bosworth. 'This sickness comes with a great sweating and stinking, with redness of the face and of all the body, and a continual thirst, with a great heat and headache because of the fumes and venoms.' Physicians of the day recommended relatives to keep the sufferer warm, and to give him no cold water but pieces of bread soaked in sugared ale. He must be kept awake, because those who fell asleep relapsed into a fatal coma. 'For in this sweating sickness death always comes, if it does come, on the first day,' More had informed Erasmus in 1517. 'I tell you, there is less danger on a battle field than in London.' Seven years later his daughter Margaret succumbed and fell into that dangerous sleep. More, on his knees in fervent prayer, thought of some remedy which was immediately ministered to her. Although 'God's marks', a sure token of death, appeared on her skin yet she recovered against all expectation. His friend Dean John Colet survived three attacks, but died from the after-effects.

Sweating sickness spread to Europe, but after raging for a year or two it petered out, apparently for ever. Then, after twenty years, in March 1551, a young man died of it in Shrewsbury. In July, Otwell reported that it had broken out in some twenty houses in his own parish of Saints Peter and Bartholomew in the City. Perhaps acting from some premonition Otwell put his business affairs in good order, and wrote on his letters: 'The Lord liveth.' Next day Otwell heard of the deaths of Harry Bostock and other familiar friends. He himself came in from the street and went to bed feeling hot at seven. Soon he was 'in extreme pain', and after drifting into a coma Otwell died at three o'clock in the morning of 10 July.

'The Lord's Visitation' scythed down many more relatives and friends that year, both in England and on the continent, but John survived an attack in Calais. 'God deliver us and be merciful unto us,' he wrote, 'for we have had a terrible time.' To make matters worse he had lost in Otwell his most able partner, and soon his business affairs began to go awry. He had increased his turnover considerably, observing that 'few in these days profit by wares but such as trade in wares continually'. He saw the war between France and the Empire, which broke out that year, as an opportunity to expand his activities in the wine trade. Although John knew it not he was overstretching himself. Storms battered one of the English ships he sent to fetch some wine his agents had bought in Spain; French warships plundered the other vessel. Yet John ignored these warnings. In vain his mentor, Anthony Cave, now old and weak, repeated to him the proverb, 'He that does not perils foresee, in perils fall.'

As Cave had invested the large sum of £1500 in some of John's ventures a note of urgency crept into his letter: 'For God's sake, look as well to th'end as to the beginning!' In reply John repeatedly asked Cave to continue his goodwill. To support the increased volume of business he offered to Cave in November 1551 the argument drawn from Luther that come what may, he ought to go on labouring diligently in his vocation.

After their southern voyages had failed John Johnson and his new partner Bartholomew Warner turned to 'Master Herring' in search of profits. They bought a thousand pounds worth of herrings on credit, only to find that they were 'so shamefully handled' and 'so falsely packed' that the profit was too small. Other ventures, such as importing raisins, Rouen cloth and molasses and sugar, proved equally unsuccessful. Within eight months of Otwell's death their business affairs had become disordered with debts exceeding £8000 and twenty or more rapacious creditors waiting to pounce upon their assets.

Johnson & Company struggled on for another year until March 1553, when they finally became bankrupt. At the end of that month John wrote to one of his creditors, the powerful Sir William Cecil, his future patron. He hoped that some order would be taken to distribute his goods among his other creditors for some were already helping themselves to his possessions. 'For God knows it is no little grief to my heart to continue in this miserable estate, beseeching God to give me grace to take it patiently as the punishment of God justly laid upon me for my sins, having deserved a great deal more, but that God in his mercy punishes me not according to my deservings . . . I beseech you for God's sake be my good master better than I have deserved, and I shall pray unto God to send you life everlasting, purchased by Christ's death and passion. Scribbled rudely, by your poor orator, John Johnson.'

With some help from Cecil and other prominent patrons as well as from his kinsmen, John Johnson lived well into Queen Elizabeth's reign, busying himself in various employments and promoting his pet scheme to create in England a market town to rival Antwerp. His son Evangelist, apprenticed in the Drapers' Company, became a successful merchant. After his marriage in 1582 he in turn fathered several children: Evangelist, Peter and a daughter named Sabine after her grandmother, and finally Emanuel. These children would never know their great-uncle Laurence Saunders, but they would certainly have read his story in Foxe's *Book of Martyrs*. For Laurence died for his faith in the great persecution of Protestants in Queen Mary's reign.

3

The Fatal Storm

Towards the end of Henry VIII's reign Edward Saunders, Sabine Johnson's eldest brother and a King's Serjeant-at-law, made it his duty as head of the family to issue a solemn warning to his younger brother Laurence. As a conservative in matters of religion Edward clearly disapproved of Laurence's faith and feared the trouble that his outspokenness would bring on the family. With his successful career as a lawyer in mind Edward doubtless did not relish the thought of being linked in the public mind with a heretic. He solemnly cautioned 'me to take very good heed unto myself,' wrote Laurence to John Johnson, 'that I be not drowned in mine own fantasy and opinion, as others have been which after repented and acknowledged their own folly.' In a long conversation Edward had said how sorry he was that Laurence was noted to be 'one of the singular sort'. Towards the end of it, as if 'to make up all, he comforted me, saying that he doubted . . . my very great familiarity with Latimer'. By this time Latimer had become a famous preacher in Luther's mould, known to his admirers as the 'Apostle to the English'.

Laurence could afford to smile at his brother's advice during the reign of Edward VI, but that proved to be but a brief interlude of tranquillity. In 1553, four months after the Johnson firm went bankrupt, the fervent and bigoted Catholic Mary Tudor came to the throne. If Edward Saunders repeated his advice doubtless Laurence again rejected it. For he deemed it 'good worldly counsel, and if I had no other end to have respect unto than this present life I would follow it, but because it agrees not to the other way, I lightly esteem it'. That 'other way' led to the martyr's stake for Laurence. Yet brother Edward, an ancestor of Bunyan's Mr Worldly-Wise, lived to enjoy a successful career. Queen Mary honoured him with a knighthood, and Queen Elizabeth made him her Lord Chief Justice of the Queen's Bench.

Queen Mary was crowned by Stephen Gardiner, now Bishop of Winchester and a prelate in high favour with her. This determined young woman had two ends in mind: to restore England to the fold of Rome and to beget a Catholic heir to the throne. Marriage to her kinsman, Philip II of Spain, promised to support the first and ensure the second. But news of their betrothal triggered off a major armed rising, which owed as much to outraged nationalism as to Protestant fervour among the 'singular sort'. Mary quelled the rebellion with Tudor courage. In July 1554 a wary Philip landed in England to claim his half-Spanish bride. According to Foxe, the Spanish king held a sword in his right hand, as if he was stepping ashore at the head of an invading army. He had the grace to shift the blade to his left hand to receive the keys of Southampton from the mayor of the town. Shortly afterwards Bishop Gardiner married the royal couple in Winchester Cathedral.

Early in 1555, Cardinal Reginald Pole, who replaced Cranmer as Archbishop of Canterbury, formally reconciled England to the see of Rome. Then Bishop Gardiner, the Queen's Chancellor, restored the laws against heresy, and the work of exterminating the 'singular sort' began in earnest. The government had given plenty of notice of its intentions. About 800 Protestant clergy and laymen had fled to the Calvinist and Lutheran centres of Geneva, Basle, Frankfurt and Strasbourg. There they imbibed far more radical doctrines than any yet accepted in England. Among them was John Foxe, the historian of that 'fatal storm', as he called it, which was about to burst upon England.

When the college at Fotheringay was finally dissolved in the previous reign Laurence Johnson had received the benefice of Church Langton in Leicestershire. From there he received a call to the London congregation of All Hallows Church in Bread Street. In the late spring of 1553, after Laurence had taken possession of his new benefice, he had gone back to Leicestershire to wind up his affairs in Church Langton. But the tumultuous events while Mary Tudor pressed her claims against the Protestant usurper Lady Jane Grey interrupted him. In these troubled weeks he preached in Northampton, boldly declaring his mind about popish doctrine. In the changed circumstances he refused to resign either of his two benefices, for he could not bear to give either into the hands of a papist. When Mary's ministers issued the royal proclamation against preaching Laurence happened to be at Church Langton, and he seems to have been forcibly prevented from entering the pulpit. Some of his friends counselled him to flee the realm, but he refused. Instead, he made his way to London.

On Saturday 14 October, as Laurence rode into the city, a privy councillor of Queen Mary's named Sir John Mordaunt overtook him. Sir John's father, Baron Mordaunt, had supported the reformation as a loyal servant of the King. Although a strong Catholic, his son had received his knighthood at the coronation of Anne Boleyn. With his father, who was a personal friend of Cromwell, he had attempted to secure a dissolved priory, yet he was among the first to proclaim Mary as Queen. Mordaunt asked Laurence where he was going. 'I have a cure in London,' he replied, 'and I go to instruct my people according to my duty.' 'I would advise you not to preach,' said Mordaunt. 'If you forbid me by lawful authority, then I must obey,' said Laurence. 'No, I will not forbid you but I give you counsel.' After they parted Mordaunt rode at once to inform Edmund Bonner, Bishop of London, that Saunders would preach to his congregation next day.

The following morning Laurence preached and in the afternoon returned to the church to deliver the customary second sermon. But the Bishop's officer arrived to escort him to Fulham Palace. Bonner stood waiting for him with Sir John Mordaunt and his 'bonner-lings', the chaplains and servants of his household. As Foxe humorously put it, 'the Bishop laid no more to Saunder's charge but treason for breaking the Queen's proclamation, heresy and sedition for his sermon.' After much talk the Bishop ordered him to put down on paper his rejection of the Catholic doctrine of the mass. Laurence did so, realizing that he was writing his own death warrant. 'My Lord, you do seek my blood,' Laurence said as he handed the paper to Bonner, 'and you shall have it. I pray God that you may be so baptised in it that you may thereafter loathe blood-sucking and become a better man.'

The Bishop then sent Laurence to the Lord Chancellor, Bishop Stephen Gardiner, 'as Annas sent Christ to Caiaphas', noted Foxe. As the Chancellor was not at home the guards held Saunders in the outer chamber for four hours. Standing bareheaded by the cupboard as Mordaunt paced up and down beside him, Laurence had leisure to observe one of Gardiner's chaplains laughing much with some gentlemen friends over a gaming table. At length Gardiner returned from court and Laurence was brought before him; he meekly knelt down and bowed courteously. The Chancellor asked him why he had ignored the Queen's proclamation against preaching. Laurence replied that he had followed the warning of Ezekiel and exhorted his congregation to persevere in the doctrine they had learned through the perilous times now at hand. He was 'pricked forward' in conscience by the apostolic requirement to obey God rather than man. 'A good conscience surely!' exclaimed Gardiner. 'Your conscience would make our Queen a bastard or misbegotten, would it not?' In denying that charge Laurence could not resist making a veiled reference to a book which Gardiner had written in King Henry VIII's reign, which declared Mary to be a bastard. The Lord Chancellor, now thoroughly annoyed, ordered, 'Carry this frenzied fool to prison.' Laurence answered that he gave God thanks for giving him at last a place of rest and quietness where he might pray for the Bishop's conversion.

For a year and three months Laurence remained in captivity. His wife came to the prison gate, with her young child in her arms, to visit her husband. The keeper, though he dare not let her into the prison, took the babe out of her arms and brought him to his father. Laurence was delighted, saying he rejoiced more to have such a boy than he would if someone gave him two thousand pounds. To bystanders Laurence made a ringing defence of clerical marriage: 'What man would not lose his life rather than by prolonging it adjudge this boy to be a bastard, his wife a whore, and himself a whoremonger? If there were no other cause for which a man of my estate should lose his life, who would not give it to avouch this child to be legitimate, and his marriage lawful and holy?'

Once delivered to the secular power, Laurence was brought by the Sheriff of London to the Counter prison in his own parish of All Hallows. By one of those strange chances of history the Sheriff that year was none other than Sir Anthony Chester, his former master. Laurence's removal to the Counter led him to rejoice that he might preach to his own parishioners out of prison as he had before done so out of a pulpit. On 4 February 1555 Bonner came to the prison to degrade him from the priesthood. It was an awesome ritual. The former priest was stripped of his vestments, struck with the crozier, and had his fingertips and top of his head symbolically scraped. When it was done Laurence said simply, 'I thank God I am none of your church.' Next day the Sheriff delivered him to a section of the Queen's Guard which had orders to take him to Coventry to be burned.

When the party reached Coventry on 7 February a poor shoemaker came to Laurence and said, 'O my good master, God strengthen and comfort you!' 'Gramercies, good shoemaker,' replied Laurence, 'I pray you pray for me, for I am the unmeetest man for this high office that ever was appointed to it. But my gracious God and most dear Father is able to make me strong enough.' He spent that night in the common gaol among other prisoners, where he passed the time praying. Next morning he was led to the place of execution outside the city, dressed in an old gown and a shirt, barefooted. Near the stake an officer asked Laurence to recant his heresies in exchange for a royal pardon: 'If not, yonder fire is prepared for you.' But Laurence remained steadfast. 'It is not I nor my fellow-preachers of God's truth that have hurt the Queen's realm, but yourself and such as you are, which have always resisted God's holy word. I hold no heresies; but the blessed gospel of Christ, that hold I; that have I taught, and that will I never revoke.' With that the tormentor cried, 'Away with him!' 'And away,' Foxe wrote, 'went Saunders with a merry courage towards the fire. He fell to the ground and prayed; he rose up again and took the stake in his arms and kissed it saying, "Welcome the cross of Christ. Welcome everlasting life"; and being fastened to the stake and fire put to him, full sweetly he slept in the Lord.'

*   *   *

Among the elect it was noticeable that the laity provided most of the martyrs. Besides five bishops and twenty-one divines, one contemporary lists the victims as follows: 'eighty-four artificers, an hundred husbandmen, servants and labourers, twenty-six wives, twenty widows, nine virgins, two boys and two infants. . . . Sixty-four more were persecuted for their profession of faith; whereof seven were whipped, sixteen perished in prison, twelve were buried in dunghills.'

Later generations of Puritan-minded apprentices in London could identify themselves, for example, with William Hunter. This lad was commanded by his parish priest to receive the mass at Easter, but refused. His master, a silk-weaver Thomas Taylor, disowned the boy and so he made his way back to his home village of Burntwood, near Lichfield. A day or two later Father Atwell, a summoner by trade, heard William reading the Bible aloud to himself in the church. 'What, are you meddling with the Bible? Can you expound the Scriptures?' William said, 'Father Atwell, I take not upon me to expound the Scriptures; but I, finding the Bible here when I came, read in it to my own comfort.' But Atwell became more angry. 'It was never a merry world since the Bible came abroad in English. I perceive your mind well enough: you are one of them that mislikes the Queen's laws. You must turn another leaf, or else you

79

and a great sort more heretics will broil for this gear, I warrant you.' William's confident answer that God would give him grace to confess his word drove Atwell to retort 'You'll go to the Devil and confess *his* name!' The apprentice replied calmly, 'You say not well, Father Atwell.'

The fuming summoner fetched Thomas Wood, vicar of South-well, from an alehouse near the church and together they told their tale to Justice Browne. After Browne had examined William about the doctrine of the sacrament he sent him up to Bishop Bonner, where he was lodged in stocks in the gatehouse of Fulham Palace for two days and nights with a crust of bread and cup of water. The Bishop asked William his age. 'Nineteen,' replied William. 'Well,' said Bonner, 'you will be burned 'ere you be twenty.' After nine months in prison the faithful apprentice was taken back to Burntwood to die. He was lodged in the Swan Inn on the eve of his execution, and there he said his farewells to family and friends. At the stake he threw his Psalter into his brother's hands, who called out: 'William, think on the passion of Christ and be not afraid.' William answered, 'I am not afraid.'

Thomas Thomkins, a weaver by occupation, was burnt at Smithfield on 16 March 1555. By disposition he was so godly that if a customer came to talk to him in his Shoreditch workroom he would begin with a prayer. Like all Christians he was against usury. If anyone wanted to borrow money Thomas showed them what he had in his purse and bade them to take it; when they returned to repay the loan he pressed them to keep it until they could better afford to do without it. Half-a-dozen of his neighbours so cherished his memory that they sought out John Foxe to tell him the full story. Thomas was arrested and taken to Fulham in July: the Bishop's servants put him to making hay. 'I like you well,' said Bonner to him one day, 'for you labour well. I trust you will be a good Catholic.' Thomas quoted St Paul's words about those who do not labour being unworthy to eat. Ah! St Paul is a great man with you,' muttered Bonner. According to Foxe, the Bishop held the weaver's hand over three or four candle flames to frighten him, but he felt no pain.

Foxe's pages abound with such homespun martyrs. Like Thomkins, many applied their religion through their callings. The doctrines of vocation clearly appealed greatly to the English middle classes. Edward Allen of Fritenden in Kent was a miller who was burnt at Maidstone. In a 'year of dearth' he sold his corn at less than half the price of his profiteering fellow millers and corn merchants. He also gave his customers 'the food of life' by reading and interpreting the Scriptures to them. On Queen Mary's accession he went to Calais, but he could not be quiet there. 'For God, he said, "had something for him to do in England".' William Wiseman (clothworker), Nicholas Hall (bricklayer), Christopher Wade (linen-weaver), George Tankerfield (cook), the wife of a brewer, the wife of a shoemaker: all were people with whom the later Puritans could identify themselves completely. A London Puritan congregation during later reigns could test their own fidelity by comparing themselves to that 'company of innocent people' who assembled in a field by the town of Islington to pray and meditate together on God's word. Officers raided the meeting and arrested 40 men and women: seven died at Smithfield, six at Brentford and two perished in prison. Nonconformists in the following reign, including the congregation of John Robinson, would claim descent from this underground church in London.

What was it really like to face death at the stake? Foxe left his Puritan readers in no doubt. The local sheriff and his men, armed with bills, glaives or halberds, usually collected the martyr from prison. After the irons had been struck off legs and arms, and sometimes a collar of iron from the neck, the prisoner was led to the place of execution. Sometimes he was drawn there bound to a hurdle, or carried in a chair if old age, illness or a prolonged diet of bread, water and salt-fish had rendered him infirm. Foxe noted that the keepers of the bishop's prisons were far less lenient with their captives than their royal counterparts. Conditions in winter were severe: Latimer could jest in the Tower to the Lieutenant that unless he let him have a fire in his room he would freeze to death before he burnt. The paradox of a martyr asking for fire amused Latimer greatly. The prisoners often encountered harrowing sights on their road. John Rogers, for instance, passed his wife and ten children, the youngest still a baby, on the way to Smithfield.

More often than not a great crowd had gathered to witness the execution. About 2000 people saw Kerby arrive at the stake wearing his nightcap. The more important spectators had seats in specially built galleries. In Gloucester they burnt Bishop John Hooper on market day. About 7000 onlookers, some swarming up trees and perched on house tops to get a better view, saw him led out to the stake near the great elm tree beside the College of Priests where he had once preached. When Christopher Wade, linen-weaver, suffered in a gravel pit near Rochester – dressed in a long white shirt sent to him by his wife – another vast crowd thronged to witness the scene. Taking advantage of a hot July day several fruiterers with horseloads of cherries did a brisk trade. Wade and his fellow martyr, Margery Pollen, arrived on horseback with their arms pinioned, singing a psalm. 'You may rejoice, Wade, to see such a company gathered to celebrate your wedding day,' Margery said to her younger companion. For it became commonplace among English Protestants to look upon their dying day as the marriage of the soul with Christ.

The victims were chained to the stake, and faggots of wood, broom and straw piled around their legs. Sometimes they stood bound to the stake by hoops of iron on a high stool or in a barrel of pitch. Bishop Hooper's friends placed a pound of gunpowder in a bladder between his legs and under each armpit to hasten his end. On that 'cold and lowering' morning the sheriff's men had already taken off his doublet and hose, and trussed his shirt between his legs with a lace taken from his hose. But the English were not good at burning people, especially when there was a wind blowing. 'Set to fire!' ordered the sheriff. But once the dry reeds or gorse used for kindling had flared up, scorching the victim's hair and eyebrows, the wind either shifted and bent the flames away from the stake or else the officers ran out of dry fuel. The green faggots or wet straw which they then cast on the fire produced clouds of choking smoke. Mercifully, many martyrs were suffocated by the fumes. Sometimes the friends of the martyr urged the sergeants to turn an ill-kindled fire so that it blew in his face. Rawlins White, sixty years old, himself reached out to arrange the straw and reed so that it would despatch him speedily. Bishop Hooper took two bundles of reeds, kissed them and put them under his arms, and indicated how the rest should be distributed, pointing to places which lacked any. Not that his precautions did him much good on that gusty February day. After three attempts the flames arose, but the gunpowder bladders broke. The wind had such power that poor Hooper stood in the fire for three-quarters of an hour. His brother Bishop Ridley, in a like predicament at Oxford, had called out piteously, 'Let the fire come unto me, I cannot burn, I cannot burn . . .'

Because burning was such a slow method of execution the martyr often had time to address the crowd. To do so Christopher Wade shouted down a friar intoning near the stake. He shifted some burning faggots to one side to make sure he had time to say his last words. The officers strove to silence or disrupt these final testimonies. A sergeant-at-arms thrust a burning furze-bush upon a pike into the face of one martyr 'to make him pray to Our Lady' rather than preach a sermon. The spectators were sometimes admonished not to pray aloud, but they would not be cheated from hearing the martyrs. That blessed word 'England' was never far from their blackened lips. Generations of later Puritans would heed the words of John Bradford, the Cambridge man whom Martin Bucer had encouraged to become a preacher. Having given his clothes away to the sheriff's poor servant, Bradford stood at the stake and addressed this prayer for his country: 'O England, England, repent you of your sins. Beware of false Antichrists; take heed they do not deceive you!' Thus through the pages of Foxe the last words of the martyrs became their most treasured relics. 'Be of good cheer, Master Ridley, and play the man,' said Hugh Latimer to his fellow victim. 'We shall this day light such a candle by God's grace in England as I trust shall never be put out.'

*   *   *

On 10 November 1558 five heretics endured death by burning at Canterbury. Three days later, Mary signed the death warrant of two London Protestants, but she died before sentence could be carried out. Her half-sister Elizabeth Tudor succeeded her to the throne. The wheel of fortune now turned in favour of the Protestants. Gardiner's successor at Winchester, Bishop White, preached Mary's funeral sermon. 'I warn you,' he told the congregation, 'the wolves be coming out of Geneva, and other places of Germany, and have sent their books before.' For some incautious words about the new chief shepherdess of the English flock delivered in that same sermon Bishop White found himself committed to prison. Times had changed.

4

Elizabethan Puritans

On the eve of her coronation in January 1559 Queen Elizabeth, a young woman of twenty-five, rode triumphantly in a litter through London for her coronation, accompanied by a thousand horsemen. The warmth of London's welcome touched her. She noticed one old man weeping and said to an attendant, 'I warrant you it is for gladness.' One shout from the crowd – 'Remember old King Henry!' – made her smile. In their tableaux the Londoners expressed their expectations for her reign. Virtue triumphing over Vice walked one stage at Cornhill; True Religion trod upon Superstition and Ignorance while a child, personifying Elizabeth, looked on with approval. At the Little Conduit another play showed Time emerging from a cave and leading by the hand her daughter Truth who carried an English Bible in her hand. Truth stepped off the stage and presented the Bible to Queen Elizabeth, who kissed it, held it up on high in both hands and then laid it on her bosom amid thunderous applause. Near the cathedral a boy from St Paul's School addressed the customary Latin oration to her, comparing the Queen to Plato's philosopher-king. The Fleet Street play showed her as Deborah, judge and restorer of Israel, taking council with her bishops, lords and commons for the good of God's people. Next day, as bells rang and cannon thundered, she was crowned in Westminster Abbey to an acclamation so deafening that one observer compared it to the last clap of time.

'Her Majesty's desire', a royal servant informed Parliament in January 1559, is 'to secure and unite the people of the realm in one uniform order to the glory of God and to general tranquillity.' Thus she commanded her subjects to eschew calling each other such names as 'heretics, schismatics and papists', for this caused displeasure and malice. Concord and unity were now the targets at which they should aim their shafts.

Shortly afterwards Parliament passed the legislation which established the Church of England under the Queen as 'the only supreme governor', and ordered the use of a revised version of the second Edwardian Prayer Book. As more orders regulating worship and church discipline appeared it became clear that Queen Elizabeth was aiming broadly at an acceptable Protestant position, one which would satisfy both the Henrician conservatives as well as more moderate disciples of the Swiss reformers. Hence the ambiguities in the 1559 Prayer Book, especially in the service of Holy Communion. The Queen looked for outward conformity, allowing individuals privately to interpret its doctrine as they pleased.

The returning Marian exiles welcomed the Protestant complexion of Elizabeth's settlement but many cavilled at the remaining warts of Romish doctrine. To the purists medieval vestments still evoked echoes of the old priestly magic of sacrificial masses. Some clergymen flatly refused to exchange their black Genevan gowns for 'the livery of Antichrist'. Wedding rings, the baptismal sign of the cross and kneeling at Holy Communion also seemed to spell a retention of the false sacramentalism of Rome.

But the home-comers did not present a united front. The Queen had in her gift bishoprics, deaneries, canonries and some of the fattest livings in the Church of England. A few exiles put conscience first and turned down her offers. But a substantial number, like John Aylmer who became Archdeacon and later Bishop of London, accepted the bait. Some donned the vestments because they believed with Luther and Bucer that such externals were 'matters indifferent'. Others may have hoped to reform the Church of England once they were living in its palaces, deaneries or canonries. These naive souls underestimated the power of institutions to change attitudes. The former poachers began to look like the old gamekeepers. Some external observers would soon see a resemblance between the Elizabethan bishops, despite their Reformed theology, and the worldly popish prelates of Wolsey's day. Lord Burghley, an acute observer of human nature, once commented to the Archbishop of Canterbury that 'he saw much worldiness in many that were otherwise affected before they came to cathedral churches that he feared the places altered the men'.

When Elizabeth succeeded to the throne the See of Canterbury was vacant, for Cardinal Pole died within hours of Mary. The Queen appointed to it a Cambridge don in his mid-fifties, named Matthew Parker, ignoring the excuses he pleaded of old age, illness and disabilities. Son of a worsted weaver in Norwich, Parker had risen to be Vice-Chancellor of his University. He had discussed Luther's theology in the White Horse Inn. Thus he represents the continuity of the English Reformation. Prudent, grave and learned, he also epitomized the new tradition of Renaissance scholarship. 'One would think that Cato or Quintus Fabius lived again in him', wrote one admiring friend. He brought to Lambeth Palace not only this impeccable background as a Reformed divine and his scholarly interests as an historian, but also an Erasmian belief in moderation, reason and peace.

Within weeks of his consecration Parker encountered those very difficulties he had probably foreseen in the quietness of his Cambridge rooms. A wave of iconoclasm, which swept across the Reformed countries of Europe at the time, visited England. Crowds gathered to smash or deface the images of saints in parish churches. These statues or pictures were seen as symbols of the old religion. They reminded the iconoclasts of indulgences, masses and shrines – the whole powerless system of salvation inflicted on mankind by Rome. While these relics of the past remained, they held, the Church of Christ, the Church of the New Testament, could not be at home in the parish churches of England. In Stratford-upon-Avon, for example, in 1564 – the year of his son William's birth – John Shakespeare, the town's bailiff, put his mark – a glover's compasses – beside a council order to deface the images and whitewash the fine frescoes in the guild chapel of the parish church.

These 'irritable precisians' or 'puritans', as Archbishop Parker called them, were especially strong in the capital. 'The world is much given to innovations; never content to stay to live well,' he wrote to a friend. 'In London our fonts must go down, and the brazen eagles, which were ornaments in the chancel and made for lecterns, must be molten to make pots and basins for new fonts. I do but marvel what some men mean, to gratify these puritans railing against themselves.' When his *Book of Advertisements* appeared in 1566, after the Queen had hesitated and delayed its publication, ordering the continued use of surplice, cope and other such outward symbols, the trouble flared up again.

Parker grumbled continually at the lack of support he received from the Queen. For influential friends at court backed these Puritan agitators. The Queen's favourite, Robert Dudley, whom she created Earl of Leicester, certainly favoured them. In the early years of the reign it was widely expected that Elizabeth would marry Leicester. Parker sensed his hand at work to restrain him. 'I may not work against precisians and puritans, though the laws be against them,' he complained. 'Know one and know all. . . . Though

I have a dull head yet I see, partly by myself and partly by others, how the game goes.'

The Queen played the game with consummate skill. A book by Erasmus, *The Education of a Christian Prince*, probably taught her the supreme importance of winning and holding the affections of her subjects. But the Queen blended the Platonic wisdom of Erasmus with the Italian realism of Machiavelli. 'Her Majesty counts much on Fortune,' wrote the Puritan Sir Francis Walsingham, 'I wish she would trust more in Almighty God.' Her restless and calculating mind was always at work, plotting a course forwards through a tangled maze of possibilities and dangers. She observed men closely and played upon their emotions as if they were the keys of her harpsichord. She alternated royal severity with feminine guile. On one occasion, when Elizabeth had said some 'hard words' to Parker in council the day before, it fell to his duty to meet her on Lambeth bridge. 'She gave me her very good looks,' wrote the bemused Archbishop, 'and spoke secretly in mine ear, that she must needs countenance mine authority before the people, to the credit of my service.' On reflection Parker felt himself to be in a well-nigh impossible situation, as he complained to Cecil: 'Her Majesty told me that I had supreme government ecclesiastical, but what is it to govern cumbered with such subtlety?'

If Parker lacked the Queen's wholehearted support against the Puritans he was also ill-served by some of his colleagues on the bishops' bench. Edmund Grindal, who was offered the key diocese of London in 1564, had himself scrupled at wearing the cope and surplice in the consecration ceremony. He wrote to Peter Martyr for advice as to what he should do, but he had accepted the bishopric before his friend could reply. Predictably Grindal was comparatively soft on the Puritans. 'He was not resolute and severe enough for the goverment of London,' wrote Parker. When Grindal was promoted to the See of York six years later, however, the Queen appointed Edwin Sandys, who was even more sympathetic to the Puritan movement. Both at London and later at York, Edwin Sandys did little to restrain any but the worst excesses of the more Puritan ministers in London.

A former Vice-Chancellor of Cambridge, Sandys had stood firm under Mary's persecution and earned honourable mention in Foxe's *Book of Martyrs* for his courage in prison. Eventually he made his way to the continent. He returned to become Bishop of Worcester before his subsequent preferment to London and York. In these dioceses Sandys showed a voracious appetite for 'fruits and fees' of office, especially lands. He provided for his family of nine children by granting them property on long-leases, much to the dislike of the Dean of York. Two of his sons, Edwin and George, would play a notable part in settling Virginia, while the tenant of a third son's property at Scrooby in Nottinghamshire, named William Brewster, would become even more famous in American history.

Despite the abusive title of 'the pope of Lambeth', Archbishop Parker was no more than a 'first among equals' as far as his fellow-bishops were concerned. From 1570, when his wife died, Parker retired more into his antiquarian studies at Lambeth Palace. Characteristically he toiled to establish the continuity of his office, tracing it back to 'my first predecessor' St Augustine. Although John Foxe and his fellow Puritans would certainly agree that the Church had existed before Luther or Zwingli, they were thinking more of a godly remnant personified by the lonely figure of Wycliffe. The idea that the Church of England stood in linear descent from the popish Church in England was a scandal to them. For the Puritans wanted no links with the Church of Rome, a mere historical aberration, but a real continuity with the Church of the English New Testament. Yet here was an archbishop priding himself on being a successor not of that great preacher St Paul but of the monkish Thomas Becket! To speed the end of the seventieth archbishop some opponents even bored holes in the archiepiscopal barge, but Parker died in his bed five years later.

Edmund Grindal, his successor, proved to be a virtually useless instrument in the Queen's hands as Primate of All England. When the Queen commanded him to suppress 'prophesyings' (local meetings at which clergymen prayed, discussed and expounded the Bible to each other before an invited audience of lay people) Grindal would only offer to regulate them. Like his fellow Marian exile John Knox in the northern kingdom, Grindal was not afraid to speak his mind to a queen, though he did so at great length, somewhat obscurely and in notably less harsh tones. 'Remember, Madam,' he wrote to her, 'that you are a mortal creature . . . and although you are a mighty prince, yet remember that He who dwells in heaven is mightier.' Queen Elizabeth would brook no such challenge to her prerogative. She gave direct orders to the diocesan bishops to stop 'prophesyings' and suspended Grindal as governor of her Church. Some seven years later, in 1583, Grindal obliged his sovereign by dying.

Queen Elizabeth turned to Cambridge yet again for her third Archbishop, John Whitgift. He was the son of a prosperous Grimsby merchant who had learnt his grammar at St Anthony's in the City. As an undergraduate at Pembroke Hall he knew the future martyrs Nicholas Ridley and John Bradford, for the latter acted as his first tutor. He became an ardent Protestant. On becoming Lady Margaret Professor of Divinity, for example, Whitgift delivered his inaugural lecture on the identity of the pope with Antichrist. In his celebrated controversy with Thomas Cartwright, which began in Cambridge, he resolutely opposed the presbyterian system, which had been developed out of Calvin's ideas by the great reformer's successor in Geneva, Theodore Beza.

Supported by the biting satire of the anonymous pamphlets known as the 'Martin Marprelate' tracts, one branch of the more extreme church Puritans had shifted its attack to the very institution of episcopacy itself. Here they were on much disputed ground. Had not Luther allowed bishops? More to the point, in England Queen Elizabeth was unequivocal in requiring her subjects to accept bishops. In this matter she would back her 'little black husband', as she called the Archbishop, with none of those hesitations which so plagued Parker.

With the Queen's complete support, Whitgift blocked the presbyterian agitation in the dioceses, while the royal ministers checked it in the House of Commons. Whitgift made much use of his Court of High Commission, although its procedures, as Lord Burghley told him plainly, 'too much savoured of the Romish inquisition'. With such a spearhead for his counter-attack, Whitgift made progress in cutting back unlicensed preaching and those potentially seditious religious meetings in private houses. Richard Bancroft, who would succeed Whitgift as Archibishop of Canterbury in 1604, first came to prominence in connection with the intelligence network which Whitgift established to ferret out the Puritan lawbreakers. That even greater future opponent of the Puritans, William Laud, was already over thirty and an ordained priest when Whitgift died. Thus the Whitgiftian tradition of Church management was destined to extend well into the next century.

As the decades passed the Church of England gradually developed a unique ethos or personality of its own, one which would be called 'Anglican' in the next century. We are accustomed to think of it as a compromise of sorts between the Catholic and

Protestant positions, but at another level it was an attempted marriage between the Reformation and Renaissance. Cambridge, the workshop which shaped its leaders, had seen both Erasmus and Martin Bucer as professors, symbolizing those two movements at work there. Forced to defend their Church against both Catholics and Protestant critics, the apologists of the Church of England from Bishop Jewel onwards turned more and more to the authority of reason. Eventually the judicious Doctor Hooker, in his *Laws of Ecclesiastical Polity*, grounded the order of both State and Church – two sides of the same coin – in natural law, whose 'seat is the bosom of God, her voice the harmony of the world'. Natural law is the expression of God's supreme reason. Everything, including Scripture, must therefore be interpreted in the light of this divine gift of 'natural understanding, wit and reason'. Churches are not static, to be frozen forever in some unchanging New Testament pattern. They grow organically, and can freely choose or adapt their forms of government to meet circumstances. Like his patron Whitgift, Hooker did not doubt that episcopacy best suited the present needs and past tradition of the English nation.

This defence of the existing order struck the Puritan opposition as an exercise not in reason but more in rationalizing the man-centredness and the various superstitious practices which still disfigured the Church of England. In a Cambridge sermon delivered in 1578 a distinguished Puritan preacher, Dr Laurence Chaderton, spoke for them all when he roundly condemned the Church as a mixture of Romish superstition and those pagan beliefs and practices inherited from England's tribal past. The latter centred upon the white and black magic which persisted in the countryside and had always existed in an underground form. The Church was, declared Chaderton, 'a huge mass of old and stinking works, of conjuring, witchcraft, sorcery, charming, blaspheming the holy name of God, swearing and forswearing, profaning of the Lord's Sabbath, disobedience to superiors, contempt of inferiors; murder, manslaughter, robberies, adultery, fornication, covenant-breaking, false witness-bearing, lying . . .' It was filled with arrogant hypocrites and renegades. Throughout the land there was a crying need for honest pastors 'to admonish, correct, suspend and execute such noisesome, hurtful and monstrous beasts out of the house of God, without respect of persons'.

*   *   *

The key to completing the Reformation in England, so the Puritans believed, lay in the multiplying of godly sermons. For them the sermon must replace the mass as the focus of popular devotion. Something of the old belief in the efficacy of numbers, however, transferred to sermons. At an early date wealthy Protestants substituted sermons for masses in their wills. In 1537, for example, Robert Barnes had served as an executor of the will of a rich London merchant Humphrey Monmouth, who left provision for thirty sermons. The practice continued. A less affluent parishioner in St Olave's in London left money for four sermons when he died in 1587, as his brass memorial plate in the church testifies to this day.

By exercising their rights as patrons Puritans among the nobility and gentry put in their parishes clergymen who could preach simply but effectively. In addition they financed 'lectureships', additional posts for preachers. The standing of their leaders at court protected them from the angry episcopal disciples of Whitgift. Lord Burghley, lord treasurer and virtually the prime minister of England, constantly intervened on behalf of Puritan preachers. More than once he spoke up for a 'reduction of the church to its former purity', despite the Queen's teasing of him and 'his brothers in Christ'.

To Puritan minds more grammar schools, providing they were properly governed and staffed, would mean more preachers. The statutes of Halifax Grammar School, founded in 1591 by a Puritan wool-merchant family, educated the young to enable some 'to become in time ambassadors of reconciliation from God to his Church'. That school numbered Sir Richard Saltonstall among its first pupils. The foundations of Sydney Sussex and Emmanuel colleges at Cambridge by prominent Puritans during the reign recorded a similar aim. The Puritan laity were certainly not to be disappointed on that score. For by the end of the century a network of Puritan preachers spread across the counties, and the 'godly' flocked to hear them.

In their zeal to do so the Puritan laity sometimes flouted the law which required them to attend their parish churches. In cities and towns they did not have to walk far, for the preaching brethren usually powerfully occupied one or more pulpits. A 'silver-tongued' preacher, like Henry Smith at St Clement Dane's in London or Laurence Chaderton in Cambridge, could draw the crowds to hear them preach for an hour. Even people of quality had to stand to hear Smith's sermons, while 'he held the rudder of their affections in his hands, so that he could steer them whither he pleased'. On one occasion Chaderton broke off after two hours in the pulpit, declaring that he proposed to trespass no longer on his hearers' patience. At that, his biographer narrated, 'the auditory cried out, (wonder not if hungry people craved more meat) "For God sake, Sir, Go on! Go on!"'

A Puritan congregation did not merely passively hear the sermon, they devoured it like holy bread. Many brought note-books so they could write down the text. They looked up the preacher's proof-texts in their own Bibles and folded the pages for discussion after dinner. In order to take down the sermon some used the art of shorthand. Timothy Bright, a country clergyman, published his *Characterie* in 1588, which became the first textbook of shorthand to be used widely. Preachers soon observed that women were much faster at shorthand than men, and one even rebuked the ladies in his congregation who had boasted about their superior deftness.

In style Puritan ministers favoured what Chaderton called 'a plain but effectual way of preaching'. Their Anglican rivals indulged in a more elaborate style in their written sermons, which the Puritans labelled 'witty' as opposed to 'spiritual'. These priests studded their addresses with elaborate word play and Greek or Latin quotations designed to impress upon the hearers the learning and wit of the preacher. Richard Greenham, a celebrated Puritan divine, dismissed such offerings as 'the swelling words and painted eloquence of human wisdom'. Like all his colleagues he attacked them vigorously as being merely 'glassy, bright and brittle . . . so cold and so human, that the simple preaching of Christ does greatly decay'. An even greater Puritan preacher, Richard Baxter, knew his flock well. They brought to church, he wrote, 'a suspicion of all that is ceremonious in God's service, of all which they find not warrant in Scripture, and a greater inclination to a rational convincing earnest way of preaching and prayers, than to the written form of words, which are to be read in churches. And they are greatly taken with a preacher that speaks to them in a familiar natural language and exhorts them as if it were for their lives.'

In contrast to preachers favoured by the bishops, who tended to speak about such topics as the divine authority of crown and mitre, or the harmony of Plato with Christ, or the advisability of virtue rather than vice, the Puritan preachers constantly brought the

Gospel down to earth. They used familiar or homely analogies to relate Christianity to everyday life. In a characteristic metaphor, for example, they spoke of themselves as 'physicians of the soul'. Sermons should reach like medicines into the souls of the congregation, said Richard Rogers, so 'that they may be merry in the Lord, and yet without lightness; sad and heavy in heart for their sins, and the abominations of the land, and yet without discouragement or dumpishness . . .' The aim was to enable each member of the congregation to lead 'a godly and comfortable life every day'. John Dod at Fawsley in Northamptonshire even held a spiritual surgery before or after the service in the church nave: 'If he thought them bashful, he would meet with them, and say, "Would you speak with me?" And when he found them unable to state their question, he would help them out with it, taking care to find the sore.'

*   *   *

'Do not, like some ungracious pastors do, show us the steep and thorny way to heaven, while he himself the primrose path of dalliance treads,' cautioned one of Shakespeare's characters. As part of their spiritual discipline Puritan preachers examined their consciences by keeping daily journals and gave advice in sermon and book so that the laity could follow their example. Richard Rogers, whose diary still exists, undertook his daily examination so that he might 'know mine own heart better . . . and to be better acquainted with the divers corners of it and what sin I am most in danger of and what diligence and means I use against any sin and how I go under any affliction'.

Among lay Puritans the diary of Lady Margaret Hoby, kept between August 1599 and 1605, has survived. Margaret received her education in the Puritan household of Catherine, Countess of Huntingdon, a sister of the Earl of Leicester. According to the Elizabethan historian Camden, her husband Henry Hastings, the third Earl, wasted his patrimony on supporting 'hot-headed preachers'; and a Stuart hand added 'probably upon those greedy horse-leeches the Puritans'. Writing to the Earl of Rutland on the latter's marriage in 1573, Huntingdon said, 'I trust that you have chosen well, and I am sure of it if the report be true that she fears God, loves the Gospel, and hates Popery.' Margaret Hoby was reared to be such a wife.

Margaret married three times. Her first husband was Walter Devereux, brother of Robert, Earl of Essex, who died young. Her second, Thomas Sidney, soon followed him to the grave. Then, at the age of 25 years, Margaret married Sir Thomas Posthumous Hoby, so called because he was born after the death of his father. Sir Thomas senior was a diplomat who achieved some note as the translator from the Italian of a celebrated Renaissance book by Castiglione entitled *The Courtier*, an influential handbook of behaviour and etiquette for the Elizabethan gentleman. He had wed Elizabeth, one of Sir Anthony Cooke's five well-educated daughters.

Cooke had stood in the tradition of Sir Thomas More, holding that 'sexes as well as souls are equal in capacity'. Consequently, in contrast to the more medieval domestic upbringing in the Hastings household, he furnished his daughters at Gidea Park in Essex with a Renaissance education. They became 'rare poetesses', skilled in both Latin and Greek. Mildred, the second wife of Lord Burghley, and Ann, who married Sir Nicholas Bacon, became models of feminine erudition. Yet Cooke's girls also received a Puritan upbringing. His first concern was 'to imbue their infancy with a knowing, serious and sober religion, which went with them to their graces; and his next, to inure their youth to obedience and modesty'. These two qualities Puritans prized above all in their wives, closely followed by some learning and proficiency with 'needle in the closet and housewifery in kitchen and hall'. Sir Anthony spoke for all Puritan fathers when he declared as his purpose 'that his daughters might have for their husbands complete or perfect men, and that their husbands might be happy in complete women'.

The mother of Sir Thomas Hoby mentioned in a letter the 'insufficiency' of her boy. In fact, even in manhood, he was so short in stature it was rumoured that he 'used to draw up his breeches with a shoeing-horn'. Unfriendly contemporaries called him a 'scurvy urchin' and a 'spindle-shanked ape'. With relentless determination Lady Russell pursued the thankless task of marrying-off this unfavoured son. Hearing that Margaret, a considerable heiress, was on the marriage market again she enlisted the help of Lord Burghley and the Earl of Huntingdon to recommend her son. Posthumous Hoby himself was despatched north to play the hot suitor, armed with a 'store of fair jewels and pearls'. An impending law-suit over her lands at Hackness, near Scarborough in Yorkshire, coupled with the friendly urgings of her elders, eventually persuaded Margaret to accept Thomas as her husband. At least he was a godly man. At their wedding on 9 August 1596 Thomas bowed to his mother's wishes and omitted all music and dancing, which anyway was contrary to his 'humour'. Instead, the couple celebrated the day by attending a sermon together and dining with their friends and families.

Sir Thomas Hoby applied himself diligently to his vocation as a magistrate. In 1635 Sir William Brereton could hold him up as 'the most understanding, able and industrious justice of peace in this kingdom'. Margaret's relationship with him seems dutifully affectionate rather than deep: in her diary she invariably calls him 'Mr Hoby'. She threaded her day with spiritual devotions of one kind or another. On a typical day in 1599, for example, she could record:

> After I was ready I took myself to private prayer, wherein it pleased the Lord to deal mercifully . . . after, I went about the house, and instructed Tomson's wife in some principles of religion, and then ate my breakfast, and then walked about till almost 11 o'clock: and after I had read 2 chapters of the bible, I went to dinner: after dinner I went to work, at which continued till 4, then I took order for supper . . . went to prayer and to write some notes in my testament, from which I was called to walk with Mr Hoby . . . and so to supper: immediately after prayer and lecture, for the diligent attention of which the Lord did hear my prayer by removing all wanderings which used to hurt me so that I received much comfort, I went to bed.

Like her husband, Margaret could never be accused of idleness. Between her religious exercises she would visit the servants at work in the house or its outbuildings, such as the pastery or granary. She walked to the fields where the men were harvesting or sat and watched them milking the herd in the long barn. Then she would spend an hour or two in her garden. Margaret's love of gardening often peeps out from this spiritual diary. In October 1599 she was busy preserving her quinces. Four years later, the day after a national fast on account of 'general mortality' in the plague, she could not resist recording that 'we had in our garden a second summer, for artichokes bare twice, white roses, red roses: and, we having set a musk rose the winter before, it bares flower now. I think the like hath seldom been seen: it is a great fruit year all over.' Three weeks later the raspberries were 'fair set again, and almost every herb and flower bare twice'.

Like Otwell Johnson in the previous generation, Lady Margaret interpreted illness or disaster as punishments from the hand of a moral God who would not spare the guilty. Luck, fortune or chance were not words that came easily to Puritan lips. For instance, a neighbour called Mr Bell was out riding when his horse fell and he broke a leg, in 'which thing, although the world account but a mischance, yet God's judgement is to be observed, for the humbling and admonition of all that hear of it . . .' Young Farley, slain by one of his father's servants with a poleaxe, deserved death. For he was 'extraordinary prophane, as once causing a horse to be brought into the church of God, and there christening him with a name, which horrible blasphemy the Lord did not leave unrevenged, even in this world, for example t'others'. The outbreak of plague in 1603, which eventually reached the nearby town of Whitby, led her to write in October: 'Lord grant that these judgements may cause England with speed to turn to the Lord.'

Sunday, or the Lord's Day, formed the centrepiece of each week. That holy day would follow a well-ordered pattern: 'After private prayers I read and then went to the church: after, I came home and prayed and then dined: after dinner I talked of the sermon, and read of the bible with some Gentlewomen . . . after, I prayed, walked and went to the church again, and after I walked a while: and so I spent some time in writings on my sermon book and at praying, and, after, I went to supper and, soon after, I heard public prayers and, lastly, when I had prayed privately, I went to bed.'

During a stay in London Lady Margaret met and dined with one of the leading Puritan preachers and theologians of her day, the celebrated Dr William Perkins of Cambridge. She had read some of his books, which were exceptionally popular with the laity. Perkins had defined theology as 'the science of living blessedly for ever', and he gave the laity clear, practical and powerful guidance. It is not hard to imagine that Margaret looked forward to meeting one of her favourite authors.

William Perkins became something of a patriarch to the English Puritans, although he died at the early age of 44 in 1602. A Fellow of Christ's College, he first achieved fame as a preacher. Members of the University and townsmen flocked to hear his sermons, which were 'not so plain but that the piously learned did admire them, nor so learned but that the plain did understand them. . . . An excellent surgeon he was at jointing a broken soul, and at stating of a doubtful conscience.' He stimulated other Puritan writers, such as William Ames, to concern themselves with the

spiritual doubts and fears of the individual. An accomplished
theologian, he was notable for espousing Theodore Beza's extreme
view of predestination, namely that Christ did not die for all men
but only for the elect. Once one of the elect is 'effectually
called' – usually through hearing the preaching of God's
word – then that status can never be entirely lost. In contrast to such
'terrors of the law and of God', Perkins came close to teaching in his
sermons that the very desire to be saved is itself a symptom of
election, a gospel that must have brought comfort to hundreds of
troubled people. His books were translated into Latin, Dutch,
Spanish and even Irish and Welsh. They exemplified the thorough
and typically Puritan standards of Biblical exposition as well as the
English concern for a practical religion, one relevant to the daily
business of living. The author's strict and pious life certainly
complemented his message. The younger generation of Puritans,
including those who would settle in America, were even more
influenced by 'Perkins our wonder' than were Lady Margaret Hoby
and her friends.

Apart from her diet of religious books by such writers as
Perkins, Margaret does not seem to have read much else. It would be
a mistake to regard her as typical in this respect. The writer of
another Puritan diary, Lady Anne Clifford, was well read in the
literature of Greece and Rome. In her portrait she is depicted with a
pile of books on the table in front of her. She could talk intelligently
'about predestination or slea-silk'. She also had a Renaissance
interest in chemistry.

Gradually Margaret seems to have found it harder to keep to the
discipline of recording each night 'my day's journey'. Words did
not come easily to her. Her journal reads more like a schoolgirl's
account of life in a spiritual boarding school than the story of a soul
voyaging on the high seas. Margaret excused those days left blank
on account of being too busy, but in April 1605 she reminded
herself sternly that people 'are unworthy of God's benefits and
especial favours that can find no time to make a thankful record of
them'. Although Margaret lived another twenty-five years her
journal, if she kept one, has not survived.

*   *   *

Perhaps Perkins had such friends as Lady Margaret Hoby in mind
when he demanded to know 'who are so much branded with the
vile terms of Puritans and Precisians, as those that most endeavour

to keep the purity of heart in a good conscience?' The 'godly sort' smarted under those common names of abuse which their contemporaries heaped upon them. They believed that the Devil or the Jesuits had introduced these names to the English language. A merchant from Antwerp named Emanuel van Meteven residing in England even named Jesuit Sanders as the culprit. For him Puritans described the people who rejected all ceremonies anciently held, organs and epitaphs, and differences of rank among the clergy.

Whatever the origin of the name Puritan it is certain that those labelled with it endured considerable outspoken criticism. The reasons are not hard to find. In the first place they constituted a deviant minority group. On the eve of the Civil War in Margaret Hoby's Yorkshire only about 138 families of gentry out of some 679 were Puritan, and there must have been fewer of them in Queen Elizabeth's day. In some places – London, the home counties and East Anglia – the proportion would have been marginally higher.

Such a minority as the Puritans, which contained its full share of vociferous zealots, was bound to cause a hostile reaction when they criticized English characteristics and customs. The English as a nation were noted for their willingness to speak their mind, to tell people the truths that no one else dared to impart, and the Puritans proved to be no exception. Although sensitive to verbal brickbats they exemplified the English independence of mind. They paid little attention to opinions of others, even though the public at large taunted them as fools and knaves. They continued to utter unpalatable home-truths to their fellow countrymen. But they did so in the teeth of an ardent nationalism which sanctified all that was English.

The frequent resort to colourful oaths and unconscious blasphemies revealed the extent of the English national character which remained both unconvinced and unconverted by the gospel according to Luther and Calvin. The flowering of the language brought with it the tares of a rich profusion of abuse. Sailors and soldiers of Elizabethan England set a fashion for cursing. 'Canst thunder common oaths like the rattling of a huge, double, full-charged culverin,' asks a character in Marston's *Scourge of Villanie*: 'Then, Jack, troop among our gallants, kiss my fist, and call them brothers.'

Apart from objecting to such blasphemies in common speech, as well as oaths in legal proceedings on the grounds that the Bible expressly forbade them, the Puritans also worked against the grain of the native English spirit in many other ways. For instance, the English loved deafening noises made by bells, drums, cannon fire or musical instruments. But the Puritans, like the Lollards before them, objected to the pealing of bells. The English excelled in dancing and music. But the Puritans condemned mixed dancing and held that all music should be excluded from church with the exception of psalms sung unaccompanied. The Church of England kept the musical genius of the nation in church with its excellent choirs. In 1592 the Duke of Württemberg attended a service in St George's Chapel at Windsor which was accompanied by an organ fitted with trumpets, together with an orchestra of cornets, flutes and fifes. He heard the choir leading the worship much as it does today, with 'a little boy who sang so sweetly amongst it all, and threw such a charm over the music with his little tongue, that it was really wonderful to listen to him'. He added, however, that the ceremonies in such places 'are very similar to the Papists'.

Foreigners also remarked upon the elegant and costly dress of the English people. Desiring novelties the English changed their fashions of clothes, hair style and beard shapes every year. As Thomas Harrison said, 'nothing is more constant in England than inconstancy of attire'. This wanton extravagance clashed with Puritan values. People who called themselves Christian should not squander money on such worldly vanities. Instead they should dress as inexpensively as their position in society would allow and give the money instead to forwarding the Gospel or for such charitable purposes as the relief of sick or poor folk. The English love of display, however, could not be easily checked. It survives to this day in the form of public ceremonial, processions and shows.

Nicander Nucius, who visited England in 1545, painted an attractive picture of the typical Englishman: tall and erect, well-made and handsome, fair complexioned, hair and beard a golden hue, eyes blue for the most part and cheeks ruddy. But he added that they were insatiable meat-eaters, 'sottish and unrestrained in their appetites'. Compared to their German cousins, who drink too much, the very hospitable English eat too much. Beef and lamb, which 'they roast to perfection', washed down with ale and beer or sugared drinks, formed their staple diet and probably gave them their red faces and thick bodies. Over-eating harms any form of spiritual life. The Puritans themselves followed the Lord's command to 'fast and pray', often keeping the traditional fast days of

Wednesday and Friday for this purpose. They began also to exhort their fellow-countrymen to forsake the pleasures of the table, drunkenness and smoking tobacco, and to take a more serious interest in their souls.

The English were inclined towards laziness. Not so laborious or industrious as the Netherlanders or French, noted Meteven, they led an indolent life for the most part, like the Spaniards. The women, who enjoyed more freedom than anywhere else in the world, spent an inordinate amount of time walking, riding, playing cards, and conversing with their neighbours and equals 'whom they term gossips'. The Puritans, believing in vocation, preached the importance of hard work and the virtue of carefully using time to be effective in God's service.

By converting a growing minority of English society through sermon and example, the Puritans made headway in altering this national tendency to lethargy. But a century after Queen Elizabeth's death Ludwig von Muralt, the first really good commentator on the common character of the English, could still identify as the chief fault of the English an inclination to both physical and mental laziness. To this trait he attributed England's credulity and astonishing indifference to conditions around them, such as the grim debtor's prisons. 'The great cruelty of the English consists in permitting evil rather than committing it.' But Muralt added perceptively that the English people's love of liberty, combined with their natural ferocity, could always rouse them from slumber when danger threatened. Owing to their passion for freedom, he wrote, the English, 'though disunited and sunk in prosperity and sloth, recover in a moment all their vigour and forget all their dissensions, in order to offer unanimous resistance to anyone who tries to subject them'.

Noticeably unwilling to serve abroad the English soldiers were martial and valorous by nature but not especially militaristic. They were bold, fiery and even cruel in war, showing remarkable courage in the face of death. With the best harbours in Christendom, Meteven had commented earlier, they also made 'good sailors and better pirates', a fact which he ascribed to their 'cunning, treacherous and thievish' qualities.

The fierceness of the English which foreigners sensed found plenty of expression at home in hunting and hawking, cock-fighting and bear-baiting, boxing and wrestling. The Bear Garden on Bankside in London was a very noisy place as the crowds watched English mastiffs snarling and snapping at bears, bulls, wolves and boars. Violence overflowed into the streets, especially at the sight of foreigners whom the English despised. Besides whipping children the English also flogged their horses. Hence the proverb, 'England is a paradise for women, a prison for servants and a hell for horses.' Again the Puritans, largely in vain, strove to change this emergent national characteristic. Bishop Latimer had preached before Edward VI against hunting and hawking, as well as dancing at banquets. As they matured in faith Puritan gentlefolk tended to abandon these customs. It is largely through the Puritans that cock-fighting and bull-baiting were eventually prohibited, but it took them decades rather than years to secure an effective ban on them.

All the national characteristics and customs, which so plainly contradicted the message of Christ which the Puritans read in their English Bibles, appeared magnified on the London stage. Oaths and blasphemy, finery and display, great noise from cannon and trumpet, idleness, excessive eating, drinking and smoking, adultery and fornication, and red-blooded violence, all could be found in the popular theatre of the *Red Bull* and a dozen other such taverns whose inner courtyards also served as settings for plays. The Puritans looked upon these places much as their secular descendants today might regard a football ground.

In 1596 a group of Puritans residing on the monastic site of Blackfriars, where Thomas More had once tested his call to the cloister, petitioned the Privy Council against a proposal to use the monks' dining hall as a theatre. Led by Sir Thomas Hoby's mother, among others, they said they feared crowds of 'vagrant and lewd persons', outbreaks of plague and the raucous noise from drums and trumpets which would disturb the congregations in neighbouring churches on Sundays. For the players compounded all their sins by opening the theatre doors on the Lord's Day. Thus they prophaned the Sabbath in the eyes of the Puritans. It was that affront above all, repeated despite government prohibitions, which attracted the implacable opposition of 'the hotter sort of Protestants' to the rival attraction. 'Will not a filthy play,' complained John Stockwood, 'with the blast of a trumpet sooner call thither a thousand than an hour's tolling of a bell bring to the sermon a hundred.'

With the plays of William Shakespeare still so much alive it is difficult for us to feel sympathy with the Puritan attitude to the theatre. But Shakespeare appealed to the more educated, middle and upper classes in society, not to the theatre-going crowds at large. Music and dancing before and during the performances drew more thunderous applause than Shakespeare's witty prose. In 1599 a foreign tourist called Platter saw *Julius Caesar* in the Globe, which had just been completed with its new straw-thatched roof. At the end of the play, 'as is their custom', some of the cast danced together with marvellous grace, two in men's and two in women's clothes. The 'jig' appealed to the audience far more than the play!

As a shrewd businessman Shakespeare wrote plays that would appeal to a wider spectrum of people than his rivals. Protestants, even Puritans, could listen to most of his plays without offence. As Shakespeare understood that people are primarily interested in themselves he reflected and magnified the values of his audience. Cordelia in *King Lear* is the portrait of a Puritan girl. Indeed Puritan fathers may well have recognized their own offspring in Shakespeare's educated girls of spirit, such as Rosalind or Desdemona, Helena or Juliet. These girls began to insist upon the right to choose their own husbands for love, a right which Luther had endorsed but conservative English parents only slowly accepted on account of the property interests at stake.

Because the Puritans formed such an influence on his potential audiences Shakespeare avoided offending them. Malvolio in *Twelfth Night* is virtually the only unsympathetic Puritan figure, and that because he appears to be against English over-indulgence. 'Dost think, because thou art virtuous,' says Toby Belch to him, 'there shall be no more cakes and ale? . . . A stoup of wine, Maria.' Falstaff, the most popular Shakespearean character with Elizabethan audiences, personified with his gargantuan girth the national sin of gluttony. But Falstaff, modelled on the Lollard rebel Sir John Oldcastle, also pays lip service to Puritan values. 'Tis no sin to labour in thy vocation,' roars the old rogue in defence of becoming a thief.

In contrast to Shakespeare's reticence other playwrights responded to the Puritan attacks with counter-charges in what became a running war of invective between stage and pulpit. Some of their jibes illuminate the growing criticism which the Puritans endured as they stood out as deviants from the English way of life. Thus they help us to know what life must have been like for the Puritans as they became the butt of such jokes. Dignity and extreme sobriety characterized most Puritans, but playwrights seized on certain oddities which some Puritans unconsciously adopted, such as a nasal twang of voice and the habit of turning the whites of the eyes up in prayer. Their precise ways, plain garments and close cut hair were all ridiculed on the stage, along with their opposition to oaths and such sins as smoking.

The discarding of time-honoured English names for descriptive epithets and strange-sounding Hebrew words was lampooned in such stage names as Zeal-of-the-Land Busy, Win-the-Fight Littlewit and Tribulation Wholesome. In fact the playwrights were not far off the mark, for the Puritans frequently used such names. They reveal how deeply the Puritan mind was impregnated with the Hebrew tradition. Such terms as 'brother' and 'sister', or even 'zealous professor' struck some English playwrights as equally risible.

The playwrights coasted around Puritanism looking for even more subjects for jest. The 'dry grace' at mealtimes, drawn out until 'the meat on the board forgot that it had been in the kitchen that day' epitomized all those 'long-winded exercises, singings and catechizings' which they abhorred. Equally lengthy was any controversy, for the Puritans seemed to love contention. They scrupled at things not radically wrong, such as the wearing of surplices, church organs and cathedral bells. Zeal-of-the-Land Busy had been a baker, but gave it up because his cakes were used at May-games around the Maypole, morris dances, marriage feasts and other sinful festivities.

Above all the playwrights voiced the common suspicion that the Puritans were more influenced by the desire for gold and worldly power than they would have men believe. Their clever casuistry was satirized in a play called *The Puritan* where one character distinguishes carefully between robbery and stealing. Although Puritans scoffed at Greek learning, apparently because it was not Hebrew, they could reason with Athenian subtlety. Hypocrisy was seen as the main ingredient in their nature. Often their hidden vice was lust. Puritans, wrote the author in *Eastward Ho* were 'the smoothest and slickest knaves in the country'. So common grew this belief that 'puritanically' became a slang word for 'secretly' or 'deceitfully'.

The Puritans smarted under this backlash of criticism and abuse from their English contemporaries, led by the playwrights and the more hostile Anglican bishops. As Elizabethan society became more secular, affluent and worldly the criteria for determining who was a Puritan became progressively weakened and widened so as to include most serious-minded Protestants who dared to question the freedom of Englishmen to say or do as they pleased on any day of the week. 'He that has not every word on oath . . . they say he is a puritan, a precise fool, not fit to hold a gentleman company,' wrote Barnaby Rich. Even in the Shropshire countryside a law-abiding and respectable man could not escape ridicule. 'My father,' wrote Richard Baxter, 'never scrupled common prayer or ceremonies, nor spoke against bishops, nor even so much as prayed but by a book or form, being not even acquainted then with any that did otherwise: but only for reading Scripture when the rest were dancing on the Lord's Day, and for praying . . . in his house, and for reproving drunkards and swearers, and for talking sometimes a few words of Scripture and the life to come, he was reviled commonly by the name of Puritan, Precisian and Hypocrite.' Although contemporaries knew it not, England had begun to divide into two camps.

5

God's Pathfinders

Late in the summer of 1536 two English ships, the *Trinity* and the *Minion*, dropped anchor off the North American coast. Present in them sailed individuals who epitomize the interests which later drew men in much larger numbers across the Atlantic to the shores of the New World. Master Hore and Oliver Daubeney, for instance, represent the London merchants and the commercial purposes that moved them. In addition Hore, who mounted the expedition, was 'given to the study of cosmography', a hint of scientific interest. This Renaissance curiosity also inspired the poet and playwright John Rastell, one of a circle of learned men who had gathered around Sir Thomas More. Armigill Wade, on leave from his post as Clerk of the Privy Council, may serve as the ardent Protestant or Puritan, for he was a close friend of John Johnson and godfather to his son.

Hunting parties from the ships rowed to the Island of Penguins and chased the 'great fowls white and grey' over the rocks. They also shot some bears, which tasted 'no bad food' after weeks of salted pork. One day, as Oliver Daubeney exercised himself by pacing the deck of the *Minion*, he caught sight of some Indians in canoes across the bay. Eager to see them at closer quarters the Englishmen rushed to launch their long boat, but the Indians paddled hard for the island where they landed and disappeared among the thick firs and pines. The only trace of them the Englishmen could find was a decorated leather boot and 'a great warm mitten' which they found beside the glowing embers of a fire.

Not long afterwards the company began to run short of food. Soon hunger drove the crews to desperate straits. One sailor on the *Minion* killed a fellow, and confessed later that he had murdered in order to eat the human flesh. The captain, a man evidently of Protestant persuasion, called the crew together and told them it was better to die in the body than to be condemned to everlasting agony in the unquenchable fires of hell. But despite this 'notable oration' the physical suffering grew to such a pitch that the sailors began to cast lots to select the next victim. Fortunately that very night a French ship, well stocked with victuals, put into the bay and anchored. The starving English company of sixteen gentlemen and ninety sailors swarmed aboard her like pirates with swords in hand, and filled their empty stomachs from her provisions. Leaving the Frenchmen with the leaking *Minion* they sailed for home. Having navigated their way through northern seas stiffened by great icebergs, they reached St Ives in October that same year. One Thomas Buts, a boy in the *Minion*'s crew, was so much altered that his own parents did not believe he was their son until he pulled down his hose and showed them a strawberry birthmark on his knee.

Not long afterwards John Rastell penned the first poem in English about the New World. He put into words the feeling of regret of such far-sighted Englishmen that Spain had already planted colonies in that region. Had the English nation stirred itself from medieval sleep sooner, then

> . . . they that be Englishmen
> Might have been the first of all
> That there should have taken possession
> And made first building and habitation
> A memory perpetual!

Many years after the voyage of the *Trinity* and the *Minion*, Oliver Daubeney and Thomas Buts told their stories to Richard Hakluyt, a young Oxford don gathering material for his first major book, *Divers Voyages Touching the Discovery of America* (1582). Hakluyt had come from a humble background but a good education at Westminster School set him upon his destined path. The Clothworker's Company awarded him a scholarship to go to Christ Church at Oxford in order to prepare himself for the Puritan ministry. There he met among his fellow undergraduates Philip Sidney and William Camden, Foxe's lay successor as the historian of England, as well as Richard Carew, later famous as the first English translator of Tasso. His fellow undergraduates called the serious boy 'Preacher Hakluyt'.

Hakluyt's vocation as preacher and his avocation as cosmographer fitted together as two eyes are joined in sight. He saw clearly the issues at stake in America long before most of his more shortsighted fellow-countrymen and preached the message in and out of season. More conscious, articulate and vigorous, he brought these Puritan characteristics to bear upon his central task of raising England from its ignorance of the New World. The imaginative idea of a new English and Protestant nation in America thus took root in at least one Elizabethan Puritan mind.

From 1582 Hakluyt served for five years as chaplain to the English community in Paris. He extended his researches there to cover the main exploratory voyages of European nations, partly hoping to move his countrymen by envy or fear to emulate and surpass their rivals. For the French Huguenots had taken the lead among the Protestants in the matter of planting colonies in North America. In 1562 Admiral Coligny sent out Captain Jean Ribault to establish the first one at Port Royal (in South Carolina). The following year Ribault took refuge in England, and published there his account of *Terra Florida*, the 'Flourishing Land'. Meanwhile the Spanish reacted sharply by massacring the remaining Huguenot settlements in Florida, Georgia and Carolina. The survivors reached England, bringing more stories and eyewitness accounts for the English presses together with samples of tobacco and potatoes. One survivor, the artist Le Moine, dedicated his illustrated book on Florida to the mother of Philip Sidney.

In 1565 Captain John Hawkins reached Florida and relieved the hard-pressed remnants of the Huguenots in Fort Caroline. He sailed again for those waters two years later in command of a squadron of six ships. At Veracruz in the Gulf of Mexico he lost three of them in a fierce fight with the Spaniards. With his remaining vessels overcrowded he sailed to a point about 250 miles north of Veracruz and then sent 114 men ashore with instructions to make their way across the isthmus. But three men – David Ingram, Richard Brown and Richard Twide – chose instead to embark upon perhaps the greatest walk in history. They resolved to head northwards until they reached the fishing settlements in Newfoundland. Their staggering journey of 2500 miles, through unexplored country inhabited by savages, took them across what is now the United States. We have no details of their route but they struck the Atlantic coast about 200 miles from Cape Breton. A French vessel took them to England, where they landed some months before the return of Hawkins.

Twelve years later, when the leading Puritan Sir Francis Walsingham and his associates were contemplating founding colonies in the unknown territory south-west of Cape Breton, someone remembered these three intrepid men. David Ingram appeared before the committee and answered a multitude of questions. Doubtless he counted himself a fortunate man, for most of his shipmates marooned by Hawkins had fallen into Spanish hands. After four years in prison they were sentenced by the Inquisition and suffered the full rigours of the first *auto-da-fé* in America. Three Englishmen perished at the stake; sixty-eight were whipped and sent as slaves to the galleys. Had Foxe ever written a supplement to his book doubtless he would have included these Protestant martyrs in his pages. Perhaps the message of Foxe, that God's providence never failed his people in their direst straits, may have sustained the English seamen in their hour of trial.

Undeterred by the open hostility of Spain the English nation redoubled its efforts to find the north-west passage. In 1576 men sympathetic to the Puritan movement, such as Leicester, Sussex, Burghley, Walsingham and Sidney, were prominent among the subscribers to the first voyage of Martin Frobisher. He threaded a way through Greenland's icebergs, battled through a tempest that knocked the *Gabriel* on its beam ends, crossed to Baffin Island and sailed up the bay that now bears his name. He found no channel through the northern landmass, but in his wanderings mapped the southern Arctic region. He carried back to England some Eskimos and a kayak. The natives' sallow skin, much like a Tartar's, helped to persuade him that he had touched Asia. Queen Elizabeth hung portraits of the wild man and women brought home by Frobisher in the gallery at Hampton Court.

A lump of ore which one of Forbisher's sailors had pocketed ashore on Newfoundland appeared to contain gold. It aroused much enthusiasm and support for Forbisher's second voyage. Sidney, like the others, was gripped by gold fever and wrote to his Huguenot friend and mentor Hubert Languet for advice on how to work the cargo of ore that came home, trying to persuade him that such knowledge might prove useful one day to 'the professors of true religion'. Despite unfavourable reports from the assayers in London, a third expedition of fifteen ships in 1578 brought back more. Yet Languet's fears that England would be crazed and emptied by a gold rush and his young Sidney corrupted as a lust for wealth swamped his natural love of goodness, mercifully proved groundless. As William Camden recorded, the worthless black ore stones were eventually used to repair potholes in the road near Dartford in Kent.

In 1578 Frobisher endeavoured, though ineffectually, to found a settlement north of Hudson's Bay. That same year Sir Humphrey

Gilbert obtained a patent from the Queen to take possession of any land he discovered in her name. His 26 year-old half-brother, Sir Walter Raleigh, commanded a small ship on his first voyage, but they accomplished nothing. Gilbert tried again in 1583 and established a colony among the fishermen who summered on the Newfoundland coast each year while they netted cod. Rather than return upon his flagship the *Delight*, Gilbert volunteered to share the hazards of an Atlantic crossing with the crew of the *Squirrel*, the much smaller consort. In one black September night of storm, 'terrible seas breaking short and pyramid wise', the watch on the larger vessel saw the lantern of the *Squirrel* bobbing up and down. Then, falling into one dark crevasse of waves, the lights disappeared from sight and were never seen again. Truly, as Gilbert had once written, 'the wings of man's life are plumed with the feathers of death'.

Queen Elizabeth, who held Gilbert to be 'a man noted of not good hap by sea', shifted her favour to his less luckless kinsman, Sir Walter Raleigh. In 1584 she granted him a similar charter. Raleigh sent out two vessels that year which discovered the island of Roanoke off the coast of a land which he named Virginia in honour of the Virgin Queen of England.

At this time the Privy Council issued an order which threatened banishment to unspecified countries for those who stayed away from their parish churches and joined the prohibited Brownist congregations. These separatists owed their name to Robert Browne, a minister who had issued a call to his fellow Puritans to waste no more time trying to reform the Church of England but to establish a holy discipline in independent congregations 'without tarrying for any'. Seeing an opportunity, Hakluyt proposed to the Queen that some of these Puritan dissidents should be transported to America. He did not doubt their loyalty. Their ministers, 'always coining of new opinions', could accompany them, for in that new continent 'they will become less contentious'. These settlers would perform an invaluable service to God by 'reducing the savages to the chief principles of our faith'. The Virginia colony, Hakluyt argued, could also serve as a place of refuge for Protestants on the old continent 'forced to flee for the truth of God's word'. Yet the Roanoke colonists of 1585–7 included few European Protestants and no English Puritans. Raleigh himself was not a Puritan. Christopher Carleil, who promoted an American colony in 1583, certainly appealed to Puritans to join him, offering that 'the godly minded . . . shall be at their free liberty of conscience'. But his expedition disintegrated the following summer before it could set sail out of Cork harbour.

The forays of Sir Francis Drake and other English seadogs upon the treasure fleets of Spain precipitated an avalanche of revenge. In 1588 King Philip despatched the Armada—a mile-wide phalanx of 130 towering galleons, great galleasses, deep-laden store ships and smaller escorts. They sailed up the Channel to the sound of drums, trumpets and chanted Latin prayers, bearing an invasion army. The defeat of this bristling, crescent-shaped monster by a combination of adverse weather and fierce English attacks by Drake, Raleigh, Frobisher and their fellow-captains gave England a breathing space in which to renew her colonizing efforts in the New World. But the Roanoke Island colony failed. Raleigh himself fell from favour under James I, who came to the throne in 1601. As a convicted traitor imprisoned in the Tower he forfeited his rights in America. In 1606 the Virginia Company received a royal charter to plant two colonies. Hakluyt, now a prebendary at Westminster Abbey, acted as consultant to the venture. Other Puritans, such as the Lord Chief Justice, Sir John Popham, gave vigorous leadership to the Virginia Company.

The settlement at Jamestown almost foundered, a fate which befell its sister colony in the north on the Sagahadoc River. But some succour from 'our mortal enemies' the Indians and the timely arrival of a supply ship saved the day at Jamestown. The second winter brought to the fore Captain John Smith, 'whom no persuasions could persuade to starve'. While blizzards swept the low and marshy lands along the Chesapeake, Smith described that Christmas which they kept 'among the savages, where we were never more merry, nor fed on more plenty of good oysters, fish, flesh, wild fowl and good bread, nor never had better fires in England than in the dry smoky houses of Kecoughtan'.

In 1609 a much-enlarged Virginia Company sent out a fleet of eight ships to the surviving colony. Off 'the still-vexed Bermoothes' a hurricane scattered it and drove the flagship upon the beach. The adventures of the ship's company on Bermuda, which mariners held to be the haunt of evil spirits, gave Shakespeare his inspiration for *The Tempest*. Some remnants of the fleet limped on to Virginia. Lacking leadership, their provisions and livestock consumed, their relations with the Indians at a low ebb (for they refused to trade except for arms, implements or utensils, and then turned on them) the colonists began to die off. Soon there remained, wrote Smith, 'not past sixty men, women and children, most miserable and poor creatures; and those were preserved for the most part by roots, herbs, acorns, walnuts, berries, now and then a little fish'. There was even an instance or two of cannibalism. 'Unto such calamity', wrote the colony's secretary, 'can sloth, riot and vanity bring the most settled estate.' At home the Virginia Council diagnosed the main cause as the unwillingness of the colonists to accept as leader any among them. 'No man would acknowledge a superior nor could from this headless and unbridled multitude be anything expected but disorder and riot.' The need for strong leadership, a lesson learnt in Virginia, would impress itself deeply on the Puritan mind.

Word began to spread in England about this disastrous mismanagement. Moreover, perhaps in order to shift the blame, it became widely rumoured that Virginia was too hostile as an environment for a colony. The Virginia Council thought it fit to publish its firm resolution to continue with the plantation. At the same time it advertised for a better quality of settlers, especially those with trades or skills. Sensing that lack of true religion was at the root of the problem, the Council appealed for 'learned divines to instruct the Colony and to teach the infidels to worship God'. They also caused to be printed the sermon preached on 21 February 1610 before the Council, the rest of the adventurers and the newly-appointed Governor, Lord de la Warr, and entitled *A New Year's Gift to Virginia*. The Puritan divine William Crashaw, who delivered it, took as his text 'Luke, 22 chapter, 32 verse: But I have prayed for thee, that they faith fail not: therefore when thou art converted strengthen thy brethren.'

Crashaw's sermon is interesting in three respects. It illustrates what has been said earlier about the clear, simple and vivid style of Puritan sermons. Then the interpretation of ends and motives is distinctively Puritan, illuminating the special emphases which men of that persuasion brought to the colonizing movement. Lastly, the sermon itself is a striking example of the social leadership provided by Puritans through their constant activity of forcefully and critically presenting issues to the Protestant public. As the structure of Crashaw's sermon shows, they appealed always to reason. To go or not to go to Virginia was debated rationally. The powerful deployment of reasons against and for the enterprise led up to a conclusion which all could accept because their minds had participated in the decision. But the Puritans were not rationalists in the modern sense, for some principal 'reasons' either way were profoundly spiritual in nature.

It is not surprising, began Crashaw, that so few had come forward to assist in the present purpose of planting Virginia. For 'the greater part of men are unconverted and unsanctified men, and seek merely the world and themselves and no further. They make many excuses and devise objections, but the fountain of all is, because they may not have present profit.' Having put his finger on the profit motive that alone moved most of his contemporaries Crashaw explained that such men were useless for spiritual work. 'Tell them how to get 20 per cent interest in the hundred. Oh! how they bite at it, oh how it stirs them! But tell them of planting a Church, of converting 10,000 souls to God, they are as senseless as stones.' He called upon all men to support the impending voyage according to their circumstances by four methods: 'countenance, person, purse and prayer'. All should bear in mind the chief end in mind, namely 'the plantation of a Church of English Christians there and consequently the conversion of the heathen from the Devil to God'.

Crashaw then listed the 'discouragements' and 'encouragements' in this great work. Under the first heading he gave seven reasons why men were being deterred from sailing to America and settling there. First was the question of lawfulness: was it right to occupy land which belonged to the Indians? Yes, because the settlers take from the savages only their surplus land and commodities, and in return give them what they must need: 'civility for their bodies' and 'Christianity for their souls'. The fact that Crashaw put this objection first suggests that many Englishmen, who saw society as founded on property, were deeply troubled in their consciences about seizing land from the rightful inhabitants.

The other discouragements Crashaw answered with equal confidence. Concerning the difficulties of distance and climate he replied that Virginia is near to England, the passage is 'fair, safe and easy' and the climate is temperate. As for the small beginnings and poverty of progress, 'for answer, I say, many greater States (than this is like to prove) had as little or less beginnings than this has'. Apart from making reference to two Old Testament texts to prove his point Crashaw buttressed his argument with a typical Renaissance flourish. 'Look at the beginning of Rome, how poor, how mean, how despised it was; and yet on that base beginning grew to be Mistress of the World.'

112

Dealing with the common report that the colonists are 'raked up out of the refuse and are a number of disordered men, unfit to bring to pass any good action,' the preacher pointed out that at least the majority of them were volunteers, and no better or worse than the stay-at-homes. God can bring great matters to pass from such unpromising beginnings. To the objection that 'we send base and disordered men' Crashaw replied – doubtless with a glance at Lord de la Warr – that 'the basest and worst men trained up on severe discipline, under sharp laws, a hard life and much labour, do prove good members of a Commonwealth.'

Then Crashaw touched on the fourth discouragement, the ill news of the country from those that come from thence. He flatly denied the truth of these reports, attributing them to those settlers deterred by the necessities of working to eat or obeying the discipline of sharp laws. The miseries of those who go in person, the fifth discouragement, Crashaw blamed largely upon the absence of governors, 'which was caused by the hand of God and the force of tempest, which neither human wit could foresee nor strength withstand'. As no great things can be achieved without enduring miseries, so this particular discouragement arose from 'baseness and cowardice of spirit'. But such want of heart was no English characteristic. Striking a patriotic note Crashaw spoke warmly of 'the ancient valour and hardness of our people'. He invited the audience to consider how the Dutch character had been altered for the better within the last century as they had struggled for freedom in the war with Spain.

The sixth discouragement, the uncertainty of profit and the long wait for it, could be easily disposed. Crashaw reiterated that 'profit is the least and last end aimed at in this voyage' but added the comforting assurance that it would none-the-less prove to be profitable in a short time.

The seventh discouragement detained him a little longer, for rumours of the 'multitude and might of our enemies' really had deterred some potential supporters. 'What enemies?' demanded Crashaw. 'They answer first the Spaniard. I answer, deceive not yourselves, we have him not our enemies: for first, he is in league with us . . . we hope they be too wise and worthy a nation to break their league and falsify the oath of God which they have made.' Had Crashaw known with what close and jealous attention the Spaniards followed the colonizing efforts of the English in America, especially through their ambassador in London, he may have been less confident on this point. The French? No, they were following England's example and planting in Canada, the same being true of other Christian nations. The Indians? No, for they invite us.

The real enemies of the enterprise, concluded Crashaw, were the Devil, the papists and the players. 'The Devil hates us, because we purpose not to suffer heathens, and the Pope because we have vowed to tolerate no papists.' Crashaw's strictures on the theatre are typically severe. 'As for players: (pardon me right honourable and beloved, for wronging this place and your patience with so base a subject), they play with princes and potentates, magistrates and ministers, nay with God and religion, and all holy things: nothing that is good, excellent or holy can escape them: how then can this action? But this may suffice, that they are players: they abuse Virginia, but they are but players: they disgrace it: true, but they are but players, and they have played with better things, and such as for which, if they speedily repent not, I dare say vengeance waits for them.' The actors hate the present company 'because we resolve to suffer no idle persons in Virginia, which course if it were taken in England, they know they might turn to new occupations'.

The first of Crashaw's three 'encouragements' sprang from the excellency of the design itself as lawful, honourable and holy. Secondly 'the friends of this action' included God, the King, the undertakers, those whom God moved to go in person, the Indians, the multitude of contributers, together with the support of God's angels and the prayers of God's Church. The third encouragement was the due consideration of the true ends of the business, namely the conversion of the savages and to appease God 'because justly offended' and to honour Him 'being by us dishonoured'. Besides strengthening our own religion, Crashaw continued,

> hereby we shall mightily advance the honourable name of the English nation, the honour whereof we ought every one to seek. Hereby we shall mightily enrich our nation, strengthen our navy, fortify our kingdom, and be less beholding to other nations for their commodities. And, to conclude, hereby we shall rectify and reform many disorders which in this mighty and populous state are scarce possible to be reformed without evacuation. And consequently, when we have achieved all these ends, we shall eternize our own names to all ensuing posterity as being the first beginners of one of the bravest and most excellent exploits that was attempted since the primitive times of the church.

As an afterthought Crashaw added for good measure the patriotic thought that 'we shall hereby wipe off the stain that sticks upon our nation since, (either for idleness or some other base fears, or foolish conceits) we refused the offer of the West Indies, made unto us by that famous Christopher Columbus, who upon England's refusal, tendered it the Prince that now enjoy them. And thus I have given you a taste of the royal encouragements which naturally and infallibly do attend this blessed business.'

Turning to the new England he saw arising in Virginia, the preacher addressed some Puritan advice to those about to 'commit yourselves to the seas and winds for the good of this enterprise'. Lord de la Warr and his companions should put Christianity first. 'You go to commend it to the heathen, then practice it yourselves: make the name of Christ honourable, not hateful unto them.' Atheists, the 'Devil's champions', were even worse, and he suggested that their blasphemy should be made a capital offence under the very first law made in Virginia. Any Brownists or other such separatists should be excluded from the colony and allowed to find somewhere else to set up the fanciful churches they had imagined in their brains. If they ever succeeded, a possibility which Crashaw obviously thought to be remote, they might give others some cause to follow them, but until then 'we will take our pattern from their betters' and stick to the Church of England.

Crashaw obviously envisaged some form of Puritan state in Virginia. He called for strict laws against swearing and other prophanity. The earth mourns because of much vain swearing by God's name, 'the common and crying sin of England', and 'your land will flourish if this be repressed. The Sabbath should be wholly and holily observed, public prayers daily attended and idleness eschewed.' Laws carefully made should be obeyed by all. By such means 'you will teach us in England to know (who almost have forgotten it) what an excellent thing execution of laws is in a commonwealth'. And so Lord de la Warr and his companions should 'go forward in the name of the God of heaven and earth, the God that keeps covenant and mercy for thousands'. To aim at less than religion and God's service would be to bring a curse, 'though not on the whole action yet on our attempt'. For human sin would not hinder the long-term purpose of God, which was undoubtedly to plant his godly English people in America.

Lord de la Warr soon succumbed to sickness in Virginia and was replaced by a tough Puritan soldier from the Dutch service, Sir Thomas Dale, who ruled the colony with a firm hand. With Dale came a young Cambridge clergyman, Alexander Whitaker, son of a well-known and extreme Calvinist theologian who had been Master of St John's College. Alexander had experienced a vocation to go out as a missionary to Virginia. A year later his *Good News from Virginia* was published in London, but he sent a foretaste of its content in letters to his friend William Crashaw. His observations of the Indians, with their eerie calls and wild rain dances, convinced him that 'there be great witches among them and they very familiar with the Devil'. Yet Whitaker felt optimistic about the prospect that God's purpose for the colony would be fulfilled now that the settlers had endured the divine chastisement of famine and death. 'I marvel more that God did not sweep them away all at once, than that he did in such manner punish them.' Let the Church of England send any of its unemployed 'young, godly and learned ministers' to reap the full and ripening harvest of souls. Yet not many responded to the call, for in 1614 he could write to his Puritan cousin in London 'I much more muse that so few of our English ministers, that were so hot against the surplice and subscription, come hither where neither is spoken of.' Alas, Whitaker himself was drowned in the James River three years later. His fate perhaps symbolizes the death of Puritan hopes for Virginia.

*   *   *

When Crashaw made that challenging reference to the separatists he may possibly have had in mind the Brownist congregation of John Robinson. Two years previously they had made their escape from Nottinghamshire to Holland, intending possibly to go further afield and settle in America. In fact ten years would pass before they did so. Then the possibility at which Crashaw hinted did come true. For the church they established there in the wilderness gave sufficient cause to the Puritans who followed in their steps to abandon the pattern of the Church of England for the congregational model. Today we know them as 'the Pilgrim Fathers'.

The story of the Pilgrim Fathers begins with William Brewster, the founder of the Nottinghamshire congregation of John Robinson. Brewster seems to have been a most attractive man. His father was bailiff of Scrooby Manor, a property belonging to the Archbishop of York. William went up to Peterhouse at Cambridge in 1580, aged about 15, and acquired knowledge of Latin and 'some insight in the

Greek'. For a time he served 'a religious and godly gentleman' called Sir William Davidson and accompanied him to the Low Countries to take possession of the surety towns of Flushing and Brill. When Davidson fell from royal favour Brewster returned to Scrooby and eventually succeeded his father as postmaster, a duty which entailed providing fresh horses and hospitality to royal messengers posting up and down the Great North Road between London and Scotland.

Brewster soon gained the friendly respect of his neighbours, 'especially the godly and religious'. He gave money generously to the poor and needy and men noted his Puritan example as 'tender-hearted'. He made diligent efforts to provide the surrounding villages with Puritan preachers. Despite such zealous activity Brewster was no stereotype or stage Puritan, sour of visage, solemn, harsh or intolerant. On the contrary he was 'of a very cheerful spirit, very sociable and pleasant among his friends'. Nor did he indulge in controversy for its own sake or overrate his own opinions, being 'of an humble and modest mind'. The only people to annoy him were those who exemplified a noted English characteristic of being proud or haughty when they had nothing to 'commend them but a few fine clothes or a little riches more than others'. In short, Brewster was a wise, discreet, godly and most gentle man, patiently 'doing the best he could, and walking according to the light he saw, till the Lord revealed further unto him'.

The author of these words, William Bradford, knew his subject at first hand. Born at Austerfield, a hamlet two miles north of Scrooby just across the River Idle in Yorkshire, Bradford had become a Puritan by the age of twelve and soon entered Brewster's circle. An orphan by background, though not without means, Bradford came to look upon Brewster as his father. The small separatist group that met for prayer in Scrooby manor house became more radical after John Robinson joined them as minister. They resolved to flee abroad and most of the congregation, numbering about 50, arrived in Amsterdam.

Why did they leave England? In his history *Of Plymouth Plantation* William Bradford hinted at the atmosphere of hostility which had surrounded them as well as the features of English life which they found unacceptable. After a brief summary of Foxe's *Book of Martyrs*, his chief authority, Bradford described the 'inveterate hatred against the holy disciples of Christ in his Church' still displayed by their enemies which rankled at the Puritans. 'And to cast contempt the more upon the sincere servants of God, they opprobriously and most injuriously gave unto and imposed upon them that name of Puritans, which it is said the Novatians [an obscure sect in the third century] out of pride did assume and take unto themselves. And lamentable it is to see the effects that have followed. Religion has been disgraced, the godly grieved, afflicted, persecuted, and many exiled; sundry have lost their lives in prisons and other ways. On the other hand, sin has been countenanced; ignorance, profaneness and atheism increased, and the papists encouraged to hope again for a day.' To support this indictment he quoted William Perkins.

In Amsterdam the exiles worshipped with an established English congregation called the Brethren of the Separation of the First English Church, better known as the Ancient Brethren, in their large new meeting house in Bruinistengange, or Brownists' Lane. After a year half of them moved on to Leyden, 'that goodly and pleasant city', where they settled down. Bradford had apprenticed himself to a French silk-maker, and in their new home he became a maker of fustian (corduroy or moleskin). Young Jonathan, Brewster's sixteen-year-old son, earned his living as a ribbon-maker. Brewster senior gave English lessons to university students and then opened a printing press behind his house in Stincksteeg, or Stink Alley, where he published Brownist tracts. Edward Winslow joined him as an apprentice. Twenty-two years old and 'of a very active genius', Winslow proved a most valuable recruit. He had been well-educated in Latin and Greek at one of the new Tudor Renaissance schools, King's at Worcester. He came from an old family, his father being a gentleman-farmer near Droitwich.

Late in 1617 John Robinson's congregation resolved to emigrate to America, not least to prevent their children from adopting the language and free-and-easy ways of their Dutch counterparts. The decision was reached after much hesitation. Again the reliance of the Puritans on the careful balancing of pros and cons in debate is an impressive testimony of the influence of the Renaissance on them. For it was the Renaissance which taught men to exercise their reason as the essential preparation for knowing God's will. They considered several other possible refuges, alternatives to 'those vast and unpeopled countries of America, which are fruitful and fit for habitation, being devoid of all civil inhabitants, where there are only savage and brutish men which range up and down, little otherwise than the wild beasts of the same.' For the possible effects on their women and aged parents of a long sea voyage, together with the change of air, diet and water, daunted them. They feared especially the savage Indians, 'a cruel, barbarous and most treacherous people' who reported practices of flaying prisoners alive with shells, or cutting off their limbs or joints and broiling them on coals in sight of the victims, caused 'the bowels of men to grate within them'. Also many precedents of ill success and lamentable miseries that had befallen others in similar designs could easily be found and were advanced in the debate. It had been hard enough to live in neighbouring Holland, the opponents urged, a civilized and rich commonwealth. How much more difficult it would be to survive in the American wilderness.

Against these reasons it was argued, wrote Bradford, 'that all great and honourable actions are accompanied with great difficulties and must be both enterprised and overcome with answerable courages. It was granted the dangers were great, but not desperate. The difficulties were many, but not invincible. For though there were many of them likely, yet they were not certain. It might be sundry of the things feared might never befall; others by provident care and the use of good means might in a great measure be prevented; and all of them, through the help of God, by fortitude and patience, might either be borne or overcome.' Moreover, those who favoured America pointed out that the twelve years of truce in the Low Countries had ended. Now 'there was nothing but beating of drums and preparing for war, the events whereof are always uncertain. The Spaniard might prove as cruel as the savages of America, and the famine and pestilence as sore here as there, and their liberty less to look out for remedy.' After a great deal of debate by the two sides, 'it was concluded by the majority to put the design for America into execution and to prosecute it by the best means they could.'

With the help of Sir Edwin Sandys, an influential member and later treasurer of the Virginia Company, they secured royal permission to sail to America but no official patent. Thomas Weston, a London merchant who set up a joint-stock company to finance the colony, seems to have favoured New England, the region north of Virginia so named by Captain John Smith. That change of plan and some new clauses which heavily favoured investors rather than colonists in the division of profits, caused some of Robinson's congregations in Amsterdam and Leyden to withdraw altogether. But the others pressed on with their plans. In

June 1620 they chartered the *Mayflower*, 'a fine ship' of about 180 tons, and then bought the smaller *Speedwell*. The latter was in bad condition and had to be refitted. On 21 July the vanguard of emigrants left Leyden. On the following day they set sail in the *Speedwell* from Delft Haven for America via England. Robinson saw them off at the quayside 'with watery cheeks'. So, wrote one of their number, they left their resting place for nearly twelve years, 'but they knew they were pilgrims, and looked not much on those things, but lifted up their eyes to the heavens, their dearest country, and quieted their spirits'.

These celebrated words of William Bradford, drawing upon the commonplace Puritan image of the Christian as a stranger and wayfarer in this world, gave rise to the first part of the equally famous name: 'Pilgrim Fathers'. The second word also comes from a sentence by Bradford written later in his history. 'May not and ought not the children of these fathers rightly say: "Our fathers were Englishmen which came over the great ocean, and were ready to perish in this wilderness."' Although they did not call themselves Pilgrims or Pilgrim Fathers it is convenient to refer to them as such today.

The *Speedwell* proved to be 'leaky and open as a sieve'. The new masts were too large for her and she carried too much sail for a vessel of 60–80 tons, so that her timbers started in a stiff breeze. On the second occasion she put back to port it was decided to leave her behind, and some passengers transferred to the *Mayflower*. But only 41 of the 102 colonists were Pilgrims: 17 men, 10 women and 14 children. These Puritans, however, provided the leadership in every sense of that word. Apart from Brewster and Bradford, both Deacon John Carver and Edward Winslow could pass as gentlemen. Carver, a former Yorkshire merchant, had four indentured servants with him, while Winslow brought two others. The only man to match up to them in natural ability as a governor of men among the main body was Captain Miles Standish. A hardened professional soldier of about thirty-six years, Standish also thought of himself as a gentleman. He did in fact come from an ancient Lancashire family traditionally Catholic in religion. Perhaps for this reason he never became a member of the Pilgrim church.

Before setting sail from Plymouth on 16 September the Puritan leaders met Captain John Smith. Although they tactfully declined his offer to go with them they may have purchased his map and book, *A Description of New England* (at least, when Brewster died there was a copy in his library). Smith noted afterwards that their 'humorous ignorance caused them for more than a year to endure a wonderful deal of misery with infinite patience . . . thinking to find things better than I advised them'.

Owing to the delays caused by the *Speedwell* the voyage of the unescorted *Mayflower* took place much later in the year than was customary. The autumnal gales buffeted the broad-beamed, double-decked ship week after week as she sailed westwards. Sometimes she drifted helplessly under bare masts, with the helmsman trying to hold her into the wind. In one storm the main beam amidships cracked with the sound of a cannon report. Someone remembered a 'great iron screw' in the hold, possibly a printing press or a lifting jack for building, and the crew used it to force the beam back into place so that it could be secured with props. After sixty-six days of such adventures at sea the Pilgrims were 'not a little joyful' when at last they dropped anchor in what is now Provincetown harbour on Cape Cod.

To counter some of the 'strangers' on board who talked of going their own way the Puritan leaders drew up the 'Mayflower Compact' to serve in place of a patent. It bound the signatories to join 'together into a civil body politic'. Then those with voting rights – the free men – elected John Carver as their first chief magistrate or governor. They spent the next ten days at Cape Cod collecting firewood, washing clothes, repairing the long-boat and reconnoitring the dunes and sparse woods near the anchorage. The first party ashore found no signs of Indians. The Pilgrims felt alone. 'They had no friends to welcome them,' wrote Bradford, nor inns to entertain or refresh their weatherbeaten bodies.' With winter at hand the coast presented to them a forbidding 'weatherbeaten face, and the whole country, full of woods and thickets, represented a wild and savage hue'.

Amid worsening weather Standish led an expedition of sixteen volunteers, each man armed with musket, sword and corselet, to search for a place of settlement. Accompanied by William Bradford and two others the armed men set off down the beach. They caught glimpses of Indians, and came across deserted huts and gardens, but after three days they returned to the ship. A second expedition proved to be equally fruitless. Then the fourth mate, Robert Coffin, the only man on board who had been to Cape Cod before, recalled a good harbour across the bay and offered to steer the shallop to it. And so on 6 December a third exploring party set off towards

Plymouth, the name Captain John Smith had bestowed on the haven six years previously.

The bitterly cold wind froze the rain and spray on their clothes until they were 'like coats of iron'. Two men fainted with the cold and many more were sea 'sick unto death' but they held their course until they ran into what is now Wellfleet Bay. Heading for the shore they spotted a dozen Indians some distance away who sped off into the woods leaving behind a black object on the sand. After a night spent on the beach, warmed by a log fire in a barricade of logs and pine branches, they walked back to the place where the Indians had been seen. They found the remains of a huge black fish about five yards long, 'some two inches thick of fat, like a hogg', called a grampus.

After a day spent exploring the vicinity the crew members and ten Pilgrims, who included Bradford, Winslow and Governor Carver, settled down for the night behind another barricade further down the beach. About midnight a 'hideous and great cry' aroused everyone. 'Arm, arm!' shouted one of the sentries as he rushed back into the barricade. They lined the fence and blazed away with their muskets at the silent, black woods. When the 'noise ceased' a sailor who had been to Newfoundland said the sound was probably the howling of wolves. At first light they roused themselves again and prayed as usual before starting to make breakfast. Disregarding the warning of Standish and others a few men took their muskets down to the shallop. The tide was still out so they laid their arms by the creek wrapped in coats and walked back for breakfast. As dawn streaked the eastern sky and the Pilgrims had begun to eat breakfast 'all on the sudden they heard a great and strange cry, which they knew to be the same voices they had heard in the night, though they varied their notes.'

'Men, Indians, Indians!' cried a sentry. A shower of whizzing arrows pursued his running figure. Some terrifying Indian war cries, strange whooping sounds like demented owls, echoed from the woods. Standish and another man fired their flintlock muskets, giving time for the others to light the long cords of match needed to ignite their matchlock pieces. Some ran down to the shallop to try to recover their weapons and with fierce whoops the painted Indians dashed out of cover to cut them off. More Englishmen attempted to succour their fellows with sword and cutlass. Soon every man had his musket ready and 'let fly amongst them, and quickly stopped their violence', But one 'lusty man, and no less valiant' had edged forward in the woods to a tree near the barricade and loosed his arrows into the clothes still draping the barricade. He withstood three musket shots in his direction. Then Standish just missed him with a well-aimed shot that scored white the bark of the tree above the Indian's head, making the splinters fly about his ears. The brave gave 'an extraordinary shriek, and away they went all of them', hotly chased by the Pilgrims and sailors for a quarter of a mile. This show of bravado, with shouts and shots, was to demonstrate that 'they were not afraid of them or any way discouraged'.

As they sailed on towards Plymouth the weather worsened, with snow, rain and a rising wind. During the afternoon gale they 'broke their rudder, and it was as much as two men could do to steer her with a couple of oars'. Outside Plymouth harbour the mast snapped in three places and went overboard with the sail into the roaring seas. As night fell they rowed the shallop into the harbour. Fearing another skirmish with the Indians they resolved at first to stay in the boat for the night, but the bitter cold drove the first mate Clarke to lead a few men ashore. They started a great wood fire on the beach, and 'the rest were glad to come to them'. After a day sounding the harbour and surveying the low hill overlooking it and the freshwater stream which flowed into the bay, the Pilgrims decided to plant their colony here. They returned to the *Mayflower* with the good news. Here Bradford heard the sad tidings that on the day after their departure his wife Dorothy had fallen (or jumped) overboard and drowned. Perhaps she could no longer endure the wintry weather and the sight of that long menacing shore.

On 26 December, fourteen weeks after leaving England and five weeks after anchoring at Provincetown, the *Mayflower* sailed into Plymouth harbour. Shore parties began work with saw, axe and adze to build the settlement of a few houses along a street leading up to a block house on the hill. Sickness ravaged them. By the beginning of spring in 1621 half of both the colonists and the ship's company had died, 'the living scarce able to bury the dead'.

For some strange reason the Indians did not attack them, a fact which surprised the Pilgrim leaders. Then one day in late March a tall, black-haired Indian carrying a bow and arrows strode boldly out of the woods and up the street towards the Common House where a meeting to discuss better defence arrangements was in progress.

'Welcome!' said the Indian in English. He asked for beer. Having none at hand they gave him some spirits, together with a meal of biscuit, butter, cheese, pudding and a piece of mallard, 'all of which he liked well'. As the Indian wore only a deerskin leather belt about his waist 'with a fringe about a span long or little more', they gave him a soldier's overcoat as a present. Samoset explained that he was a sachem or chief from the land north of Massachusetts Bay. He had come to visit his friend Massatoit, sachem of the Wampanoags, who lived some forty miles away on Narragansett Bay. He had learnt his broken English at fishing stations in the region known now as Maine. The Patuxet Indians who had formerly lived around Plymouth, he explained, had all died in the great plague a few years previously.

Within a short time Samoset returned with several other Indians with furs to trade and finally came to announce that Massatoit with sixty warriors was waiting nearby for the Pilgrim leaders to meet him. After a ceremonious greeting the Pilgrims concluded with Massatoit a treaty of mutual assistance which assured the survival of the colony and indeed gave peace to Massachusetts Bay for forty years. It was an astonishing turn of events.

Its providential face can be seen most clearly by constrasting the destiny of the Pilgrims with the fate of a group of the English Ancient Brethren from Amsterdam who had emigrated to Virginia. A quarter of them died during the sea voyage and the remainder ceased to be a community on arrival. One or two may have found their way eventually to Wolstenholme, a settlement on the James River founded in 1619 by the Martin's Hundred Society who had obtained a patent for 20,000 acres. The first 220 settlers built a fort: a four-sided building with towers at two corners and a gun platform facing the river. Unlike the later log forts on the frontier, with posts closely set side by side to keep out arrows, here the posts were spaced apart and joined by vertical planking, like a ship's side. A low platform ran round the inside of the pallisade to enable the defenders to fire their muskets over the parapet. Not that anyone expected trouble from the Alonquian Indians of Virginia. But at dawn on Friday 22 March 1622 they struck with their tomahawks through the colony. By sunset 350 Europeans lay dead out of the total population of perhaps 2500. Seventy-eight of them died in Wolstenholme, and fifteen women were carried off. Excavations of the abandoned site of the fort reveal something of the horror even today. One grave yielded a skeleton of a hastily-buried thirty-year-old male settler, his skull smashed by a tomahawk. Several clay pipe bowls littered the soil around him, together with ash from the burnt buildings. Inside the fort lay a discarded helmet, complete with cheek pieces and visor, an entire backplate of a suit of armour, firing mechanisms of five matchlock muskets and some 140 lead bullets which had been stuffed into a small hole beside the pallisade. A mud-daubed wasp nest, doubtless once high in the timbers of the fort, had been baked brick-red by the fire which the Indians had set to the walls.

By contrast Edward Winslow could write at Plymouth, 'we, for our part, walk as peacefully and safely in the wood as in the highways of England'. In this comparative security the colony of New Plymouth took shape. Seven dwelling houses and four other buildings, all of timber construction with thatched roofs, now stood along the little street, while the others were in process of construction.

Carver died a week or so after the *Mayflower* left for England in April, and William Bradford was elected in his place. Now aged 32, Bradford not only personified the qualities admired by the Puritans but he also possessed outstanding gifts as a leader.

One day Samoset had brought into the Pilgrim settlement an Indian called Tisquantum, or Squanto. He had been seized from New England in 1614 by an English sea captain, but made his escape and way home some four years later. After Massatoit returned home Squanto stayed with the Pilgrims, for they now occupied his homeland. The last of the Patuxet tribe, Squanto had once helped to clear the Indian fields around Patuxet (Plymouth) Bay which the Pilgrims had now inherited. He showed them how and when to plant Indian corn and where to find the best fishing places. Until his death in 1622 Squanto gave them invaluable service. Although not without some Indian faults of character, he was a true friend and guide. Bradford called him 'a special instrument sent by God for their good beyond their expectations'.

The Thanksgiving in October 1621, a semi-pagan festival imported from rural England, celebrated the first harvest from some twenty acres of cornfields. The fifty-one Pilgrims, with two new babies in their mothers' arms, entertained Massatoit and his warriors to a feast of venison, roast duck and turkey, possibly with cranberries gathered as today in the low boggy fields where they grow in abundance. Like many later participants in this national celebration they rather over-did the eating and drinking, and ran short of food for weeks to come. Not until 1863 did President Lincoln appoint the last Thursday in November as national Thanksgiving Day.

Although they knew it not, the Pilgrims had even more cause for thanksgiving upon that autumnal day. For they had established the first real Puritan bridgehead in the New World. Those that followed them in the great migration of the 1630s would look upon the Pilgrims as God's pathfinders. As William Bradford reflected in his journal, 'As one candle may light a thousand, so the light here kindled has shone into many, yea in some sort to our whole nation. Let the glorious name of Jehovah have all the praise.'

6

'This Wanton Heart of Ours'

'In my youth,' wrote John Winthrop, 'I was very lewdly disposed, inclining unto and attempting (so far as my heart enabled me) all kinds of wickedness, except swearing and scorning religion, which I had no temptation unto in regard of my education.' Winthrop wrote his 'Christian Experiences' in 1636 and 1637, but an earlier journal covering a few years and dating from 1606 has also survived. Together with a full cache of letters these diaries reveal the spiritual workings not merely of John Winthrop but also of his Puritan contemporaries in the new generation which came to maturity in the reign of James I.

They received an education from their first- or second-generation Puritan parents, complemented by the vocational labours of godly schoolmasters in the new grammar schools, designed to make them Puritans from a tender age. John's grandfather was a prosperous Suffolk clothier who had purchased Groton Manor after the great Abbey of Bury was dissolved. His son Adam became a lawyer and married the sister of Archbishop Matthew Parker's former chaplain, Dr John Smith, who later became Master of Trinity College at Cambridge and then Bishop of Bath and Wells. When she died Adam married the daughter of a local clothier, who bore him four daughters and a son. He named the boy John, probably in honour of the Puritan Dr Still.

Adam brought up his children in the religious or godly way advocated by the Puritan preachers. Young John accepted the doctrines and attitudes taught to him without question, but he was troubled from an early age by pride. He possessed a strong natural sense of self which sat uneasily with a faith which preached total reliance upon God. When he was fourteen and a student at Cambridge University, for example, he fell into a lingering fever. Deprived of his 'youthful joys', he wrote, 'I betook myself to God, whom I did believe to be very good and merciful, and would welcome any that would come to him, especially such a young soul, and so well qualified as I took myself to be; so as I took pleasure in drawing near to him.'

Even more troubling, this emerging and imperious self was accompanied by powerful sexual desires. The only acceptable remedy lay in an early marriage. On 17 April 1605, when he was little more than seventeen years old, he wed Mary Forth at Great Stambridge in Essex. Ezekiel Culverwell, a famous Puritan divine and vicar of the town, conducted the service. Afterwards John lived with his parents-in-law for a time. He listened with deepening attention to the plain, powerful preaching of Culverwell, of whom he became a zealous disciple and 'could have kissed his feet'. From this beginning he developed a true Puritan's insatiable thirst to hear the word of God preached, and would not miss a good sermon, though many miles off, especially one which 'searched deeply into the conscience'.

Yet neither marriage nor the ministrations of Ezekiel Culverwell and his colleagues brought peace to the young man's heart. The spiritual zeal for self-improvement, which would last his lifetime, had begun to burn like the fires in the Suffolk corn stubble after harvest. In February 1606, a few days before the birth of his first child, John confessed in his journal: 'Worldly cares, though not in any gross manner outwardly, yet secretly, together with a secret desire after pleasures and itching after liberty and unlawful delights, had brought me to wax weary of good duties and so to forsake my first love, whence came much trouble and danger.'

Constant introspection led to much greater self-awareness. Like most Puritans John became more scrupulous as he sensed the effects of even the smallest sins on his spiritual life. For example, the postponement of Bible reading and prayer until three o'clock one day for the sake of completing some needless work, thoroughly unsettled his heart. 'It is wonderful how the omission of the least duty or commission of evil will quench grace and estrange us from the love of God.' Even in Groton Church, listening to a sermon one Sunday in March, 'I let in but a thought of my journey into Essex, but straight it delighted me, and being not very careful of my heart, I was suddenly, I know not how, so possessed with the world, as I was led into one sin after another, and could hardly recover myself, till taking myself to prayer before I was too far gone, I found mercy.'

The apparently simple requirements of the Christian faith have always proved extremely difficult to transfer into practice. In some ways Winthrop and his fellow Puritans seem to be recapitulating the moral and spiritual struggle of Luther prior to his conversion. But there is a vital difference. Thanks to Luther and the Reformation apostles, the English Puritans already knew that no saving merit abides in good works or self-made virtues. They had learnt the master principle of salvation by faith alone. What they needed to feel or experience for their peace of mind was the power of Christ's spirit already at work in their souls, both as an earnest of salvation and as a transforming agent leading them to Christian perfection. But they could not be passive recipients of such grace. They had to co-operate in faith and by good will, even though at times they could not be sure whether it was Christ or the old unregenerate self which stirred within them. For Christ is always hidden in the soul to the eyes of introspection.

The co-operative nature of this relationship with Christ found expression in covenants, an idea borrowed from the Old and New Testaments. On 20 April 1606, for instance, John made a new covenant with the Lord with these terms: 'Of my part, that I would reform these sins by his grace: pride, covetousness, love of this world, vanity of mind, unthankfulness, sloth, both in his service and in my calling, not preparing myself with reverence and uprightness to come to his word. Of the Lord's part, that he would give me a new heart, joy in his spirit, that he would dwell with me, that he would strengthen me against the world, the flesh and the Devil, that he would forgive my sins and increase my faith. God give me grace to perform my promise and I doubt not but he will perform his. God make it fruitful. Amen.'

The covenant should be read as a statement of John's goal. He continued to catalogue instances of those sins over the next two years, which he manfully combatted with renewed repentance and prayer, the encouraging words of Scripture and wisdom from the pages of such divines as Thomas Cartwright and William Perkins. His conscience became still more sensitive. For instance, his practice of shooting wildfowl along the stream began to trouble him. Again he resorted to the schoolroom method of ostensibly rational debate to resolve his dilemma. He marshalled eight natural reasons against shooting, including the law of the land, but added honestly that for his part he usually came home from a shooting walk with little or 'most commonly nothing' in his game bag towards his costs and labour.

If Winthrop foreshadows those modern wildfowlers who have laid aside their guns in order to watch or paint birds rather than kill them for sport, so also he prefigures the later legions who have resorted to dieting to combat the quantity and richness of food available in England. In September 1612, for instance, he noted that the variety of food offered at dinner drew him to eat more than was good for him. He resolved to eat no more than two dishes at any one meal, whether fish, meat, fowl, fruit or cheese. To keep the flesh from growing 'jolly and slothful', he put himself on a sparse diet, consisting mainly of bread and beer. He found that it reduced his weariness and wandering thoughts at prayer and left him far more fit and cheerful for the duties of his 'calling of magistracy' and his other responsibilities. Thus for spiritual reasons (which we have merely secularized) the Puritans as exemplified by Winthrop renewed the struggle against the ingrained English characteristic inclination to gluttony.

Winthrop took up his father's profession as a lawyer. But he considered seriously the possibility of becoming a Puritan preacher. For 'I grew', he wrote, 'to be of some note for religion (which did not a little puff me up), and divers would come to me for advice in cases of conscience; and, if I heard of any that were in trouble of mind, I usually went to comfort them: so that upon the bent of my spirit this way, and the success of my endeavours, I gave myself to the study of divinity, and intended to enter into the ministry if my friends had not diverted me. But as I grew into employments and credit thereby, so I grew also in pride of my gifts and under temptations, which set me on work to look to my evidence more narrowly than I had done before.' John's vocation did not survive the rigorous testing. He had discerned motives and tendencies in his character – probably sexual in nature – incompatible with a true calling to the ministry. Yet for the remainder of his life he pursued, largely unconsciously, an avocation as a Puritan prophet, preacher and pastor. He epitomized 'the priesthood of all believers', one of Luther's cardinal doctrines.

The journals of John Winthrop tell us little about his pastoral activities. He was not interested in recording his good works. Nor do they tell us much about the worldly life which he evidently enjoyed too much. Thus the diaries have given to some unsympathetic modern writers the impression of John Winthrop as an unhinged, morbidly introspective individual, visited on occasion by religious mania. Nothing could be further from the truth. His notebooks certainly record in a perceptive way the psychology of temptation and sin as he experienced them and his longings to be free of them. Thus the journals show us John Winthrop gradually becoming detached from the anchor ropes of his world. Yet in May 1613, when he penned as the second of twelve Puritan rules for himself the words 'I will live where he appoints,' he could not have foreseen where God would eventually direct his steps.

*   *   *

Mary Winthrop, 'a right godly woman', bore her husband six children, the eldest being named after him. She died in June 1615. Six months later John married Thomasine Clopton. She soon became pregnant and on Saturday 30 November the following year John wrote, 'my dear and loving wife was delivered of a daughter, which died the Monday following in the morning. She took the death of it with that patience, that made us all to marvel, especially those that saw how careful she was for the life of it in her travail.'

Next day a fever seized Thomasine and she haemorrhaged. By Wednesday those about her bedside began to fear for her life. They sent for a relative called Duke who had some medical knowledge. When Thomasine learnt of it she told John that she hoped he would deal plainly with her and not feed her with vain hopes. Winthrop's strong emotions burst their bounds and he wept. She asked him to be content. 'You break my heart', she said, 'with your grievings.' Winthrop answered that he could do no less when he feared to be stripped of such a blessing. She replied, 'God never bestows any blessing so great on his children but still he has a greater in store.'

Thomasine asked that the bell of Groton Church should be tolled for her, so that her neighbours should know she lay on her deathbed and would visit her or pray for her. By Saturday the fever had become stronger. She prayed vehemently to God to overcome the tempting Devil and not to remove his loving kindness from her, 'as we might see by her setting of her teeth, and fixing her eyes, shaking her head and whole body'. Then, like a child going to sleep, she asked for the curtains to be drawn. She was much grieved in her remaining hour to be without daylight or candlelight. But she could not even endure to look at the firelight, saying that it was of too many colours like the rainbow.

The dying woman then exercised her prerogative of speaking her mind to her family and household. She called on them to serve God above all. She bade farewell to her mother and to John's parents, blessed each of his children individually and had the youngest, baby Mary, brought to her for a kiss. Next the servants received their thanks or admonitions. She released Elizabeth Crouff from service, but told Anne Pold that she was a stubborn wench and exhorted her to be obedient to Winthrop's mother. 'You have been in bad serving, long in an alehouse,' she said to Anne Adams, 'you make no conscience of the Sabbath; when I would have had you gone to church you would not.' To Mercy Smith she added 'You are a good woman; bring up your children well. You poor folks commonly spoil your children in suffering them to break God's Sabbaths . . .'

John continued to pray by her bedside. In the early hours of Sunday morning, wrote Winthrop, 'I discoursed unto her of the sweet love of Christ unto her, and of the glory that she was going unto, and what a holy everlasting Sabbath she should keep, and how she should sup with Christ in Paradise that night.' If life was set before her now, she said, she would not take it. At five o'clock 'she fetched two or three sighs and fell asleep in the Lord.' On Wednesday 11 December John buried her in the chancel of Groton church by the side of his first wife. They disinterred Thomasine's baby daughter and laid her beside her mother's body, and there they lie to this day.

*   *   *

Winthrop's spiritual life had now progressed to the point where he, like all true Puritans, saw clearly the central issue in existence as a choice now between centering his being on God or self-centredness. He felt that God would not allow him to live with 'a heart halting between God and the world'. If he stole any affection from God to set it again on the world, 'roaring after pleasure, glory, profit, etc.' God abhorred him and his service, 'so as I see that if he may not have my heart he will have nothing'.

Winthrop persevered. He endeavoured on his knees to 'get my faith strengthened, or my heart humbled and broke, or the feeling of the love of God shed abroad in my heart'. Feelings or emotions, as always in spiritual life, proved to be fleeting, with doubts and anxieties chasing joys and assurances like darker clouds following white ones across the great Suffolk sky. By constant prayer and reflection, however, God 'taught me to trust to his free love, and not to the power or self worth of my best prayers, and yet to let me see that true prayer, humble prayer, shall never be unregarded'.

Sometimes answers to prayer came in unexpected ways. One day John came across some old letters that his first wife had written to him. As he read them his mind filled with recollections of the

132

'entire and sweet love' that had existed between them. Prayer changed the memory into a meditation upon the mystical union of Christ and his soul. His thoughts so gripped him that he forgot about his supper. Mary had been probably no more than fourteen or fifteen when she wrote these letters. John smiled at 'the scribbling hand, the mean congruity, the false orthography and broken sentences'. Then he 'yet found my heart not only accepting of them but delighting in them, and esteeming them above far more curious workmanship in another, and all from hence, that I loved her. It made me think thus with myself: Can I do thus through that drop of affection that is in me, and will not my Lord and husband Christ Jesus (whose love surpasseth knowledge, and is larger than the ocean) accept in good part, the poorest testimonies of my love and duty towards him?'

Throughout 1617 Winthrop strove to discipline his mind. In February, when he rode to London about his legal business, he used the time in the saddle to pray, sing psalms and meditate. For a local Puritan minister had persuaded him that a Christian is bound to make use of what he has learned in the Sabbath throughout the week. If any 'special affections' are stirred up by a particular reading, prayer or meditation, 'we should work upon them in the week days; for certainly the Sabbath is the market of our souls.' Such dedication had made him sober company to his fellow justices of the peace when they met for the Quarter Sessions the previous month. While the Suffolk gentry enjoyed the opportunity to dine well and exchange social or political gossip Winthrop continued to 'refrain my mouth, eyes and ears from vanity'. He accepted that others – true Christians – did not share his call to limit themselves in those lawful comforts which constitute our outward happiness. But he himself observed the principle that the more a man's behaviour differs from the common course of the world, 'the more occasion and matter there is of the observation of God's work in him'. The outward deviations in behaviour served to reassure him of inward grace.

The Puritans attracted criticism as anyone who differs from the social herd will do. They possessed bold tongues and a rich vocabulary of abuse. Winthrop's journal records the kind of adverse comments made about the godly by their less stringent neighbours. 'He will shorten his days,' said one. 'He will be overcome with melancholy,' added another. Certainly the Puritan spiritual condition in this stage could look like the English disease of

133

melancholy to the observer. When Oliver Cromwell in a like state of mind consulted Sir Thomas Mayerne, a famous London doctor, in 1628 his unease was described in the casebook as 'valde melancholicus'.

'Methought,' wrote Winthrop, 'I heard all men telling me I was a fool to set so light by honour, credit, wealth, jollity, etc. which I saw so many wise men so much affect and joy in, and to tie my comfort to a conversation in heaven, which was no where to be seen, no way regarded, which would bring my self and all my gifts into contempt.' He prayed to God to keep him from being discouraged. 'Thou assurest my heart that I am in a right course, even the narrow way that leads to heaven.' God and all experience told him that in this way there is least company. Those who 'walk openly' in this way will be reviled and 'made a gazing stock, called puritans, nice fools, hippocrites, hairbrained fellows, rash, indiscreet, vainglorious,' but that was as nothing compared to what God's excellent servants had been tried with, 'neither shall they lessen the glory thou hast prepared for us'.

Winthrop's diary illustrates how the Puritan habit of self-scrutiny developed a remarkable perception into the inner workings of the human heart. Take, for example, 'the usual cause of the heaviness and uncomfortable life of many Christians'. As he wrote one day, it is not the religion of these Christians or their want of outward comforts, but because conscience drives them to leave some beloved unlawful liberty before their hearts are fully resolved to forsake it. 'Whereas if we could deny our own desires and be content to live by faith in our God, the Christian life would be the only merry and sweet life of all.' Before the week was out he tasted the truth of his own words. Having abstained from 'such worldly delights as my heart most desired, I grew very melancholic and uncomfortable'. He allowed his mind some moderate 'outward recreation'. Afterwards his wily heart took advantage of the precedent, under the 'benefit of Christian liberty', to grant him a similar indulgence where there was no real need.

Also Winthrop came to understand the paradoxical truth that it is easier to be a Christian in times of affliction than prosperity. Puritan self-discipline can be seen as a kind of self-imposed affliction designed to maintain the feeling of dependence on God in each minute. He compared the process to the taming of a wild colt, so that a child can back him to the plough. So 'this wanton heart of ours' must be broken in by affliction and disciplined by the duties in callings that are neither pleasing or easy to the flesh. Then it will stand meek and gentle, waiting for the master's will.

This insight helped to wean Winthrop away from constant, solitary introspection into the world of action. For if affliction alone bred the feeling of faith in God the best place to find it lay in the world. Far from turning away into what Milton would call 'a fugitive and cloistered virtue', the Christian should engage himself fully in the midst of life. As Winthrop wrote to himself at this time, he that 'would have sure peace and joy in Christianity, must not aim at a condition retired from the world and free from temptations, but to know that the life which is most exercised with trials and temptations is the sweetest, and will prove the safest. For such trial as fall within compass of our callings, it is better to arm and withstand them than to avoid and shun them.' All Puritans, in the great tradition of Luther, came to the same conclusion through personal experience.

These spiritual struggles, it must be emphasized, were not a prelude to John Winthrop's eventual conversion. He was converted already, probably from childhood where he first learnt the language of Protestant religion. These turmoils are the stuff of his Christian life. This is what it felt like to be a Puritan. Again like Luther, a Puritan such as John Winthrop knew himself to be always sinning, always doubting, and always fearful. But he experienced also grace overshadowing sin, faith containing doubt, and love constantly at work to cast out fear.

*   *   *

When spring came in 1618 John Winthrop felt himself ready to embrace again the cause of his most severe afflictions, holy matrimony. He was still only about thirty years old when he became engaged for the third time. His betrothed, Margaret Tyndal, came from an Essex family distantly linked with the famous translator of the English Bible. His first letter to her begins on an ecstatic note: 'My only beloved Spouse, my most sweet friend, and faithful companion of my pilgrimage, the happy and hopeful supply (next Christ Jesus) of my greatest losses, I wish you a most plentiful increase of all true comfort in the love of Christ, with a large and prosperous addition of whatsoever happiness the sweet estate of holy wedlock, in the kindest society of a loving husband, may afford you.' Their love as yet in 'this springtime of our acquaintance can put forth as yet no more but the leaves and blossoms, whilst the fruit lies wrapped in the tender bud of hope'.

John brought Margaret to Groton Manor for the first time on 24 April 1618, possibly the day after their wedding in Great Maplested Church. Old Ezekiel Culverwell wrote to John in a 'weary shaking hand' to assure him of his prayers, having heard the news from him in 'letters which well resemble their parent in constancy of true Christian love'. He counselled the young couple to let God have their hearts, 'and he will give them back each to the other'. In March the following year, despite his asthma and other ailments, the faithful pastor took up his pen to write again a few days before Margaret gave birth to her first child, a son called Stephen. With a father's pride Culverwell could not forbear to add in his postscript:

> I hope you have heard of my daughter's fruitfulness, two at a birth: 4 which could not make 2 years. 7 living. The poor man has his hands full, yet I thank God he thrives both ways which is rare and good.

Marriage and growing spiritual maturity gradually set John more free for others. He became a warm friend to his 'loving neighbours' at Groton and in the surrounding villages. Local ministers began to consult him about church appointments. He was diligent in his calling as landowner, lawyer and magistrate. Always he was ready for the unexpected opportunity to serve his neighbour. In December 1623, for instance, he apologized to Margaret for a delay in returning home, 'for coming to Childerditch upon Saturday last, I found my cousin Barfoot very ill, and decaying so fast as on Monday morning I could not leave him, so staying with him about noon he comfortably and quietly gave up the Ghost. I saw God's providence had brought me thither to be a stay and comfort to her in that sudden trial, when none of her friends were with her'.

That same year John's father Adam died in his seventy-fifth year. A delightful man, Adam had enjoyed his grandchildren to the full. Knowing that his death would come as an especial blow to the first-born of them, John, an eighteen-year-old student at Trinity College in Dublin, Winthrop broke the news gently. 'He has finished his course,' wrote Winthrop in his letter, 'and is gathered to his people in peace, as the ripe corn into the barn. He thought long for the day of his dissolution, and welcomed it most gladly. Thus is he gone before; and we must go after, in our time. This advantage he hath of us – he shall not see the evil which we may meet with ere we go hence.'

Both John and Forth Winthrop proved to be exemplary Puritan sons, but Henry caused his father much concern. In 1627 he sailed to Barbados to become a tobacco planter. Shortly afterwards his brother John, who had left Trinity and just returned from taking part in the Duke of Buckingham's ill-starred expedition to relieve La Rochelle, departed again on a fourteen-month grand tour of Italy and the Levant. At home in Suffolk Margaret looked after little Deane and baby Samuel while her husband worked hard in his office as an attorney in the Court of Wards. 'I have many reasons to make me love you,' she wrote to him, 'whereof I will name two: First, because you love God; and, secondly, because that you love me. If these two were wanting, all the rest would be eclipsed. But I must leave this discourse, and go about my household affairs.' She added a postscript: 'I did dine at Groton Hall yesterday; they are in health, and remember their love. We did wish you there, but that would not bring you, and I could not be merry without you.'

Two years later Winthrop reached the momentous decision to sell Groton Manor and move his family to London. He discussed with Margaret the possibility of taking a house at Isleworth, a parish in Middlesex on the Thames nearly opposite to Richmond. In the light of their later and infinitely more hazardous voyages across the Atlantic it is amusing to read Margaret's anxiety about the thought of her husband commuting a few miles to his chamber in a Thames rowing boat. 'But I must allege one thing,' she wrote, 'that I fear in your coming to and fro, lest if you should be ventrous upon the water. If your passage be by water which I know not, it may be dangerous for you in the winter time, the weather being cold and the waters perilous. And so I should be in continual fear of you lest you should take any hurt. I did confer with my mother about it and she thinks you had better take a house in the City, and so come home to your own table and family; and I am of the same mind, but I shall always submit to what you shall think fit.'

Despite her resolution to stay at Groton for the winter, 'in regard that my little one is very young and the ways very bad to remove such things as we shall stand in need of', Margaret came to London in the autumn of 1628 to nurse her husband through a serious illness which he had contracted on top of suffering from a gangrenous finger. Apart from serving to deepen his religion Winthrop also recorded that the illness cured him of his addiction to smoking tobacco. With a surprise that betokens his modesty, he wrote also that he experienced then the love of God's people 'towards me in all places where I was known, testified by their much inquiring after me, mourning for the fear which was conceived of my death, and earnest praying for my recovery'. Clearly he had become a leader among the 'godly people'.

During the summer of 1629 an event occurred which made Winthrop abandon his plans for moving to London. In June he told Margaret, 'I think my office is gone, so I shall not wrong you so much with my absences as I have done.' A few days later he confirmed the fact and added that he had lost his chamber as well. We can only speculate on the reasons for his dismissal, for none was given. During the rest of that month Winthrop was busy putting his affairs in order in London but he was also thinking and praying much about the future. What should he do?

Probably about this time Winthrop was in touch with the council of the Massachusetts Bay Company in London, but he had not as yet decided to emigrate. By the end of July in 1629 he rode into Lincolnshire to visit Isaac Johnson and to consult with him about the great Massachusetts enterprise. Like the Pilgrim Fathers before him Winthrop carefully listed the reasons for and against emigrating to America. His paper in several versions was widely circulated among Puritans. Sir John Eliot, for example, now a prisoner in the Tower after the forced dissolution of parliament that year, possessed a copy. It is evident that Winthrop believed that God's judgement gathered over the land would shortly break out into a terrible storm. America would be a place of refuge for all the churches of Europe in their desolation. Their present mission might be to prepare that haven in the wilderness ready for the hour of need.

Chief among his more 'particular considerations' was the fear of burying his talent in England. In fact his decision to emigrate had a great effect upon the enterprise. On the very day that he rode into Lincolnshire to confer with Isaac Johnson the General Court met in London to consider a proposition 'to transfer the government of the plantation to those that shall inhabit there, and not to continue the same in subordination to the Company here, as it now is'. After some debate the matter was left unresolved and adjourned to the next meeting on 28 August. Clearly those in favour of the proposition began to press men such as Winthrop to commit themselves before that date, subject to the powers of government being granted to the plantation.

Despite some pressures from friends to stay at home John Winthrop put his signature beside those of Sir Richard Saltonstall, Thomas Dudley, Isaac Johnson, John Humphrey, Increase Nowell, William Pynchon and five others to the celebrated Cambridge Agreement. With suitable safeguards this paper bound its signatories to embark for the plantation by 1 March 1630, providing that the whole government and the charter for the colony be transferred to them and its future inhabitants. After further discussion on 28 August the General Council met next day and passed by a show of hands the necessary proposition to set them on their way.

Perhaps Saltonstall expected to be elected governor. He was two years older than Winthrop, and had some relevant experience as a member of the Virginia Company. Indeed Captain John Smith had died in Saltonstall's house. He had signed the Cambridge Agreement first. Yet by the 19th of the next month, not Saltonstall but Winthrop had been chosen for that office. Clearly Winthrop had deeply impressed the Council. Thomas Dudley spoke in a letter of his piety, liberality, wisdom and gravity. Perhaps the Council sensed also his wholehearted commitment to the venture. Here was a leader all could accept. 'So it is that it has pleased the Lord to call me to a further trust in this business of the Plantation, than either I expected or find myself fit for, being chosen by the Company to be their Governor.'

*   *   *

John Winthrop spent that winter in preparation for the voyage to America. Meanwhile the Spanish attacked in the West Indies. 'Some would discourage us with this news,' he wrote, 'but there is no cause, for neither are we in the like danger; and, besides, God is with us, and will surely keep us.' His son John acted as his aide and agent. John junior possessed a marked interest in technology and science. In him the strand in the Renaissance heritage personified by Leonardo da Vinci surfaced visibly. In Colchester he copied down into his notebook the dimensions of a fort. He sent to his father an account of a windmill he had invented. In New England he would establish an iron-works, making him one of the founding fathers of American industry.

By January 1630 Winthrop and the Assistants (or Governors) of the Company had a full list of colonists for the fleet which would sail from Southampton in March. Winthrop's second son Henry had also elected to join them, having sold his estate in Barbados and married a cousin, Elizabeth Fones. The decision may have improved relations with his father, which had remained poor. 'I know not what he does nor what he intends,' Winthrop had complained to his wife, 'I mourn for his sins and the misery that he will soon bring upon himself and his wife.' Little did he know the grief which Henry had in store for him as a father as well.

At the end of January John began to prepare Margaret for 'our long parting, which grows very near'. He had correctly guessed that Margaret would be falling into a state of anxiety. Before he could send a letter to reassure her he received one from her which 'dissolved my head into tears'. He wrote in reply: 'If I live I will see you ere I go. I shall part from you with sorrow enough. Be comfortable my most sweet wife, our God will be with you.' Nine days later, St Valentine's Day, he listed for her all the separations and dangers they had survived together through God's all-powerful providence. He ended his letter with a charming postscript: 'You must be my valentine, for none has challenged me.'

John returned home to Groton Manor at the end of February to say farewell to Margaret. He also said goodbye forever to the house, Suffolk fields and village of his boyhood, that friendly environment where he had lived for most of his forty-two years. Then he set out for Southampton. In his last letter to Margaret from London, dated 10 March, he wrote: 'My dear wife, be of good courage; it shall go well with you and us. The hairs of your head are numbered. He who gave his only beloved to die for you, will give his angels charge over you. Therefore raise up your thoughts, and be merry in the Lord. Labour to live by your faith. If you meet with troubles or difficulties, be not dismayed. God does use to bring his children into the straights of the Red Sea, that he may show his power and mercy in making a way for them. All his courses towards us, are but to make us know him and love him . . .'

7

The Prelude

'The Church and Commonwealth here at home has more need of your best ability in these dangerous times than any remote plantation,' wrote Robert Ryece, a venerable old Suffolk antiquarian whom Winthrop consulted before taking his decision. Moreover, he was too old for such enterprises. 'Plantations are for young men, that can endure all pains and hunger.' Nor should a man of his wisdom and long experience contemplate adventuring his whole family upon such uncertainties. It would be ·hard for one brought up among books and learned men to live in a barbarous place, where there was no learning and less civility. The grave and prudent Ryece solemnly counselled his friend to stray not 'out of your vocation, committing yourself to a world of dangers abroad'. These reasons failed to convince Winthrop, yet similar arguments would anchor the majority of Puritans in their beloved native land.

Among Winthrop's generation who stayed at home were three men who can most aptly exemplify the kind of leadership which the Puritans supplied to their Protestant countrymen during the Great Revolution. If we imagine that upheaval as a drama in three parts, each played a leading role in one of the parts and a subsidiary role in the others. John Hampden was prominent among the leading group of Puritans in Act One: the Prelude. During Act Two, the Civil War itself, Sir William Waller best illustrates the vigorous military leadership provided by the Puritan gentry. In the third Act, the Aftermath, the stage is dominated by Oliver Cromwell.

Providence had equipped all three men to play their parts on the English scene in ways denied to John Winthrop. Both Hampden and Waller were first-born sons in wealthy families of ancient lineage. Hampden owned extensive lands in Buckinghamshire and the neighbouring shires. He rated as one of the richest commoners in his county. Waller inherited the lucrative office of Chief Butler of England, which allowed his agents to tax certain wine imports on his behalf. Their fathers, both Puritans, had died in their youth. Hampden's mother was the second daughter of Sir Henry Cromwell, a Huntingdonshire gentleman whose father had changed his name from Williams to Cromwell as an act of gratitude to the Tudor minister who had bestowed on him some monastic spoils. Her brother, Oliver's father, owned a small estate, about a third the value of Hampden's though three times larger than Winthrop's property. But in 1636 Cromwell's uncle on his mother's side died, bequeathing to him the bulk of his estate including a house in Ely. Cromwell had joined his cousin as a man of substantial property.

All three received an English gentleman's education: a mixture of Renaissance and Reformation learning in the context of the traditional medieval curriculum. Waller was brought up in Dover Castle, where his father served as Lieutenant, and he probably studied under a tutor. Hampden boarded at the comparatively new grammar school at Thame, less than ten miles from the family manor house on a Chiltern beech-hill at Great Hampden. A square oak bedstead which he occupied survives to this day in Aylesbury Museum. It links him with William Waller, for it bears an inscription carved by a schoolboy's penknife 'E.W. 1617'. The initials stand for the poet Edmund Waller, a scion of the Waller family at Beaconsfield and a cousin of Hampden's by marriage. Cromwell attended the free school at Huntingdon, where he came under the lasting influence of a Puritan clergyman–schoolmaster called Thomas Beard.

Waller and Hampden went on to Oxford University, to Magdalen Hall and Magdalen College respectively. Standing on the edge of Anglican and Royalist Oxford, as if ashamed of such company, Magdalen College looked towards the Puritan home counties for its students. Lord Clarendon, a later Chancellor of the University and a Laudian layman, thought Magdalen an unfruitful place, 'the discipline of that time being not so strict as it has been since, and as it ought to be'. He may have had in mind academic laxity as well as Puritan fervour. Thomas Hobbes, who matriculated a few years after Hampden, seems to have spent many hours reading travel books and snaring jackdaws in the deerpark, a comparatively harmless pastime by the standards of the day. Yet the fellows of these two Oxford colleges did not neglect their duties. At Magdalen Hall, John Crowther, the tutor of the Ralph Verney, one of the Verneys of Claydon in Buckinghamshire, sent him a sheaf of astronomical notes, which he had compiled especially for his pupil. In addition Crowther prepared for him a general scheme of the Arts and a genealogy of the kings of England, and exhorted him 'to devote to logic and divinity from three to four hours a day'.

A contemporary called Magdalen at Oxford 'a very nest of Puritans' but it could not compare with the Cambridge colleges as a breeding-ground of men so persuaded. Emmanuel, Sidney Sussex and Christ's, where Winthrop's younger son Forth was a contemporary of John Milton, had become bywords as hotbeds of Puritanism. No painted saints gazed upwards in windows or perched in niches in the chapel of Sidney Sussex when Cromwell first entered it as an undergraduate. Samuel Ward, the Master, had helped to translate the King James Bible. Yet his comfortable office altered this mild, slow-spoken divine. A conservative in politics, he responded to the crisis in the next reign by sending the college silver to King Charles.

Cromwell cut no figure as a scholar of the classics. He preferred cosmography, mathematics and history on the grounds that these subjects fit a man for public services. Among history books Sir Walter Raleigh's *History of the World* was immensely popular with such young Puritans, not least because it chronicled the fall of so many tyrannous regimes. For Raleigh wrote history as a commentary on present political events. The Puritans admired such a Renaissance mind that could encompass all historical knowledge in one volume. 'Tis a body of history,' wrote Cromwell to his son Richard later, 'and will add much to your understanding than fragments of a story.' Foxe wrote the spiritual story of England, but Raleigh set the nation's history in a universal context. This moral struggle, shot through with the silver threads of providence, began in the days of Greece and Rome and was moving now towards its climax.

Hampden shared his first cousin's interest in recent history but far excelled him in learning. 'He had a great knowledge both in scholarship and in the law,' wrote Sir Philip Warwick, who knew him in later years. 'He was very well read in history, and I remember that the first time I ever saw that of D'Avila of the civil wars in France it was lent me under the title of Mr Hampden's *Vade-Mecum*, and I believe that no copy was liker an original than that rebellion was like ours.' (A vade-mecum was a book carried constantly about with a person.)

After university Hampden became a student at the Inner Temple in London. In the widely-influential Renaissance treatise on the education of a gentleman entitled *The Governour*, Sir Thomas More's son-in-law Sir Thomas Elyot had advocated such a course of legal studies to prepare for public service. He held that law was the

fittest profession for a gentleman. Even if not practised profession-
ally, as in Hampden's case, it equipped him to manage the legal side
of land-owning and to serve as a justice of the peace. Moreover, the
law trained a gentleman to speak with 'the sharp wits of logicians,
the grave sentences of philosophers, the elegancy of poets, the
memory of civilians [students of the Civil Law], the voice and
gesture of them that pronounce comedies'.

*   *   *

William Waller, like Hampden's younger brother Richard, chose to
complete his education with a grand tour on the continent. In the
'Experiences', a list of special providences which Waller composed
later in life, he noted that in Padua he very narrowly escaped an
epidemic of burning fever, while near Gradisca in Friuli an
overcrowded boat ferrying him across the River Isonzo began to
sink: 'I was fain to leap out, and falling short of the bank, I had been
carried away by that swift stream, but that I caught hold of a bough
of a tree, which supported me, till I was helped out.' At Bologna, on
the way from Venice to Florence, a priest, who had travelled with
him in the same party, informed against him to the Inquisition. 'I
was searched, my trunk, wherein I had nothing but clothes, was
rifled to the bottom, but it pleased God to so order it, that they let
along a box, wherein I had some papers, which might have exposed
me to question; when they had it in their hands ready to open it.'

Not long after his return to England he responded to a call to
rescue Queen Elizabeth of Bohemia from the clutches of the Catholic
powers. Elizabeth, the eldest daughter of James I, had inherited the
charm of her grandmother Mary, Queen of Scots. During the
disappointing reign of her father, Elizabeth and her brother Prince
Henry (before his premature death in 1612) became the focus of
Puritan hopes. Her marriage to Frederick, the Elector Palatine, on St
Valentine's Day in 1613 was universally popular, especially among
the Puritans who had much to admire in the Calvinist Prince. Also it
was hoped that he would lead a major advance of Renaissance
learning.

Frederick and Elizabeth soon ran into trouble. His action in
accepting the throne of Bohemia, the birthplace of John Huss, called
upon his head a Habsburg storm. Indeed he triggered off the Thirty
Year's War. For three decades the Puritans in old and New England
would watch the changing fortunes of this epic struggle with
fascinated attention. In the opening move the Imperial army

brushed aside the Bohemian forces. Thus it seemed imperative to the English Puritans that this Protestant David and his lovely wife should be rescued from the unequal struggle with the ungodly Goliath. Reluctantly James I bowed to pressure and in January 1620 he authorized Sir Horace Vere to raise 2,000 soldiers to secure their safety. An ardour for the task ahead gripped the young Puritans who volunteered to go with Vere. At Gravesend that summer Waller met for the first time two men who would play important parts in his later life: Robert Devereux, the twenty-nine-year-old Earl of Essex, and Ralph Hopton from Somerset, who was five years younger than Essex.

After reaching the Palatinate, Vere sent forwards a troop of sixty gentlemen, including Hopton and Waller, to serve as the Lifeguard of Queen Elizabeth. In Bohemia they saw scenes of devastation and rapine as the national forces fell back before the Imperial army. As these regiments of Walloon, Polish, Irish and Cossack mercenaries drew near to Prague, the Queen's Lifeguard skirmished with them. 'I had a miraculous escape out of the hands of the Cossacks,' wrote William, 'when in a skirmish my horse was killed under me, and in the clearing of myself from him, I fell with my foot hanging in the stirrup, in making my way through them, I had several shot made at me, at a close distance, yet it pleased the Lord, none wounded me; only one grazed lightly on the top of my head, and I came off with safety.'

After the battle of the White Mountain in November 1620 the royal couple fled their capital. The English volunteers escorted the 'Winter Queen' through the falling snow, and when deep drifts halted the coaches and baggage waggons Ralph Hopton carried the Queen of Bohemia behind on his horse for forty miles. On 5 December, the Queen, pregnant with her second son, rode into Frankfurt-on-the-Oder, accompanied by her Lifeguard.

As the campaign was virtually over Waller returned to England. In June 1622 the King knighted him. Two months later he married Jane, sole daughter and heiress of an eminent lawyer Sir Richard Reynell, who had built himself a gracious house near Newton Abbot. William and his bride moved into Forde House and lived with them. For the next fourteen years he enjoyed a quiet life as a country gentleman. 'They that have been acquainted with the passages of my little world, in the former course of my life,' he wrote after the Civil War, 'can bear me witness how little I have affected great things . . . and have desired no greater preferment that to be mine own man. God has blessed me with a competent fortune, and given me a mind (it is his gift) fitted to enjoy that blessing. In that retired way, I enjoyed myself freely, *Nella Signoria di me*, as the Italian says, in the kingdom of mine own mind, without other thoughts than such as might arise from quiet senses, looking upon public affairs, as men use to look upon pictures, at a distance . . .'

* * *

A seat in the House of Commons gave John Hampden a grandstand view of public events. Puritans such as Sir John Eliot provided leadership for those more Protestant-minded subjects opposed to the interwoven religious, domestic and foreign policies of James I and his favourites. Hampden served his political apprenticeship to Eliot. He spent most of 1627 as a prisoner with Eliot in the Gatehouse for refusing to pay the forced loan demanded by the ministers of the new king, Charles I. He worked actively on parliamentary committees designed to maintain the uncompromising Protestant character of Church and Commonwealth. His quick and subtle mind, his ability to listen, his knack of guiding the discussion, his knowledge and wisdom, and above all his Christian character made him stand out as one destined for greatness. In 1629 he observed those tumultuous events in the Commons when Speaker Finch announced the royal command to adjourn. 'No, No!' roared the opposition. Denzil Holles rushed forward and held Finch down in his chair as Eliot condemned for the last time those who made popish or Arminian innovations and who advised the paying of illegal taxes as traitors. Within days the ringleaders found themselves in the Tower of London. Parliament would not meet again for eleven years.

The seven members of Parliament so detained were kept in close confinement. Some visitors wandered about inside the Tower trying to find the whereabouts of the prisoners by shouting up at the windows, until the warders apprehended them and escorted them out of the fortress. Two friends of Eliot, Sir Oliver Luke and a companion, who had requested in vain for the opportunity to see him, did actually catch sight of Denzil Holles across a green lawn. With nothing to read, Holles had whiled away the long hours by exercising with dumb-bells and whirling a top. He held them up for Luke to see, and make 'antick signs and devoted salutations at their parting'. Within a few months, however, all except Sir John Eliot were released.

Eliot corresponded copiously with his friends. Hampden wrote frequently. A letter from him survives which asked Eliot to send 'the paper of considerations concerning the Plantation' (as noted, almost certainly a version of Winthrop's original). Eliot replied that Hampden's letters possessed a great virtue; besides signifying health and love, they 'imparted such variety of happiness in his counsels and example that it made a degree of liberty to have them'. Hampden's merits placed so great an obligation on him, he wrote, that no command or opportunity to serve him should be neglected or refused. Three weeks later Hampden returned the paper, and his accompanying letter reveals that Eliot's two sons were spending their first Christmas vacation from Oxford enjoying the 'rough-hewn entertainment' of Hampden House. Meanwhile in the Tower their father received a cart-load of logs sent up from Bedfordshire by the thoughtful Sir Oliver Luke to warm his 'little thin carcass'.

Having been found guilty, and refusing to pay his fine, Eliot settled down as best he could in the Tower. Young Richard Eliot's behaviour at Oxford caused him much concern. In a fatherly letter Eliot asked him to remember that his enemies would make political capital out of Richard's misbehaviour if they could 'to extract some scandal or disadvantage against me'. He begged the boy not 'in the sea of vanity to make shipwreck of all my hopes' and urged him to recover his 'gravity and composure'. Eliot's humanist philosophy, child of both the Renaissance and the Reformation, shines forth from the letter. Beasts have affections, wrote Eliot, but man alone has reason. Therefore 'propound goodness not pleasure for your object. Lose not yourself for liberty, or rather make not liberty a vice'.

For some reason Eliot's daughter was removed from school and lodged with Sir Oliver Luke, where Hampden visited her. He thought Lady Luke would not send her back. 'Not for any particular blame she can lay upon her,' he added, 'but that in such a mixture of dispositions and humours as must needs be met with in a multitude, there will be much of that which is bad; and that is infectious, where good is not so easily diffusive. And, in my judgment, there is much more danger in such a nursery than in a school of boys, for, though an ill tincture be dangerous in either, yet it is perfectly recoverable in these, hardly or never in the other.'

Eliot exercised his mind by writing a book entitled *The Monarchy of Man*, a treatise in the Renaissance tradition of Erasmus to prove that monarchy was the best form of government. The work was tediously long, as Eliot cut nothing out. He made over 400 quotations from more than fifty classical authors, compared with barely thirty references from the Bible. It contained no original thought. In fact, despite the inordinate influence in favour of such enlightened monarchy stemming from such thinkers as Plato and Aristotle, their witness came in the golden evening of Greece. The much stronger classical tradition over the previous centuries stood hostile to kings and in favour of republics of sturdy independent men ruled by educated oligarchies. The ancients' love of freedom could not bend to a tyrant, the Greek word for king. To Sir John Hampden, a generation younger than Eliot, *The Monarchy of Man* must have seemed no more than a literary exercise. After reading the first part, which Eliot sent to him for comment, he replied with tact that he judged it to be 'an exquisite nosegay, composed of curious flowers, bound together with a fine a thread. But I must in the end expect honey from my friend – somewhat out of these flowers digested, made his own, and giving a true taste of his own sweetness: though for that I shall await a fitter time and place'.

But that opportunity never came. In 1632 Eliot fell ill. The King refused a petition from Eliot asking him 'to set me at liberty, that, for the recovery of my health, I may take some fresh air'. For Eliot offered no submission: he intended to return to the Tower as soon as he had recovered his health, 'there to undergo such punishment as God has allotted to me'. In a vindictive mood, the King would grant no mercy. On 27 November Eliot died in his cell. When his son John petitioned for the right to bury the corpse of his father at the family home of Port Eliot, King Charles himself wrote on the document: 'Let Sir John Eliot's body be buried in the Church of that parish where he died.'

*   *   *

During the early 1630s Hampden played a prominent part, along with many other Puritan noblemen and members of the Lower House, adventurers, religious refugees and London merchants, in schemes for colonizing the western hemisphere. The principal projects which concerned him were the colonies on Providence and Henrietta Islands in the Caribbean, and the settlement at the mouth of the Connecticut River. In the event the former never prospered. The islands eventually fell into Spanish hands and then became a nest of pirates. The latter fared a little better. A fort was built and named Saybrook but the Connecticut Company could not even

1 Sir Richard Saltonstall by an unknown artist, thought to have been painted in Holland in 1644. He was then 58 years old.

2 The martyrdom of Laurence Saunders at Coventry. One of the many woodcut illustrations which helped to make Foxe's *Book of Martyrs* such a popular work.

3 Puritans in the wilderness of New England on their way to church. A painting by the nineteenth century artist G.H. Boughton.

4 An Indian brave as sketched by Captain John White in
Virginia. In 1587 Sir Walter Raleigh launched his second attempt
to plant a colony in Virginia with White as Governor. Three
years later, when he returned from England with supplies, White
could find no trace of the settlers. Probably they had perished at
the hands of the Indians.

5 Sir John Eliot, dressed in his nightshirt and holding a tortoise-shell comb. This portrait was painted shortly before his death in the Tower of London in 1632.

6 Sir William Waller at the height of his fame during the English Civil War, painted by Robert Walker.

7 Governor John Winthrop. This portrait, by an unknown artist, was probably painted before Winthrop left England for America in 1630.

8 John Winthrop the younger, who became Governor of Connecticut. He took an active interest in technology and practised as a physician. He was one of the New Englanders elected a Fellow of the Royal Society.

9 The Chapel of Littlecote House in Berkshire, the home of Colonel Alexander Popham during the Civil War. It is the only complete example of a Puritan chapel in a private house, and shows the typical arrangement of all Puritan places of worship, with the elevated pulpit standing in place of an altar.

10   A ten-year-old Puritan schoolboy, by an unknown artist, dated 1657.

11 Edward Winslow, painted by Robert Walker in London, 1651. It is the only portrait of a Mayflower 'Pilgrim Father' that has survived.

12 William Pynchon. He sailed with Winthrop in 1630 to America, but returned to England to end his days.

Hugh Peters Chaplain to Oliver Cromwell

13 Hugh Peter, who returned from New England to serve the Commonwealth. A committed supporter of Oliver Cromwell, he met a horrible end in 1660 as a regicide.

keep it supplied, let alone develop the colony. In course of time it was absorbed by the settlers who came from Massachusetts Bay into the new colony of Connecticut.

In the absence of any parliament these company meetings provided opportunities for leading Puritan nobles and gentlemen to confer together about politics. The Earl of Warwick, president of the government's Council for New England, played an influential part in their deliberations. Despite his irregular personal life, Warwick served as a patron of the Puritans. In the Civil War he would command the navy of Parliament. The leading Puritan peers involved in both companies were Lord Saye and Sele and young Robert Greville, Lord Brooke, who had succeeded to his title in 1629 on becoming twenty-one. Other Puritans, such as Sir Benjamin Rudyerd, Sir Gilbert Gerrard, Sir Edward Harwood, Richard Knightley and John Pym, were among the commoners in the Providence Company. Sir William Waller joined it as an investor somewhat later. Six of the Providence shareholders also put money into the Connecticut venture. The patentees of the latter included not only John Hampden but also Sir Richard Saltonstall, now safely returned from Massachusetts Bay.

A top turret room in Broughton Castle, Lord Saye's home, is still pointed out as the place where committees of the two companies held some of their meetings. Although Hampden did not have shares in the Providence Company, he maintained close links with the governing body of patentees. Two of them are named executors in his will: Richard Knightley and Sir Gilbert Gerrard. Some of his trustees are also appointed in Pym's will of 1637. Thus it is clear that the colonial enterprises of these years formed the matrix for the friendships which would have considerable political significance in the coming constitutional crisis.

During the 1630s both Hampden and Waller experienced the deepening, purifying affliction of bereavement. Lady Jane Waller was even smaller in stature than her short husband. As so often happened in those days she experienced difficulties in childbirth. Her first labour began in January 1631. William stayed at his wife's bedside until his growing tears on her behalf drove him from the room. 'I could not but be very apprehensive of the weakness of her condition; and having retired myself to prayer, and earnestly besought God to strengthen her, and being desirous to comfort myself with some portion of God's word, I took the Bible to read, and letting it fall, with some passion, upon the table (but without any particular design at all upon one place more than another) it opened upon the 128 Psalm, in the singing Psalms, "Like a fruitful vine on they house side, so doth thy wife spring out."' Two more falls of the Bible convinced William that this was no accident, and in a few hours Jane gave safe birth to a son, Richard. Two years later she presented her husband with a daughter, whom they called Margaret. The new baby was baptised in February 1633, in Exeter Cathedral, as her brother had been before her. But this time Jane never recovered from her exertions, and the next spring William dutifully recorded the loss of his 'virtuous, discreet, loving and beloved wife'.

John Hampden had married Elizabeth Symeon of Pyrton in Oxfordshire on Midsummer Day. The long embroidered white kid gloves, edged with gold lace and lined with pink taffeta she wore then have survived to this day. English ladies were careful to protect their fair complexions by wearing hats and gloves, and they became important items of apparel. Black gloves were worn at New England funerals by Puritan ladies, and given afterwards to the minister as part of his remuneration. Elizabeth bore her husband nine children before she died in childbirth in 1634, the same year as Jane Waller's death.

The two husbands differed in the kind of monuments they raised to their wives. Hampden followed stricter Puritan custom by erecting in Great Hampden Church a plain wall tablet with an inscription. It exemplified the Puritan belief in the significance of words. The inscription was carefully composed by Hampden himself as a memorial to their human love which was now transcended as his partner had found her true fulfilment in union with God. In words of finely-chiselled classical letters Hampden recorded that 'her sorrowful husband' had dedicated this monument on 20 August 'to the eternal memory of the truly virtuous and pious Elizabeth Hampden', wife, daughter and 'the tender mother of a happy offspring in 9 hopeful children':

> In her pilgrimage,
> The staie and comfort of her neighbours,
> The love and glory of a well-ordered family,
> The delight and happiness of tender parents –
> But a crown of Blessings to a husband.
> In a wife, to all an eternall paterne of goodness
> And cause of love, while she was
> In her dissolution

> A losse invaluable to each,
> Yet herselfe blest, and they fully recompenced
> In her translation, from a Tabernacle of Claye
> And Fellowship with Mortalls, to a celestiall Mansion
> And communion with a Deity.

Family pride sometimes mingled with Puritan piety and produced a more elaborate monument. Waller commissioned a noted Herefordshire sculptor named Epiphanius Evesham to build a tomb worthy of his wife and himself in the north transept of Bath Abbey. Working in black and white marble Evesham created a tomb not unlike a four-poster bed, with four Corinthian pillars supporting a classical cornice. Sir William in alabaster effigy leans on one elbow in a life-like position gazing down into the face of Jane. At their head and feet kneel the two children in the long skirts of childhood. The tablet at the rear which would have contained his epitaph is blank, for William is buried elsewhere. But his gracious verse on Jane is still a delight to read:

> Sole issue of a matchless paire
> Both of their state & vertues heyre
> In graces great, in stature small,
> As full of spirit as voyd of gall;
> Cherefully grave, bounteously close
> Holy without vain-glorious showes:
> Happy and yet from envy free:
> Learn'd without pride, witty yet wise.
> Reader this riddle read with mee.
> Here the good Lady Waller lyes.

During the Civil War the Puritan animosity against religious images in church spilt over into a destruction of all statues and pictures. Doubtless the soldiers, mostly illiterate, thought it best to be on the safe side and to leave no suspicious statuary unmarked. Even Waller's own troopers defaced his effigy with their swords during their stay in Bath. There is a bust to their little boy placed in a church just outside Peterborough during the war which bears the words:

> To the courteous Souldier:
> Noe crucifixe you see, noe Frightfull Brand
> Of superstitious here, Pray let mee stand.
> Grassante bello civili.

151

But the message was lost upon the unlettered soldiers and their swords have defaced this statue too.

*   *   *

The eleven years after 1629 when King ruled without Parliament can hardly be labelled a tyranny. In many ways Charles proved himself an enlightened despot. The country enjoyed a decade of peace and relative prosperity. But the Church of England moved steadily towards what would later be called a High Church stance. In William Laud, who became primate in 1633, the King found a prelate after his own heart. 'I laboured nothing more,' Laud wrote later, 'than the external public worship of God – too much slighted in most parts of this kingdom – might be preserved, and that with as much decency and uniformity as might be, being still of the opinion that unity cannot long continue in the Church where uniformity is shut out at the Church door.'

The last of the great Elizabethan churchmen, Laud believed passionately in outward uniformity. He worked immensely hard to secure it. He began by reviving the custom of an archiepiscopal visitation, sending officials to inquire into the condition of every diocese in his southern province. All communion tables were removed back to the east end of the church, and fenced with rails to keep out the dogs which habitually accompanied their masters to church. Every clergyman was obliged to conform to the Prayer Book. Ritual acts, vestments, music and stately processions, designed to emphasize the sacraments and generally to convey 'the beauty of holiness', all came into favour as the Laudians pressed on with their reforms.

Laud's interference with parochial freedom varied in its effectiveness from diocese to diocese. Certainly it helped to swell the stream of Puritan emigrants to New England. Hampden himself almost fell into Laud's wide-flung net. In October 1634 Sir Nicholas Brent, Laud's Vicar-General, reported that Hampden had been reprimanded for holding a muster of the county trained volunteers in the churchyard at Beaconsfield. The Laudians disliked any use of consecrated ground for such secular purposes. Parish church and churchyard, however, all possessed secular functions and those could not be easily erased. Villagers stored their arms and armour in the parish church. Legal contracts were often exchanged there. The Puritans could justify theologically this time-honoured English custom of regarding churches as secular buildings. In this respect they worked with the grain of English character.

The unpopularity of Laud's attempted changes is reflected in the spleen vented by the Buckinghamshire gentry on the informer against Hampden, Sir Edmund Verney and their fellow deputy lieutenants. Both Hampden and Verney had also fallen short in the matter of attending their parish churches. They travelled further afield to hear the best available Puritan preacher each Sunday. Brent received assurances from Hampden which apparently contented him. Yet a contemporary clergyman records that the instructions of the Vicar-General were kept for a few days and then quietly ignored.

Brent's visitation of Sussex the following year shows how Puritanism had become rooted in the towns. His report is written in a humorous vein – after the Civil War he worked for the Puritan leaders and carried out for them a survey of the University of Oxford. In Chichester 'Mr Speed of St Pancras confessed his error of being too popular in the pulpit; the mayor and his brethren are puritanically addicted, which caused me to admonish one of the aldermen for putting his hat on during the service.' In Arundel he prohibited three clergymen 'vehemently suspected to be non-conformitants' from preaching. One of them in the pulpit 'spake unto four of his neighbours who sat before him in one seat that he was certain three of them should be damned. The fourth was his friend, and therefore he saved him.' In Lewes 'I inhibited one Mr Jennings to preach any more for particularising in the pulpit. He called one of his parishioners "arch-knave", and being questioned by me answered that it was but a lively application. The man abused did think he had been called "notched knave" and fell out with his barber who had lately trimmed him.'

Without Parliament the Puritans had no public forum in which to voice their opposition to Laud's policies. As the years passed the English gentry as a whole increasingly resented the King's high-handed action in suspending Parliament. The Stuart king had withdrawn both their traditional court for redress of grievances and the ancient, hard-won right of free Englishmen to participate in national government. The Puritan gentry not only felt the consequences more than their neighbours, they also interpreted the deeper political or constitutional issue at stake. They suspected that Charles Stuart had the makings of a tyrant, and that he might try to bury English liberties for good, but they were not sure. He had certainly begun to behave as if the doctrine of the divine right of kings was true. The ceiling painted by Rubens in the new Whitehall banqueting house, a magnificent Renaissance building, conveys to this day the grand image of monarchy, the king as a demi-god, which inspired the enthusiasm of royalists throughout Europe.

But Rubens had to be paid, as did all the other contractors who supplied the stately splendour of the Court or the services which government needed daily. Money came not from heaven but from the productive labours of subjects. Without Parliament to grant him taxes King Charles and his ministers resorted to various expedients which technically lay within the royal prerogative. He revived the old forest laws, for example, which enabled him to levy heavy fines upon those who had enclosed fields within the bounds of the old royal forests. Yet these measures did not provide enough money. Then his lawyers identified one tax which, if successful, would secure him financial independence from Parliament. In times of war ports in medieval England had been asked to supply ships or money in place of them. Writs for Ship Money, as it was called, had been issued to coastal towns earlier in the reign, but in 1635 the Privy Council extended the principle and sent them to all inland counties as well. They justified this innovation by reference to the ferocious activities of Dunkirk privateers in the Channel.

The Ship Money tax bore heavily on the common people. According to a Herefordshire return of arrears 'many of the defaulters are very poor; many have gone into New England'. In Norfolk another group of defaulters departed to the same haven, together with their minister. Apart from its economic burden on the poor the tax posed a political challenge.

The Puritan leaders saw the issue more clearly than the rest of the gentry. They determined to oppose it. The meetings of the Providence Company gave them an opportunity to formulate a plan. They agreed that two of their number – a peer and a commoner – would fight test cases in the courts. In the event the Crown did not proceed against Lord Saye, and the full force fell on John Hampden for refusing to pay his assessment in Buckinghamshire. The case came before the Court of Exchequer Chamber – the twelve principal judges of England sitting together – in the autumn of 1637.

After days of legal argument over such issues as what constituted a national emergency the judges began to deliver their verdicts and the reasons for them. Sir Thomas Trevor, for example, agreed upon the importance of the case 'for the sum is but 20s. but the weight thereof is of far greater extent: it concerns the whole kingdom'. He agreed that in normal circumstances it would be best for the King to summon Parliament to grant money for war, but cited the instances of the Armada in 1588 and the 'Gunpowder Treason' of 1605 as ground for preserving the Crown's independent powers. 'Alas, it is not Parliaments can keep us safe,' he said. Then Trevor firmly rejected any notion of popular control over the King. 'This Kingdom has been always monarchical: a democratical government was never in this Kingdom.' Parliament was too slow to be an instrument against danger, and could not supplant the King as the chief means of preventing it. Ships provided our best defence, and the royal fleet now contained ships of greater size and strength, all better furnished than ever before. 'All of which redounds to the King and Kingdom's honour. The ship, called the *Sovereign of the Seas*, may be termed the *Sovereign of All Ships*.' At least Trevor was right on that point, for the *Sovereign of the Seas*, launched the previous summer at Deptford, measured 254 feet long and carried 144 cannon. As for the Ship-Money tax, Trevor concluded: 'I wish it may be paid by all cheerfully.'

Five judges had now given judgement for the King, and a resounding royal victory was in sight when Sir George Croke, Justice of the King's Bench, rose to give his verdict. As a Buckinghamshire fellow-countryman of Hampden's and as one of the two doubtful justices in a consultation about the legality of the tax, Croke was a key figure in the trial. If he allowed himself to be swayed by the majority opinion, the case would turn into a triumph for King Charles. A contemporary wrote that Croke's wife and nearest relations had brought pressure to bear upon him to speak from his conscience. More than any of the other judges, however, Croke showed that he had grasped the political and constitutional significance of the trial and his own chief part in it. 'I must confess, this cause is a very great cause, and the greatest cause that ever came into question before any judges,' he began. 'And for my own part I am sorry it should come in question in this place; more requisite it was to have had it debated in a public assembly of the whole State, for on the one side, it concerns the King in his prerogative and power royal; and on the other side, the subject, in his lands, goods and liberty, in all that he has, besides his life.'

Doubtless to their delight, Hampden and his friends then heard Croke first apologize before proceeding to differ from his brother judges, which he must do because their views 'do much trouble me'. As for the apparently convincing case of the King's two counsels, he observed that when he had himself spoken as an advocate the argument had seemed clear-cut, but that it looked quite different from the judge's seat. Croke, who was a Puritan, then said he would follow 'God's direction and my own conscience', hardly legal language. 'I desire God to guide me to a true judgment, and though, for the reasons aforesaid, I doubt myself, yet I am not of the same opinion as my brothers, but according to my conscience, I think that judgment ought to be given to the defendant.'

We can only imagine the immense stir that these words must have caused in the Exchequer Chamber and later in the kingdom. Whatever the majority verdict, nothing could erase the fact that one judge, guided by God and his conscience, had declared in public in favour of John Hampden and the non-payment of Ship Money. In the Inns of Court it would be said that the King had Ship Money 'by hook but not by Croke'.

In the end the Crown won by the narrowest possible margin of seven to five. Moreover, the arguments of Hampden's lawyers, Oliver St John and Robert Holborne, which were as 'full of rare and excellent learning', had become the talk of London. Even before the trial ended, their effects, and still more the opinions of Sir George Croke and Sir John Hutton, had renewed the flagging opposition to Ship-Money. By the spring of 1638 it had spread throughout the country, being especially strong in Essex, Oxfordshire, Buckinghamshire and Gloucestershire. The Privy Council heard reports that Sir Alexander Denton, the new Sheriff of Buckinghamshire, had not pressed the matter because he listened too much to his kindred and friends. Although men accepted that the judges had condemned Hampden on legal or technical grounds, they certainly felt that the true merits of his case had not been rejected. In 1639, when writs for Ship Money went out again and Buckinghamshire was assessed for £4500, no one seems to have paid. By 1640, only a third of Ship Money was received by the Treasurer of the Navy, and sheriffs in almost every county encountered a stiffening resistance to it.

Ship Money caused 'a wonderful murmuring', as Richard Baxter described it, because the nobility and gentry interpreted it as an attempt to overthrow the constitution of the kingdom and a threat to the concept of private property. Hampden lost the case and he duly paid up the sum for which he had been assessed. But the King won a Pyrrhic victory. Hampden's 'carriage throughout that agitation', concluded Clarendon, 'was with that rare temper and modesty that they who watched him narrowly to find some advantage against his person, to make him less resolute in his cause, were compelled to give him a just testimony. And the judgement that was given against him infinitely more advanced him than the service for which it was given.'

Hampden and his Puritan 'brothers', as they called each other, had now become marked men. That turncoat Parliamentarian Sir Thomas Wentworth, Lord Deputy of Ireland and later Earl of Strafford, wrote as much in anger to Archbishop Laud: 'Mr Hampden is a great Brother, and the very genius of that nation of people leads them always to oppose civilly as ecclesiastically all that authority ever ordains for them. But, in good faith, were they right served they should be whipped home into their right wits; and much beholden they should be to any that would thoroughly take pains with them in that sort.' He added that 'as well as I think of Mr Hampden's abilities, I take his will and peevishness to be full as great.'

Strafford had a point. The Puritan identity did emerge in opposition, and in those days civil and ecclesiastical politics could not be divided. Their separation would indeed be the ultimate answer, but that lay in the future. When the Puritans came to power in the middle of the century, with no one to oppose, the seeds of 'declension' soon became evident. Puritanism thrived best in opposition.

The Ship Money affair certainly made Hampden's name known. Before that historic stand, wrote Clarendon, 'he was rather of reputation in his own country than of public discourse or fame in the kingdom, but then he grew the argument of all tongues, every man inquiring who and what he was that durst at his own charge support the liberty and property of the kingdom, and rescue his country from being made a prey to the court'. Thus Hampden was established as the Puritan successor to Sir John Eliot when the King's dismal failure to impose the Prayer Book on the Scots led to the recall of Parliament.

Clarendon's portrait of Hampden on the eve of the Long Parliament is an unforgettable evocation of the Puritan spirit. It is paradoxical that Hampden was one of the heroes of the Royalist *History of the Great Rebellion* unless one recalls that Clarendon was a Parliament man who understood the finer points of the leadership needed in that assembly of equals. He saw Hampden's potential greatness. In his youth, wrote Clarendon, he enjoyed all the sports, exercises and company 'used by men of the most jolly conversation'. As his awakened conscience led him to abandon these activities Hampden retired 'to a more reserved and melancholic society, yet preserving his natural cheerfulness and vivacity, and above all a flowing courtesy to all men'.

The Long Parliament met in November 1640 and embarked upon a programme of reform which swept away the various instruments and pillars of prerogative government. The majority of the Lower House, leavened by the Puritan group led by John Hampden and John Pym, clearly enjoyed overwhelming support in the country for these measures which occupied the next twelve months. 'When this Parliament began', concluded Clarendon on the subject of Hampden, 'the eyes of all men were fixed on him as their *Patriae pater*, and the pilot that must steer their vessel through the tempests and rocks which threatened it. And I am persuaded that his power and interest at that time was greater to do good or hurt than any man's in the Kingdom, or any man of his rank has had in any time. For his reputation for honesty was universal, and his affections seemed so publicly guided that no corrupt or private ends could bias them.' Significantly, James I had asserted that the title 'Father of his country' 'was ever and is commonly used of kings'. Now, for the first time in English history, it was accorded to a commoner who had emerged as a national leader.

*   *   *

The outbreak of the Irish Rebellion in October 1641 precipitated the real crisis. The Puritan leaders feared that the army which would have to be raised to suppress it might be employed first against them. But to challenge the King's right to appoint his military commanders would be to summon the very citadel of the royal prerogative, and many moderate members of the House of Commons now hesitated. The Grand Remonstrance, Pym's attempt to establish the King's fundamental unreliability, revealed the growing division.

At 9 am on 22 November the Commons began a long discussion on the Remonstrance, taking its 204 clauses one by one. Characteristically Hampden waited until late in the day before speaking. At 9 pm when he rose to his feet, the candles had burned low and many of the older and more infirm members had made their way home. Yet some 300 members heard him describe the Remonstrance as 'wholly true in substance and a very necessary vindication of the parliament'.

An earlier speaker had defended episcopacy on the grounds that without a few large prizes in the lottery of preferment few men would take holy orders. 'If any man could cut the moon out into little stars', he had argued, 'we might still have the same moon, or as much in small pieces, yet we should want both light and influence.' Hampden now replied to him by asking by what authority they should suppose that God valued the moon more than the stars. Were the clergy less useful to the Church than the bishops? Quoting the Book of Revelation, he spoke of the vision of the Church as the Bridge of Christ, clothed with the sun, with the moon as a footstool and the stars as a crown about her head.

At about 2 am the Remonstrance was put to the House and passed by 159 to 148, a majority of only eleven votes. As soon as the result was declared, Hampden moved that the Remonstrance should be printed. In other words, he intended to make it an appeal to the people. This possibility infuriated those who had already opposed the Bill, and may have alarmed some who had supported it. Hyde stood up and asked for leave to register a formal protestation against this unprecedented action. A friend of his, Geoffrey Palmer, then shouted out 'I do protest!' and others called out 'All! All!' Weariness and hunger had frayed tempers to a breaking-point. Members were on their feet, hurling their hats in the air; some took their swords in their scabbards from their belts and rested them on the ground with their hands on the pommels. Palmer argued that the chorus of 'All! All!' meant that he spoke for all the rest and justified a protestation.

In the dim, candle-lit chapel with its lofty, cavernous roof above them, 'I thought', wrote Sir Philip Warwick, 'we had all sat in the valley of the shadow of death; for we, like Joab's and Abner's young men, had catch't at each others locks, and sheathed our swords in each others bowels, had not the sagacity and great calmness of Mr Hampden by a short speech prevented it.' Hampden began by quietly asking how Palmer could know other men's minds. His brief speech brought silence to the House, and it was agreed to leave the matter of printing the Remonstrance undetermined until the morrow.

As the members walked out into the cold morning, Falkland walked beside Oliver Cromwell, who sat as one of the members for Cambridge. On the previous morning Cromwell has asked Falkland why he had wanted to postpone the debate on the Remonstrance until the next day. 'There would not have been time enough, for sure it would take some debate,' replied Falkland. 'A very sorry one,' commented Cromwell. Now, with fourteen hours of debate behind them, Falkland could not resist asking Cromwell if he was well satisfied. Cromwell answered that he would take Falkland's word another time, and whispered in his ear that if the Remonstrance had been rejected he would have sold all he had next morning and never seen England again, and he knew many other honest men of the same resolution.

At this time few men perceived the worth of Oliver Cromwell. The courtly young Sir Philip Warwick had noticed him in November:

> I came one morning into the House well clad, and perceived a gentleman speaking . . . very ordinarily apparelled; for it was a plain cloth suit, which seemed to have been made by an ill country tailor; his linen was plain, and not very clean; and I remember a speck or two of blood upon his little band which was not much larger than his collar; his hat was without a hatband: his stature was of a good size, his sword stuck close to his side, his countenance swollen and reddish, his voice sharp and untunable and his eloquence full of fervour . . .

Such men as Warwick prized exquisite clothes, polished manners and silver oratory: the Huntingdonshire squire jarred upon both their eyes and ears. The most elegant member in the House, Lord George Digby, laughed derisively at 'that sloven', with his untidy suit and harsh voice. 'Pray, Mr Hampden, who is that man? For I see that he is on your side by his speaking so warmly today.' Hampden answered: 'That sloven whom you see before you has no ornament in his speech; but that sloven, I say, if we should ever come to breach with the King (which God forbid!), in such a case, I say, that sloven will be the greatest man in England.'

Two weeks later, one of the Puritan leadership group named Sir Arthur Heselrige introduced the Militia Bill. If passed, it would take the supreme command of the military forces to be raised for Ireland out of the King's gift. A Lord General and Lord Admiral would be nominated in the Bill. It was a revolutionary proposal.

While matters stood thus in January 1642 the King confirmed the worst fears of Pym's supporters by his personal attempt on 4 January 1642 to arrest the Five Members: Pym, Hampden, Holles, Heselrige and Strode. This abortive *coup* 'was interpreted as such a horrid violation of privilege,' Sir William Waller later wrote, 'that although his Majesty was pleased to withdraw the prosecuting of it and to promise a more tender respect for the time to come, yet nevertheless this spark (as his Majesty terms it) kindled such flames of discontent as gave occasion first to the raising of guards and afterwards to the levying of an army. Clarendon observed that after the attempt Hampden 'was much altered, his nature and carriage seeming much fiercer than it did before'.

Parliament's action in issuing the Militia Bill as an Ordinance in March made the breach an accomplished fact. Asked by a peer if he would cede control of the militia to Parliament for a while, Charles replied, 'By God, not for an hour!' Nor would he permit any reform or abolition of the institution of episcopacy in the Established Church as proposed by some Puritans in the House of Commons. The King's obstinacy now became a virtue, swinging the conservative pendulum in his favour. By June 1642 he had found a party; by August he could raise an army.

Many Puritans sensed that God in his wrath was about to loose upon England a second fatal storm. Sir William Waller, who entered Parliament as a member for Andover in May 1642, had heard as much from his old friend Sir Bevil Grenville, a Cornish Puritan. 'I wonder nothing at what the Divine justice does threaten the iniquity of the present times with,' he wrote to Waller, 'but I rather wonder (all things consider'd) that it has not sooner happen'd. Let others look upon secondary causes; I contemplate the originals and do believe the evils are deserved, but perchance silence is best.'

The division of England into two sides supporting King or Parliament presented such men as Grenville with a cruel dilemma. The roots of the English gentry were interwined with the Tudor monarchy. The king symbolized the people: he was their image. Despite the personal failings and lack of judgement displayed by the first two Stuarts, this aura had transferred from Queen Elizabeth to them. The convenient fiction that the ills of the kingdom stemmed from evil advisers, not from Charles himself, enabled even the most ardent opponents to maintain intact their mental picture of a social order crowned by a revered king. Men of Puritan conviction, such as Sir Bevil Grenville and Sir Edmund Verney, could not bring themselves to abandon their ingrained English loyalty and fight against their lawful monarch.

For Hampden, Cromwell, Waller and the great majority of Puritans, however, the interests of God's continuing reformation and the need to preserve the traditional freedom of the English people took precedence over loyalty. They now addressed themselves to the challenge of providing the supporters of Parliament with

161

the same energetic leadership in war they had shown in debate. Resolution and commitment informed all their actions. As Clarendon said of Hampden, 'without question when he first drew the sword he threw away the scabbard'.

8

America: Land of Promise

On 4 November 1631 the *Lion* dropped anchor off the New England coast. There came in her Margaret Winthrop with Mary, Stephen, Deane and Samuel. John gave them a royal welcome. As the ship fired a salute, on shore the captains drew up some companies of militia as a guard of honour. After Margaret landed she was entertained by the people from the nearer parts of the plantation. They laid out a feast of fat hogs, kids, venison, poultry, cheese and partridges, 'so as the like joy and manifestation of love and never been seen in New England'. Winthrop thought it 'a great marvel that so much people and such a store of provisions could be gathered together at so few hours' warning'.

Winthrop took his wife and children home to their new stone house on the Mystic River near Boston. Next spring Margaret may have accompanied him on some of the expeditions he made to explore the surrounding country. In January, for example, Winthrop boated up the Charles River. He named the first tributary on the north side above the falls Beaver Brook, for beavers had shorn down great trees to make their dams. A stone cleft in a great rock he called Adam's Chair after his son. Another high and rocky prominence received the name of Mount Feake in honour of Robert Feake, who had married his widowed daughter-in-law. Evidently it became hard to think of names for all the natural features. A year later, for example, Winthrop called one lofty outcrop Cheese Rock, on the grounds that when they sat down to eat there they found nothing but cheese in their haversacks. The Governor's servant had forgotten to pack the bread and other victuals. Such incidents evoke an atmosphere of a second springtime in Winthrop's life. Warmed by his reunion with Margaret, he evidently delighted in the vast potential of this new land.

But even this 'other Eden' was not perfect. In the summer swarms of mosquitoes plagued them and the woods abounded in rattlesnakes. Winthrop always carried some snake-weed in his pocket as a remedy against snakebite. But a more deadly serpent soon shattered their peace: discord among Puritan friends. During 1632 Winthrop fell out with Deputy Governor Thomas Dudley, eight years his senior. Dudley had lent someone $7\frac{1}{2}$ bushels of corn in order to receive 10 back at harvest time, which Winthrop and some others held to be oppressive usury. The Governor also felt that his deputy had set a bad example by panelling and adorning the inside of his house at the beginning of the plantation. Dudley replied that he had done it for warmth, and besides it had cost little as he used only clapboards nailed to the wall. Dudley in turn resented Winthrop's decision to move the timber frame of his town house from Newtown to Boston. By September 1632 they had apparently settled their differences and 'ever after kept peace and good correspondence together, in love and friendship'. Later, one of Winthrop's sons would marry Dudley's daughter. But Dudley voiced first the growing envy felt among the gentry at Winthrop's prominence in the colony. Perhaps Sir Richard Saltonstall had resented it, too, but if so he had returned home rather than raise the matter. In addition, Dudley also felt critical about Winthrop's relative leniency in sentencing offenders, preferring a much tougher approach.

Increasing numbers of settlers also subtly began to change the character of New England, as both Bradford and Winthrop sensed. For hundreds of emigrants were arriving each year from England. Some came to enjoy the liberty of worship, others sought land and economic opportunity in the New World. The learned Puritan divine John Cotton, minister of Boston in Lincolnshire and a leading exponent of the 'plain but effectual way of preaching', was the most prominent figure among the 1633 emigrants. His first son was born on the voyage and Cotton called him Seaborn, 'to keep alive in me, and to teach him, if he live, a rememberance of sea-mercies from the hand of a gracious God'.

Cotton's sermons in New England stimulated the first spate of religious conversions in American history. His message served also an important political or social function by checking the home-sickness which afflicted his fellow emigrants. One of them, Captain Roger Clap, told how 'the Lord Jesus Christ was so plainly held out in the preaching of the Gospel unto poor lost sinners, and the absolute necessity of the new birth, and God's holy spirit in those days was pleased to accompany the word with such efficacy upon the hearts of many, that our hearts were taken off from Old England and set upon heaven'. Except for a few, who could not forget the lush green fields and smiling countryside of their former home, people no longer asked 'How shall we go to England?' but 'How shall we go to heaven? Have I true grace wrought in my heart? Have I Christ or no?' Clap witnessed the shedding of many tears in the Dorchester meeting-house at such times. Conversions now swelled the membership of all the churches up and down the plantation.

The English settlers brought with them all manner of human failings. The General Court countered with a social discipline modelled upon English laws and punishments. In 1634 it issued orders against tobacco smoking and the wearing of costly apparel or immodest fashions. They proved as ineffectual as their counterparts in England. For drunkenness Robert Cole was ordered to wear a red D on his chest for a year. Three persons were whipped and banished for adultery. In this case the church elders argued that the legal death penalty for this crime was sufficiently known and should be executed, but the civil magistrates gave the offenders the benefit of doubt. Philip Ratcliff, a servant of Winthrop's predecessor Governor Craddock, was also whipped and had both ears cut off in Boston. 'I saw it done,' wrote Roger Clap. But these punishments were no worse or better than those which Winthrop and his fellow magistrates had meted out in the shires of England.

Indeed Winthrop looked upon Massachusetts Bay as being an English county enjoying much the same sort of virtual independence from the central government in London as, say, Suffolk or Yorkshire. Englishmen had strong local loyalties: they habitually called the county their 'country'. With the vast Atlantic ocean between them and with the help of their Puritan friends at home, who now included Sir Richard Saltonstall, it was not difficult for Winthrop and his colleagues to maintain almost complete freedom from King Charles's government. But English shires contained nobles as well as gentry. Should New England follow suit? It seemed a logical development. During June 1634 a fleet of fourteen great ships arrived in the Bay. Apart from more ordnance, muskets and powder bought by public subscription they carried a company of emigrants which included Mr John Humphrey and his wife Lady Susan, one of the Earl of Lincoln's sisters. 'For godly people in England,' wrote Winthrop, 'began now to appreciate a special hand of God in raising this plantation, and their hearts were generally stirred to come over.' The new arrivals brought letters from 'some persons of great quality and estate', declaring their intention to join the exodus if they could be satisfied on certain points.

Lord Saye and Lord Brooke, the principal authors of the

questions, received answers largely composed by John Cotton, who seems to have had that task delegated to him by the General Court. The New Englanders accepted their proposed condition that the chief power in the commonwealth should reside in two houses representing the ranks of gentlemen and freeholders, which would meet both separately and assembled together. They responded favourably also to the parliamentary model proposed by the peers. But they baulked at the ninth request, that the two peers and their companions should be admitted with their heirs in perpetuity as 'gentlemen of the country'. The criterion for rank and office, replied Cotton, was membership in one of the churches. 'Hereditary honours are all very well, but hereditary power cannot be accepted.' Perhaps this principle deterred the two peers. Although Winthrop called the social structure of New England a 'mixed Aristocracy', the 'democratic' tendencies hostile to any form of hereditary power were nevertheless quite pronounced from the beginning.

Although they remained friendly to the Puritans in Massachusetts Bay the noblemen directed their efforts more towards the rival settlement on Providence Island. They endeavoured to attract colonists to the warmer climate and more fruitful soils of the Caribbean rather than to the Bay despite Winthrop's expressed displeasure. In reply, Saye upbraided Winthrop for comparing the New England colonists to the Children of Israel, and implied that they had not restrained themselves from criticizing the Providence project. For his part Winthrop clearly regarded the latter as a worthless enterprise. History would soon support him.

At this time, the year 1634, the English government became thoroughly alarmed at what was happening under their noses: the exodus of politically dangerous men to New England and rumours that more, such as Saye, Brooke and Hampden, would shortly follow. Doubtless acting on instructions Governor Craddock wrote to Winthrop asking for a return of the charter. In December Winthrop and his colleagues debated what they would do if a Governor-General was sent out from England. They resolved that they would not accept him, but defend 'our lawful position'. John Endecott, the Salem magistrate, chose this sensitive time to commit an act of Puritan extremism. He defaced the national flag by cutting out the red cross that occupied the top left-hand quarter. For the red cross, he declared, was first given to the King of Spain by the Pope as an ensign of victory. So it was a superstitious thing, a 'relic of

Antichrist'. The General Court reacted cautiously with only a mild punishment. They feared the deed would be taken as an act of rebellion, but also doubted the lawful use of the cross in the ensign once the issue had been raised. The following year the cross disappeared from all the militia colours, but the royal standard still flew over Castle Island at Boston. The red cross was temporarily restored during the English Civil War as a mark of solidarity, but only 'till the state of England shall alter it'.

The outspoken views of Roger Williams posed a still more serious threat to good relations with England. Son of a London merchant tailor, Williams was employed first by Sir Edward Coke, the great jurist, who helped him to secure a Cambridge education. He landed in New England in 1631 and was chosen as 'teacher' of the church at Salem. Objecting that the church was not clearly separated from the Church of England, he refused the office and went to Plymouth. In 1633 he returned to Salem and became a minister. But he continued to demand loudly that the churches of New England announce their separation from the Church of England. He attacked the charter, declaring that the King had no right to grant the colonists the land of America. Massachusetts belonged to the Indians and should be purchased from them. He denied that a magistrate should be allowed to tender an oath to an unregenerate man, thus calling into question the judicial system. He advocated that magistrates should have no power to punish persons for their religious opinions. The civil power should restrict itself to enforcing the second 'table' of the decalogue, the commandments relating to moral behaviour.

In October 1635 the court banished Williams. Rather than face deportation to England, he acted on a suggestion from Winthrop and in January fled into Narragansett country through the deep winter snow. Thus he became the founder of Providence, Rhode Island. For the rest of his life he served as its principal guide and statesman. He became a Baptist in 1639, but soon renounced that commitment. Williams now called himself a Seeker. The Seekers believed that no true church had existed since the spirit of Antichrist gained the upper hand in the church on earth. God in his own good time would ordain new apostles and prophets to found a new church. The Seekers did not think it right to hasten the process, an attitude in tune with the Quakers. Like this later sect the Seekers suffered persecution. In 1612 Bartholomew Legate, one of their preachers, was burnt in London for heresy. New England had no need of such punishments when it could exile deviants beyond its boundaries, where their protest would be lost in the vast continent. Out of sight, out of mind.

On 14, 15 and 16 August the greatest hurricane in the living memory of the Indians struck New England. It blew down many thousands of trees, overthrew some houses and drove ships at anchor in the Bay aground. Those at sea fared even worse. The *James* of Bristol, with a hundred 'honest people' from Yorkshire, narrowly escaped shipwreck on the rocky Isle of Shoals. Twenty-one passengers, including a minister called Avery from Wiltshire, his wife and six children drowned when a barque was cast away on Cape Ann. The minister's cousin, Anthony Thacher, a tailor from Salisbury in Wiltshire, barely survived the disaster. His letter, written to his brother in England, testifies not only to the struggle of the early settlers against the brute forces of nature. It is also evidence of that belief in special providences which sustained the Puritans even in their darkest hours.

When the hurricane struck them at about ten o'clock at night on 14 August the barque dragged her night anchor and tossed helplessly before wind and waves. As the company sat 'comforting and cheering one another in the Lord' the ship was grounded between two high rocks. There the heavy seas pounded the vessel to pieces. As they sat awaiting certain death parents and children continued to bewail, but without screaming or crying, for all 'as silent sheep, were contentedly resolved to die together lovingly, as since our acquaintance we had lived together friendly'. Soon only the families of the minister Avery and Thacher had not been washed away. Yet safety lay not far distant for by the grey light of dawn Thacher caught sight of tree tops.

With desperation the parents and children clung to the rock as the waves dashed over it. As their strength ebbed the children were swept off into the boiling sea and drowned. In the water Thacher, who could not swim a stroke, clung to a plank from the ship. Eventually he staggered ashore. There he found his wife who had also saved her life by grasping hold of some wreckage. To escape the cold and the roaring of the sea they went up into the land and took shelter under an uprooted cedar tree. As the wind slackened the castaways returned to the shore to look for their children, dead or alive.

> You condole with me my miseries, who now began to consider of my losses. Now came to my remembrance the time and manner how and when I last saw and left my children and friends. One was

severed from me sitting on the rock at my feet, the other three in the pinnance; my little babe (ah, poor Peter!) sitting in his sister Edith's arms, who to the uttermost of her power sheltered him from the waters; my poor William standing close unto them, all three of them looking ruefully on me on the rock, their very countenances calling unto me to help them; whom I could not go unto, neither could they come at me, neither would the merciless waves afford me space or time to use any means at all, either to help them or myself. Oh I yet see their cheeks, poor silent lambs, pleading pity and help at my hands. Then, on the other side, to consider the loss of my dear friends, with the spoiling and loss of all our goods and provisions, myself cast upon an unknown land, in a wilderness, I knew not where, nor how to get thence. Then it came to my mind how I had occasioned the death of my children, who caused them to leave their native land, who might have left them there, yea, and might have sent some of them back again, and cost me nothing. These and such like thoughts do press down my heavy heart very much.

But I must let this pass, and will proceed on in the relation of God's goodness unto me in that desolate island, on which I was cast. I and my wife were almost naked, both of us, and wet and cold even unto death. I found a knapsack cast on the shore, in which I had a steel, and flint, and powder-horn. Going further, I found a drowned goat; then I found a hat, and my son William's coat, both which I put on. My wife found one of her petticoats, which she put on. I found also two cheeses and some butter, driven ashore. Thus the Lord sent us some clothes to put on, and food to sustain our new lives, which we had lately given unto us, and means also to make fire; for in a horn I had some gunpowder, which, to mine own, and since to other men's admiration, was dry. So taking a piece of my wife's neckcloth, which I dried in the sun, I struck fire, and so dried and warmed our wet bodies; and then skinned the goat, and having found a small brass pot, we boiled some of her. Our drink was brackish water. Bread we had none.

There we remained until the Monday following; when, about three of the clock in the afternoon, in a boat that came that way, we went off that desolate island, which I named after my name, *Thacher's Woe*, and the rock, *Avery his Fall*, to the end that their fall and loss, and mine own, might be had in perpetual remembrance. In the isle lies buried the body of my cousin's eldest daughter, whom I found dead on the shore.

The island lies about two miles east of the south-east point of Cape Ann and to this day it is called Thacher's Island.

*   *   *

In 1635 two ships, the *Defence* and the *Abigail*, dropped anchor in the Bay. They brought three Puritans of note with them. John Winthrop junior had returned with a commission to begin the plantation on the Connecticut River and to be governor there. Hugh Peter, pastor of the English Church at Rotterdam, had escaped this way from a persecuting ambassador, who would have imposed on him 'the English discipline' of Archbishop Laud. Winthrop described the third passenger, Henry Vane, as 'a young gentleman of excellent parts'. Despite being son of a prominent servant of King Charles he felt called as a Puritan to obey the gospel, forsaking all honours and preferment. He crossed the Atlantic, wrote Winthrop, in order 'to enjoy the ordinances of Christ in their purity here'. The King reluctantly granted him a licence to do so for three years. Vane brought more letters from Lord Saye and Lord Brooke threatening that if insufficient land awaited them in Connecticut they would go elsewhere.

Vane and Peter soon stirred up trouble. Hearing about the discord that simmered beneath the outward show of politeness between Winthrop and Dudley they convened a meeting to secure 'a more firm and friendly uniting of minds'. In some surprise – actual or simulated – Winthrop spoke of 'his brother Dudley' and said he thought they were reconciled already. Dudley averred as much. Then the real business began. Governor John Haynes, elected the previous year, ventured to say that Winthrop had been remiss in one or two matters during his term of office, notably by being too lenient. Next morning the church ministers in Boston ruled that strict discipline in criminal and martial affairs was more necessary in plantations than in settled states. Winthrop bowed to the pressure and gracefully acknowledged his failing. The magistrates renewed their mutual love. They promised 'to express their difference in all modesty and due respect to propound their difference by way of question'. They would be more familiar amongst themselves, avoiding all jealousy and suspicion, 'not opening the nakedness of one another to private persons'.

Not long afterwards Henry Vane was elected Governor in the annual election. The fact that he was son and heir to a privy councillor in England doubtless influenced the electors as much as the young man's evident zeal. But he came into office without experience at a time when new troubles arose. The fierce tribe of Pequod Indians in Connecticut arose in arms and gave the Puritans their first real taste of an Indian war. Militia companies marched away from Massachusetts Bay to deal with them. The English were characteristically bold, courageous and fiery in attack. In 1637 the English soldiers dispersed the Pequods, who lost 800 or 900 braves in the war.

In Boston Henry Vane soon enmeshed himself in a theological wrangle. Mrs Anne Hutchinson, 'a woman of ready wit and bold spirit', was a midwife by calling, and, finding that many women with babies could not attend church on Sunday, she began to hold meetings for them at her house during the week at which she expounded the sermons she had noted down. But she soon began to add her own commentary on the preacher's words. This practice illustrates a deep-seated tendency in the Puritan movement. By stressing the spiritual equality of men and women the Puritans had advanced the day of social equality between the sexes. They themselves still retained the traditional assumption, supported by the Bible, that a woman should be subordinate to her husband in all things. It was a male function, for example, to preach in public, or to lead prayers and explain sermons heard or read to his family. Women had begun to encroach on this function. The Renaissance educational movement, which gradually included more and more girls, produced women of developed intelligence as well as Puritan spirit. Anne Hutchinson possessed both.

Justification by faith alone, without any reliance on good works, constituted the central doctrine of Puritanism from the days of Luther. Puritans were always sensitive to any hint of a deviation from that basic tenet. In old England they had discerned it first in the practices and customs retained in the Elizabethan Church. Then they saw an even more grave threat to it in the pernicious teachings of Jakob Hermandszoon, a Dutch Reformed theologian better known as Jacobus Arminius. The Puritans used his name to label the anti-Puritan doctrinal tendencies in the Church of England under Archbishop Laud. Arminius had interpreted the Epistle to the Romans in such a way as to cast doubt on the doctrine of predestination, the theological buttress of justification by faith alone. He wrote a refutation, for example, of a treatise by William Perkins on that very subject. The Arminians were attempting to square God's sovereignty with human freedom. Against the English Puritan's view, which stemmed from Calvin's successor Theodore Beza, that Christ died only for the elect, they reasserted Calvin's belief that he died for all men. That fact must alter our evaluation of man. Thus they did what they could within the tight framework of

Calvin's system to reintroduce a sense of the significance of man and the individual's contribution to his own salvation.

The Puritan preachers and articulate laity of New England had unhesitatingly rejected this onslaught. They embraced the extreme version of justification by faith alone which the English theologians such as Perkins had evolved. They felt themselves secure within the citadel of faith. Then, to their horror, Anne Hutchinson accused the bulk of them of falling victims to the old enemy of legalism. According to Captain Roger Clap, this 'instrument of Satan' declared that they were 'legal preachers'. By contrast she and her growing band of disciples stood up as champions 'for free grace and for the teachings of the Spirit', and in particular that the Holy Spirit unites himself with the soul of a justified person. Sanctification, or the growth of a Christ-like character after conversion, does not constitute evidence that a person is justified.

In old England Anne had been a parishioner of John Cotton. Now she exempted him from her general charge. According to her, Cotton was almost alone in preaching the true gospel. Cotton found it difficult to disentangle himself from her skirts. He certainly believed that the Spirit dwelt in the justified person, but he stopped short of the idea of any indissoluble union between the Spirit and human souls. Like Luther he preached that good works will grow from faith like fruit from a tree. Yet by pushing the Puritan gospel to its extremes Anne had exposed its ultimate illogicality. Despite the intellectual commitment to justification by faith alone, expressed in such doctrines as predestination, almost all Puritan preachers in practice assumed some form of effort – valuable effort too – on the part of their listeners. Although they developed a remarkable sensitivity to the inner spiritual life by keeping journals, Puritans found it difficult to distinguish whether these human 'works' preceded or issued from the free gift of grace. As those applying for church membership in New England had to testify to their justification by grace in public, the Puritans faced the task of trying to discern the precise stages of spiritual development in others. Their various textbooks did describe the supposed sequence of events but not in close agreement. Nor did human nature always conform to the textbook.

The counter-attack to Anne Hutchinson advanced along some well-established lines. They flung names at her, especially 'antinomian'. To accept her extension of the Reformation principle, they said, would encourage men and women to flout the moral law and to indulge in all kinds of immorality. The only tenable defence of her position, the one put forward by St Paul and Luther before her, would be to argue that faith and reason operate on different planes. Although rationally the consequences of the total emphasis on God's work might be immorality, in the order of faith the Christian would not so abuse his freedom. But no Puritan divine, as son of both Reformation and Renaissance, would admit that faith and reason could lead to different conclusions. In the steps of St Thomas Aquinas the Puritans held to the view that a near-perfect intellectual and spiritual theology existed which harmonized the two paths of knowledge.

The controversy begun by Anne Hutchinson soon spilt over into politics. Governor Henry Vane supported her views on the union of the Holy Spirit with the justified person's soul, while Winthrop sided with the orthodox view. In October 1636 Vane announced to the General Court that he had been summoned home to secure his estates. With the Indians at war on one side and a French menace in the north, one of the Assistants – doubtless a Vane supporter – voiced 'some pathetical passages' on the consequences of his departure. Vane broke into tears, and under pressure gave a further reason for going. He feared 'the inevitable danger he saw of God's judgements to come upon us for these differences and dissensions, which he saw amongst us, and the scandalous imputations brought upon himself, as if he should be the cause of all'. The Court silently assented to his departure. But Vane then changed his mind. The Hutchinson faction, which had now captured the Boston church, sent a deputation to bid him stay. Vane 'expressed himself to be an obedient child of the church', and announced that he dared not go away without its leave.

Vane's continued presence kept the controversy boiling. He expressed displeasure at hearing the ministers had met without his knowledge to draw up the issues where they suspected John Cotton differed from them. Hugh Peter told him plainly that 'it saddened the ministers' spirits that he should be jealous of their meetings or seem to restrain their liberty'. Vane excused himself. Peter then said that before Vane arrived the church had been at peace. The light of the gospel brings a sword, replied Vane piously, and the children of the bondwoman would persecute those of the freewoman. Peter besought him humbly to consider his youth and short experience in the things of God. Let Vane beware of peremptory conclusions, 'which he perceived him to be very apt unto'. For his part, he blamed the rise of new opinions, both in the Low Countries and in New England, upon pride and idleness.

By now both the spokesmen of Puritan orthodoxy and John Cotton, whose ambivalence lent a cloak of respect to the Hutchinson camp, had so qualified their views on the relation of justification and sanctification that no one could tell where they really differed. Yet it became common for the Hutchinson supporters to label men as being children of either a 'covenant of grace' or a 'covenant of works'. Perhaps, unconsciously, the extremists were seeking a substitute in New England for those arch-protagonists of the 'covenant of works', the papists. For psychological reasons they needed an official opposition in order to experience their identity, just as the individual Puritan needed affliction to feel God's presence in his soul.

In 1637 the freemen re-elected Winthrop to the governorship. Vane and his two closest associates were pointedly not chosen as Assistants. Not long afterwards Vane returned to England. Anne Hutchinson became even more provocative in two lectures a week in her house as she sensed the tide turning against her. She said it had been revealed to her that she would be persecuted in New England and that God would ruin the colony because of it. The Sabbath, she said, is like any other day. There is no resurrection of the body. The protracted religious debate fuelled by these radical views unhinged some people's minds. Winthrop recorded two incidents of religious mania. In February a Weymouth man lept out of bed crying 'Art thou come, Lord Jesus?' He jumped from the window and ran seven miles through deep snow, pausing to kneel and pray in several places. Next morning his neighbours found his frozen corpse. In Boston a woman in spiritual despair threw her child down a well.

Margaret Winthrop felt the depression which fell upon the community. From 'Sad Boston' that year she wrote to her husband during his absence at Newtown:

> Dear in my thoughts, I blush to think how much I have neglected the opportunity of presenting my love to you. Sad thoughts possess my spirits, and I cannot repulse them; which makes me unfit for any thing, wondering what the Lord means by all these troubles among us. Sure I am, that all shall work to the best to them that love God, or rather are loved of him. I know he will bring light out of obscurity, and make his righteousness shine forth as clear as the noon day. Yet I find in myself an adverse spirit, and a

trembling heart, not so willing to submit to the will of God as I desire.

In 1638, after a trial in which she claimed to speak with the authority of the Holy Spirit, Mrs Hutchinson was formally excommunicated and banished. She and her family made their way to Rhode Island and eventually to Long Island, where she died at the hands of the Indians.

Outwardly New England seemed to be growing. Emigration from old England had now reached a peak, with twenty ships that year bringing some 3000 settlers. But the canker of the Hutchinson affair remained below the surface. As if signalling divine anger an earthquake tremor shook New England with a sound 'like a continued thunder or the rattling of coaches in London'. John Cotton preached at a general fast kept as a mark of penitence. Significantly it was held on account of the apparent decay in the power of religion and the decline of 'professors to the world'. Another unbalanced woman, Dorothy Talbye, was hanged for murdering her own daughter in a fit of melancholy or spiritual delusion. In Salem a Puritan woman called Mrs Oliver, who excelled Anne Hutchinson both as a speaker and in her apparent zeal, objected to giving satisfaction about her faith before being admitted to 'the Lord's Supper'. She stood up in church and protested her rights. Endecott threatened to send for constables to eject her. After a court appearance she was imprisoned and eventually whipped, a punishment she bore with 'a masculine spirit'. Where Anne Hutchinson had led others followed.

These internal wranglings may have helped to stimulate the exodus from Massachusetts Bay to found new colonies in neighbouring places. Several pastors and their congregations, for example, marched into Connecticut. John Humphrey accepted an invitation to become the next governor of Providence Island. His party disparaged New England, but for John Winthrop it remained the land which 'God had found out and given to his people'. Lord Saye replied that New England was only a place of temporary refuge. A better place had been found in the Caribbean. All Puritans should remove there. But when Humphrey's two vessels reached Providence Island heavy cannon fire from the guns of the newly-arrived Spanish conquerors drove them back. William Peirce, the master who had brought Margaret Winthrop to America in the *Lion*, and one other sailor lost their lives in that fierce salute.

*   *   *

In government Winthrop believed in firm leadership, preferably by himself. After all, he had come to New England primarily in order to use his talent for ruling. Although he never initiated changes in constitutional matters he maintained his position by conceding them gracefully when they become political issues. In 1641 it was not so much the degree of participation in government which the freemen demanded which troubled the political waters. A more immediate issue was the power which the governor should enjoy in relation to the leading magistrates or rulers. A younger generation of men, such as Saltonstall's son Richard, had now become magistrates. They chafed at the inequality they found in government. That year Richard Bellingham was chosen as Governor, a candidate who favoured their opinion.

Beneath the surface lay different models or assumptions about government. Still deeper lay the ultimate question of authority. In 1641 the people chose Nathaniel Ward, the minister of Ipswich, to preach the election sermon. Winthrop noted that it was the Governor's right to choose the preacher on these occasions, but he let it pass. Ward referred to Greek and Roman government, presumably stressing the more equal distribution of political power in those polities. Winthrop dismissed the appeal to the authority of classical models as gross error. Christian religion and the Bible, he said, make us wiser than the ancients. Our times have the advantage of learning from all that has gone before us in experience and observation. We may better frame rules of government for ourselves than receive others on the bare authority 'of those heathen commonwealths'.

Winthrop's confidence that his own generation could far outstrip the ancients seems to accord well with the Renaissance spirit. But his low estimate of any contributions stemming from 'heathen' Greece or Rome and the high value he placed on the other root of our civilization, the Hebraic tradition, stamp him as a child of Luther rather than Erasmus. In his sermon Nathaniel Ward had advised them to keep all magistrates equal in power and honour. Winthrop noted in his journal that to do so would be against Israelite practice, for the Hebrews appointed rulers of tens and of thousands. Moreover, he added, it would be contrary to the custom of all nations ever known and recorded.

Nathaniel Ward also opposed the practice of trying legal cases in private hearings before the magistrates without the benefit of advocates. Winthrop defended the practice on the grounds that no lawyers had settled in New England. But the Puritans as a whole were fairly hostile to lawyers as a body. The private hearing method doubtless accorded better with their reading of scripture. Ward had a small axe to grind, for he practised law before turning to the church.

Ward's learning in the law led to a request from the magistrates. Would he draw up a code of statutes for them? After three years of study Ward produced such a collection. His 'Body of Liberties' contained a hundred laws, and they can be seen in hindsight as a link in the chain between the statutes of old England and the principles of the future Declaration of Independence.

Among the 'liberties' which New Englanders enjoyed was the right to be executed for adultery! Although English law supplied the spirit (and most of the letter) in the 'Body of Liberties' the Puritan influence is apparent in the clauses supported by Biblical references which carry the death penalty. By comparison with England, however, the total number of capital offences was reduced. Of the new ones, added because the Old Testament incontestably required them, most were rarely carried out. It is as if the Puritans sensed that executing people for adultery or serious sexual offences was wrong, but had no means at hand of extricating themselves from the logic of their wholehearted acceptance of the Old Testament.

In 1642, when the English Civil War broke out, the Puritans in New England naturally sided with their brethren who were supplying dynamic leadership to Parliament's cause. It is true that a Captain Jenyson in the Watertown militia did incautiously express some scruples about the legality of Parliament's revolt. He accepted that Parliament stood for 'the more godly and honest part of the Kingdom', yet doubted that he would side with them against their prince if he was in England. If the King attacked us, he hastened to add, he would defend New England with his life. Soon, however, he was able to tell the magistrates that he had changed his mind. Once again friendly and reasonable persuasion – or social pressure – from the Puritan brethren had restored unity. But the captain's fellow citizens did not merely express moral support for the English Puritans. Some returned home to preach or fight alongside them.

The presence of Americans in the English Civil War is a little known but fascinating fact in the relations between the two countries. Winthrop's son Stephen was among those who returned home. In 1645 he joined the New Model Army. In 1646 John

Winthrop wrote in a letter to his eldest son: 'Your brother has sent again for his wife, and it seems means to stay in England with his brother Rainsborough, who is governor of Worcester, and he is captain of a troop of horse.' Rainsborough was an extreme republican who wanted no negotiations with the King and a wider participation in politics than the constitution had hitherto permitted. The New Englanders seem to have been naturally attracted to this radical leader, who eventually commanded a regiment and became a major-general. Cromwell placed much trust in him. Israel Stoughton became the lieutenant-colonel in Rainsborough's regiment, while Nehemiah Bourne – a ship's captain – was major to him.

Winthrop's grandson, Fitz-John, who succeeded his father as Governor of Connecticut, served as a captain in the Commonwealth army. John Leverett and William Hudson were respectively captain and ensign in the same foot company. Another New Englander acted as surgeon to the Earl of Manchester's Lifeguard. Doubtless many other American colonists of lesser social rank served in the armies of Parliament. One of them, a servant of a gentleman in Dorchester, returned home with some money in his purse to enlist only to be waylaid and robbed by the Cavaliers.

Ministers also responded to the call. George Downing, son of Emmanuel Downing of Salem, returned to England via the West Indies and became a preacher in Colonel Okey's regiment of dragoons in the New Model Army. Hugh Peter rendered even more significant public service as a preacher in the train of artillery and as Cromwell's messenger to Parliament. Peter committed himself completely to the cause. Indeed he signed the King's death warrant and would be eventually executed as a regicide.

Peter possessed boundless zeal and energy. His mind teemed with projects. He was the first American activist. Not long after his arrival in New England, for example, Peter actively tried to raise money to establish a fishing industry. He pressed for John Cotton to be given a sabbatical in order to unravel the 'knotty passages' of scripture. He wanted Foxe's *Book of Martyrs* to be brought up to date. He urged the compulsory employment of people in winter, for he feared that idleness would be the ruin of both church and commonwealth. He confessed once that he drove himself to work unremittingly in order to forget his wife's mental illness. Their daughter had married one of Winthrop's sons. In keeping with the prevailing custom Winthrop and Peter regarded themselves as related and called each other 'brother'.

The outbreak of the revolution in England heralded a change in the expectations of the brethren who remained in New England. The European war between Catholics and Protestants, which broke out in 1618, had seemed to them the first signs of an impending thunderstorm of divine judgement on the Old World. Against the darkest hour God had prepared a haven for his people, using the Puritan colonists as his instruments. During the 1630s, when some 20,000 people emigrated from England to the Bay colony, it seemed as if that expectation was being realized. But by 1642 the picture had changed. The European war had become no more than a nationalistic struggle for dominance, behind a smokescreen of religious propaganda. As for refuge, the English Puritan leaders had made it plain that they looked more to the islands of the Caribbean than to New England. The act of revolution, however, ushered in a new possibility. If the armies of Parliament proved victorious, then some form of a holy commonwealth would be certainly established in England. Could not the 'New England Way' of congregational church discipline now serve as its model? Surely it would be seen as a better alternative both to the Church of England and to the presbyterian system? For the Puritans in Massachusetts Bay in 1642 it seemed as if their day of spiritual leadership had at last begun to dawn.

9

This War Without an Enemy

'My passion for the Parliament embolden'd me to offer my service as far as to the raising of first a troop and after of a regiment of horse', wrote Sir William Waller. During the summer of 1642 both King and Parliament recruited armies for the next act in the drama – the Civil War. The Puritans continued to provide the leaven of leadership in the lump of Parliament's supporters. They were the more active soldiers, brimming with zeal for a cause which they looked upon as the work of God.

The road from London to the battlefield of Edgehill in Warwickshire was a long and dusty one for the army of Parliament as they marched along it in the hot summer of 1642. Each weary mile drew them nearer to the great battle which they believed would resolve the Civil War at a stroke. The letters of Nehemiah Wharton, a sergeant in the Redcoats regiment of Colonel Denzil Holles, capture the mood among the Puritans in the rank-and-file of the army. At Chiswick the soldiers burned the Laudian altar rails in the church. At Hillingdon they tore up the vicar's white surplice for use as handkerchiefs. After entering Buckinghamshire, 'the sweetest country that ever I saw', Wharton recalled the burning of more altar rails, and the accidental death of a maid shot by a careless musketeer at Wendover. 'From hence we marched very sadly two miles, where Colonel Hampden, accompanied with many gentlemen well horsed, met us, and with great joy saluted and welcomed us, and conducted us into Aylesbury.' With loaves and cheeses looted from papists' houses stuck on their swords they marched on towards Northampton. On the way Wharton killed a fat buck in the park of Hillesden House, home of the Royalist Sir Alexander Denton, and speared its head on his sergeant's halberd like a trophy of war.

Some thirty miles west of Northampton lay Warwick Castle. There Lord Brooke had already drawn upon himself a formidable Royalist besieging force. The King set out to join the siege, pausing to bombard Coventry on the way. To relieve the city Hampden and Sir Arthur Goodwin with their regiments of foot and horse together with Holles' Redcoats, made a rendezvous with Lord Brooke and his Purplecoats and Lord Saye's Bluecoats. Hearing that the Earl of Northampton with a Royalist force was at hand, the Parliamentarians 'gave a great shout, with flinging up of their hats and clattering their arms, till the town rang again with the sound'. Spurning food and lodging they marched out to the fields. At daybreak they found Northampton's men drawn up, and 'being on fire to be at them' advanced under Hampden's command. After a brisk skirmish the Royalists turned tail and fled.

As the King's main forces had withdrawn to Nottingham, Hampden led the advance guard back to Northampton. The Redcoats had already secured the dismissal of their lieutenant-colonel, Henry Billingsley. Like many professional soldiers he swore profusely. The custom of prefacing remarks with 'God damn me', so common among the Cavaliers, especially grated on Puritan sensibilities. Wharton called him a 'Godamme blade, and doubtless [he will] hatch in hell'. Tutored by such officers the common soldiers indiscriminately plundered five or six gentlemen's houses. Thoroughly alarmed at this 'insolency' Hampden and other senior officers sent Sir Arthur Heselrige to inform the Earl of Essex of the need for a code of martial law. The Lord General arrived at Northampton shortly afterwards, bringing his own coffin and winding-sheet with him.

Once discipline had been restored the army marched on to Warwick. The Redcoats arrived too late to claim beds; they slept on straw and became lousy with fleas and bugs. The drill-conscious Sergeant Wharton says that these 'backbiters' seemed to march 'six on breast and eight deep at their open order'.

From Warwick the army trudged some twenty-eight miles westwards through incessant rain to Worcester. Wharton notes 'such foul weather that before I had marched one mile I was wet to the skin'. In the city of Worcester the soldiers refreshed themselves on perry made from Worcestershire pears at one penny a quart, and wandered around the streets as well as looking over the cathedral and the churches. Wharton compared this Royalist city to Sodom and Gomorrah: he considered it to be rather more heathen than Algiers or Malta. But he was even more shocked by the Welsh oaths in the streets of Hereford, where he marched in September with a commanded party of 900 soldiers. The men attended the Laudian clergy's morning service in Hereford Cathedral and danced to the organ music in the choir while the 'puppets' of the choir sang away.

When a robed canon prayed for the King a soldier roared out, 'What! Never a bit for the Parliament?' After this 'human service' conducted by the Baalists, wrote Wharton, the men then marched off to a 'divine service' where they heard a rousing sermon from the chaplain of the Redcoats, the eminent Puritan divine, Mr Obadiah Sedgewick. Back in Worcester once more, Wharton and his men were put to work constructing fortifications around the city, and so they missed the great battle at Edgehill.

On 23 October the two armies faced each other at Edgehill. Both generals disposed their infantry in the centre with squadrons of horse on the wings. In battle the Royalist cavalry proved superior. They carried all before them in the charge but could not be easily reformed. The Parliamentarian foot stood their ground and fought stoutly. Sir Edmund Verney lost his life in preserving the King's Standard. Hampden's brigade came into the field late in the day. Several of the scattered troops of horse, including Oliver Cromwell's, had now regrouped and they accompanied Hampden forwards. Hampden and other Puritan leaders, such as Sir Philip Stapleton who commanded the Earl of Essex's Lifeguard, urged their general to attack again either that evening or next morning. But Essex heeded the 'old soldiers of fortune', notably a Frenchman called Dalbier who served as Quarter-Master-General of Horse, who persuaded him against such a course.

As the two armies marched southwards in a race towards London the Puritan officers seethed with anger at the failure to win the war at a stroke. In effect they blamed it upon the mercenary generals. Was not Dalbier's real motive, for example, a desire to prolong the war? Moreover, the ranks of Essex's army contained soldiers recruited in towns, often from the unemployed. They enlisted for pay or plunder. The Cavaliers had at least displayed the natural fighting characteristics of Englishmen: valour, dash and boldness in attack. Some of Parliament's regiments had equalled them, but too few had shown the spiritual zeal of their Puritan leaders who fought not for money or plunder but only for the cause.

Years later Cromwell recalled a conversation with his first cousin Hampden during this post mortem on Edgehill.

> I had a very worthy friend then; and he was a very noble person, and I know his memory is very grateful to all – Mr John Hampden. At my first going into this engagement, I saw our men were beaten at every hand. I did indeed; and desired him that he would make some additions to my Lord Essex's army, of some new regiments:

and I told him I would be serviceable to him in bringing such men in as I thought had a spirit that would do something in the work.

This is very true that I tell you; God knows I lie not. 'Your troops', said I, 'are most of them old decayed serving-men and tapsters and such kind of fellows; and', said I, 'their troops are gentlemen's sons, younger sons and persons of quality. Do you think that the spirits of such base and mean fellows will ever be able to encounter gentlemen, that have honour and courage and resolution in them?' Truly I did represent to him in this manner conscientiously; and truly I did tell him: 'You must get men of spirit, and take it not ill what I say – I know you will not – of a spirit that is likely to go on as far as gentlemen will go – or else you will be beaten still.' I told him so; I did truly. He was a wise and worthy person; and he did think that I talked a good notion, but an impractical one. The result was I raised such men as had the fear of God before them, as made some conscience of what they did.

Hampden was too preoccupied that autumn to attempt a reconstitution of Parliament's cavalry, even if he had the power to do so. Apart from acting virtually as chief-of-staff to Essex he sought to infuse aggressive vigour into the tired limbs of the army. Clarendon's estimate of Hampden's leadership qualities could be extended to other Puritan colonels: 'He was very temperate in diet, and a supreme governor over all his passions and affections, and had thereby a great power over other men's. He was of an industry and vigilance not to be tired out or wearied by the most subtle or sharp; and of a personal courage equal to his best parts; so that he was an enemy not to be wished wherever he might have been made a friend . . .'

On 12 November Prince Rupert led the Royalist advance guard through an early morning mist to attack Brentford. The Redcoats of Denzil Holles and Lord Brooke's regiment bore the full brunt of the attack. 'Freeborn John' Lilburne, a captain in the latter, was among those forced to surrender. Hampden led his Greencoats in a fierce counter-attack which stemmed the Royalist tide. Next day the Royalist army turned away from the combined forces of Essex and the London trainéd bands, drawn up on Turnham Green. Again the Puritan leaders pleaded with Essex to fall upon the enemy. But again Essex, listening to such advisers as the Earl of Holland and General Dalbier, chose inaction. Thus, without hindrance, the Royalists marched off to Oxford, which they made their headquarters. They protected it by a ring of fortified outposts and strong quarters. Far from finishing the Civil War, the Edgehill campaign merely marked the end of the beginning.

*   *   *

In order to protect London the Earl of Essex interposed his army between the capital and Oxford. In the spring of 1643 Parliament much reduced his forces by authorizing the despatch of certain officers and their regiments or troops to stiffen local supporters in the regions. These regiments from the parent body formed the cores of some important regional armies. In the army of the Eastern Association Captain Cromwell applied the Puritan principle of selection as he increased his troop to a regiment. At the same time Sir William Waller began his spectacular career as a general. He marched into the west to form the army of the Western Association. Lord Brooke received command of the associated counties of Warwick, Stafford, Leicester and Derby.

On the occasion of the 'election' of his captains and junior commanders – the commissioning ceremony – Brooke delivered a speech to them in the hall of Warwick Castle which was subsequently printed in London. It must be read not simply as a well-constructed and finely-worded oration in the style of Pericles or Cicero, the fruit of a full Renaissance education. It also served as the Puritan manifesto. If we want to know what the Puritans felt and thought in the early months of the war then Lord Brooke's speech provides a clear answer.

'Gentlemen, country-men, my noble friends and fellow soldiers,' he began. 'We behold the flourishing and beauteous face of this Kingdom, overspread with the leprosy of a Civil War in which we are forced for the safeguard of our lives, the preservation of our liberties, the defence of God's true religion (invaded by the practices of Papists and Malignants) to become actors: I doubt not but each of you will play your part with that noble resolution and Christian courage as the greatness and the meritoriousness of the work does challenge.'

Echoes of both the Renaissance and the Reformation blended in Brooke's appeal to patriotic and religious motives as well as to the ties of friendship. 'No man is born for his own use only, said that great Commonswealth man of the Romans, Cicero. His friends and countrymen claim an ample share in his abilities, as your friends, your country, nay your religion and God himself demand in yours. And surely it would be both unnatural and impious to deny such powerful suitors your assistance.' The papists are the chief enemies. Will 'their insatiate avarice and thirst of blood' be satisfied with their recent plunderings, of estates and inhumane acts? 'No, Gentlemen, they aim at you, at all our ruins. Desolations and deaths are machinated by these vipers, who would gnaw a passage to their ambitions through the entrails of their mother the Commonwealth, whose destruction they have pursued as craftily and violently as is possible to be expected from persons of such much acrimony and spleen to the subject's liberties, and aversion of true religion and all goodness.'

Thus Brooke identified the papists as the real leaders of the opposing side. In this respect he was proved to be wrong. It is true that the Catholics to a man did support the King. Also many prominent Catholic laymen, such as the Marquess of Winchester, were wholehearted adherents in the field. But the Catholics never played a leading role comparable to that which the Puritan brothers performed among the equally diverse supporters of Parliament. In 1642, however, the red rag of a papist plot served to whip up fury among the 'hotter sort of Protestants'. Bred on Foxe's *Book of Martyrs*, they could see clearly the hand of the Catholics at work to encompass their downfall.

To counter this religious threat Brooke wanted officers who were prepared to fight with motives as lofty as his own. If any man was not moved by the justice of the cause, their commander would 'rather have his room than his company'. In a prophetic vein several years ahead of its time Brooke saw clearly the ultimate issue in contention – freedom of conscience. 'Your religion and freedom of your consciences, which far transcends your corporeal liberty, invokes you to stand up its champions against these Papistical Malignants, who would strike at God through the very heart of his known truth, so long practised among us. And surely nothing can be dearer to any of conscience, than the security of conscience and its invaluable freedom.'

Brooke knew that 'going against the King may stagger some resolutions', but he offered this defence against the charge of disloyalty, if not treason: 'Tis for the King we fight, to keep a crown for our King, a Kingdom for our sovereign and his posterity, to maintain his known rights and privileges, which are relative to the people's liberties, from a sort of desperate State incendiaries, that in seeming to fight for his Majesty brandish open arms against his sacred crown and dignity.' In the adverse army they will observe these notorious papists or popishly affected people. With their thoroughly 'devilish plots and hellish stratagems' such men now around the King had threatened 'not only his precious life, but the lives of his predecessors, Queen Elizabeth and his father of sacred memory, as that never to be forgotten (Gun)powder Plot shall for ever testify to their shame and confusion'. Brooke linked these domestic treacheries to such foreign attempts as the Armada in 1588 'to root out from the face of the earth' all those who opposed the papists in doctrine.

Finally, Brooke and his fellow Puritan leaders intended that the war in hand should be conducted in a decent and humane manner. Hence his apprehension about employing veterans from the Thirty Years War who had offered him their services.

> I must needs thank the gentlemen for their kind proffer, and yet desire licence to be plain with them, hoping they will not take it as a disparagement to their valours, if I tell them we have now too woeful experience in this Kingdom of the German wars; and therefore cannot so well approve of the aid of foreign and mercenary auxiliaries. In Germany they fought only for one spoil, rapine and destruction; merely money it was and hope of gain that excited the soldier to that service. It is not here so required as the cause stands with us. We must employ men who will fight merely for the Cause's sake, and bear their own charges, (rather) than those who expect rewards and salaries.

To hire mercenaries would mean 'we shall never have a conclusion of these wars. For it is obviously in their self-interest to spin out our war to a prodigious length, as they have done in other countries, rather than see them quickly brought to a happy end'.

'We must despatch this great work in a short time or be all liable to inevitable ruin,' concluded Brooke. All the Puritan leaders shared that sense of urgency, not least because they were men of property. 'I shall therefore freely speak my conscience', continued Brooke. 'I had rather have a thousand or two thousand honest citizens that can only handle their arms, whose hearts go with their hands, than two thousand of mercenary soldiers that boast of their foreign experience.' Instead of making money the end of their endeavours, 'these well-affected citizens will fight for the Cause, which is 'for Almighty God, their religion, the laws of the land, the subjects' liberty and safety'. They know that good deeds are their own reward, even 'if God be not pleased to give a blessing to the work in hand by a fair and honest accommodation between his Majesty and Parliament to give a cessation to these wars'.

While his officers bowed their heads Brooke turned from discourse to pray aloud that God Almighty would arise and maintain his own cause, scattering and confounding the devices of his enemies, not suffering the ungodly to prevail over his poor innocent flock. 'Lord, we are but a handful in consideration of thine and our enemies,' he said. 'Therefore, O Lord, fight thou our battles. Go out as thou didst in the time of King David before the hosts of thy servants, and strengthen and give us hearts, that we may show ourselves men for the defence of thy true religion, and our own and the King and Kingdom's safety.'

Lord Brooke personified the active qualities of spirit and character that the Puritans looked for in their soldiers. The day after his speech he visited Northampton to raise recruits. He would not allow plunder, cashiering a cornet for stealing some money from a woman. Later in the week he engaged the enemy in a skirmish at Stratford. In order to subdue Staffordshire he marched to Lichfield and began an assault on the Cavaliers who occupied the cathedral close. It was scarcely an engagement which merited a general's presence but the Puritan leaders such as Brooke and Hampden possessed such a burning desire to finish the war that they would hazard their persons in any skirmish. A Royalist musketeer, possibly perched high on the cathedral roof, doubtless could not believe his eyes when he saw Lord Brooke in his sights and well within range. A moment later Brooke lay dead in the street.

*   *   *

Gradually the forces of Parliament recovered from the shock of Lord Brooke's death. The war continued to surge back and forth in the regions. Only on the main stage – the no-man's land between the main armies of Essex, west of London, and King Charles in Oxford – did nothing much happen. The Puritans both in army and Parliament had now almost lost patience with the stolid, cautious Earl of Essex. They talked of replacing him with a Puritan candidate, such as the victorious Sir William Waller or their noble leader John Hampden.

Hampden's national fame, his political position as co-leader of the House of Commons with John Pym, and reputation for aggression in the field, certainly qualified him for high command in the eyes of Puritans. Whether or not Hampden shared that view we do not now know. Certainly he laboured to maintain good relations between the Earl and his supporters in Parliament, notably Sir Philip Stapleton, and the more 'violent' Puritan members who wanted more aggressive action in the field. For he saw clearly the need to maintain unity. For the failure of Essex to win the war within the first six months brought the signs of a dangerous split in the Puritan leadership. The Puritans may have the same values, including a high value placed upon friendship and unity, but they now found themselves deeply divided over the conduct of the war.

In April the army of Essex captured Reading after a somewhat inglorious siege but failed to press on towards Oxford. On 17 June Prince Rupert led a flying column of Cavaliers on a night raid behind enemy lines. When the alarm was given in Thame, the Parliamentarian headquarters, Hampden was among those who instantly volunteered to ride out and attack them. With a democratic touch he asked the officers and common soldiers of a troop of horse if they would accept him as their leader. They freely and unanimously consented, and 'showed much cheerfulness that they could have the honour to be led by so noble a captain'.

The hastily-assembled Parliamentarian troops of horse caught up with the Cavaliers on Chalgrove Field. During the fierce cavalry action Hampden received a fatal wound in the shoulder. A Cavalier trooper had ridden up and shot him from behind with a double-loaded carbine or pistol. The two balls bit deep into the flesh behind his shoulder blade. Shocked and growing weaker as his blood stained his shirt and buff-coat, Hampden found it difficult to stay upright on his horse. A Parliamentarian trooper, taken prisoner later that day, told his captors 'that he was confident Mr Hampden was hurt, for he saw him ride off the field before the action was done, which he never used to do, and with his head hanging down, and resting his hands upon the neck of his horse, by which he concluded he was hurt.' In this state Hampden rode five miles to the security of Thame, where he took to his bed.

At first it seemed as if all would be well. *A True Relation*, the account of the great fight printed in London within a day or two of it, reported: 'it is certain that Colonel Hampden that noble and valiant gentleman, received a shot with a bullet behind in the shoulder, which struck between the bone and the flesh, but is since drawn forth, and himself very cheerful and hearty, and it (through God's mercy) more likely to be a badge of honour, than any danger of life'.

Almost certainly, however, Hampden's shoulder or arm had been shattered. Within a day or two complications developed. Inflammations and spasms, or possibly gangrene, caused serious concern to the doctors. On 22 June a letterwriter noted that three physicians went from London to Hampden's bedside. However, he never regained his full senses and died on Saturday 24 June, his wedding anniversary. On the following day his body was borne ten miles to Great Hampden for burial in the parish church at the side of Elizabeth, beneath the chancel. Probably the Greencoats accompanied their slain leader, marching before and behind the cart bearing the coffin.

Hampden's friend Arthur Goodwin had stood by his bedside at Thame. On the day after the funeral, Goodwin wrote to his daughter Lady Wharton as follows:

> Dear Jenny,
>
> I am here at Hampden in doing the last duty for the deceased owner of it, of whom every honest man hath a share in the loss, and therefore will likewise in the sorrow. In the loss of such a friend to my own particular, I have no cause of discontent, but rather to bless God that he hath not according to my deserts bereft me of you and all the comforts dearest to me. All his thoughts and endeavours of his life was zealously in this cause of God's, which he continued in all his sickness, even to his death. For all I can hear the last words he spake was to me, though he lived six or seven hours after I came away as in a sleep. Truly, Jenny, (and I know you may easily be persuaded to it), he was a gallant man, an honest man, an able man, and take all, I know not to any man living second. God now in mercy hath rewarded him. I have writ to London for a black suit, I pray let me beg of you a broad black ribbon to hang about my standard. I would we all lay it to heart, that God takes away the best amongst us. I pray the Lord to bless you. Your ever, dear Jenny, most affectionate father,
>
> Arthur Goodwin
>
> Hampden, June 26th, 1643

By the end of August, not eight weeks after the funeral, Arthur Goodwin had also died. By this time Puritan morale stood at its lowest. Two of their champions had fallen. Defeat, desertion and disease had sapped the strength of Parliament's armies. They looked with increasing urgency for a more vigorous Puritan general to promote beside or in place of the Earl of Essex. That summer their interest focused upon Sir William Waller.

*   *   *

From the outset Waller had demonstrated the active spirit of a true Puritan soldier. He dedicated himself totally to the cause. In September he captured Portsmouth, a vitally important arsenal and port. At Edgehill he shared the fate of the Parliamentarian cavalry. His major, inappropriately named Sir Faithful Fortescue, began the day badly by riding forwards with his men and changing sides. When Prince Rupert's Cavaliers broke the right wing Waller had his horse shot under him but he survived unhurt. Before the year's end he had secured for Parliament the southern counties by seizing Farnham Castle in Surrey, Winchester in Hampshire and Chichester in Sussex. The House of Commons gave him public thanks for his 'valour and fidelity', while the Londoners shouted 'William the Conqueror! William the Conqueror!' when he rode through their streets.

In February 1643 Waller received command of the newly-formed Western Association. Marching mainly by night to conceal his small force from the enemy he reached Bristol in March. From there he launched himself upon a campaign of singular boldness and imagination. A night march led him to Malmesbury, which he took by storm. Then he crossed the Severn by a pontoon bridge and fell upon a Welsh Royalist army besieging Gloucester. After a brief attack Waller captured 150 officers and 1444 common soldiers. April found him marching into Wales. Monmouth and Usk fell easily, but the Welsh seemed solidly Royalist. In Chepstow harbour he seized the *Dragon of Bristol* as a prize. Meanwhile Prince Maurice was rallying an army to intercept his return to Gloucester. After another night march through the Forest of Dean the 'Night Owl', as the Royalists now called Waller, brushed his way past Prince Maurice's forces at Little Dean. Once in Gloucester he attempted to turn the tables on them by occupying the bridge over the Severn at Tewkesbury, but the Cavaliers beat him to the next bridge at Upton. The two armies fought at Ripple. The Royalists had the better of the day. Waller withdrew to Gloucester towards the end of April. He made another night march to take Hereford. Meanwhile the King withdrew his remaining garrisons in the region in order to strengthen the army to relieve Reading. Thus Waller found himself undisputed master of the Severn valley.

In May Sir Ralph Hopton transformed the military situation by breaking out of the Cornish peninsula at the head of a Royalist army. The King sent the Marquess of Hertford with a strong body of horse to meet him. Hopton and Hertford met at Chard in Somerset on 4 June. Waller and his general of horse, Sir Arthur Heselrige, marched down to Bath. As the armies quartered near each other, skirmishing in the Somerset hills, Hopton wrote to Waller proposing a meeting. Doubtless he hoped to persuade his old friend to change sides. Waller, who now knew that the eyes of all Puritans were fixed upon him as a possible successor to the over-cautious Earl of Essex, showed political commonsense in refusing the invitation. His carefully drafted reply, later printed, is a thoroughly Puritan letter. The high value which Puritans placed upon friendship permeates its sentences. Like Lord Brooke, Waller identified the cause of Parliament with God and religion. Again, like him, he advocated a limited and humane war.

To my noble friend Sir Ralph Hopton at Wells.
Sir,
    The experience I have had of your worth and the happiness I have enjoyed in your friendship are wounding considerations when I look upon this present distance between us. Certainly my affections to you are so unchangeable that hostility itself cannot violate my friendship to your person, but I must be true to the cause wherein I serve. The old limitation *usque ad aras* holds still, and where my conscience is interested all other obligations are swallowed up.
    I should most gladly wait on you according to your desire but that I look upon you as you are in engaged in that party beyond a possibility of retreat and consequently incapable of being wrought upon by any persuasion. And I know the conference could never be so close between us but that it would take wind and receive a construction to my dishonour.
    That great God which is the searcher of my heart knows with what a sad sense I go upon this service, and with what a perfect hatred I detest this war without an enemy. But I look upon it as *opus domini*, which is enough to silence all passion in me. The God of peace in his good time send us peace, and in the meantime fit us to receive it. We are both upon the stage and must act those parts that are assigned us in this tragedy. Let us do it in a way of honour and without personal animosities. Whatsoever the issue be, I shall never willingly relinquish the dear title of
your most affectionate friend
and faithful servant
William Waller.

Early in July the Royalist army advanced on Bath. Waller faced them first on a hill west of the city and then transferred his forces under cover of darkness to the commanding heights of Lansdown on the north side. 'Indeed that general of the rebels', wrote an admiring Royalist colonel, 'was the best shifter and chooser of ground when he was not master of the field that I ever saw, which are great abilities in a soldier.' On 5 July the Royalists closed upon the steep hill. Waller unleashed a strong 'forlorn hope' to attack them. Captain Atkyns, a Cavalier troop commander, called it 'the boldest thing that I ever saw the enemy do, for a party of less than 1,000 to charge an army of 6,000 horse, foot and cannon in their own ground at least a mile and a half from their body'. As the Cornish foot stormed the crest of Lansdown Sir Bevil Grenville was killed at the head of his regiment. With great difficulty the Royalists drove Waller's men back from the brow of the hill to their second line of dry stone walls. In the middle of the night the Parliamentarians withdrew into Bath, leaving the field to the enemy.

The Royalists could not do more. Hopton was badly hurt. He had ridden to view some prisoners, who sat smoking their pipes in a wagon of gunpowder barrels. One of them dropped his match and Hopton was blown up with them. The army marched away to Devizes, where Waller encircled them. But the King heard of their predicament and sent three brigades of horse to succour them. On Roundway Down this fresh force inflicted a shattering blow on Waller's army. As Oliver Cromwell wrote 'Sir William Waller, whom some called "William the Conqueror", has been beaten all to pieces.'

*   *   *

In the first year of war Waller had exemplified the zealous activity which most distinguished the Puritan approach to the Civil War. He also demonstrated remarkable humanity. To Lord Arundel, seeking his children, he replied that 'I was a mere stranger both to their taking and removal and therefore not accountable. I presume your nobleness will impute nothing to me in either.' At Lansdown the lieutenant of Captain Atkyns' troop was captured unhurt and then cruelly shot twice with pistols by a Scot. He told Atkyns later that Waller 'seemed exceedingly angry at the inhumane action that befel him, and sent for his own chirugeon immediately, and saw him dressed before he went away. He gave the inkeeper charge that he should have whatever he called for, and he would see him païd; that whatever woman he sent for to attend him should be admitted, and lent him ten broad pieces for his own expenses'.

In one respect, however, a major question now stood by Waller's name as the Puritan candidate to succeed Essex: Did God favour him in battle? Individual Puritan preachers such as Richard Baxter scorned the idea that success or failure in battle had any spiritual significance. But the Puritans had become so imbued with the practice of reading God's providential blessings or chastisements into events great and small that they could not draw the line at battle. Thus a reversal in the field plunged a Puritan general into a spiritual crisis. Had God turned against him? Was he indeed one of the elect? Where had he fallen into culpable sin?

After 'my dismal defeat at Roundway Down' Waller fell into a state of near-despair. 'This was the most heavy stroke of any that did ever befall me', he wrote later. 'General Essex had thought fit to persuade the Parliament to compromise with the King, which so inflamed the zealous that they moved that the command of their army might be bestow'd upon me. But the news of this defeat arrived whilst they were deliberating on my advancement, and it was to me a double defeat. I had nearly sunk under the affliction, but that I had a dear and sweet comforter. And I did at that time prove according to Ecclesiasticus, chap xxvi: "A virtuous woman rejoiceth her husband . . . As the sun when it ariseth in the high heaven, so is the beauty of a good wife."'

Lady Anne, Waller's second wife, was the unlikely daughter of Sir Thomas Finch, the Speaker held down in his chair by Denzil Holles before the dissolution of the 1629 parliament. 'I humbly besought God to provide such a wife for me,' wrote Waller, 'as might be a help to me in the way of his service, and that I might have a religious woman or none.' Anne Finch was certainly zealous in religion. She proposed that they spend a day together in prayer to seek God's blessing on their marriage. 'It pleased the Lord', Waller added, 'to answer our prayers in as full a measure of comfort as ever was poured upon a married couple. And though at first there was some little differences in our natures and judgements as to some particulars, yet within a little while that good God wrought us to the uniformity that I may say we were but as one soul in two bodies.'

Lady Anne belonged to the new generation of Puritan women, represented in America by Anne Hutchinson, who wished to participate in the traditional world of men. The Royalist newspaper published in Oxford, *Mercurius Aulicus*, accused her of preaching in public. Anne wrote to the editor denying the charge, 'for as yet (she protests) she never preached, but says she knows not what we may drive her to'. According to the newspaper she had only interpreted some difficult passages of Scripture, 'which her Ladyship called undoing hard chapters; according to which phrase her husband's army is quite expounded'. Through his wife's connections Waller had acquired Winchester Castle as their new home before the Civil War. The Royalist newspaper recalled that when the couple attended religious meetings in Winchester Cathedral Anne took the dominant part. If William 'offered to speak about doctrines or uses, her Ladyship would rebuke him, saying "Peace, Master Waller, you know your weakness in these things" '. If that is true it suggests that Waller did not share his wife's more extreme Puritan views.

In war Lady Anne ranged herself beside her husband like a lioness. The Royalists even insinuated that she 'has usurped the general's baton'. She would probably have loved to command the army. Certainly she enjoyed her position of prominence and influence as the General's lady. After a service in Abingdon church the following year, reported a Royalist, she called out, 'Stand off, good people, that the soldiers may see me.' She actively supported a move to appoint as governor of Reading Colonel Henry Marten, the later republican and regicide. The fact that Sir William allowed her such a share in his work underlines the changing concept of marriage pioneered by the Puritans.

In Bath after Lansdown Lady Anne had ecstatically predicted a great victory in the offing. She shared her husband's deep despondency after Roundway Down as they rode first to Bristol and then to London. But her strong spirit rallied him. In the capital they found that the Earl of Essex had fallen still further in popularity. With John Hampden dead the 'vehement' or 'violent' party in Parliament and City had no real alternative but to support Waller, a general of proven competence. His defeat in the West could be blamed on scapegoat Essex for failing to prevent Lord Wilmot's sally from Oxford. Had not Essex deliberately allowed it to encompass Waller's ruin? Giving Waller the benefit of all doubts Puritan London rallied to him. 'In that heat, as the sun is ever hottest after a cloud,' wrote Waller, 'I had an offer . . . of a very considerable army to be raised and put under my command, with a constant maintenance of it.' The proud and truculent Earl of Essex delayed for as long as possible before sending the House of Commons a commission which would make Waller virtually equal to himself. Even then he left a blank space for the recipient's name. The House ordered the Clerk to insert into it 'Sir William Waller'.

Not until 29 August did Waller have this necessary authority to issue commissions to his officers.

The selection of officers strained Waller's relations with the Puritan coterie who acted as promoters of the new 'Flying Army'. It included such later radicals as Henry Marten and Sir Henry Vane. These men adhered to the Puritan principle enunciated so clearly by Lord Brooke and now actively pursued by Colonel Cromwell in the Eastern Association, namely that only godly men should be chosen as officers. For his part Waller placed more value on professional experience. He reminded the committee that although he desired zealous men about him 'there went more to the making up of an officer than single honesty'. In his opinion 'a good man might make a good soldier, but there must go the good men and the good soldier to the composition of a good officer'. He told them also that he would be answerable with life and honour for the service of the army, and 'that it would be a poor plea for me to say it was the officers' fault, when it might justly be retorted upon me as my fault that I took such officers'.

Eventually the committee accepted a compromise assurance from Waller that officers with both piety and ability would be preferred before all others. But if sufficient numbers of such men did not present themselves, he would be free to commission experienced officers 'although they were not otherwise so refined men as I could wish'. To appease them further he appointed Sir Arthur Heselrige to be president of a selection board for officers, with power to cross out the names of all those judged to be unfit or unworthy to be employed.

According to Waller's *Vindication*, written in 1649 in a prison where Cromwell had incarcerated him, this solution still did not satisfy his sponsors. 'I then found they had it in their design', he wrote, 'to model and form an army that should be all of their own party and devoted to their own ends. Upon this we differed. I trusted not them, nor they me, and so we agreed. From that time forward I may date the expiration of their friendship'. Viewed from the other side, however, the lukewarmness of the sponsors for Waller's new army is understandable. Waller promoted foreign mercenaries. A Dutchman, Jonas Vandruske, and a Frenchman, Francis Duet, both received commissions to raise regiments of horse. But the Scots professionals fared the best, receiving command of five out of eleven regiments as well as the train of artillery.

To Waller's mind the Scots fully met the compromise criteria of combining religious zeal and soldierly competence. 'I acknowledge that I have, and ever have had, a particular respect and value for that nation,' Waller wrote. 'I love their constancy to their covenant, their steadiness in their counsels, their gallantry in the field. Some of them I have had the honour to command, and braver men I am confident no man could command.'

Although military necessity drove the House of Commons to conclude the Solemn League and Covenant with Scotland that autumn few of the Puritan members shared Waller's enthusiasm for that nation. The Englishman's characteristic dislike for all foreigners embraced the Scots. Perhaps reacting against the Englishman's sense of innate superiority they appeared quarrelsome and braggart. Major William Carr, who had a commission from Waller for a regiment of horse, quarrelled so violently with Heselrige that he was committed to the Compter prison in Southwark. Matters gew far worse in Essex's army. Next year several prominent Scots officers secured a transfer of themselves and their units to Waller's command.

Apart from this long-standing mutual animosity the Puritan nucleus supporting Waller would have no truck with the Presbyterian system. Sir Henry Vane, Marten and Heselrige, like Oliver Cromwell, favoured something along the lines of the New England model: autonomous congregational Puritan churches, loosely grouped together in fellowship but firmly independent of any higher church authority. Thus they became known as Independents. Their tradition stemmed from English separatism as taught by Robert Browne. By contrast the Calvinist Presbyterian system as adopted by the Scots would impose upon the necks of the local congregations a yoke of regional and national synods. Even in the summer of 1643 a small number of Independents were looking ahead to the time after the war was successfully concluded. They saw more clearly than their contemporaries that control of the army was the key to unlocking the future. Indeed they may have already been scheming to impose their version of a Puritan commonwealth on the nation. Neither the Scots nor Sir William Waller and other Puritan leaders shared this vision. They envisaged instead some form of presbyterian organization, with or without bishops, which would maintain a measure of uniformity. They in turn would be labelled 'Presbyterians'. Although in 1643 the united ship of Parliament had not foundered on this issue, yet that dark jagged rock lay beneath the surface.

If Waller liked and admired the Scots professionals under his command, some of their characteristics would offend the more sensitive consciences among his Puritan soldiers, such as their love of finery. Waller's Sergeant-Major-General of Foot and Dragoons, James Carr, was taken prisoner in 1643. His captured wardrobe included a suit of Spanish cloth edged with silver lace, a long riding coat of the same material, a Dutch coat lined with fox fur and a steel cap covered with scarlet cloth worked with more silver lace. Waller did not care about such externals. He gave Carr a commission to raise a regiment in the new army, 'for he is an honest man and brave old soldier'. The habit of swearing, common among all professional soldiers, caused more irritation. Major-General Andrew Potley, a distinguished veteran under Gustavus Adolphus, attracted criticism on that score. Lieutenant-Colonel John Birch, commander of Heselrige's new regiment of Bluecoats, blamed one reverse in the coming campaign on the fact that Lieutenant-Colonel Leighton 'did swear too hard to have God with him'.

John Birch represents the sort of officer favoured by such Puritan commanders as Brooke and Hampden, Heselrige and Cromwell. In his native Bristol he was described as the most active man in town for the Parliament. He possessed religious zeal and an English proclivity for all-out war. Like John Hampden's former shepherd, Thomas Shelbourne, who rose to become a colonel in Cromwell's Ironsides, Birch came from a humble background. Even when he entered the Commons he still talked in the language of a carrier of wine, but with a simple beauty and eloquence familiar to us in the pages of Bunyan. 'He spoke always with much life and heat', wrote Bishop Burnet later. 'But judgement was not his talent.' Eventually Birch adhered to the Presbyterian political party and like Waller suffered imprisonment at the hands of Cromwell.

*   *   *

In September 1643 Essex bestirred himself and relieved Gloucester, the last stronghold of Parliament in the West. Essex now felt strong enough to secure a return of Waller's commission to form an independent army. But Lord Hopton, now recovered from his wounds, threatened the southern counties. Waller received a new commission to be Sergeant-Major-General of the Southern Association. His army would consist of diverse elements: his remaining regiments from the West, some new units raised in London that summer, county forces and two or three regiments of London trained bands.

As Lord Hopton's army had not yet appeared, Waller occupied

his men by laying siege to Basing House, the strongly fortified lair of the Roman Catholic Marquess of Winchester. The garrison stoutly resisted. On Sunday 12 November Waller led his soldiers in a vain attempt to storm the place. In their confusion the front rank of one London regiment fired their muskets out of range, and then caught the volleys of the second and third ranks because they did not turn away speedily to reload. Within a few minutes some sixty citizen soldiers lay dead or wounded. This ill success and the cold weather dispirited the Londoners. As the rain poured down that night Waller slept among them on a straw bed. A mutiny broke out when he mustered the army to face Hopton's advance. 'As I was riding about to give orders,' he wrote, 'I was saluted with a mutinous cry among the City regiments of "Home, Home!" So that I was forced to threaten to pistol any of them that should use that base language, and an enemy in the field so near.' As the Londoners refused to obey the decision of the council of war to fight Hopton, Waller retired to Farnham.

Early in the morning on 27 November a large brigade of Royalists neared Farnham, as Hopton said, 'to see the countenance of the enemy'. Most of Waller's forces lay abed in their quarters in the surrounding villages. But 'at Farnham God appeared wonderfully for me'. Despite the mistake or neglect of his Adjutant-General (a post which the poet John Milton coveted) and the slackness of his men in drawing to the rendezvous, it seemed to Waller that his army was saved by the special providence of a morning mist. 'In that extremity the Lord took opportunity to show himself for me, by sending a mist all the morning, that by reason thereof the enemy durst not give on.' As Hopton withdrew his rear column, he wrote that he was 'very smartly entertain'd' by the Parliamentarians, in a manner he described as 'very soldier-like'.

With his own morale restored Waller now took the offensive. The Royalists made the mistake of dividing their army between several winter quarters. After a brilliant night march through thick woods Waller fell upon the nearest Cavaliers at Alton. They fought well. To this day the inside walls of the parish church, where they made their last stand, are pitted with lead from musket and pistol bullets. 'I must acknowledge that I have lost many brave and gallant men', wrote Hopton to Waller. 'God give a sudden stop to this issue of English blood, which is the desire, Sir, of your faithful friend.' Yet Waller had no thought of sheathing his sword now. 'Great was my exultation', he recalled, after this victory. To seal the success 500 common soldiers among the prisoners now took the Covenant and fought for Parliament.

Four days later Waller led his army to attack the Royalist quarters at Arundel. His regiments stormed the earthworks in front of the castle. 'In the middle of the danger and difficulty of the assault', wrote an officer, 'our noble, vigilant and heroic commander Sir William Waller did so cheer up our resolutions and put such new fire into our blood as it raised in us the spirit of fortitude to fall upon our enemies.' So inspired, the Parliamentarians beat the enemy back into the town and then the castle. In the fighting Birch was hit in the stomach. In a memoir addressed to its subject his secretary recalled the command Birch received to pursue the enemy. 'At which instant Sir William Waller's Lieutenant Colonel, who but then you encouraged by clapping your hand on his shoulder, your hand no sooner off but he was shot dead. And yourself not gone above 20 paces further received that wonder of God's mercy the shot in your belly, which deliverance to you was so great that I cannot speak of it without admiration.' Birch stopped the hole with his finger until he had drawn his men into the town. Then he collapsed and was laid on the floor of an inn with many other wounded.

The Royalists cooped up in the castle held out for sixteen days. Then, with provisions running out, they sued for terms. During the negotiations Waller courteously invited the ladies in the castle to dine with him. After the surrender he had netted about 1,000 prisoners, half of whom entered Parliament's service. He treated the Royalists well. A Royalist colonel who refused to sign the capitulation noted that he could have been put to the sword 'had General Waller been cruel'. In the London streets later that month Waller received a rapturous greeting.

By now the Scots had entered the war in the belief that the English had agreed to introduce Presbyterianism. In fact Sir Henry Vane had introduced a let-out phrase in the treaty, promising a reform of the church 'according to God's word'. Despite objections from Essex, the strategic direction of the war was entrusted to the Committee of Both Kingdoms. Pym had died a few days before Alton. Like Hampden he had exercised an invaluable leadership by maintaining unity, especially between the moderate, peace-seeking supporters of Essex and the more active, vigorous Puritans who wanted speedy and decisive victory in the field. The latter now moved into the ascendancy. Prominent members of that faction, including Sir Henry Vane, Heselrige and Cromwell occupied some eight of the fourteen commoner seats on the Committee. Waller was also a member, while Essex sat as one of the six elected peers. Two of Essex's senior officers, Sir Philip Stapleton and Sir Gilbert Gerrard, were chosen as well.

In March Waller faced Hopton and his co-general Patrick Ruthven, Earl of Forth, in the fields beside the village of Cheriton. Their armies were roughly equal in strength with about 10,000 men on each side. The fight began with a long-range attempt by Waller to dislodge the Cavaliers from the commanding heights of Cheriton wood. As the Parliamentarians watched the London volunteers running back in disorder down the hillside Heselrige turned to Birch, now recovered from his wound, and said 'Now, Colonel, have you fighting enough?' With true Puritan spirit Birch replied, 'Sir, this is but a rub; we shall yet win the cast.'

Birch proved to be right. The Cavalier horse found it difficult to deploy after they had edged their way down two narrow lanes from the hill. Waller's cavalry, formed into nine fair bodies, successfully charged them and inflicted the first great defeat they had ever suffered – sweet revenge for Roundway Down. Waller rode about in the thick of battle, trailed by his Lifeguard. 'I reckon it a mercy that upon a sudden occasion that day,' he recalled, 'charging without my headpiece and being known to the enemy, as I afterwards understood from some of them, I came off safe and unhurt.' By evening the Royalists had retreated westwards. They carried away the mortally wounded, among them Lord John Stuart and Major-General Sir John Smith, but left 300 soldiers dead on the field. In Waller's army the only man of note badly wounded was a Puritan lieutenant-colonel whose leg had been blown away by a cannon ball. He declared to those about him that 'he had yet another leg to lose for Jesus Christ'.

On 21 March, a week before the battle of Cheriton, Prince Rupert had relieved Newark. In order to retrieve the situation the Earl of Manchester's army marched into the Midlands to link up with a brigade sent by Essex. As Essex had also supplied Waller with a brigade of horse his army could hardly have protected the capital from a determined thrust. Thus Cheriton was fought and won at a time of great vulnerability for Parliament. Waller hoped to follow up his victory by marching into the West. Instead he received orders to converge on Oxford with Essex and bring the King's main army to decisive battle.

The summer campaign of 1644, however, turned out to be a chapter of disasters. The two armies failed to complete the encirclement of Oxford in time to prevent the King breaking out towards Worcester. Essex then ordered Waller and Heselrige to pursue the King while he marched into the West to raise the siege of Lyme Regis. This plan surprised Waller and infuriated Heselrige. The latter rode to London to complain to the Committee of Both Kingdoms. In the meantime Waller obeyed his Commander-in-Chief and set out after the King. For his part Essex angrily shrugged off the directions of the Committee that he should retrace his steps to Oxford and leave the West to Waller.

After weeks of marching and counter-marching on the King's heels Waller at last came within sight of the Royalists as they marched northwards along a road on the far bank of the River Cherwell. Waller gave orders for two columns of horse to attack across the river at Cropredy bridge. The Cavaliers repulsed them. They fell back to the bridge. Meanwhile the 1200 foot who had passed over the bridge, mainly pikemen, now ran back from the enemy musket fire crying 'The field's lost! The field's lost!' They left behind them eleven cannon, much to the jubilation of the Royalists. But Waller's men fought savagely to hold the bridge. A soldier called James Sleamaker 'received a cut from the enemy through the face and had his bowels trod out with a horse and was then run through with a sword to the unparalled hazard of his life'.

Waller withdrew to a strong position on Bourton hill. Just before sunset the King sent a trumpeter asking if a herald could proclaim 'a gracious message' to the Parliamentarian regiments. Waller refused permission. The trumpeter then gave him a private letter which 'to my great shame and surprise,' wrote Waller, came from a lady well-known to him. 'In it she besought me to betray my cause, and this she did so wittily and kind that I had much ado to be angry. Before this lady's marriage I had been her suitor, and did dearly love her, and she remembered me of this, and of some soft passages. Whether or not she was put on this by some greater than herself I never knew. But I returned for answer that as I had never been traitor to my love so I would not to my cause, which I should be, if I did as she would advise. And after this I heard no more.'

After suffering the 'dishonourable blow' at Cropredy bridge Waller resumed the work of shadowing the King's army. Morale had fallen low. 'During these two days march I was extremely plagued by the mutinies of the City brigade', he informed the

Committee. The Londoners had cried out their old song of 'Home! Home!' Waller told the Committee that an army compounded of such men will never go through with their service. 'Till you have an army merely your own that you may command, it is in a manner impossible to do anything of importance.' Again the King slipped away like an eel towards Worcester. Waller followed. 'I am of the opinion before this business be done', he wrote, 'we shall be the longest winded army in England. I hope we shall never be weary of well doing, let the way be never so long and rugged.'

News that the combined armies of the Scots and the Eastern Association had defeated Prince Rupert at Marston Moor on 2 July stopped King Charles in his tracks at Evesham. The King then marched south-westwards to attack Essex in the West country. Waller received orders to leave his foot and remaining guns at Abingdon and despatch the bulk of his cavalry to render assistance to Essex. At Lostwithiel in Cornwall the King's army gave Essex a sound beating. Waller interposed his weak forces as 'a gallant forlorn hope' between the capital and the victorious Royalist army advancing from the West. The Committee decided to concentrate the armies of Waller and Manchester, together with the remnants of Essex's army, to give battle.

On 27 October they engaged the King at Newbury. Waller led three brigades under Skippon, Cromwell and Balfour in a night march designed to bring them upon the enemy's rear. But the Parliamentarian attacks lacked co-ordination. The King watched the fighting from the top of Donnington Castle and then withdrew his army intact to Oxford. A few days later he coolly returned to recover his artillery from the castle. The Parliamentarian council of war could not agree on what to do. Manchester urged caution. 'If we fight 100 times and beat him 99 he will be King still, but if he beats us but once, or the last time, we shall be hanged, we shall lose our estates and our posterities be undone.' His subordinate General of Horse Oliver Cromwell replied, 'My Lord, if this be so, why did we take up arms at first? This is against fighting ever hereafter. If so, let us make peace, be it never so base.'

Rather than conclude such a peace the vigorous Puritan leadership piloted the Self-Denying Ordinance through Parliament. The time had come, Cromwell declared in the House of Commons, to cast off 'all lingering proceedings, like those of soldiers of fortune beyond the sea, to spin out a war'. Aimed at removing Manchester and Essex from command the Ordinance also in theory ended the military careers of all members of Parliament, including Waller. 'Truly, I was so little fond of the trade of a soldier (not withstanding the temptations of honour and profit that accompanied it)' he wrote, 'that I gladly gave my vote to the Self-Denying Ordinance and the New Model.'

In January 1645 Waller received command of a caretaker force to oppose General Goring in the West. With the help of Cromwell and Ireton, with some 2000 of Manchester's mutinous horse, he succeeded in capturing Sir James Long's regiment of Cavaliers. But the chief interest for Waller in this 'hopeless employment into the West', as he called it, lies in the fact that he could observe the eagle in his nest. At this time Cromwell had never shown any extraordinary abilities, 'nor do I think that he did himself believe that he had them'. Although Cromwell was blunt and outspoken he did not bear himself with pride or disdain. As an officer he was obedient and never disputed Waller's orders not argued about them. 'He did, indeed, seem to have great cunning. And whilst he was cautious of his own words, not putting forth too many lest they should betray his thoughts, he made others talk until he had as it were sifted them and known their inmost designs.' He discerned that a captain high in Essex's favour would soon desert the cause, 'although his words were full of zeal and actions seemingly brave'.

Waller gave another instance of Cromwell's perceptiveness. 'When I took Lord Percy at Andover, having at that time an inconvenient distemper, I desired Colonel Cromwell to entertain him with some civility; who did afterwards tell me, that amongst those whom we took with him (being about thirty), there was a youth of so fair a countenance that he doubted of his condition; and to confirm himself willed him to sing. Which he did with such a daintiness that Cromwell scrupled not to say to Lord Percy that being a warrior he did wisely to be accompanied by *Amazons*. On which that Lord, in some confusion, did acknowledge that she was a damsel. This afterwards gave cause for scoff at the King's party, as that they were loose and wanton, and minded their pleasure more than either their Country's service, or their master's good.'

To the end Waller maintained the best relations he could with the opposing Royalist commanders. When Goring's troopers beat up his quarters in Wiltshire he wrote this characteristic letter: 'Noble Lord, God's blessing be on your heart, you are the jolliest neighbour I have ever met with. I wish for nothing more but an opportunity to let you know I would not be behind in this kind of courtesy. In the mean time, if your Lordship please to release such prisoners as you have of mine for the like number and quality that I have of yours, I shall esteem it as a great civility, being your Lordship's most humble and obedient servant, William Waller.' Without a body of foot Waller could not make much headway against Goring, let alone march to the relief of beleagured Taunton. In later years he suspected that the campaign had been proposed by those who 'wished to lessen me in my reputation and expose me to ruin.'

Looking back from a prison cell some five years later on his military career Waller could accept his dismissal. 'It was just with God to lay me by from all employment, as a broken vessel, in regard of the corruption of my heart in my first engagement, and neglect of reformation in the officers and soldiery under me.' In other words he acknowledged that he had fallen short of the Puritan principles described by Lord Brooke. He had sensed worldly motives at work in his enthusiasm for the cause. He had not promoted godliness actively enough. As to 'secondary' causes, he had failed to follow up his successes. His army suffered from divided loyalties and chronic shortage of pay. Like Sir Walter Raleigh in his *History of the World* before him he also recognized that luck played an important part in human affairs, 'the dice being no where as uncertain as in the field'. Oliver Cromwell, less influenced by the Renaissance than Waller, would not have allowed such a role to fortune in war. But no Puritan could fault Waller for lack of effort. 'I strained myself in missing my aim,' he concluded, 'and my failing was my punishment.'

*   *   *

The New Model Army consisted of the better regiments of the three armies of Waller, Essex and Manchester. Sir Thomas Fairfax, a religious man and a valiant leader in battle, became commander-in-chief. Still on active service Cromwell received several extensions of his commission. Then, with a battle impending, he escaped completely the axe of the Self-Denying Ordinance. Fairfax appointed him Lieutenant-General of Horse. 'Ironsides is come to head us', said the troopers, greeting him 'with a mighty shout'. Next day the New Model took on and defeated the King at the battle of Naseby. 'When I saw the enemy draw up and march in gallant order towards us, and we a company of poor ignorant men,' wrote Cromwell, 'I could not, riding alone about my business, but smile out to God in praises, in assurance of victory, because God would, by things that are not, bring to naught things that are.' The soldiers of the New Model, seasoned by several campaigns, were far from being the simple, godly men of Cromwell's imagination. But his deeply Puritan spirit played down human skill and courage in order to prove that, as he said, 'God did it'.

The King now had no field army, except that under Goring in the west. In July Fairfax scattered this army at Langport, the last pitched battle of the Civil War. Then he subdued the west by taking the remaining strongholds and fortified cities one by one. A spirit of unity now held together the New Model, the fruit in part of continued success in the field. After the fall of Bristol in September, Cromwell reported as much to Parliament: Presbyterians, Independents, all had here the same spirit of faith and prayer; the same pretence and answer; they agree here, know no names of difference: pity it should be otherwise anywhere. All that believe, have the real unity, which is most glorious, because inward and spiritual, in the Body and to the Head. As for being united in forms, commonly called Uniformity, every Christian will for peacesake study and do, as far as conscience will permit; and from brethren, in things of the mind we look for no compulsion, but that of light and reason.

In October three Royalist garrisons in Hampshire and Wiltshire fell to Cromwell. Sir William Waller witnessed the fall of Winchester Castle, his former home. Basing House offered a stiffer resistance. General Dalbier had already besieged it for some weeks. After pounding it with five great guns and some 16-inch mortars, Cromwell's force of 7,000 men made ready to storm the place. According to Hugh Peter, chaplain to the train and the most prominent preacher with the army, Cromwell spent much of the night in prayer. In the heat of the assault about a hundred Royalists died and several more suffered serious wounds in trying to protect their friends when Cromwell's men fell to plundering the house. 'They were most of them Papists,' wrote a Parliamentarian, 'therefore our muskets and swords did show but little compassion.' When Peter tirelessly reasoned with the captured Marquess of Winchester he spoke out stoutly, 'If the King had no more ground in England but Basing House, I would adventure as I did and maintain it to the uttermost.' His family motto – 'Love Loyalty' – gave Basing its name of Loyalty House.

When Langport House in Wiltshire fell next, six Parliamentarian soldiers were arrested for robbing Royalist officers contrary to the terms of surrender. Cromwell had them tried by a council of war. The judges sentenced one to the gallows and sent the other five to Oxford to endure the pleasure of the Royalist governor. Cromwell lacked Waller's deep humanity and easy humour in dealing with the Royalists, but he had not abandoned the Puritan principle of conducting the war as humanely as possible.

In 1646 the New Model continued to stamp out resistance in the west. Lord Hopton succeeded in raising 3,300 horse and 1,900 foot to relieve Exeter. Fairfax and Cromwell beat him from Torrington. On 14 March Hopton yielded his sword at Truro. Oxford held out until 24 June, but the King's last field army surrendered a week after Hopton at Stow-on-the-Wold. Silver-haired old Lord Astley, the Royalist general, shrewdly saw that the tangible common task of beating the enemy had united the diverse elements on Parliament's side. Now that unifying purpose had been accomplished would not their latent divisions and the inclination to controversy tear them apart? 'Gentlemen,' said Astley prophetically to his captors, 'you may now sit down and play for you have done all your work, if you fall not out among yourselves.'

10

A Confusion Called a Commonwealth

Victory in the field gave to Parliament the appearance of un-challengeable political power. After the long war, had not the time come to gather the fruits? Perhaps the Puritan gentry would establish a holy commonwealth, modelled on the experiment in Massachusetts Bay. It would be ruled by a suitably chastened and penitent King Charles, shorn of his popish advisers and dependent upon the Puritan leaders for both the political counsel and the social style of his reign. But these hopes proved stillborn. Astley's prediction that the Parliamentarians would publicly fall out among themselves came true within months. Nor would the stubborn and shifty King Charles play the role now assigned to him, the part which alone would allow the old constitution to survive.

Early in 1647 Parliament voted to reduce the size of the New Model Army, recruiting from the redundant soldiers a second army to quell Ireland. A member in the House of Commons proposed Sir William Waller as the Commander of the latter but he in turn suggested Skippon, which was agreed. In March Waller arrived at the Army headquarters with a parliamentary deputation to per-suade the Army to accept this plan. But the officers wanted more information and assurances which Waller could not give. The disgruntled officers embodied their requests in a petition which they sent up to Parliament. But Waller's mission had at least revealed a potential division in the Army. Many of Waller's old officers, such as Quarter-Master-General Richard Fincher, joined those who declared their willingness to serve in Ireland. But the majority – led by Commissary-General Henry Ireton, 'that cun-ningest of Machiavellians', as Lilburne called him – stood re-solutely opposed to these propositions made to them. In the Commons debate Ireton coolly replied to Waller's charge against him as being the ringleader by calling it 'a pure fiction'.

Parliament was led by a large group of Presbyterians, a coalition of Puritan members who broadly favoured some form of Pres-byterian church organization. They felt sure the Westminster

Assembly of divines would eventually advise them on some such scheme. Politically they were conservatives, upholding the social order and striving for a workable negotiated compromise with the King which would perpetuate the familiar constitutional framework while retaining power in their hands. The Army posed a growing threat as it talked itself into a more radical posture under the leadership of such men as Ireton, Hammond, Lilburne and Pride. The Independents, those who believed passionately in the congregational way together with a general toleration for all Puritans, gradually tightened their grip upon it. At first they stuck to issues which immediately affected the soldiers, notably pay. But they soon broadened this bridgehead of opposition as Parliament, with a singular lack of political commonsense, attempted to impose its will concerning the Irish service without even settling the Army's arrears of pay. As a former commander Waller saw the folly of that. 'I may say,' he wrote, 'I was for it to the uttermost farthing,' holding as he did 'that a soldier's pay is the justest debt in the world.'

Led by its skilful political leaders the Army closed ranks against the plan. With their connivance Cornet Joyce seized the King at Holmby House and brought him to Newmarket, thus securing a principal piece in the chess game of power. The Army called for a purge of Parliament and then impeached the eleven Presbyterian leaders, among them Sir William Waller. Hesitating fatally between conciliation and defiance Parliament made some half-hearted efforts to defend itself. Waller, Browne, Poyntz and Massey, the former military commanders in the Presbyterian group, would lead an army composed of the London trained bands and 5000 horse, recruited from unemployed officers and 'gentlemen of quality'. On 3 August Waller received command of this army, but it was already too late. Three days later the New Model Army occupied London. Waller, together with Denzil Holles, Sir Philip Stapleton and other Presbyterian leaders, took ship for the continent. A warship caught their vessel outside Calais and escorted them back to the Downs. But a council of war held aboard Vice-Admiral William Batten's flagship discharged them. After a revolt in the navy that October the new rulers, upon Sir Henry Vane's insistence, replaced Batten with Thomas Rainsborough. Batten said that his dismissal was all of a piece with the way that experienced and proven army commanders, such as Waller and Poyntz, had been cast on one side.

At Calais Sir Philip Stapleton caught the plague. At great personal risk Waller visited the dying man, holding his hand not five or six hours before the end. Waller then removed to the Hague, where he paid his respects to the Queen of Bohemia as well as exchanging civilities with some Royalist exiles. Meanwhile in England the King's political intrigues precipitated the Second Civil War. According to Sir Hardress Waller, a key role in the plan for the rising in the South-West, which never came to fruition, was to be played by two of Sir William Waller's ex-officers, one of whom had been a Major-General.

During 1648 the New Model Army defeated the King's weak forces and his far stronger Scottish allies. While Cromwell lingered in the north the Presbyterian majority in the Commons sent commissioners to negotiate with Charles in the Isle of Wight. He eventually agreed to an experimental form of Presbyterian church government, combined with a modified episcopacy. Waller returned from exile and on 5 December 1648 added his vote for a settlement on the basis of these terms. But Cromwell, much influenced by Ireton, had convinced himself that Charles must die. For Charles had behaved like the more odious despots in the Greek and Latin school books. Milton argued persuasively that even if a king was not a tyrant the people still had the right to depose him. But only a tyrant, reasoned Cromwell, would plunge his country into a second civil war. That year they issued a gold medal with John Hampden's portrait on the face, bearing on its reverse the motto *Inimicis Tyrannis* – 'Enemy of the Tyrant'. According to Richard Baxter, who served as chaplain in Edward Whalley's regiment until 1647, the Army radicals now 'took the King for a Tyrant' and 'intended to master him absolutely'. As the Earl of Essex had said in relation to Strafford, 'Stone dead has no fellow.' By the end of 1648, nerved by Renaissance learning, the Army leaders had resolved upon punishing what they saw as a clear case of tyrannicide.

The day after the Presbyterians in the Commons had voted to accept the Treaty of Newport they experienced the Army's retribution. Colonel Pride and Colonel Sir Hardress Waller (William's cousin and a former colonel in his army) turned away 96 members at the door and arrested 45 others, including Sir William Waller. He remained a prisoner in St James's Palace for eighteen months, the state prison where King Charles was held the night before his execution in January 1649. Most probably Waller looked upon that 'memorable scene' as Charles strode briskly across St James's Park, through lawns white with hoar-frost, to face the headsman's axe.

The King's execution certainly shocked Waller and other

moderate Puritans. For in that other religion of the Puritans, the religion of England, the person of the monarch occupied a central place. His death precipitated England into 'a confusion called a Commonwealth', as Waller described it, which can be said to have lasted until the Restoration in 1660. Just as the King had ruled without a Parliament for eleven years, so it happened that Parliament, propped up by the Army, now attempted to govern without a King. Its rule also lasted a mere eleven years.

The name of Parliament cloaked the real power which was the Army. Just as Charles had kept his chief opponent, Sir John Eliot, in prison, so Cromwell ordered the continued detention of Sir William Waller. He was moved from London to Windsor Castle. There old Sir Robert Harley, whose eldest son Edward – once a regimental commander under Waller – also languished in prison – sent him some notebooks. 'It is a duty which these sad days call for,' Harley wrote, 'that we should help to lessen one another's burden, especially when we can say we suffer not as evil doers.' Waller replied in true Puritan vein: 'I see by your enclosed you are in very good company when you are alone. I wish I may edify by the good example. It is the chemistry of a true Christian to extract good spirits out of the evils of this world. The Lord sanctify his hand to us all and teach us to learn righteousness out of his judgements.'

After a second spell in St James's, Waller said he was 'tossed like a ball into a strange country, to Denbigh Castle in North Wales, remote from all my relations and interests'. There he would almost certainly have met Sir Richard Saltonstall, who now lived in Denbigh. But Waller's greatest consolation was the presence of his wife, the fiery Lady Anne. 'She came to me disguised in mean apparel,' wrote Waller, 'when I had groaned in my bonds seven months, thinking it the duty of a wife to risk all things for the satisfaction of her husband. Much difficulty had she in coming, and was frequently on the brink of being discovered. But at length over mountains and unknown roads, sometimes with a guide and sometimes with none, she arrived at my prison. And she seemed when she discovered herself to me, to be like the angel who appeared to Peter in like circumstances. She did not bid my prison gates fly open, but by her sweet converse and behaviour she made those things seem light which were before heavy and scarce to be borne.'

Lady Anne certainly restored her husband's sense of humour if he had ever lost it. In September 1651, after thirty-two months of imprisonment, he wrote cheerfully to Colonel Edward Harley in London: 'I know not into whose hands these presents may come, but if any be so impertinent to open them, I would have them know from the highest to the lowest, from cat to bobtail, that I am, Sir, your most affectionate and ever faithful friend.'

*   *   *

Meanwhile the Westminster Assembly debated on. The English Puritans had developed a love of measured, rational discussion. This exercise of intellect, however, combined with a resolute obedience to sensitive conscience, led them to perceive more clearly their real differences. 'The humour of this people is very various and inclinable to singularities, to differ from all the world, and from one another, and shortly from themselves,' wrote Robert Baillie, one of the Scottish commissioners at the Assembly. 'No people have so much need of a Presbytery,' he concluded. Baillie could not help admiring the standard of debate among the 121 divines and 30 laymen chosen by Parliament to sit in the Assembly. He praised their 'learning, quickness and eloquence . . . the great courtesy and discretion in speaking'. But he noted their English tendency to prolong the argument, never closing upon an agreement.

The Westminster Assembly had been summoned to advise Parliament on how to complete the great original enterprise of Puritanism, namely the further reformation of the Church of England. Parliament told it to begin by revising the Thirty-Nine Articles in a Puritan direction. By the time they reached Article 15, however, the Solemn League and Covenant was concluded, which presupposed doctrinal agreement between England and Scotland. Thus Parliament suspended the revision and ordered the framing of 'a Confession of Faith for the three Kingdoms, according to the Solemn League and Covenant'. After twenty-seven months the large commission had completed the Westminster Confession, which both kingdoms accepted. As a statement of Puritan theology it exercised a deep influence on all the Puritan churches, including those of New England.

Apart from the Confession, the Longer and Shorter Catechisms and a substitute for the Book of Common Prayer called the *Directory of Public Worship*, the Assembly achieved little else. The Presbyterians and Independents wrangled over the sacraments and the jurisdiction of church courts. As for church polity, the majority certainly favoured a presbyterian parochial system, but the minority of Independents stood firmly for the right of congregations to be gathered regardless of parish boundaries. Thus the Westminster Assembly spread its 'unhappy and unamenable prolixity' over 1163 sessions before 1649 without reaching a consensus on church organization. It finally petered out in 1653, having concerned itself latterly mainly with the trial of ministers. Yet as far as possible the Westminster Assembly had served its purpose. The Church of England had been partially remodelled on Puritan lines.

Behind the polite but interminable debates so beloved by the English Puritans lay some deep disagreements at the level of values. The roots of the values in question go back to the springs of the Reformation and Renaissance, and back into the water tables of antiquity. The slow process of growth took place and the first green shoots appeared in the hundred years before the Civil War as values which were held by the few became the common property of the many. School and pulpit, teaching and preaching, had done most to spread these values. The sudden heat of that conflict produced an almost tropical rate of growth which flowered in the immediate aftermath of the war. The hot sun and warm rain, however, also brought up tares as well as wheat, values of a more secular nature, such as nationalism and avarice, which were intertwined with those of Erasmus and Colet, Luther and Calvin. It is possible to distinguish the strands or varieties among the luxuriant green growth, tracing them back to their sources on the one hand and relating them to present-day values on the other. Certainly Puritan contemporaries were far too excited and inspired by the present moment to carry out this kind of historical analysis. They still took for granted the integrity of their inheritance. Patriotism, the Reformation and the Renaissance flowed into their present consciousness like three rivers tumbling down into a single English lake. 'The late times of civil war,' recalled Thomas Sprat, 'brought this advantage with them, that they stirred up men's minds . . . and made them active, industrious and inquisitive.'

John Milton, the supreme Puritan poet, captured the mood. In 1644 he failed to secure the post of Adjutant-General in Sir William Waller's army, but if his sword remained idle his pen never rested. That year he wrote his *Areopagitica*, a written speech addressed to Parliament persuading them to withdraw the new law against unlicensed printing. Milton's strange title referred to the Areopagus, a hill near the Acropolis in Athens where the highest judicial tribunal of the city met. Milton was invoking the values of Athens, which he now held to be truly English.

In his magnificent concluding exhortation addressed to the 'Lords and Commons of England' Milton reminded his readers of the nation's special calling. 'Why else was this nation chosen before any other, that out of her as out of Zion should be sounded forth the first tidings and trumpet of reformation to all Europe? Now once again, by all concurrence of signs and the general instinct of holy and devout men, God is decreeing to begin some new and great reformation in his Church, even to the reforming of the Reformation itself. What does he, then, but reveal himself to his servants, and (as his manner is) first to his Englishmen?'

If the meeting of the Westminster Assembly inspired this vision of a fuller Reformation in England in his mind's eye Milton saw also the Renaissance renewed as well. The intelligence and creative vigour of England had been so stimulated by the Civil War that the poet could see it as the birth-pangs of a nation. 'Methinks I see in my mind a noble and puissant nation rousing itself like a strong man after sleep, and shaking her invincible locks. Methinks I see her as an eagle renewing her mighty youth, and kindling her undazzled eyes at the full midday beam.'

The sources of Milton's ideas are not hard to find. For Milton had received a fine classical education at St Paul's School and Christ's College Cambridge, as well as being steeped from childhood in the Puritan faith. It is not surprising that like Lord Brooke (whom he warmly commends in *Areopagitica*) he had taken on board the high Renaissance value placed upon man and his reason. In *The Nature of Truth*, which Milton had recently read, Brooke had proclaimed his confidence in reason to guide man as far as man can go himself. Milton developed this theme. He saw Englishmen as noble creatures, possessed of reason and 'so pliant and prone to seek knowledge'. Much truth still remained to be discovered. God would yet unfold more of his mind to the wrestling Jacobs among his children. (John Robinson had told the departing Pilgrim Fathers as much.) Therefore the pursuit of truth demanded freedom of debate. 'Give me the liberty to know, to utter, and to argue freely, according to conscience, above all liberties', cried Milton.

The road signposted by Lord Brooke and Milton led towards the emergence of an even greater individualism. The Reformation and Renaissance had already both reflected and reinforced the sense of being an individual, a unique and self-conscious person rather than merely a functional cog in the mill of medieval society. In New England some years earlier Roger Williams had already exemplified the national tendency of the English towards an uncompromising religious individualism. As Milton followed the guidance of conscience and reason he also came to see himself as a solitary Seeker, one of those 'singularities' so abhorrent to Baillie's tidy Presbyterian mind. As people said, Milton *was* a sect.

Set against this tendency towards greater individualism was the value traditionally placed upon order and discipline. 'Order is the soul of Commonwealths and societies', as one Puritan said. Ultimately that reflected the high value of society itself in Christian thought. In both Church and State the debates after the Civil War revolved around the central issue of how to reconcile the interests of the individual with those of society as a whole. Those who believed in the reasonableness and natural goodness of the individual tended to insist upon the maximum amount of freedom, while those who feared or distrusted the mixed instincts of human nature demanded order and discipline. It is a perennial issue in life.

Like Winthrop and the other leaders of the Massachusetts Bay Colony as well as the majority of the Puritan ruling class at home, Waller belonged firmly in the second camp. In his *Vindication*, written in Denbigh Castle during 1649, he castigated the 'promiscuous toleration of all sects' under the present regime. In his opinion the resulting divisions formed 'the principal cause of atheism in this our age, wherein men of corrupt minds, taking offence at the discordant and cross opinions that are among us, do grow to a contempt of all religion'. Like the New England Puritans, Waller would not allow toleration to those tenets which are destructive to the fundamentals or essentials of religion. Nor did he like to see all order abandoned in church services in the name of 'the Christian liberty of primitive times'. But who would determine the boundaries of these 'essentials' or lay down an acceptable order? That is still the central problem of modern Christian theology. Without much confidence Waller hoped that an enlarged Westminster Assembly might provide the answers. As we know, his hope was not fulfilled.

Cromwell and his family of generals shared the basic values of society and the individual but gave them a different interpretation. They had noted that men of unorthodox opinions, such as Anabaptists, had fought valiantly among the godly for the Good Old Cause. Why should the same men not live and work with them as amicably in peace time? The writings of Lord Brooke had buttressed this rational deduction. Under the growing influence of Renaissance reason, educated Englishmen of all persuasions came to believe that a relatively few 'fundamentals' existed upon which all could agree, while they could safely be allowed to argue and differ about the inessentials. Luther had held the same view, it might be added. What had gone wrong, they said, was to extend the boundaries of the fundamentals. Among Anglican divines William Chillingworth had argued as much in *The Religion of Protestants: A Safe Way to Salvation* (1638). On the plea that 'the Bible only is the religion of Protestants' he had extended rights of reason and free inquiry in religion, thus denying to any church the title to infallibility. Apart from challenging the authority of visible churches he also laid himself open to the charge of Socianism. After being captured by Waller's soldiers following the fall of Arundel Castle, Chillingworth lingered on his deathbed while the rival Puritan chaplains strove in vain to persuade him of the errors of his thought. Did he conceive, asked his arch-rival Francis Cheynell, that a man living and dying a Turk, Papist or Socinian could be saved? 'All the answer I could gain from him was, that he did not absolve them and would not condemn them.' Finally, in his displeasure, Cheynell could do no more than fling a copy of *The Religion of Protestants* into the grave on top of Chillingworth's coffin.

Cromwell had not realized how far a common aim, such as winning a war, in itself creates cohesiveness. Remove that aim and unity flies apart. After the New Model Army had achieved victory in the field men no longer felt the need to suppress their natural differences. The debates in the Army's camp after the war revealed these disagreements over theology, politics and even values among soldiers who could only unite against Charles Stuart and the Papist threat. The Army debates at Putney dug deep into the nature of liberty and the basis of all authority in society. The Levellers began to look dangerous when they called into question the common law and the institution of private property. They interpreted the liberty that comes from the free grace of God offered to all men in Christ as having the direct implications of greater political democracy. In 1649 Cromwell broke them under the useful pretext of restoring discipline in the Army.

The Diggers, an offspring of the Levellers formed in 1649 by Gerrard Winstantley, held the view that Christianity required a communist mode of life. Under his leadership some fifty men set to work digging up common land and planting crops on St George's Hill at Weybridge. By this prophetic act they sought to encourage God to bring in the day when all men would live as equals in a society bonded by love and subsisting on a communal economy. The Diggers soon faded away.

The Fifth Monarchy Men posed a more serious threat to English society, just as Munster's Anabaptists had done in Luther's Germany. For this extreme Puritan millennial sect took more forceful means to usher in Christ's Second Coming and thousand-year reign on earth. In 1653 Vavasor Powell told his congregation to go home and pray, 'Lord, will you have Oliver Cromwell or Jesus Christ to reign over us?' They envisaged a holy commonwealth ruled by the saints under Christ. When prayer failed to remove the government a wine cooper named Thomas Venner led risings of Fifth Monarchy Men in 1657 and 1661 in order to make way for Christ. After the second attempt he was beheaded.

The Civil War produced a crop of self-appointed preachers who had fed deeply on the Bible and reached their own interpretations. John Bunyan, son of a tinsmith, was drafted into the Parliamentary army at sixteen. In 1653 he joined an independent church. 'I was never out of the Bible either by reading or meditation', he wrote. If this particular unlicensed preacher proved to be the finest Puritan popular author of all time there were scores of others who merely retailed distortions of the Christian faith. Like Bunyan they attempted to make the Puritan faith more tangible, concrete or definite – in a word more popular – but unlike him they failed miserably. In fact the two parts of *Pilgrim's Progress* were not published until 1678 and 1684, and so that great work shines as the evening star of the Puritan movement.

The fictional names of characters in *Pilgrim's Progress*, such as *Valiant-for-Truth* and *Mr Great-Heart*, are celebrated. It is not so widely known that names of this kind were common in Puritan England when Bunyan was a young man. They reflect the spread of Puritan teaching among artisans. A Sussex jury list, for example, includes Be-courteous Cole, Safety-on-High Snat, Search-the-Scriptures Moreton, Increase Weeks, Kill-sin Pemble, Fly-debate Smart, Fly-fornication Richardson, Seek-wisdom Wood, Much-mercy Cryer, Fight-the-good-fight-of-faith White, and The-peace-of-God Knight. Hertfordshire could field Lamentation Candle, Mephibosheth Lamprey and Humiliation Scratcher.

Characteristically the sects who attracted artisan support

developed one aspect of the Bible until it took leave of all reality. Ludovic Muggleton and his cousin John Reeve, for example, claimed to be the 'two witnesses' mentioned in chapter 11 of the Book of Revelation. They believed that Cain's parents were Eve and the Devil, while Abel's parents were Eve and God. Thus God had arranged to have a people fathered by the Devil whom he could destroy. They also held that reason was the Beast in the Book of Revelation. As the heavenly messengers they could decide who would be saved or damned. Strangely enough, the Muggletonians survived as a very small sect until 1868.

All these radical groups who plucked and enlarged one Puritan theme at the expense of the rest eventually died out. A group of lasting significance, however, was the Society of Friends, better known as the Quakers, under George Fox. Like so many other sectarian leaders Fox came from the lower middle class. His father was a weaver, and he was apprenticed at first to a shoemaker. In 1646, after long inner struggles, Fox entrusted himself to the 'Inner Light' of the living Christ. He abandoned church-going and began to preach that truth is to be found by direct experience of the inner voice of God speaking to the soul. He was frequently imprisoned, first at Nottingham in 1649, but his enthusiasm and magnetic leadership soon attracted followers whom he organized in a stable way. Though Cromwell had a respect for George Fox personally the Quakers were persecuted for their refusal to pay tithes. They also refused to take off their hats in public, which could be interpreted as disrespect to those in authority. With their programme of no minister, no sacraments and no liturgy, they had pushed the Puritan logic of extinguishing the remnants of popery to its ultimate limit.

Even the Quakers had to contend with the problem of heretics who developed their own doctrine of the indwelling Christ beyond the bounds of common sense. After James Nayler had retired from the Army in 1651 he was converted by George Fox and rapidly became the second leader of the movement. About four years later he came under the influence of a group of Ranters, a sect of extremists who believed that God's grace had made them incapable of sin. Martha Simmonds began to persuade Nayler that his unity with God through the spirit meant that he was Christ. In Exeter gaol, where he was confined as a Quaker, he was accredited with having raised a woman from the dead. Prompted by Martha Simmonds, he broke away from George Fox. Upon his release from prison in 1656 he made a triumphal entry into Bristol with his followers, modelled upon Christ riding in to Jerusalem on Palm Sunday. The second Protectorate Parliament ordered him to be punished cruelly for blasphemy – his tongue was bored with a hot iron, he was whipped on two occasions and given two years hard labour in prison. On a happier note, he was later reconciled with Fox and restored to much of his former popularity.

The sheer diversity of popular religious beliefs, garbled mixtures of Reformation, Renaissance and native folklore, springing up from the ranks of tradesmen and shop-keepers, proved the need for more instruction in Christianity. Preaching on a fast day before the House of Commons in August 1646, Jeremiah Burroughes reminded the members that people cannot be forced to believe before they are taught. To attempt force is 'to seek to beat the nail in by the hammer of authority, without making way by the wimble of instruction.' With Englishmen such blind compulsion would fail. 'Consider you have to deal with English consciences; there is no country so famous for firm strong oaks as England; you will find English consciences to be so.'

Cromwell certainly promoted the preaching ministry. For he looked upon the Word of God expounded by godly ministers as the chief instrument in transforming England into Richard Baxter's 'land of saints and a pattern of holiness to all the world'. Never had the parishes of England seen more Puritan preaching than under the Commonwealth. Unlike Massachusetts, however, the pulpit was not supported by the civil power enforcing theological orthodoxy. Cromwell's closest religious advisers, John Owen and Thomas Goodwin, were both Independents and disciples of John Cotton. But they accepted a different challenge. 'The reformation of England,' boasted Owen, 'shall be more glorious than of any nation in the world, being carried on neither by might nor power, but only by the spirit of the Lord of Hosts.'

'Of the three sorts of godly men,' said Cromwell, 'Presbyterians, Baptists and Independents, though a man be of any of these judgements, if he had the root of the matter in him he may be admitted.' This policy certainly gave England a preaching ministry. As a compromise each of the three sorts implicitly accepted that they could not lord it over the other two. For, as Owen put it, it was better for 500 errors to be scattered among individuals than one error to have power and jurisdiction over all the others. Thus Presbyterians such as Baxter in Worcestershire were free to organize their parishes into voluntary associations governed by presbyteries if they pleased. The *Directory of Public Worship* (1645) gave general instructions rather than set forms of service. The morning service consisted of prayers, two lessons, Psalms and a sermon. The Holy Communion was received afterwards, the people sitting round the table. Thus the church of the nation had become a broadly comprehensive Puritan church centred upon the common institution of the sermon. In time Cromwell came to see himself as the chief village constable of England, maintaining law and order while 'the spirit of the Lord of Hosts' did its work in the pulpits. Popery and prelacy were banned officially, but the Church of England was far too deeply rooted to be seriously disturbed. It continued to find ways of offering the Prayer Book services to the faithful. Even Baxter, no friend of the Lord Protector, acknowledged that under Cromwell 'godliness had countenance and reputation also, as well as liberty'.

Meanwhile the search continued to find a consensus of faith, one which would unite the warring branches of the Christian church. Although men had returned to Luther's distinction between fundamentals and inessentials they still could not agree on the extent of the fundamentals. For reason worked like an acid on the copper base of Christian belief. The Israelites among the Puritans strove to stop the floodgates which their Graecian brothers were busy opening. 'Learn', wrote Francis Cheynell in 1644, 'the first lesson of Christianity, self-denial. Deny your own will and submit yourselves to God's. Deny your reason and submit to faith. Reason tells you there are some things above reason and you cannot be so unreasonable as to make reason judge of those things that are above reason. Remember that Master Chillingworth did run mad with reason, and so lost his reason and religion both at once. He thought he might trust his reason to the highest points. His reason was to be judge: whether or no there be a God? Whether that God wrote any book? Whether the books usually received as canonical be the books, the Scriptures of God? What is the sense of those books? What Religion is best? What Church purest?'

But some Puritans, more inclined than Cheynell to trust rational inquiry, had also embarked upon the Protestant quest for the unassailable fundamentals. Secondary theological doctrines which had been allowed almost to overshadow the 'root of the matter', justification by faith alone, could now be seen by a few enlightened men as matters for a proper Christian agnosticism. With regard to predestination, Baxter asked 'May not all common Christians well take up a contented ignorance here?' He thought that 'enlarging our Creed and making more fundamentals than God had ever made' had been the main cause of fiery controversies which rent the Reformed churches. In a conference in 1654, which met to agree upon the essentials of Christian faith, Baxter argued for the Apostles' Creed, the Lord's Prayer and the Decalogue alone. When other commissioners complained that 'a Socinian or a Papist will subscribe to all this, I answered them "So much the better!"' In a later comment upon a theological book Baxter added the immortal words, 'I am a Christian, a mere Christian . . .'

But plain Christianity would do away with the need for a learned ministry and threatened the civil order. As one Puritan wrote, the issue now had become 'No Minister, No Magistrate'. A further revolution seemed imminent, this time to establish the rule of the people. By his firm action against the Levellers in London and the Army in 1649 Cromwell prevented his opponents, the Presbyterians, from making too much political capital out of the growing social unrest. The conservative interpretation of the way things were going was clearly voiced by Denzil Holles in his *Memoirs* that year: 'The meanest of men, the basest and vilest of the nation, the lowest of the people, have got the power into their hands, trampled upon the crown, baffled and misused the Parliament, violated the laws, destroyed or suppressed the nobility and gentry of the Kingdom.' Holles spoke for a large section of the gentry. Few could equal his credentials as a Puritan leader. But Holles was also the second son of an earl. He believed passionately in the need to preserve the social order.

His friend and fellow Presbyterian leader Sir William Waller was also putting pen to paper in 1649, although in the less congenial setting of a remote castle prison in North Wales. Waller wrote his *Vindication* primarily to defend himself against the charge 'that from the time I quitted my employmen in the field I took leave of my first principles and deserted the godly party, siding with those who had the pestilent tokens of malignancy upon them'. Like Sir John Eliot before him he summoned up an array of Greek and Roman authors to prove the worth of monarchy as the keystone in the arch of a mixed form of government comprised of aristocracy and democracy. But he admitted that the appeal to antiquity had no real force. 'These are ancient things,' he wrote, 'and the remaining memory of them appears unto us no otherwise than like a crack'd mouldered picture, whereof we may discern here and there some decayed lineaments and touches, but cannot possibly make out the full and entire proportion.' This may be Waller's way of saying that the message of antiquity about kingship was at best ambiguous. Certainly Puritans such as Waller and Winthrop were not open to persuasion by appeals to the classical past when that contradicted their firmly-held assumptions about the social order. Ultimately Waller wished to see the government of King, Lords and Commons restored because England had 'happily flourished' under it previously. In short, he wrote, 'I was born under a monarchy, and I desire to die under it.'

Testing or demanding situations, such as adversity provides in plenty, revealed the Puritan spirit at its best. Stripped of secondary theological elements the pure gold of an active Christian faith at work to accept and transform hostile circumstances still shines out to illumine our own lives. Waller's reflections on imprisonment remind us of John Donne's sermons, which he may well have heard in his youth. 'I am both a prison and a prisoner to myself,' Waller wrote at Denbigh. 'The world is but a common gaol . . . a prison wherein those that have greatest power and authority have greatest bonds upon them and are greater prisoners than those whom they imprison. . . . In the straitest confinement that can be put upon me it is the refreshing of my soul that I can walk with God and have my conversation in heaven. I may be shut up, but God cannot be shut out.'

Waller's *Vindication* is a noble Puritan work, too much ignored by historians. He showed outstanding courage in condemning the rule of the purged Long Parliament, known as the Rump, as a usurpation and a tyranny, indeed as 'treason in the highest degree'. Waller saw himself as a martyr for Parliament, the guardian of English freedom. 'My affection to the Parliament (that is the Public) was no morning dew,' he wrote. 'Though the sun has looked upon me and scorched me to a degree of blackness, though I have suffered many ways in my estate, in my liberty, in my reputation, yet nothing has been of force to exhale that. They write of Creon in the tragedy that he hugged his beloved daughter in his arms in the midst of the fire and would not quit his hold, but when he could not help her willingly perished with her. I have embraced the Parliament cause in the hottest flames of the war, and by the grace of God so long as I can retain my soul within my teeth I will never desert it. And if I can do it no further, I shall contentedly mingle my ashes with it.'

As subsequent events showed, it was Waller at Denbigh Castle and not Cromwell at Whitehall who spoke for the majority of the Puritan gentry in England. A minority among them, allied to the Army and drawing moral support from New England, certainly held sway. But they had broken the unwritten contract between the Puritans and the spirit of the English nation. For England was a monarchy and to alter that fact challenged the whole nature of English society as well as trampling on its deeply conservative spirit. Having executed the King in the heat of the hour the ruling Puritan minority cast around for a rationale for their act. Some, like Sir Henry Vane, embraced the doctrine of republicanism. But Cromwell seems to have remained unconvinced. In his English heart he remained a monarchist. He refused the Crown himself but would not abide another Stuart on the throne. Only death rescued him from his dilemma.

The defeat of Charles II at Worcester in 1651 effectively removed the possibility of restoring the monarchy by force. Consequently Cromwell could afford to give his political opponents, the Presbyterian leaders, their liberty. In exile Holles had turned down the office of secretary of state from Charles II and he accepted the opportunity to return home and live a quiet life. Waller was also set free. 'After all the endeavours to find out a matter of charge against me,' he wrote triumphantly, 'I came off with an entire innocency, not only uncondemned but unaccused.'

Lady Anne had died that winter and William resolved upon his third marriage. 'I besought God for his direction in my choice, who heard my petition and sent me the Lady Harcourt to repair the breach in my poor family, which was so rich a blessing both to me and my children that I can never sufficiently acknowledge it.' After a Puritan upbringing in the household of her father Lord Paget, Anna had married Sir Simon Harcourt whom she described as 'a useful and much desired man'. A Royalist officer, he was killed in the Civil War. 'I was in such a condition that I needed him most', wrote Anna about William in her journal. Her estate in jeopardy, her children grown up, her mind worn out with troubles, Anna's health had begun to suffer. 'Then did God give me a religious, wise and faithful loving husband.'

Anna mothered William's younger children William, Thomas and Anne. In her diary she could be thankful that they 'prove so hopeful and do improve daily under my care'. She bore her husband a son, Walter, and a year or two later a daughter, Moll Waller.

About this time Waller wrote his 'Experiences', listing all God's special providences to him from his boyhood. Only one version, written in his own hand, survives today. It was written for his eldest daughter Margaret (who had married Sir William Courtenay of Powderham Castle in Devon). By comparing it to a copy of an earlier version it is possible to see Waller's Puritan spirit at work contending with self. When he looked again at his first draft he clearly felt that he had not always achieved his aim, which was to 'set up' God for his family's praise, not himself. So he omitted many of the stories about himself and rephrased others to elevate God's part. For example, 'At the Devizes when I beat the Lord Marquess of Hertford . . .' becomes 'At the Devizes when it pleased God to grant me that success . . .' Any grounds for pride or self-satisfaction in the section entitled 'several prosperous successes' were edited out.

In the year of his release Waller composed a vow or personal covenant with God. In exchange for God's 'infinite mercy and goodness' in all these experiences he undertook to transmit them in writing to his family in order that neither he nor posterity should ever forget them. He renewed his vows against 'every gross sin or the allowance of any, though never so small'. He also renewed his practice of giving a tenth of his income to pious or charitable uses, in addition to the £100 devoted to these ends as a thanks offering for his release from prison. To mark the blessing and happiness of his marriage he added another £100, to be employed as his 'godly friends' directed. He made some further provisions for the work-house he had set up at Newton Abbot in Devon to give employment to the poor.

At the centre of his 1652 vow Waller expressed with great simplicity the true core of the Puritan faith. There is no overt theology in it, just a burning desire for a God-centred life rather than a self-centred life. 'I humbly devote my life to God', wrote William, 'who has so preserved it and so many ways blessed it, resolving by his grace to do all I can for the setting of him up in my heart: to love, fear and trust him more; to pray, read and hear more, and more zealously than I have done hitherto; to walk in my particular calling uprightly, constantly, cheerfully, fruitfully; and to endeavour to become better in all relations, both to the public in church and state whensoever I shall be in a capacity to serve them, and in private as father, husband, master etc.' That is what it meant to be a Puritan.

As a father William resolved to bring up his children 'in the nurture and admonition of the Lord, teaching them his fear both by precept and example, with a spirit of meekness that they be not discouraged'. In similar vein he encapsulated in a few words a Puritan husband's duty: living with his 'dear yokefellow according to knowledge, loving her as mine own body, as mine ownself, as Christ loved the Church, so taking care with her for the things of this world that as we study to please one another we may likewise remember the homage we both owe to God and labour above all things to please him'. As a master he intended to carry himself towards his servants as 'knowing that I also have a master in Heaven'. He would refrain from threatening, giving them what is just and equal, and make provision for 'my family', as he called them, according to his duty.

*   *   *

Under the Puritan Commonwealth, stage plays, May Day ceremonies, church-ales and morris dances were all forbidden by law, along with cards and dicing. Some of these activities – such as Whitsunales and May-games – were already in decline in parts of England, but others were growing in popularity. Even the great Lord Fairfax was fined five shillings in 1655 after it was proved that he had been present at a comedy or stage play the previous Christmas. The Puritans objected to the English customs and pastimes partly on religious and partly on rational grounds. Pagan fertility customs, such as morris dancing, obviously attracted their opposition. They disliked also apparently innocuous customs, such as church ales or even drinking healths at dinner, which led to drunkenness. Fiddlers and minstrels found in taverns were declared vagabonds and treated as such. For religious as much as secular motives they took issue with the Englishman's sin of gluttony. But often they called into question customs which were simply meaningless or irrational, and thus beneath the dignity of a free Christian man. Two examples – wedding days and Christmas day – will suffice.

The English wedding was an elaborate affair, governed by old customs and accompanied by lavish hospitality. The bride wore her hair loose, crowned by a circlet of myrtle or corn ears. Her dress was usually white or russet, sewn with knots of coloured ribbons which young men pulled off after the ceremony to wear as bride favours in their hats. All the guests wore bright scarves. The bridegroom gave fringed and gauntleted gloves to his friends. Elizabeth Hampden's pair of bride's gloves have survived and can be seen in Aylesbury museum: they are exceptionally beautiful. These would have been given to the bride-men who led her to the church. The ring might be a jewelled or enamelled hoop with a motto engraved inside. Plain gold rings appeared in the Commonwealth and are tokens today of the Puritan quest for simplicity. The stricter Puritans, of course, emulated their New England cousins and wore no rings.

In the country churchyards the guests carpeted the path with flowers and rushes. Two bride-men led the bride into the church, while the bridesmaids escorted the groom carrying bouquets of rosemary, the flower of constant love. After the ceremony the married couple and witnesses observed the custom of drinking wine with sops in it. When the procession came home they dined at a laden table, accompanied by music and dancing. At night the company all drank glasses of sackposset, made of wine, milk, eggs, sugar and spices. When bed-time came the bride-men pulled off the bride's hanging garters and then the bridesmaids took her up to the bedroom and undressed her while the bridegroom's friends did the same for him in an adjoining room. When the couple were in bed the wedding guests poured into the room to wish them joy, and perform more customs such as flinging the stocking. Music, feasting, drinking, dancing and kissing continued to the early hours of the morning. At daybreak the local musicians assembled under the window of the newlyweds in order to wake them with a lively tune.

As John Winthrop made plain in his letters to Margaret before their wedding, much of this time-honoured jollity troubled the Puritan conscience. They preferred a simple ceremony, shorn of its pagan customs. The Puritans retained the sermon and prayer but abandoned the rest. Believing that marriage was primarily a civil contract they would not accept marriage as lawful unless it was performed by a magistrate. Anne Murray, an ardent Royalist, described such a civil ceremony when she married Sir James Halkett in 1656 at the house of a Justice of the Peace in Woolwich. 'The Justice performed what was usual at that time, which was only holding the *Directory* in his hand, asked Sir James if he intended to marry me. He answered yes; and asked if I intended to marry him, I said yes. Then says he, "I pronounce you man and wife." So, calling for a glass of sack, he drank and wished happiness to us. And we left him, having given his clerk money, who gave in parchment the day and witness and attested by the Justice that he married us. But if it had not been done more solemnly afterwards by a minister I should not have believed it lawfully done.'

Perhaps nothing strikes us as stranger today than the Puritan attempt to suppress both the secular and religious celebration of Christmas. In 1647 all festivals and holy days were abolished, and replaced by strictly controlled recreation days for servants and apprentices. In New Plymouth colony the Puritans had insisted on treating Christmas as a normal working day from the start, much to the dismay of the other settlers under their government. The Scots had banned Christmas celebrations as long ago as 1583, though they had not found it easy to stop snowballing, football, guising, carol-singing and other profane pastimes. Lady Margaret Hoby devoted Christmas day to prayer, Bible-reading and self-examination. Why did the Puritans feel so strongly about this church festival?

Christ-mass – 'Christ-tide, I pray you,' said Ben Johnson's Puritan Ananias in *The Alchemist* – carried all sorts of Popish overtones. In addition, the English made it the occasions for over-indulgence in food and drink, as well as pastimes which seemed reprehensible to the Puritan mind. 'Who is ignorant,' Philip Stubbes asked in the *Anatomie of Abuses* (1583), that at Christmas time 'more mischief is committed than in all the year besides?'

In 1644, in deference to their new Scots allies, Parliament directed that Christmas (which fell on a Wednesday) should be kept as a fast day, but few observed the order. Next year the *Directory of Public Worship* abolished the religious but not the secular celebration of Christmas. 'O blessed Reformation!' commented a friend to Sir John Oglander, 'the church doors all shut, and the tavern doors all open!' Parliament met as usual. Major-General Richard Browne, who had commanded the London brigade at Cheriton, proclaimed the abolition of Christmas and ordered his soldiers at Abingdon to work normally on that day. But the Puritans were flying in the teeth of some settled English national characteristics which found expression at Christmas. In 1647 serious rioting broke out at Ipswich, Oxford and Ealing. Ten thousand men of Kent ominously resolved that 'if they could not have their Christmas day, they would have the King back on his throne'. In Canterbury crowds defiantly played football in the streets, preventing the Mayor from opening the market. The mob swarmed into twelve shops that had opened and threw their wares 'up and down'.

If such riots became uncommon the English continued to disregard the law. Moderate Puritans, the vast majority, did not oppose some of the Christmas customs, including even dancing and the theatre within limits. Yet the Puritan leadership could not entirely ignore the constant pressures from extremists or disregard the political implications of ill-judged toleration. In the reformation of manners, morals and customs they pursued a middle course, taking a stricter line in London than elsewhere. Their ministers urged them to stand firm. Anthony Burgess, preaching to Parliament, admitted that the people held 'that the reformers are the troublers of England,' but insisted that this unpopularity should not blunt zeal. Evoking the examples of the Prophets and Christ, Luther and Calvin, he declared 'better it is to endure the rage of the people than the anger of God.' The blessings that follow reformation would cure all complaints.

Royalist propaganda exaggerated the effects of the Puritan attempt to reform the popular national holiday. 'Old Christmas now is come to town,' said the broadsheet *Mercurius Democritus* in 1652, 'though few him do regard.' The theme of a pamphlet called *The Vindication of Christmas* in 1653 was the rejection of old Father Christmas and his failure to find anyone to welcome him until he reached a remote farm in Devonshire. Here Christmas was being kept in the old style and in pursuits that could give offence to nobody. The author defended the ancient Catholic policy of accepting and using pagan customs, providing they were harmless. Was not kneeling at prayer a practice borrowed from the heathen? Yet as early as 1646 Ralph Josselin tells us that many London families were weaned from the old sports and pastimes.

What happened behind the closed shutters of London shops on Christmas Day? Ralph Josselin heard in 1652 that Londoners brought 'bay, holly and ivy wonderfully for Christmas, being eagerly set on the feast'. A botanical work published in 1656 mentions mistletoe being brought long distances for sale at Christmas-time. Not a few Englishmen believed with Sir Andrew in *Twelfth Night* that life 'consists of eating and drinking'. He blamed the ordinariness of his wit on the fact that 'I am a great eater of beef'. The English Christmas was an orgy of roast beef, goose, turkey, plum-broth and mince-pie. According to the *Vindication of Christmas*, the Puritans assumed 'power and authority to plunder pottage-pots, to ransack ovens, and to strip spits stark naked'. A minister in Scotland in 1659 did search houses in order to rid them of the Christmas goose, but there is little evidence of quite such diligence in England.

'This nation makes a God of its belly', wrote a Puritan in 1652. The Puritans could make but little headway against the English passion for good food in plenty. That national characteristic often proved too strong for the godly. None other than Hugh Peter was accused in 1652 of preaching against Christmas Day and then consuming two large mince-pies for his dinner. The English continued to enjoy their beef. Bishop Duppa said 'though the religious part of this holy time is laid aside, yet the eating part is observed by the holiest of the brethren'.

*   *   **

'I love old England very well,' sighed Ralph Verney in 1655, 'but as things are carried here the gentry cannot joy much to be in it.' For the Royalist gentry there was indeed little to be thankful for. That year Cromwell divided England and Wales into twelve military districts, each ruled by a Major-General. The Major-Generals had three main duties. First, they had to maintain law and order, preventing tumults, plotting and insurrection; secondly, they had to impose a tax on all known Royalists to go towards the expenses of their soldiers; thirdly, they were directed to 'promote godliness and virtue' by enforcing the laws against drunknness, blasphemy and immorality of every kind. The system lasted for little more than a year but it gave rise to the post-Restoration myth that during the Commonwealth the Puritans destroyed Merry England and imposed their own brand of gloomy godliness on their fellow countrymen. In 1659 a Frenchman could write that 'the religion of England is preaching and sitting still on Sundays'.

Like most myths there was an element of truth in it. Primarily to prevent gatherings of Royalist sympathizers the Major-Generals received orders to stop horse-races, bear-baitings and cock-fights. But the latter were suppressed also because of their association with 'gaming, drinking, swearing, quarrelling and other dissolute practices, to the dishonour of God'. For the same reasons of security and morality they closed solitary or disorderly ale-houses. They also enforced the legislation for Sabbath observance which had been on the statute book since the 1620s. They fined men for swearing or gambling and punished them for drunkenness. Some of the convicted protested at this infringement of freedom. A Bury man, for example, arrested for tippling, declared that the laws of England had been 'new modelised and Cromwellysed'. But the twelve Major-Generals or their deputies varied widely in their Puritan zeal. Even the most enthusiastic were hampered by the level of indifference they found in the shires entrusted to them. 'Our ministers are bad, our magistrates idle and the people asleep,' complained Major-General James Berry from the Welsh border counties. On another occasion he reported from Monmouth: 'I am much troubled with the market towns; everywhere vices abounding and magistrates are fast asleep.' One has the impression that in most parts of England as long as a man was not a notorious drunkard or profligate his morals were regarded as his private concern. The history of Cromwell's 'poor little invention', as he called the institution of the Major-Generals, hardly justified his bold claim that it 'has been more effectual towards the discountenancing of vice and settling religion than anything done this fifty years'. The Puritan rulers had certainly demonstrated their reforming intentions, but they would effect no lasting social transformation, especially among the poorer classes.

'I have lived in a country where in seven years I never saw a beggar, nor heard an oath, nor looked upon a drunkard,' declared Hugh Peter in a sermon before a joint assembly of Parliament and the Westminster Assembly. Let England look across the Atlantic to the example of her daughter New England. 'Why should there be beggars in your Israel where there is so much work to do?' With unemployment increasing it was an urgent question. In place of indiscriminate charity or poor relief, based on the medieval notion that poverty is not a social evil to be removed by human effort but a visitation from the hand of God, the Puritan reformers proposed a new approach of social discipline and training, designed to equip the poor with the necessary mental attitudes and skills to find work. The poor must learn the doctrine and practice of self-help. The magistrates would administer this national programme of work houses, family means tests and the apprenticing of pauper children to trade. In order to finance the scheme there were various novel suggestions for raising taxes not on property but upon men's income, wealth or luxury goods, such as coaches or kennels of hounds. The *Perfect Diurnall* in 1652 envisaged three to six workhouses in each country, a county bank and professional overseers in place of the parish churchwardens. One Puritan even proposed a 'poor man's office' or labour exchange. The example of Holland, which had a thriving fishing industry and no unemployment, was also invoked. Why not use the English poor in our fishing industry? Or set up joint stock companies in order to create jobs for them?

Yet the Puritan reformers set their faces against helping the 'obstinate, ungodly poor'. One Puritan pamphleteer told a story of a

Scotsman, Dutchman and Englishman who shared the same prison, condemned to die. Three masters begged their lives successfully in order to put them to work in their respective trades. The Scotsman and Dutchman eagerly accepted the offers of the first two employers. But the third benefactor encountered a peculiarly English attitude, one which has since then caused other nations to shake their heads in disbelief. For the Englishman 'told his master in plain terms his friends never brought him up to gather hops, but desired that he might be hanged first, and so he was'. Such vagabonds were self-evidently fit only for the house of correction or the colonies, said the reformers.

The theoretical discussion ran far ahead of policy or practice. The Vagrancy Act of 1657, the only measure that became law, declared that all travellers on the road without means of subsistence shall be deemed beggars, whether begging or not, and suppressed as vagabonds. Some houses of correction and Bridewells were repaired and built, but the administration of the poor law under the Commonwealth remained as sleepy and inefficient as it had been when the Stuarts reigned. Had the rule of the Puritans lasted longer the story might have been different.

*   *   *

In 1654 Waller acquired Osterley House in Middlesex. It was the former home of Sir Thomas Gresham, the famous London merchant, and it stood as a mute reminder of the glories of the golden reign of Elizabeth. Early the following year some Royalist plotters approached him at his town house in Aldersgate Street. Whatever his reply another opposition Puritan leader, Lord Willoughby of Parham, could promise the Royalists that both Waller and Browne would support them in the planned uprising. According to Cromwell's informers, Browne would command the London trained bands while Waller led those of Westminster and Middlesex. But when Penruddock's Rising collapsed in the West Country that spring Waller was not implicated. He gave thanks to God 'that he preserved me in so ensnaring a time'.

In March 1657 the Lord Protector sent messengers to search Waller's house in London, seize his papers and to bring him in safe custody to Whitehall Palace where Cromwell lived in state. The Lord Protector examined Waller himself concerning 'many particulars'. He sent him home that night, 'which was a mercy quite above my hopes', wrote Anna in her diary 'and contrary to the

230

expectation of all people and a thing very unusual with those in power'. Waller adds an illuminating footnote. Cromwell, he said, 'did examine me as a stranger, not as one whom he had aforetime known and obeyed, yet he was not discourteous'. That bond of shared values, the gift for friendship which had bound the Puritan brotherhood together in the war, had receded into the background.

It was the visit of the Marquess of Ormonde, a prominent Royalist, to the capital which had triggered off Waller's arrest. Major Robert Harley admitted under interrogation in the Tower that he had discussed the visit with Waller. 'It is certain Sir William Waller was fully engaged,' wrote that Spymaster-General Thurloe to Henry Cromwell. After the Lord Protector's death in 1659 the Royalists at home and abroad stepped up their activity to bring home Charles from Holland. Waller now worked hand-in-glove with the conspirators, drawn in more deeply by his links with the entourage of the Queen of Bohemia. On their behalf he even approached Richard Cromwell, who had abdicated as his father's successor after eight months with the restoration of the Rump. Richard merely informed Thurloe. Then in the summer Booth's Rising collapsed. On 5 August Thurloe's troopers arrested Waller in the middle of the night at Tunbridge Wells, where he had gone to take the waters for his health. After a fortnight's detention he was sent to the Tower of London. Fortunately neither Sir George Booth nor any other Cavalier leader informed on Waller. After ten weeks spent in a comfortable house within that grim fortress he and Anna regained their freedom.

In the discussions among the Presbyterian party and the Royalists Waller favoured on the whole an unconditional restoration. He said that Charles's 'sweetness of disposition and temper' would soon persuade the next free Parliament to restore fully his rights and prerogatives. Others of his persuasion urged the King's acceptance of the Treaty of Newport as the necessary condition for the royal return. Military means having failed Waller now resorted to political action. The Army had ejected the Rump while he was in prison but restored it again in December. The politically moderate Puritan leaders – Waller, Sir Gilbert Gerrard, Sir Richard Onslow, William Prynne and 17 or 18 of the other excluded members – demonstrated by demanding admission in vain at the doors of Parliament. Only General Monck's march southwards from Scotland preserved the unpopular and unrepresentative Rump.

Monck soon secured the agreement of the excluded members to

his programme for settling the divisions within the Army and calling a free Parliament. Then he ordered their readmission as the first step to those ends. In February 1660 a crowd gathered to watch the excluded members returning like heroes to their seats. Young Samuel Pepys, a clerk in the Exchequer, had begun to keep his diary seven weeks before. He saw the procession. 'Mr Prynne came in with an old basket-hilt sword on, and had a great many shouts.' Waller had the misfortune to be walking behind that crop-eared veteran. 'As he went into the House,' wrote Pepys, 'W. Prynne's long sword ran between Sir William's short legs and threw him down, which caused laughter.'

At the end of May the capital welcomed King Charles II from exile. The Restoration of the monarchy was the last great triumph of the mainstream Puritan leadership of the English nation. The mantle of that leadership had fallen on the shoulders of the political Presbyterians. As Baxter wrote, 'the word Puritane is now vulgarly changed into Presbyterian.' Waller, Holles, Manchester and the others survived the usurpation of the Independent-led Army and the subsequent half-hearted attempt to turn England into a holy republic. What they voted to restore was the rule of law in the State, English freedom as guaranteed by a freely-elected Parliament and a greater measure of discipline in the Church. In 1660 they had every reason to believe that the progress in introducing Puritan standards would continue within the Church of England despite the imminent return of a modified episcopacy. King Charles II promoted conciliatory measures so as not to expel the Puritans from the Church. In the event he was thwarted by reactionary laymen in the provinces and in the Cavalier Parliament, whose decisions resulted in the restoration of the Church of England as it was before the Civil War. On St Bartholomew's Day in 1662 the purge of Puritans took place. Some 1760 ministers and 150 college fellows and schoolmasters were ejected as dissenters.

Thus events after the Restoration dashed the hopes of conservative Puritans for a modified episcopal system, such as had been suggested in 1641 by the late Archbishop of Armagh, James Ussher. Cromwell had given this dignitary a state funeral in Westminster Abbey. Puritanism now had to survive in a hostile environment. The Corporation Act eliminated many Puritan magistrates. The Conventicle Act of 1664 punished any person over sixteen years of age for attending a religious service not conducted according to the Book of Common Prayer. The Five Mile Act of 1665 prohibited any ejected preacher from living within five miles of a corporate town or place where he had formerly ministered. Puritan preachers arrested by the authorities faced fines and imprisonment.

'I believe', wrote the New England Puritan John Davenport in 1647, 'that the light which is now discovered in England will never be wholly put out, though I suspect that contrary principles will prevail for a time.' Under the Restoration the forces of reaction did seem to triumph. But the processes of reform and change in both Church and State with which the Puritans had identified themselves would continue under new men. Moreover, the Puritans had not merely personified and led the English nation, they had also influenced and changed it. As their power faded the seeds they had planted in the English character grew and put forth secular leaves and branches, bearing fruit down to this present time.

*   *   *

Sir William Waller had now retired completely from public life, applying himself to family affairs, reading and writing. He wrote to Robert Harley, once a young officer under him at Lansdown and now Governor of Dunkirk, entrusting his second son Thomas to his care. 'You will find him to be of flexible, ductile disposition and ready, I hope, to embrace your good counsel, if his easiness do not betray him to ill company.' Waller only feared the youth's love of gambling, which had already landed him in debt. His eldest son William had already left home 'in a rebellious way'. He was in Calais, and must be prevented from meeting with Thomas and debauching him. Like so many other Puritan fathers in both England and New England, Waller clearly looked upon his sons as disappointments. John Hampden's eldest son and heir Richard – 'one of the learnedest gentlemen I ever knew', wrote Bishop Burnet – succumbed to rationalist influences in Paris and became a Deist. In 1696 he committed suicide by cutting his throat with a razor.

In October 1661, freed at the end from 'a slavish fear of death' which had long troubled her, Lady Anna died. At Waller's request the celebrated presbyterian preacher Edmund Calamy of Aldermanbury preached her funeral sermon, which was later printed. Calamy praised Anna for her Puritan virtues: her support of preaching ministers, her attendance at the two Sunday sermons, her catechism of servants, her monthly reception of the Lord's Supper. Little Moll had died before her. Nor did Walter or a baby sister, born in 1657, survive for more than a few years.

Echoes of these family tragedies are to be found in Waller's reflections, published after his death as *Divine Meditations upon Several Occasions: With a Daily Directory*. Their subjects, such as 'Upon the contentment I have in my books and study' or 'Upon an entertainment of godly friends', suggest the ordered life of a Puritan gentleman. Contrary to the modern stereotype of a Puritan as a sour and solemn man Waller not only possessed a sense of humour but praised it. In the delightful society of 'conscientious friends', he held, mirth is 'a divine thing', an anticipation of the joys of Heaven. 'It is one of the Devil's lies', he wrote, 'that religion is a dull, flat, melancholy thing. Whereas in truth there is no such clear delicate mirth as that which comes from the springs above.'

An attack of gout and his recovery from it, sunrise and sunset, hunting and fishing, a fair house and a pleasant garden, good music and pictures in a gallery, a prancing horse and even a parrot in a cage, all these inspired separate meditations. Waller summoned up his old Civil War sobriquet as 'the Night Owl' to embroider a characteristically Puritan stress upon the importance of regular hours and hard work: 'How strangely do those people live that begin their morning at noon and their noon at night, that turn day into night and live backward? But it is no wonder to see owls fly abroad at late hours! O my soul, God never created you to live in a feather-bed! Life consists in action; idleness is but a living death.'

Death itself now held no terrors for Waller. 'Methinks, I have had a long day's journey in the world and a wearisome, accompanied with blustering weather and rugged ill ways, and now a bed would do well,' he wrote. 'Nay, I am not only dead, but in a great part buried. How much of myself is already laid in the dust? Death has taken three of my ribs from me, and so many of my limbs as I have lost children at his stroke. My dearest relations are gone to bed before me. To what purpose serves this fragment, this remainder of me here? Lord, take all to thee. Let me not lie half in the bed and half out. Thy bed is not too little nor thy coverlet too narrow but thou hast room enough for me.' His words can be given a wider interpretation. For Brooke and Hampden, Winthrop and Cromwell had all 'gone to bed' before him. Waller, the last of that great Puritan generation, died in 1668. He was buried in the New Chapel in Tothill Street near to the Parliament he had loved so dearly.

* * *

The northerly breezes of rationalism cooled the religious climate in the closing decades of the seventeenth century. A new generation of thinkers continued the work of William Chillingworth and Richard Baxter. John Locke's *The Reasonableness of Christianity* (1695) sought out the rational parts of Scripture in the hope that all might agree upon them and abandon their dogmatic divisions. Locke was a Puritan by parentage and upbringing. His father had served as a captain in Colonel Alexander Popham's regiment in Sir William Waller's army. Locke's pious mother died when he was a child, but he wrote that his father 'lived perfectly with him as a friend'. With Popham's help he was sent to Westminster School, now the rival of St Paul's School in London. He saw King Charles beheaded in Whitehall. At Oxford he read the works of Descartes, the philosopher who had first appeared on stage of European history as a common soldier in the Imperial armies which assaulted Bohemia at the outset of the Thirty Years War. Cartesian rationalism and the new experimental science, practised by such men as his friend Robert Boyle, deeply influenced his thought, as became clear in such major works as *On Toleration* and the *Essay Concerning Human Understanding*. Locke's denial of the divine right of kings, his statement of the principles of natural rights and property rights, and his defence of a balanced constitution, all had a profound effect on both sides of the Atlantic.

It became clear that the price of religious unity, in the opinion of Christian rationalists such as Locke, amounted to no less than the surrender of belief in the divinity of Christ. Puritanism was essentially God-centred, not Christ-centred. By emphasizing the direct and personal relationship of the believer with God, Luther had inadvertently reduced the need for a present mediator. Christ's work of redemption lay in the past. Christ dwelt in the soul of the Christian by faith, but could he distinguish by introspection Christ's spirit from the Holy Spirit, or indeed from reason – the light that lightens every man?

The shift of consciousness towards a Renaissance view of man and his world gained momentum. To those who saw man as a noble, god-like creature, imbued with divine reason, the mental apparatus of the Fall, the Atonement and eternal punishment fell away like the spent casing of a large rocket firework. Men such as Locke and Newton, Adams and Jefferson, abandoned belief in the Trinity. They became Christian Unitarians or Deists.

The sons of the classically educated Puritan gentry, such as Waller, Hampden and the younger John Winthrop, would not themselves become Puritans. Indeed that name seems inappropriate after the Restoration; it lost all meaning as a specific description of some men and women in Church and State. After 1660 many in the younger generation made haste to distance themselves from it, at least as a political movement. Samuel Pepys had been reared in the Puritan tradition at St Paul's School. John Langley, the Highmaster for seventeen years after 1640 was a Puritan schoolmaster of distinction, a learned antiquarian and theologian. Thomas Fuller, Edmund Calamy and Sir Robert Harley all had sent their sons to be educated by him. In 1657 all the pupils attended his funeral, which in keeping with Puritan teaching was performed without ceremony. They wore their best black suits and gloves, a common custom at Puritan funerals in both old and New England. One evening after the Restoration Pepys was dining at Sir William Batten's house where he met an old schoolfriend named Christmas. The latter remembered 'that I was a great Roundhead when I was a boy'. He became hot with fear that Christmas would soon blurt out to the company what Pepys had said on the day of the King's execution, namely that if he was a preacher he would choose as his text 'The memory of the wicked shall rot'. Fortunately for Pepys, it happened that Christmas had left St Paul's School before that fateful day.

The diary of Pepys is a secular development of the daily journals kept by the Puritans for spiritual purposes. It gives a vivid picture of a man shaped by Puritan values but drawn irresistibly to the pleasures and rewards of this world. The Puritan in him is never far below the surface. His industry as an administrator of the navy was prodigious, an early example of the effects of the Puritan work ethic. Even in his amorous exploits and numerous infidelities Pepys cannot forget his Puritan teachers, as his human pangs of conscience testify.

*   *   *

If Pepys felt worried about his Roundhead indiscretions as a schoolboy it is not surprising that those Puritans who were deeply committed to Cromwell and the Commonwealth feared for their lives after the Restoration. In fact, capital retribution was reserved only for the regicides and one or two others. Sir Henry Vane went to the scaffold to be beheaded in a black suit and cloak, with a scarlet waistcoat, on the anniversary of the battle of Naseby. His religious faith and his patriotism, together with a characteristically English contempt of death, kept him steadfast and defiant to the end.

Two of Cromwell's Major-Generals who were regicides, Edward Whalley and his son-in-law William Goffe, fled to America. Governor John Endecott warmly welcomed them in Boston, expressing his surprise that more such godly men did not join them. When Endecott received the royal warrants for their arrest he made a pretence of searching for them. The two fugitives found refuge with their friends and relatives in the hinterland, living in caves in the woods when the chase came near. They settled down eventually at Hadley in Massachusetts. During the Indian War of 1675, according to tradition, Goffe emerged as the leader of the settlers in the hour of crisis. The man who had commanded Cromwell's own regiment at Dunbar, and at push of pike repelled the stoutest foes that day, could be relied upon to remain calm before a few hundred Indians. Under an assumed name Goffe kept up a correspondence with his wife, who remained in England with his three daughters.

Hugh Peter was among the ten regicides executed in the first year of the Restoration. Just as William Laud had been executed as a symbol of popish prelacy, so Hugh Peter would die because he personified the militant Puritan movement. After his trial his daughter Elizabeth visited him every day in the Tower of London. A minister to the end, he preached to his fellow prisoners and composed *A Dying Father's Last Legacy to an Only Child.* 'My child', he wrote, 'to believe things incredible, to hope things delayed, and to love God when he seems angry, are Luther's wonders, and mine, and thine.' He urged Elizabeth to read the Scripture daily and meditate fervently upon them. 'I say read with delight, not as under a cloud, or as a labourer.' Knowing that she would shortly be destitute he could foresee the problems she would face in making a suitable marriage. Nevertheless she should aim to do so, 'only marry in, and for, the Lord.'

It was 'my very great mercy,' Peter said, 'that temptations never led me from that honest, old, godly, Puritan profession of the everlasting truths of the Gospel.' Alas, his zeal had led him to 'trample' into politics. In working as a staff officer under Cromwell in Ireland, for instance, the minister from New England had accepted a commission as colonel of a regiment of foot. He blamed most of his temperamental failures and errors of judgement on his ill health: recurrent bouts of fever which led his mind to become temporarily deranged. He claimed that he had avoided politics for a year or more, a change of heart that came too late. But Peter protested vehemently that he had engaged himself in civil affairs only in order to promote goodness and religion, to forward sound learning and to help the poor so 'that there may not be a beggar in Israel, in England'. Yet, as the judges pointed out, he was not on trial for work done towards these laudable ends, but for his errors and complicity in the King's death.

Through jeering English crowds, eager as ever to see blood on that October day in 1660, Hugh Peter was drawn on a hurdle with John Cook to Charing Cross, that 'idol of popery'. There they made ready for the barbaric death reserved for convicted traitors: being hanged by the neck, cut down and disembowelled, the corpse beheaded and then quartered for display in different parts of the land. One account says that Peter showed visible signs of fear, shrinking back from the scaffold. But others testify that at sixty-two and in poor health, Peter faced death bravely. Cook suffered first. After disembowelling him the executioner came to Peter, rubbing his bloody hands, and exclaiming, 'Come, how do you like this, Mr Peter, how do you like this work?' Far from being unnerved his next victim replied calmly: 'I am not, I thank God, terrified at it. You may do your worst.' Poor Hugh Peter! Had he not once urged that Foxe's *Book of Martyrs* should be brought up to date? Now he wrote a fitting climax for such a work in his own blood.

Many other New Englanders in England, such as John Leverett and Francis Willoughby, now made their way home. A young minister named Increase Mather was among the more notable of them. The son of a minister and born in Dorchester, Massachusetts, Mather had visited England after graduating at Harvard and become chaplain to the Governor of Guernsey at the age of twenty. Ahead of him lay long years as pastor of the South Boston congregation, the largest in New England at that time, together with political leadership in the struggle with England to preserve the charter, as well as prolific authorship of nearly 150 works and the presidency of Harvard. He represents the last generation of Puritans, those who would seek now to pass on their inheritance in the free air of America. What kind of country did they find upon their return home?

11

Dear New England, Dearest Land To Me!

As these words by the Puritan poet Michael Wrigglesworth suggest, English patriotism had been transplanted to New England's stony soil. Over the decades the love of old England which so characterized the English settlers was gradually transferred to their new country. They no longer regarded it as their backyard wilderness, as if looking homewards towards England across the seas. It became for them a land of beauty, a vast, undiscovered continent full of promise. As the colonies – Connecticut, Rhode Island, New Haven, New Hampshire – multiplied, the Americans began to face inwards to the hinterland. They became more conscious and proud of their distinctive Puritan way of life, which they determined to defend. In their love of liberty – the desire for freedom from outside interference – they would eventually show themselves to be more English than the English.

The fires of Puritan zeal were already beginning to burn lower in New England when Increase Mather and his friends returned to Boston. New England grew by the cellular division of congregations, and the wider that Puritans spread on the ground the thinner it tended to become. Moreover, the province could not isolate itself from the religious and intellectual ferment in England after the Civil War. Ships brought boxes of books and tracts, as well as unwelcome immigrants to expound them. In his journal Winthrop tells the story of one Captain Partridge, who had fought for Parliament in the Civil War before coming to America. On board ship he had broached and zealously maintained several points of antinomianism and familism. He refused to answer the magistrates about them but agreed to discuss his opinions with John Cotton. The Boston minister reported back that Partridge, an honest but ignorant man, might well change his mind completely after further discussions. But the majority of magistrates insisted upon an instant retraction. Partridge would not agree to do so until he was clearly convinced in his conscience of his error. Despite winter being at hand they forced Partridge, his wife and children, to depart to Rhode Island. 'This strictness was offensive to many, though approved by others,' noted Winthrop.

The difference between the congregational way as practised in America and the presbyterian system advocated by the majority in the Westminster Assembly paled into insignificance beside the issue of toleration. For both of these rivals preached or practised a degree of church order and orthodoxy which was abhorrent to the Independents who seized the fruits of victory after the Civil War. After a visit to the British West Indies in 1645 a relative of the younger John Winthrop wrote to advise him that 'the law of banishing for conscience makes us stink everywhere'.

The wafted odour of such criticism did not cause Winthrop's father to waver in his conviction that the godly had a right and duty to govern the ungodly. Nor did he question that the New England church had an equal right and duty to maintain its orthodoxy. But his race was almost run. In 1647 Margaret succumbed to the illness which subsequently killed her. 'Thus the Lord is pleased to keep us under', wrote Winthrop to John, 'and all in love and for our own good, that he may wean us from this world and draw our hearts more after Christ Jesus and those riches which will endure to eternity.' After a time of mourning Winthrop married his fourth wife, a Boston shipmaster's widow who bore him his sixteenth child. In 1649, after struggling for six weeks with 'a feverish distemper' he died aged sixty-one. 'Our honoured Governor, Mr John Winthrop, departed this life,' wrote John Hall, a young Boston goldsmith in his diary: 'a man of great humility and piety, an excellent statesman, well skilled in the law, and of a public spirit.' The Boston militia fired a salute of cannon at his funeral.

Winthrop's successors, notably Governor John Endecott, stood firm on the issue of toleration for as long as they could. About the year 1650 Sir Richard Saltonstall took up his pen at Denbigh in North Wales, and wrote to protest against New England's intolerance to Cotton and Wilson, the preachers of the Boston church. Although he wrote in the warm vein of friendship he did not mince his words:

> Reverend and dear friends, whom I unfeignedly love and respect:
> It does not a little grieve my spirit to hear what sad things are reported daily of your tyranny and persecutions in New England, as that you fine, whip, and imprison men for their consciences. First, you compel such to come into your assemblies as you know will not join with you in your worship, and when they show their

dislike thereof or witness against it, then you stir up your magistrates to punish them for such (as you conceive) their public affronts. Truly, friends, this your practice of compelling any in matters of worship to do that whereof they are not fully persuaded is to make them sin, for so the Apostle (Rom. 14 and 23) tells us, and many are made hypocrites thereby, conforming in their outward man for fear of punishment. We pray for you and wish you prosperity every way, hoping the Lord would have given you so much light and love there that you might have been eyes to God's people here, and not to practice those courses in a wilderness which you went so far to prevent. These rigid ways have laid you very low in the hearts of the saints. I do assure you I have heard them pray in the public assemblies that the Lord would give you meek and humble spirits, not to strive so much for uniformity as to keep the unity of the spirit in the bond of peace.

When I was in Holland about the beginning of our wars, I remember some Christians there that then had serious thoughts of planting in New England desired me to write to the governor thereof to know if those that differ from you in opinion, yet holding the same foundation in religion, as Anabaptists, Seekers, Antinomians, and the like, might be permitted to live among you, to which I received this short answer from your then governor, Mr. Dudley: God forbid (said he) our love for the truth should be grown so cold that we should tolerate errors. And when (for satisfaction of myself and others) I desired to know your grounds, he referred me to the books written here between the Presbyterians and Independents, which if that had been sufficient, I needed not have sent so far to understand the reasons of your practice. I hope you do not assume to yourselves infallibility of judgment when the most learned of the Apostles confesseth he knew but in part and saw but darkly as through a glass. For God is light, and no further than he doth illuminate us can we see, be our parts and learning never so great. Oh that all those who are brethren, though yet they cannot think and speak the same things, might be of one accord in the Lord. Now the God of patience and consolation grant you to be thus minded towards one another, after the example of Jesus Christ our blessed Saviour, in whose everlasting arms of protection he leaves you who will never leave to be

Your truly and much affectionate friend in the nearest union,
RICHARD SALTONSTALL

Cotton's reply, a striking apology for the New England Way, soon moved from defence to attack. The men referred to by

Saltonstall had suffered justly. One of them, Obadiah Holmes, was an excommunicate person who had baptised adults 'against the order and government of our churches established (we know) by God's law and (he knows) by the laws of the country'. He chose to be whipped rather than pay his fine. As for the imprisonment of Holmes and his associate, 'they fared neither of them better at home, and I am sure Holmes had not been so well clad of many years before'.

As for compelling men to worship, that did not make them sinners if the worship was lawful. Indeed the magistrate who did not put men to their Sabbath duties would be the greater sinner than a passive worshipper. Better to make men hypocrites than allow them to continue as profane persons. 'Hypocrites give God part of his due, the outward man, but the profane person gives God neither outward nor inward man.'

If 'our native country were more zealous against horrid blasphemies and heresies than we be, we believe the Lord would look at it as a better improvement of all the great salvations he hath wrought for them than to set open a wide door to all abominations in religion, wrote Cotton with mounting fervour. 'Do you think the Lord hath crowned the state with so many victories that they should suffer so many miscreants to pluck the crown of sovereignty from Christ's head? Some to deny his God-head, some his manhood; some to acknowledge no Christ, nor heaven, nor hell, but what is in a man's self? Some to deny all churches and ordinances, and so to leave Christ no visible kingdom upon earth? And thus Christ by easing England of the yoke of a kingdom shall forfeit His own kingdom among the people of England. Now God forbid, God from heaven forbid, that the people and state of England should so ill requite the Lord Jesus. You know not if you think we came into this wilderness to practice those courses here which we fled in England. We believe there is a vast difference between men's inventions and God's institutions. We fled from men's inventions, to which we else should have been compelled; we compel none to men's inventions.'

Cotton concluded by pointing out that a degree of toleration did exist in New England. The Presbyterians had certainly established themselves in Connecticut and some congregations in Massachusetts Bay inclined that way. Governor Dudley's answer to Saltonstall's letter from Holland had been short but zealous, for Puritan enthusiasm will always seem quite different from that coldness condemned in Scripture.

In their determination to maintain 'the foundation of religion' the Puritan ministers of New England were no respecters of persons. William Pynchon came from an ancient family which could trace its lineage back to the Norman Conquest. His grandfather had married the heiress of the wealthy Sir Richard Empson, a notorious minister of King Henry VII. His father, the second of six sons, settled at Springfield in Essex, where William was born about 1590. He had signed the Cambridge Agreement and must be counted among the founding fathers of America. He was one of the leaders of the settlement at Roxbury, where he engaged in the fur trade. Then with several others he founded Springfield where he continued to prosper as a merchant. The townsmen even granted him the privilege of storing his corn in the loft over the meeting-house room, providing he promised to prop up the roof if it began to sag! With some breaks he served annually as a magistrate until 1650, when he was in his sixties.

The cause of his dismissal and exile lay within the covers of his book *The Meritorious Price of Our Redemption*. Four years before, a law had been passed which condemned to fine and banishment anyone who should subvert the Christian faith by maintaining certain 'damnable heresies', such as 'denying that Christ gave himself a ransome for our sins'. On this score the General Court in October 1650 condemned Pynchon's book, which had been printed and sold in England.

The book itself is worthy of more than a passing notice. It is the scholarly work of a very intelligent layman, who knew Latin, Greek and Hebrew. Pynchon applied his reason and learning to unlocking one of the central mysteries of the Christian faith. He rejected the view of Beza and Perkins, that the sins of the elect were imputed to the Saviour, who suffered the torments of hell for that purpose. He quoted Luther, Calvin and St Augustine to support his case, and ten other English and continental theologians for good measure. As for proof texts, he compared the variant readings in the Geneva, Tyndale and King James's versions of the Bible. Pynchon held that Christ's perfect obedience unto death had redeemed the world, not merely the elect. Christ did not suffer the wrath of God, but he did the will of God. We may be saved because the law, which was broken by disobedience, was honoured and restored by the obedience of the God-man.

The General Court commissioned a reply to Pynchon's book, and advised him to confer with its author Norton and two other ministers, including Cotton. The usual attempt at friendly and gentle persuasion failed to move Pynchon in the desired direction. He appeared before the General Court in May 1651 with a paper to show that he was taking the counter-arguments seriously, but he failed to turn up again as requested in October or the following May. For Pynchon had returned to England. Part of his family accompanied him, but his son John remained behind in Springfield and succeeded in time to his influence and authority. Several letters, including one from Sir Henry Vane, arrived from England protesting at the treatment of Pynchon. To many readers in England the tenets of his book, wrote Vane, appeared 'as disputable and to some of note, probable'.

On arriving in England, William Pynchon settled down at Wraysbury, on the Thames in Buckinghamshire. It lies about three miles above Windsor Castle, directly opposite Magna Carta Island and Runnymede. He spent the remaining ten years of his life there studying and writing. He dedicated his rejoinder to Norton's reply, published in 1655, to Oliver St John, the lawyer who had defended Hampden in the Ship Money case. In it he conceded that the sufferings of Christ had some link with 'the due punishment of our sins, by way of satisfaction of divine justice', but his challenge to the narrow, Hebraic categories of late Puritan theology remained firm. He died in 1662, aged seventy-two years, and was buried in the shadow of the ancient parish church.

But the magistrates could not silence the new breed of Puritan deviants. In New England the Quakers took toleration by storm. The first Quakers in Massachusetts Bay confirmed the worst fears of the magistrates. They interrupted sermons and practised the Ranter habit of strolling naked down the aisles as part of their demonstrations. Governor Endecott castigated them for their 'presumptuous and incorrigible contempt for authority'. Fines did not deter them; when banished they simply returned. In 1659 two such persistent Quakers were executed. A third, Mary Dyer, was standing on the scaffold with her arms bound and face covered when she was reprieved. Yet she came back from exile to find the martyrdom she so obviously wanted. 'She hangs there like a flag', wrote one eyewitness. After six Quakers had died in Massachusetts Bay the 'Cart and Whip Act' of 1661 introduced a less odious form of punishment. The Quakers spread rapidly in America. In 1674 Rhode Island elected its first Quaker Governor. By 1681 a Baptist congregation in Boston had also won the right to toleration, though fifty years passed before a second one was established there.

The Quakers soon attracted leaders from among the Puritan gentry. That they saw themselves in direct line of succession to the main Puritan tradition can be illustrated by a 'letter from me (Mary Pennington) to my dear grandchild Springet Penn, written about the year 1680, and left to be delivered to him at my decease.' Mary's first husband, Sir William Springet, had died of typhus after the siege of Arundel Castle. Her second husband, son of the vigorously Puritan Lord Mayor of London, joined the Quakers in 1657 and suffered imprisonment in 1660 for refusing the oath of allegiance. His wife followed in his religious footsteps with enthusiasm. Although she wrote with full appreciation of her first husband's intense Puritanism, she quietly lamented that he had not embraced the whole truth. Her daughter Gulielma married William Penn, founder of Pennsylvania, and her letter was addressed to their eldest son Springet Penn: 'Dear Child, You bearing the name of your worthy grandfather Springet, I felt one day the thing I desired was answered, which was the keeping up his name and memory, not in the vain way of the world, who preserve their name for the glory of a family, but in regard that he left no son his name might not be forgotten . . .'

Mary drew a vivid pen-portrait of Sir William as a Puritan gentleman. He is such a fine example of the class that produced the Puritan Fathers of New England, such as John Winthrop, Sir Richard Saltonstall, John Endecott and William Pynchon, that it is worth examining his life through her eyes. Her letter makes it clear that upbringing and education played a vital part in producing these flowers of English Puritanism in the early seventeenth century. His widowed mother supplemented her income by practising medicine. She kept several poor women hard at work in her dispensary making oils, salves, balsams, syrups, conserves, purges, pills and lozenges, as well as 'drawing spirits, distilling of waters'. She kept an Independent minister at her brother's house in Kent where she lodged with her three children, and allowed people to come twice a week to hear him preach. She counselled her son William not to marry for an estate and disregarded various offers from wealthy parents of girls, 'urging him to consider what would make him happy in a choice. She propounded my marriage to him because we were bred together of children, I nine years old and he twelve, when he first came to live together . . .'

William's mother educated him and her children 'in the fear of the Lord, according to the knowledge given in that day, and took great care in placing him both at school and university. She sent him to Cambridge (as being accounted more sober than Oxford) and placed him in a Puritan college called Katherine's Hall'. After brief studies in the Inns of Court he returned to Kent. Before he was twenty-one they married, 'and without a ring, and many of their formal dark words left out (upon his ordering it) he being so zealous against common prayer and such like things. . . . When he had a child he refused the midwife to say her formal prayer, and prayed himself, and gave thanks to the Lord in a very sweet melted way, which caused great amazement.' He never went to the parish church but went many miles to hear one Wilson, who had been suspended for not conforming to the bishops, 'an extraordinary man in his day. Nor would he go to prayers in the house, but prayed morning and evening with me and his servants in our chambers, which wrought great discontent in the family (we boarded with his uncle Sir Edward Partridge) . . .'

In his 'zeal against dark formality and the superstitions of the times,' William had a commission sent to him to be the colonel of a regiment of foot. He raised 'without beat of drum' 800 men, most of them Puritans or sons of Puritans. Like his own company of sixty volunteers, young men of substance, William took no pay. At Newbury a spent bullet wounded him. When his own native county, Sussex, was in danger of spoil by the Cavalier party, who had taken Arundel, his regiment took part in the siege of the town and castle under Sir William Waller.

After the surrender William succumbed to the disease of the soldiers. He sent for Mary, who came to him despite the appalling winter conditions and being pregnant with Springet's mother. When he saw her William sprang up from bed, saying, 'Let me embrace you before I die. I am going to your God and my God.' For two days Mary sat by him, cooling his parched lips with her own cool lips, often for hours at a time, regardless of infection and of great pain in her condition. At length he died. 'When he was dead,' recalled Mary, 'then I could weep.'

*   *   *

Behind a determined rearguard action against the sects and various theologically unorthodox views, the New England Puritans faced a serious internal problem: the gradual decline of zeal. Their retention of infant baptism plunged them into damaging controversies as the baptised children of church members, not themselves among the elect, brought their own babies for baptism. As the century neared its end there were other troubles which could be interpreted as God's judgement against New England. In 1675 Governor John Leverett rebuked Increase Mather for one of the growing number of sermons interpreting events as a divine judgement on the loss of 'purity' in religion.

The Governor's irritation is understandable. The preachers of New England undoubtedly exaggerated the decline of religion. They did so partly for dramatic effect and partly in order to frighten men into taking their duties more seriously. The same message had been on the lips of Puritan preachers for decades. Fifty years earlier John Preston had told a Cambridge congregation that God evidently had a 'controversy' with England which required action from every man. 'If we look back upon that generation of Queen Elizabeth, how are we changed! They were zealous, but here is another generation come in their room that is dead and cold.'

But the Puritan heat was ebbing away almost imperceptibly. In 1680, after droughts, fires and the worst Indian war in New England's history, the ministers who met in synod listed the symptoms of 'declension': neglect of religion in church and family, intemperance, worldliness and lack of public spirit. Yet the process remained so gradual that the same themes could be preached for many years. 'It is too evident to be denied', said Samuel Whitman in another election sermon in 1714, 'that religion is on the wane among us . . . Is not religion degenerating into an empty form?'

Puritanism was too deeply rooted in the soil of New England to wither suddenly on the bough. The outward forms remained although the Puritan spirit was ebbing away. In 1680 Jasper Danckaerts, a member of a sect in the Dutch Reformed Church, visited his brethren who had settled in Maryland and Delaware. He then sailed with a Dutch companion to Boston to take ship for Holland. The captain of the vessel which brought them from New York entertained them politely at his house. It was Sunday, 'which it seems is somewhat strictly observed by these people, there was not much to do today', he wrote. On the following Friday, a fast day, they experienced their first Puritan service.

> We went into the church, where, in the first place, a minister made
> a prayer in the pulpit, of full two hours in length; after which an
> old minister delivered a sermon an hour long, and after that a

prayer was made, and some verses sung out of the Psalms. In the afternoon, three or four hours were consumed with nothing except prayers, three ministers relieving each other alternately; when one was tired, another went up into the pulpit. There was no more devotion than in other churches, and even less than at New York: no respect, no reverence; in a word, nothing but the name of Independents; and that was all . . .

On the following Sunday they heard sermons in three churches, the best of them by 'a very old man named Mr John Eliot', the celebrated 'Apostle to the Indians'. As they could not obtain his Bible in the Indian language from the Boston booksellers they walked next day to Roxbury to buy one from the author. Conversing partly in Latin and partly in English, Eliot told them he was seventy-seven years old and had been forty-eight years in these parts.

He deplored the decline of the church in New England, and especially in Boston, so that he did not know what would be the final result. We inquired how it stood with the Indians, and whether any good fruit had followed his work. Yes, much, he said, if we meant true conversion of the heart; for they had in various countries, instances of conversion, as they called it, and had seen it amounted to nothing at all; that they must not endeavour, like scribes and Pharisees, to make Jewish proseltyes, but true Christians. He could thank God, he continued, and God be praised for it, there were Indians whom he knew, who were truly converted of heart to God, and whose profession, he believed, was sincere.

The old minister accompanied them to the limits of Roxbury and bade them farewell.

John Eliot lived for another ten years, an example of the extraordinary longevity of many Puritans in New England. He confessed once to having a pleasant fear that those two dearest neighbours of his – John Cotton of Boston and Richard Mather of Dorchester – who had got safely to Heaven before him, would suspect him to be gone the wrong way because he stayed so long behind them. According to one who saw him die, 'his last breath smelt strong of Heaven'.

A visit to Harvard University failed to impress Jasper Danckaerts.

We went to it (he wrote) expecting to see something unusual, as it is the only college, or would-be academy of the Protestants in all America, but we found ourselves mistaken. In approaching the house we neither heard nor saw anything mentionable; but, going to the other side of the building, we heard noise enough in an upper room to lead my comrade to say, 'I believe they are engaged in disputation.' We entered and went up stairs, when a person met us, and requested us to walk in, which we did. We found there eight or ten young fellows, sitting around, smoking tobacco, with the smoke of which the room was so full, that you could hardly see; and the whole house smelt so strong of it that when I was going upstairs I said, 'It certainly must be also a tavern.' We excused ourselves, that we could speak English only a little, but understood Dutch or French well, which they did not. However, we spoke as well as we could. We inquired how many professors there were, and they replied not one, that there was not enough money to support one. We asked how many students there were. They said at first, thirty, and then came down to twenty; I afterwards understood there are probably not ten. They knew hardly a word of Latin, not one of them, so that my comrade could not converse with them. They took us to the library where there was nothing particular. We looked over it a little. They presented us with a glass of wine. This is all we ascertained there. The minister of the place goes there morning and evening to make prayer, and has charge over them; besides him, the students are under tutors or masters.

Before leaving Boston the Dutch traveller wrote his unflattering impressions of Puritan religion in this late stage of its story.

All their religion consists in observing Sunday, by not working or going into the taverns on that day; but the houses are worse than the taverns. No stranger or traveller can therefore be entertained on a Sunday, which begins at sunset on Saturday, and continues until the same time on Sunday. At these two hours you see all their countenances change. Saturday evening the constable goes round into all the taverns of the city for the purpose of stopping all noise and debauchery, which frequently causes him to stop his search, before his search causes the debauchery to stop. There is a penalty for cursing and swearing, such as they please to impose, the witnesses thereof being at liberty to insist upon it. Nevertheless you discover little difference between this and other places. Drinking and fighting occur there not less than elsewhere; and as to truth and true godliness, you must not expect more of them than of others.

*   *   *

249

A visitor such as Danckaerts could only form a superficial impression of Puritan New England, such as the quality of sermons and the observance of Sunday. In order to find out how the New England Puritans and their English cousins viewed life we can do no better than reconstruct their views and practices concerning love and marriage, for here we draw continually upon their legacy.

It is best to start with the young unmarried Puritan man and woman. The Puritan ideal for them both was chastity, and Milton was its most articulate champion. As a sensual youth he had felt the full force of sexual temptation. Why should not he give himself

> To sport with Amaryllis in the shade
> Or with the tangles of Neaera's hair?

His masque *Comus* is a verse sermon on chastity. Comus pleads the case of what we would call sexual intercourse before marriage, which he represents as freedom. The Lady defends chastity first on the level of natural reason. Then she rises with 'sacred vehemence' to propose the religious end of 'sun-clad' chastity as a visible sign of the Christian's faith in God. Submission to lust, she says, merely enslaves people under the specious promise of liberty:

> Love virtue, she alone is free,
> She can teach ye how to climb
> Higher than the sphery chime;
> Or, if virtue feeble were,
> Heaven itself would stoop to her.

When the Puritans established their holy commonwealth in New England they punished fornication, or sexual intercourse between unmarried couples, just as the Church of England continued to do at home. The standard penalty, a £10 fine or a public whipping, applied equally to both parties. But it invariably produced a strong feeling of guilt and a fear of general retribution in a young person reared in a Puritan home. 'By this sin', declared Tryal Pore before Middlesex County court in New England in 1656, 'I have not only done what I can to pull down judgement from the Lord on myself but also on the place where I live.'

Not all shared Milton's lofty Puritan idealism, but everyone agreed that fornication should be discouraged because it tended to produce bastards who could be financial burdens on the community. Young girls had a habit of 'laying' a child upon a complete stranger. In order to protect innocent men and to identify who should be held financially responsible midwives used to choose the time at the baby's delivery when the mother was at her weakest and then 'charge it upon her to tell whose the child was'.

The Puritans in New England were realists who knew that courtship included more than words. In order to give a couple privacy and yet keep them warm during the long, bitter winter evenings, they allowed the practice of 'bundling' or 'tarrying'. In the foreroom or parlour, which had no fire, the couple would lie in two blankets sewn together down the outer sides and middle – in effect a double sleeping bag. Here, away from the hubbub of the kitchen, the young people could talk and kiss.

When it came to the choice of a marriage partner the Puritans were guided not by romantic passion but by rational love. The affections, those 'underservants of the soul', had to be kept in their place. Feelings should be commanded by the will and guided by reason. The Puritans would recognize the modern cult of romantic love as a debased or secular form of their belief. When love is worshipped as an end in itself it becomes demonic. Thus love in advance was by no means essential. Far from being the cause of marriage the Puritans saw love as more the product of it. They entered matrimony not primarily for an existing love, though they obviously took such feelings into account, but because they judged that they *would* love each other.

Normally the man or woman decided to marry without a particular person in mind. In choosing a suitable person the Puritans desired to be equally yoked in terms of social rank and wealth. Women tended more than men to marry above their class. As in the case of most major decisions the Puritans employed reason. They debated the pros and cons until the decision emerged. The New England poet Michael Wrigglesworth addressed just such a rational proposal in a letter to Miss Avery. He gave her two reasons for marrying him. First, after their short meeting, 'my thoughts and heart have been toward you ever since'. Secondly, she is 'the most suitable person'. Then he raised two possible objections and answered them.

Sometimes the couple were swayed more by their friends than reason. Hugh Peter, that emotional, clownish and melancholic man, approached his second marriage to a widow, Mrs Deliverance Sheffield of Boston, with many 'fluctuations'. Another lady in his Salem congregation, Ruth Ames – daughter of the celebrated theologian William Ames – also desired to marry him. The experienced widow countered by pretending disinterest. John Endecott wrote to Winthrop describing her stratagems in the language of a Shakespeare comedy: 'I find she now begins to play her part, and, if I mistake not, you will see him as greatly in love with her (if she will but hold of a little) as ever she was with him; but he conceals it what he can as yet.' In his anguish Peter wrote to Winthrop, whose son had married his stepdaughter, asking for advice – 'Let me not be a fool in Israel'. But Winthrop had often told him he could not leave her now. The unwitting suitor desperately looked for some spiritual assurance to desist or continue. If only England would call for his unmarried services. . . . But eventually Peter martyred himself to honour.

After a period of trial or espousal, corresponding to our engagement, the wedding took place. For the Puritans marriage was an ordinance of God, but it was not a sacrament. It was a natural state, but particular persons received a specific gift of grace to transform it into a spiritual union. It rested upon a covenant, a mutual engagement between two parties. As it involved questions of ownership, inheritance and residence the Puritans regarded marriage as a civil matter. In New England the civil magistrates continued to perform all weddings until 1686, when the ministers reclaimed their traditional function. They normally took place in the bride's house. As for the service itself, any fitting words from Scripture and prayers would do. Although wanton dancing and riotous merry-making were forbidden under the law in Massachusetts, feasting, wedding cakes and sackposset or rum added to the natural mirth and joy.

In the Puritan imagination the ideal relationship between a godly husband and his wife was a complementary one. In more traditional thinking the man exercised 'the priesthood of all believers' in his family by occupying some sort of intermediary position between God and 'the weaker vessel', his more practical, earth-bound wife. As Milton wrote, 'he for God only, she for God in him'. The relationship of Adam and Eve gave Biblical authority to this traditional assumption of male leadership (although the ancient makers of that myth were probably only trying to explain the origin of what they observed in human society). The Puritan wife looked to her husband for headship and guidance:

> O thou for whom
> And from whom I was formed flesh of thy flesh
> And without whom I am to no end, my guide
> And head!

The Puritans insisted that in heaven all relationships in this life no longer continue in the same manner. As Thomas Hooker told his Connecticut congregation, in heaven the king remembers not his crown, the husband his wife or the father his child. The only relation which endures beyond this life is that which exists between a believing man and his final end, God in Christ. This was 'the only marriage that cannot be dissolved'.

In consequence a man 'ought to make God his immediate end', not his wife or children. The Puritans distrusted the uxorious man, for he had allowed his love to become inordinate. Immoderate grief after a bereavement was also interpreted as a symptom of inordinate love. Yet if there was no marriage in heaven the believing couple would find all their joys restored, enlarged and shared in the wider communion of saints. Because they were human, Puritans still looked for a 'journey's end in lovers meeting'. Richard Baxter, who married late in life Margaret Charlton, a Shropshire woman in his congregation some twenty-one years his junior, said that she told him 'oft of her hopeful persuasions that we should live together in Heaven'.

The Puritan emphasis upon the community emerges in our time in secular clothes in the sense of growing unease at the exclusiveness of modern marriage, the way in which it cuts off or divides the 'nuclear family' from wider society. Because of the Puritan within us we instinctively feel that it is wrong to invest too much significance in marriage, however happy our particular experience of it may be.

Characteristically and persistently, Puritans struggled to know the ends of activities or practices, the purpose they served in the order which God had created. They were practical Aristotelians, not ascetics. The Puritan could enjoy a good bed because he knew that the end of all sleep and rest was refreshment for activity. To love sleep and ease for their own sake was to mistake their end. Meat and drink existed not for the purpose of pleasure, but so that we might serve God better. If a man's mind delights in eating and drinking for their own sake, he has succumbed to the lust of the flesh. In enjoying good things the Puritan kept in mind why they had been ordained.

In marriage the purpose was now procreation, now companionship, depending on the chapter in the story. The Puritans put much more emphasis than their contemporary churchmen on friendship in marriage. They based this interpretation on God's wish to remedy Adam's loneliness in Eden. In an age of a growing self-consciousness, a sense of possessing unique individuality, more men experienced the reverse face of individualism, which is loneliness. Marriage seemed to be God's gracious solution to that problem. But this emphasis upon friendship as the primary end represented a radical shift from the traditional position, and brought some unforeseen consequences which will be described later.

The Puritans accepted that fallen human nature made it difficult for men to order their loves to proper objects and in proper proportions as all Christian thinkers since St Paul and St Augustine had recommended. Puritan preachers, the first marriage counsellors, told their flock not to expect too much of each other in marriage, for 'you marry a child of Adam'. Margaret found that Richard Baxter possessed an impatient temper of mind and habit of sharp speaking which she called his 'over-selfish querellousness'. To cope with such faults the pastors advised the common virtues of goodness, kindness, patience, meekness and a forgiving spirit. 'Look not for perfection in your relation,' said one preacher to a couple, 'God reserves that for another state where marriage is not needed.' Yet a Puritan spouse should endeavour to gather up the seeds of irritation before they could grow like rank weeks in the soil of human depravity. Who would want a wife who allowed herself to become 'sullen, pouty, so cross that she'll scarce eat or speak sometimes'? Love remained always as a solemn obligation to God as well as a mutual duty. As Hugh Peter wrote to his daughter, the conjugal yoke 'must still be lin'd with more love to make the draught easy'.

Being a woman, Peter added to his daughter, she should keep at home and not be like the squirrels in the New England woods, 'leaping from tree to tree, and bough to bough'. Although wives and mothers for natural reasons did spend much of their time in the home, the Puritans did much to make straight the way for the emancipation of women. In New England the majority of the members of the church were women, and this participation opened new doors for them. In the home, their main sphere of influence, women had in effect equal authority with their husbands over the children and the servants.

Like any parents they saw their first duty as providing food, shelter and protection. The Puritan magistrates took a stern view of any cruelty or neglect involving children. In September 1660 the Essex County court admonished Francis Urselton and his wife 'for leaving their children alone in the night in a lonely house, far from neighbours, after having been warned of it'. Puritan parents reasoned with their children, prayed with them, and taught by word and example the godly life. They used homely language. As 'the little needle will draw a long tail of thread after it', wrote Hugh Peter for his girl, so 'little sins may be followed with great sorrow', but a little grain of faith like mustard seed will do wonders. For all its glory the world has a principle of decay in it – 'dote not on it, my poor child'.

A tender sympathy often informed the relations of parents and children. 'Diverse children have their different natures,' wrote Anne Bradstreet, 'some are like flesh which nothing but salt will keep from putrefaction; some again like tender fruits that are best preserved with sugar.' Unfortunately the schools set up in America perpetuated at first the English tendency to use the birch rod far too liberally.

Sometimes a bright schoolboy could help his less gifted fellow. Richard Mulcaster, High Master of St Paul's at the end of Queen Elizabeth's reign, possessed a pedagogue's sense of humour. Having bent one boy over to cane him he looked up at the class in his 'merry conceit' and said, 'I ask the banns of matrimony between this boy his buttocks of such parish on the one side and Lady Birch of the parish on the other side, and if any man can shew any lawful cause why they should not be joined together let him speak, for it is his last time of asking.' An intelligent boy stood up and said, 'Master, I forbid the banns.' Mulcaster stood silent for a moment, and then said, 'Yea, sirrah, and why so?' 'Because all the parties are not agreed,' replied the boy. To his credit Mulcaster spared them both.

Puritan parents in New England seem to have modified the English characteristic of toughness towards school boys. The Dorchester school rules in 1645 accepted 'the rod of correction' as an ordinance of God, but gave parents the right to 'friendly and lovingly' expostulate with the master who used the stick too much. Should they disagree, the case could be referred to the wardens. 'The greatest cruelty of the English consists in permitting evil rather than committing it', a German visitor to England had written in 1694. At least the Puritans set their face against cruelty to children.

The English characteristic of aggressiveness also surfaced in the home, especially in the ill-treatment of wives. Under English law it is still difficult for the law to intervene in what is deemed to be a domestic affair. By contrast the Puritan government in New England held it to be a crime for a husband to strike his wife or command her to do anything contrary to the laws of God. The Plymouth magistrates punished one man 'for abusing his wife by kicking her from a stool into the fire' and another for 'drawing his wife in an uncivil manner on the snow'. The court sentenced John Dunham to a whipping for 'abusive carriage towards his wife in continual tyrannising over her, and in particular for his late abusive and uncivil carriage in endeavouring to beat her in a debased manner'. At the request of Dunham's wife the sentence was suspended. With commendable regard for equality Puritan magistrates also protected the husband. In 1655 Joan Miller of Taunton appeared before a court charged with 'beating and reviling her husband, and egging her children to help her, bidding them knock him on the head, and wishing his victuals might choke him'.

Wilful desertion constituted a ground for divorce, but the more common one was adultery, 'that most foul and filthy sin . . . the disease of marriage'. Although the Puritans in both England and New England passed laws based upon the Old Testament making the offence a capital one, the death sentence was carried out very rarely and only in the most flagrant cases. The usual punishment was a severe whipping and having to wear the cloth letters A.D. sewn upon one's upper garments. A double standard did operate here, for a married man would not be charged with an infidelity committed with a single woman. The chief concern was to prevent a woman from being unfaithful to her husband, for that not only violated marriage but also threatened the social order.

For the vast majority of Puritan gentlemen or ministers, as opposed to those ordinary English folk who lived under them in New England and swore allegiance to the laws of Massachusetts Bay, divorce for any other reason than adultery was unthinkable. Not long after their marriage Hugh Peter's wife Deliverance went mad. In deep despair he left her and their baby daughter in New England while he sailed home to serve as a chaplain in the New Model Army. Years later, when awaiting execution in the Tower, he counselled his daughter to bear in mind that affliction keeps us awake 'as the thorn to the singing bird', and conscience calls us to labour 'as the day the lark, and the lark the husbandmen'. Driven by the thorn in his side of a tragic marriage, Hugh Peter threw all his extraordinary nervous energy into work. Under Cromwell, whom he served as a popular spokesman, he rose to be a chaplain of the Council of State and contemporaries dubbed him the unofficial 'Vicar General and Metropolitan of the Independents both in New and Old England'. In July 1654 Roger Williams visited him in the suite of rooms in Whitehall Palace which had once belonged to Archbishop Laud. They met in the prelate's book-lined library. In his letter describing the visit Williams told John Winthrop that Peter now 'cries out against New English rigidities and persecutions', especially their unchristian dealing with him in excommunicating his distracted wife (on the grounds that she must be possessed by the Devil). 'Surely, Sir, the most holy Lord is most wise in all the trials he exercises his people with,' wrote Williams. Hugh Peter 'told me that his affliction from his wife stirred him up to action abroad, and when success tempted him to pride, the bitterness in his bosom comforts was a cooler and a bridle to him.'

At Cromwell's funeral Hugh Peter walked side-by-side in the procession with John Milton, a man who had responded very differently to the affliction of an unhappy marriage. Milton had not only dedicated himself to poetry but exemplified in his life the themes of his pen, such as chastity. 'He who would not be frustrate of his hope to write well hereafter in laudable things,' he wrote in 1642, 'ought himself to be a true poem; that is, a composition and pattern of the best and honourablest things.' The following year, when he was thirty-five, he decided to marry and chose as his bride Mary Powell, the seventeen-year-old daughter of a Royalist in Oxfordshire, whom he had known as a girl. Within a month of their wedding Mary left him and returned home. Despite the Civil War which now raged, Milton struggled to reconcile his Puritan ideals and his sad experience with the existing teaching on divorce. In his book on divorce he argued for a new doctrine and discipline. The Westminster Assembly replied by demanding that Milton's book should be publicly burnt.

Milton wrote with feeling about the plight of a chaste man, with little experience of women, who marries because the friends of the bride persuade him that 'acquaintance' will breed love. Such a 'sober man, respecting modesty and hoping for the best, often meets, if not with a body impenetrable, yet often with a mind to all other due conversation inaccessible, and to all the more estimable and superior purposes of matrimony useless and almost lifeless'. Milton argued that even an adulterous wife could be forgiven and taken back, but nothing could be done about 'indisposition, unfitness or contrariety of mind'. Surely here was 'a greater reason for divorce than natural frigidity'.

Milton's concept of marriage is deeply Puritan. A woman's

rights are the same as a man's. Authority rests in the husband, except where he acknowledges that his wife is more prudent and intelligent than himself, when 'a superior and more natural law comes in, that the wiser should govern the less wise, whether male or female'. But marriage is above all a spiritual affair, 'a divine institution joining man and woman in a love fitly dispos'd to the helps and comforts of domestic life'. Milton puts the social end of marriage first, prizing above the procreation of children 'the apt and cheerful conversation of man with woman to refresh him against the evil of a solitary life'. That 'rational burning' for a companion has its remedy in marriage. It follows that a sexual relationship without the marriage of true minds is worthless. The only course then is to divorce and remarry.

Influential though Milton's view of divorce has been in our own times, he could not prevail against the overwhelming conservative opposition from all quarters to a change in the Christian law. At the end of the Civil War the Powell family, ruined by the King's defeat, asked Milton to take Mary back. He relented and she joined him at a house in the Barbican, where she bore him three daughters over the next few years. Shortly afterwards Mary's father died, and Milton's mother-in-law came to live with him bringing her remaining eight children! In 1652 Mary died. Then his second wife died in childbirth. Four years later, with blindness coming upon him, Milton married Catherine Woodcock. Through 'knowledge of good bought dear by knowing ill' he had made an excellent choice. After Catherine died, also in childbirth, he recalled her in a dream which inspired a moving sonnet. He declared his hope that he would see again in heaven 'my late espoused saint'

> . . . vested all in white, pure as her mind.
> Her face was veiled; yet to my fancied sight
> Love, sweetness, goodness, in her person shined
> So clear as in no face with more delight.
> But, oh! as to embrace me she inclined,
> I waked, she fled, and day brought back my night.

Ultimately the hope of all Puritan married couples centred upon their 'wedding day' with the divine Bridegroom. For in union with him they trusted that they would discover new depths of communion, both with each other and all the saints in heaven. When one spouse died the other waited eagerly for their greater wedding day. At Colworth Church in Bedfordshire there is a monument erected in 1641 to Sir William Dyer and his wife, Lady Katherine. He died first and she wrote this verse, where is carved in marble behind his effigy:

> My dearest dust, could not thy hasty day
> Afford thy drowszy patience leave to stay
> One hower longer: so that we might either
> Sate up, or gone to bedd together?
> But since they finisht labour hath possest
> Thy weary limbs with early rest,
> Enjoy it sweetly: and thy widdowe bride
> Shall soone repose her by thy slumbring side.
> Whose business, now, is only to prepare
> My nightly dress, and call to prayre:
> Mine eyes wax heavy and ye day growes cold.
> Draw, draw ye closed curtaynes: and make roome:
> My dear, my dearest dust; I come, I come.

*   *   *

The Puritan virtues in family life survived longest not in busy ports like Boston but in the small villages (or towns, as they were called) set deep in the wilderness away from the coast. Haverhill in the northern part of Massachusetts Bay was such a Puritan frontier town. It was situated on the juncture of the Great River, the Merrimac, with the Little River. An Indian village called Pentucket – 'the place by the winding river' – had stood there. Nathaniel Ward had planned the settlement for his son John and his son-in-law. A deed whereby John Ward and three others paid three pounds and ten shillings to Passaconoway's tribe for a tract eight miles west from the Little River, six miles east and six miles north still exists, dated 15 November 1642. The place was named after Nathaniel's birthplace, a market-town in Suffolk. Some months earlier the first sermon was preached on the site under a great spreading oak tree. The church when it was formed consisted of only eight men and six women. John Ward accepted the call to be their minister. His was the twenty-sixth church in Massachusetts, Haverhill being the twenty-third settlement.

The setting of Haverhill possessed a wild natural beauty. The colonists grew English herbs and flowers in their gardens, hearts-ease and mignonette, rue and rosemary, while the trees in their orchards bore fine cooking and eating apples. But the severe winters and disease took a fearsome toll. Thirteen children died in the hamlet before 1644, and twenty-seven more in the next twenty years. In 1648 the settlers erected a small log meeting house with no gallery. Every Sunday a drum or horn summoned the congregation to church, the men carrying their muskets. They would pause to read laws or public notices posted on the church door. The colonists also perpetuated an even more ancient English custom of nailing the heads of marauding wolves on the front of the church.

As the decades passed the services in this meeting house hardly changed. In 1694 a meeting house twice the size, 50 by 42 feet, was erected. Haverhill had become a straggling town of some 100 houses, with six garrison houses for defence against the Indians.

On the committee appointed to view the new meeting house was Nathaniel Saltonstall, one of Sir Richard Saltonstall's grandsons. His father, Richard, had engaged in New England politics. He actively sought a wider spread of power among the magistrates, opposing its relative concentration in the hands of Winthrop, Dudley and Endecott. Yet if the Puritan enterprise in New England inspired him its accomplishments seem to have left him as dissatisfied as his father. In 1649 he had returned to England with his wife and three daughters. With his father he served the Commonwealth in various capacities. After his father died in 1661 Richard went back to Ipswich in New England. He went home again for eight years, and then returned once more to Ipswich. Finally, aged seventy-seven, he sailed for England in 1687 and died in Lancashire seven years later. And so Nathaniel was the first Saltonstall to take root in New England. At Haverhill he fulfilled the destiny of founding a family in America originally envisaged by his grandfather, Sir Richard, in the reign of King Charles I.

We can imagine Nathaniel attending town meetings in the new meeting house, debating with his neighbours such matters as land divisions, applications to join the town, the state of local industries and the minister's salary. John Ward preached in the frontier hamlet until the year before his death in 1693 at the ripe old age of eighty-eight – the longevity of the Puritans was a source of much pride to them. Benjamin Rolfe of Newbury accepted the call to take his place. Nathaniel saw him mount the pulpit Sunday by Sunday, dressed in long black robes and his white preaching bands, black stockings and silver-buckled shoes. During the service the gentlemen would be approached first by the deacons with the collection plate, followed by the elders, all married men and single persons. After the afternoon service the congregation would attend

Dear New England, Dearest Land To Me!

to the trial of offenders or hear the penitent confessions of transgressors. Only a few years earlier John Hutchins' wife was admonished for wearing a silk hood, while two daughters of Hannah Bosworth were fined ten shillings each for wearing silk. These sumptuary laws, imported from Europe, were intended primarily to maintain the outward distinctions between the social orders, not for religious purposes.

One topic of conversation increasingly dominated the conversation as the Puritan families ate their dinners on the grass and fed their horses between services each Sunday – the Indian menace. Except for the troubled time of King Philip's War the frontier town had enjoyed unbroken peace. Now anxiety mounted. In 1690 the town meeting even debated whether or not to abandon Haverhill altogether. The inhabitants sensed the coming storm. The Puritan experience included coping with the constant fear that one day the Indians would swoop down upon them.

On 15 March 1696 the Indians struck at Haverhill. Shortly after dawn painted war parties attacked and burnt nine houses, killing twenty-seven people including thirteen children. Thomas Duston's house stood two miles north-west of the meeting house. He was riding in a far part of his farm when he caught sight of some armed Indians in the woods. He galloped back to the house and seized his musket. His wife was still in bed, having given birth to her twelfth child a few days earlier. Duston hustled away his seven surviving children towards the garrison house of Onesiphorus Marsh. To protect his family he rode back between them and the Indians, dismounted and, resting his musket on the saddle, he opened fire.

Meanwhile some of the Indians reached the open door of Duston's house. Mary Nelf, the nurse, barely had time to rip some woven cloth off the loom in which to wrap the baby before the Indian braves burst in. They seized her and then dragged Hannah Duston from bed. Whooping and shouting, the braves then fired the house with torches they lit from the fire in the brick kitchen fireplace. Soon the war party had regained the cover of the silent forest. The baby began to cry loudly in Mary's arms. An Indian warrior snatched it from her arms and dashed it to death against a tree.

After a nightmare journey the Indian war party camped on a small island in the Merrimac. There the two women had an opportunity to talk to Samuel Leonardson, a boy captured at Worcester in the autumn of 1695, aged twelve. His mother had died of anxiety and grief. He explained that once they reached the main camp the women would be made to run the gauntlet naked before being sold into captivity. Having digested this information Hannah resolved on action. She told the boy to ask the Indians how they killed a person with a single blow and took scalp locks. Samuel came back an hour or two later with the answers. Just before dawn Hannah, aided by Mary and Samuel, put their new knowledge to grim use. They crept up to the sleeping braves and killed all of them with sheath knives. Only one wounded squaw escaped and they also spared an Indian boy. Gathering provisions from the wigwams they loaded them into a canoe. Having scuttled the other canoes they began paddling down the river as day broke. After a few hundred yards Hannah turned back. She had forgotten to scalp the dead Indians. Later she and her husband used the bounty money they received for the scalps in order to rebuild their house.

Mrs Hannah Duston died in 1736, aged seventy-nine. In 1724 she had applied for admission as a church member. For evidence of saving religious experience she cast her mind back to those terrible days in the hands of the Indians. 'I am thankful for my captivity,' she wrote, 't'was the comfortablest time I ever had.'

*   *   *

What became of the Puritan churches in America? For a while the 'elect' in New England resisted Baxter's conclusion that 'saints should not dream of a Kingdom of this world, or flatter themselves with the hopes of a golden age or reigning over the ungodly.' But eventually the Puritan churches in America succumbed to the same general influences as their brethren in England. For the English nation on both sides of the Atlantic experienced a definite shift of consciousness which gradually cooled the holy fever of Puritanism. Secular concerns – national expansion, commercial rivalry, worldly success – came to the forefront of men's minds. Reason and toleration triumphed as ideas in both countries. Without the benefit of any organization beyond schools, the highest values of Greece and Rome, centred upon an elevated view of man and the supremacy of reason, eroded the ramparts of Reformation orthodoxy.

The Catholic Church had fought the Arian heresy and Calvin followed suit by burning Servetus. But the ferment in England hatched after the Civil War among the Puritans a new sect, the forerunners of the Unitarians, who rejected Christ's divinity on

Biblical grounds. John Biddle graduated in 1638 at Magdalen Hall, Oxford, that nest of Puritans, before becoming a schoolmaster in Gloucester where he wrote his first tract 'against the deity of the Holy Ghost'. After 1652 his adherents, known variously as Biddellians, Socinians or Unitarians, began to meet for regular Sunday worship. To save him from more imprisonment at the hands of Parliament, Cromwell took a leaf out of New England's book and banished Biddle to the Scilly Isles. Returning to London after the Restoration he was again sent to prison, where he died.

Eventually the Unitarians moved the grounds of their faith from the Bible to reason itself, although they did not entirely abandon the claim of Scriptural authority. Reason and conscience became the ultimate authorities. In the eighteenth century Unitarian views spread widely among the dissenting congregations, notably the English Presbyterians. In America the first Unitarian congregation met at King's Chapel, Boston. Yet William Ellery Channing, perhaps the greatest American Unitarian theologian, retained the Puritan emphasis on church, not sect. He regarded himself as belonging 'not to a sect, but to the community of free minds'. Ralph Waldo Emerson was the son of a Boston Unitarian minister and became one himself for a time before he developed his own version of the Unitarian faith. When he visited William Wordsworth in the Lake District the two men fell into a heated discussion about Unitarianism. By then many Congregational churches in New England had accepted this thorough-going brand of rationalized Puritanism. During the nineteenth century Unitarianism remained the chief cultural and social influence in Boston and the other major towns. The First Church of Salem is a symbol of the triumph of this tradition. Built upon its present site in 1835, it proclaims on a board to passers-by that it is America's oldest continuous Protestant church. Gathered in 1629, it numbered Roger Williams and Hugh Peter among its ministers. It now belongs to the Unitarian and Universal faith.

As the New England churches tackled dwindling numbers by gradually lowering the requirements for church membership, so revival movements sprang up as reactions. Frenzied enthusiasts such as James Davenport in the eighteenth century religious revival known as the Great Awakening hurled themselves around the pulpit as they preached hell-fire and damnation in order to win souls, an approach totally alien to the Puritan tradition. Davenport claimed that he could immediately detect the elect from the damned: he called the former 'brothers' and the latter 'neighbours'. Jonathan Williams, later head of Princeton College, assured thousands of hearers that the long-awaited millennium would shortly dawn in New England. For years afterwards itinerant preachers proclaimed the imminence of the New Jerusalem and urged men and women to walk up the sawdust trail of salvation.

If the non-conformists in England and the later Congregational churches in New England stand in the same relation to Puritanism as vinegar does to wine, then the popular fundamentalist revival movements taste more like the dregs. In America it is far too late in the day to bolt the door against the universal and humanist spirit emanating from the Renaissance. Religion has to live with reason or die.

Both George Whitefield and John Wesley preached in America. In his attempt to reform the Church of England from within Wesley continued the main Puritan English tradition. But for an historical accident the Puritans might have been called Methodists, for methodical was a term for preciseness in living. In 1605 Marston poked fun at the word 'methodical' in the *Dutch Courtezan*. Mrs Mulligrub appears as a Puritan. She is against smoking tobacco, she says. 'I can tell you so methodically. Methodically! I wonder where I got that word? Oh! Sir Aminadab Ruth bade me kiss him methodically.' Wesley's Methodists held no new doctrines: they emphasized the practical side of faith. The only qualification for a potential member was a desire to save his soul. The movement soon spread widely in America.

The destiny of the Puritans in America could be further described in terms of their grand-daughter churches, or those national movements – such as the abolition of slavery or temperance campaigns – which drew inspiration from them. But the really interesting story lies between the lines of modern American social history. It centres upon the Puritan who lives within us today. Many of the values which still inform our beliefs and attitudes today – notably in work and marriage – stem from the common Puritan heritage of England and America.

12

The Puritan Within Us

Measured by generations, the Puritan age is not all that remote from us. Therefore it is not surprising that Puritan values and attitudes survive today. For the epic story of the Puritans had no dramatic or sudden end: the river just fades away into the sands, seeping down to the water-table which still feeds the springs of our values today.

Perhaps the best starting-point is the Puritan ethic of work. The English adopted and made peculiarly their own the doctrine of vocation as expounded by Luther. The Christian must work hard in his calling in the world, for his labour is the means whereby the love of Christ in him can reach out to his neighbour. Luther and the Puritans assumed, of course, that men were Christians and that they lived in natural communities, such as villages, where they knew their neighbours personally. Over the centuries, however, religion faded into the background in men's minds and secular concerns moved to the forefront of consciousness. Cities grew in size, drawing in labour from the rural communities. As labourers produced goods for people they did not know, toiling for long hours in factories to make profits for their employers, they experienced a growing alienation from work and even from society itself.

Among the middle classes, the heirs of the Reformation and Renaissance tradition through education and home upbringing, the sense of vocation survives in more-or-less secular forms. The Puritan virtues of industry, thrift, sobriety, frugality, reliability, temperance and punctuality are still there, but they serve social, material or worldly ends. Religion and economics both sanction such virtues. Failure to recognize and use one's talents is felt to be a sin against oneself and society. This restless desire to serve others by employing one's abilities to the full is the hallmark of the Puritan attitude to work. As Richard Sibbes said, 'Christianity is a busy trade.' Laziness or idleness is unacceptable. The Puritan in modern man seeks to be constantly active. He feels an inward sense of duty – 'stern daughter of the voice of God', as Wordsworth called it – which drives him to be busy. Benjamin Franklin wrote the creed of the self-made man in one sentence: 'God helps those who help themselves.'

There are more specific illustrations from the world of business which show how Puritan practices have been successfully transferred to secular ends. Women first learned shorthand to record Puritan sermons. The Puritan preachers exhorted men to study how they spent time in order to make better use of it. 'Time is precious', said Baxter, 'Lord give me skill and wisdom to redeem it.' Sir Matthew Hale, a Puritan judge in Restoration England, sat down each morning and planned his day carefully. Baxter thought that six hours sleep should suffice any man. Franklin recommended a disciplined use of time for achieving wealth: 'Remember that time is money.' Today there are business courses specifically on the management of time. For secular ends the teachers seek to arouse the same awareness of the shortness and value of time in today's managers as the Puritan preachers induced in their congregations, while the sands in the hour-glass at their elbow slipped away to illustrate their point.

Yet the competitive qualities – the desire to move up the economic and social ladder, the obsession with winning – are not traceable to the Puritan spirit. One manifestation of that win-or-lose attitude – making as much profit from one's neighbours as possible – struck them as both unchristian and immoral. Indeed, the 'Puritan work ethic' is too often made a scapegoat for modern qualities and ideas which the Puritans actually abhorred and discouraged. The common idea that Puritans looked upon success, especially material riches, as sure evidence of their election is well off the mark. If they fell into that trap, which savoured of salvation through works, their preachers quickly pointed out the error. 'This life is the time of striving, of running, of acting,' said John Preston, 'it is not the time for being rewarded.'

The Puritan belief in God's providence, however, meant that they constantly translated what befell them into the language of God's gracious dealings with his children. As Cromwell wrote to his cousin Hammond in November 1648, 'If you will seek, seek to know the mind of God in all that chain of Providence, whereby God brought you thither. . . . My dear friend, let us look unto providences; surely they mean somewhat. They hang so together; have been so constant, clear and uncluded.' Yet in 1649 some forty-seven Presbyterian ministers wrote to Cromwell and his officers to point out to them that military victories signify little. For 'God does not approve the practice of whatsoever his providence does permit.' If it was not easy to interpret the complex pattern of victories and defeats, gains and losses, in the wars, it was just as hard to do so in the multifarious activities of a busy, tumultous peace.

Because the Puritan was taught to think clearly about ends and also to discern his own motives by introspection he was in no danger of confusion about money. God, not wealth, was the true end of work. 'God makes us rich, by being diligent in our callings,' said John Preston, 'using it to his glory and more good, he does cast more riches upon us. Man makes himself rich when he makes riches the end of his calling, and does not expect them as a reward that comes from God.' It all depends upon keeping the 'right uses' of money in mind. To be more effective in doing good, a man has a duty to increase his estate. Thus a desire to be rich, providing it is not inordinate, can share the bed with faith.

The Puritan attitude to work and material success reflects the paradox at the heart of Luther's teaching about vocation and work. 'There is another combination of virtues strangely mixed in every lively holy Christian, and that is, diligence in worldly business, and yet deadness to the world; such a mystery as none can read, but they that know it,' said John Cotton in a sermon. The godly merchant will take all his opportunities, lose no occasions 'and bestir himself for profit,' but at the same time 'be a man dead-hearted to the world.' Because his heart is not set on material things 'he can tell what to do with his estate when he has got it'. Such is the holy worldliness of the true Christian. But when religion decays, what is left but worldliness? The paradoxes of faith collapse into mere contradictions. Writing of Plymouth Colony, though his words apply to New England, Cotton Mather concluded: 'Religion begat prosperity and the daughter devoured the mother.'

If the Puritans resolved to work 'as ever in my great Task-Master's eye' they did not ignore the need for recreation. The general calling to be a Christian took precedence over any particular calling. If the first should ever demand it, the second must be surrendered. Thus they were responsible more by accident than design for the modern obsession with work. Work served religious and social ends; it was not an end itself. Apart from banned pastimes, such as card-playing or dice, there were plenty of harmless activities for recreation. Together with the sports and games they brought with them, the New Englanders adopted, for example, skating and sleigh-riding from their Dutch neighbours.

The Puritans practised a rigid Jewish form of sabbatarianism because they took the Old Testament seriously. The Jewish religious laws reflect experience and common sense. The Puritan within us still values having one day a week which is a genuine break from the rest of the week's pattern. A quiet day once a week makes sense in terms of mental and physical health, which is our way of saying that it accords with God's law.

*   *   *

Our present attitudes owe a great deal to the Puritans as far as relationships between the sexes, and especially marriage, is concerned. The myth that the Puritans were prudish or condemned sex should be dismissed once and for all. They could not bear to remain unmarried for long. One Puritan widow remarried within twenty-four hours of her husband's decease. But they did set their face against sexual relations outside marriage.

It is difficult to capture the particular ethos of a marriage between two Puritans beyond saying that it tended to be a deep union of spirit and mind as well as body. Both man and woman valued this spiritual companionship. The husband was accepted as the natural leader, but on the spiritual and often intellectual levels the Puritan wife thought of herself as his equal. 'Souls have no sexes,' preached Robert Bolton. At the core of their union lay their communion with Christ, who was both within them and in Heaven. As they looked daily towards God and approached him on their life's pilgrimage, so they grew closer to each other.

The Puritans placed much weight on friendship, but it was eclipsed in their eyes by marriage. Hugh Peter urged his daughter to seek a 'soul-friend'. More important, he expected her to become such an 'experienced Christian friend' herself to her husband. 'If such a one you can find, you shall enjoy their experiences freely, you shall constantly be carried to God in their prayers, you shall have sympathy and help in your trouble,' he wrote. 'To such open your heart clearly, who will never upbraid you for confessions; and know when foundations shake, you will need a master-builder or workman. Such is a good friend and wife.'

Whatever their religious views, many people seek for themselves and their children this kind of marriage. The theological language in which the Puritan couples expressed their love may have become less common. But people seek a marriage based upon shared values and interests. Even beyond that, the Puritan within us looks in marriage for a certain almost indefinable quality of love. Such marriages were commonplace among the Puritans. They were grounded in a union not of this world but of the world to come. In the first important book of poems written in America young Anne Bradstreet, the daughter of Thomas Dudley, could pen these words:

TO MY DEAR AND LOVING HUSBAND.
If ever two were one, then surely we.
If ever man were lov'd by wife, then thee;
If ever wife was happy in a man,
Compare with me ye women if you can.
I prize they love more than whole mine of gold,
Or all the riches that the East doth hold.
My love is such that rivers cannot quench,
Nor ought but love from thee, give recompence.
Thy love is such I can no way repay,
The heavens reward thee manifold I pray.
Then while we live, in love lets so persevere,
That when we live no more, we may live ever.

In our own day Milton's incipient Puritan doctrine of divorce has been pushed to the limits and beyond. One Baptist minister in America is on record for having married twenty-four times; each time he tired of his bride! Such absurdities are far from the Puritan spirit. But divorce on the grounds of what we would call incompatibility did seem to be a rational corollary of the Puritan view of marriage, at least to Milton. As modern man seems to possess a less sure hope of enjoying the communion of saints in heaven, it is not surprising that many resort to the divorce courts to remedy paradise lost.

It is comparatively easy to dissolve an unhappy marriage today, but more divorce does not necessarily mean better marriages. The decline of religion may account in part for this loss of quality in marriage. Conversely, secular marriages may cumulatively detract from our understanding of God. For the Puritan's experience of marriage helped them to know God not as some inscrutable, distant, almighty potentate, but as Father and Husband. Increase Mather could call God the 'wisest and richest Bridegroom' – an image beloved of the English Puritans. Perhaps we might add Bride as well. Had not John Donne written of his Anne:

The admiring her my mind did whet,
To seek thee Lord, as streams do show the head.

269

The Puritan within us is often mistaken as a philistine. In fact the Puritans were far from being hostile to culture. With respect to the arts it is not my intention to cover them with whitewash, a substance they applied so liberally to the medieval wallpaintings of English churches. They would wish their portrait to be painted 'warts and all'. They were certainly iconoclasts. In 1642 Parliament ordered the defacing of any person of the Trinity in churches or church yards. A brief tour of the churches of East Anglia alone will show how wildly William Dowsing and his troopers exceeded their orders. Fortunately they spared the chief glory of the region, the medieval stained glass in King's College Chapel, Cambridge. But in fifty days Dowsing smashed his way through 150 old churches. In one day his men broke 1000 windows and pictures, oak figures of the twelve apostles and twenty cherubim. In Blythburgh Church the floor tiles are cracked where the troopers' horses were stabled for the night; the great angels on the painted beams of the soaring roof still bear the wounds inflicted by musket shot. Yet the church has a wonderful simplicity. Clear glass windows and walls white from floor to roof give an unforgettable impression of space and light.

Where the Puritans worked against the grain of English national character they made little headway. They may be forgiven for opposing much of Elizabethan drama, but the English revealed a genius for this particular art form. Milton, who could recognize great poetry when he met it, praised 'my Shakespeare' in a lyrical sonnet. The English also excelled in music and loved dancing. As related above, the English Puritans followed the Swiss reformers in banning musical instruments from church as unscriptural (Amos 5. 23), probably because they liked it so much and feared that its sensual appeal would distract them from understanding the words of prayer or scripture. Outside church the Puritans, like all Englishmen, delighted in music. Cromwell would listen for hours to an organ played in the hall of Hampton Court; he arranged musical concerts in the Cockpit at Whitehall; he even had a small orchestra at his daughter's wedding who played while the guests danced the night away. The marriage of drama and music would prove irresistible to the English. Opera was devised in Italy, but the first London performance took place under Cromwell. Milton is said to have secured the release from the Tower of a Royalist playwright called Sir William D'Avenant, who obtained permission in 1656 of an 'entertainment after the manner of the ancients' called 'The Siege of Rhodes' which was the first English opera. In 1674 the poet John Dryden came to Milton to ask for permission to turn *Paradise Lost* into 'an heroic opera' in rhyming couplets. Milton agreed. For some years Dryden's operatic version sold far more copies than Milton's original!

In New England the singing of psalms unaccompanied 'in such grave tunes as are most used in our nation' ran into trouble. The earliest colonists could sing by note more than a score of tunes, but these gradually dwindled to five or six. By about 1720 the churchgoers had reduced their repertoire to the tortured renderings of three or four tunes, so musical instruments were introduced and singing schools began. As in England, the love of good music eventually conquered obedience to the letter of the Old Testament.

Apart from paintings or statues of 'idols' the Puritans in New England had no objection to the visual arts. But they had little leisure or money to spend upon them. In the seventeenth century they limited themselves to expressing their artistic sense in the design and ornamentation of functional objects. Their meeting houses, with clapboard exteriors, shingle roofs and window shutters, possessed a simple grace. Used for town meetings as well as worship they resembled English town or market halls. In time they became embellished with such details as corner pendants, decorative iron door latches and hinges, while gables both enhanced the appearance and gave extra room.

Sir William Waller had confessed his 'vanity in furniture' and John Hampden interested himself in architecture. Many Puritans shared the concern for good craftsmanship in such functional objects as houses, chairs, tables and chests. In domestic artistry Puritan women excelled in fine needlework, making not only patchwork quilts but embroidered hangings. In particular the Puritans adorned their houses with texts from Scripture. At Chester in England there are still houses which bear such sentences painted above their shop fronts. Similar texts were also embroidered by the women and hung indoors. They used the needle, which was invented in Elizabeth's reign, and their skilful industry drew humorous comment from the playwrights. In *The Citye Match*, a play performed in 1639, Jasper Mayne could say: 'Nay, Sir, she is a Puritan at her needle too. Indeed, she works religious petticoats; for flowers she'll make church histories. Besides, my smock sleeves have such holy embroideries, and are so learned, that I fear in time all my apparel will be quoted by some pure instructor.'

Devotion to the Word, and the close study of it, fed the Puritan love of words. In his old age Governor Bradford undertook the study of Hebrew to 'see the ancient oracles of God in their native beauty'. The same Puritan virtue of simplicity without unnecessary adornment, the hallmark of 'the plain but effectual way' of preaching, inspired their poetry and prose. For us, looking back, Puritan literature is dominated by Milton and Bunyan. Together with Shakespeare and the King James's Bible, these Puritans of genius have taught generations of Englishmen and Americans the music of the English language. From Daniel Defoe and onwards, there is hardly a poet or writer of distinction in either country who has not something of the Puritan within. The English-speaking world cannot miss the Puritan rhythms in our language and thought:

We must be free or die, who speak the tongue
That Shakespeare spake; the faith and morals hold
Which Milton held.

Both the American environment and their ideas led the Puritans to emphasize the simple and the functional. The gentry who could afford paintings bought portraits of themselves or their families because they were useful. They did not bother with landscapes or classical scenes. Unlike the Stuarts they tended to patronize English artists, such as Robert Walker and Samuel Cooper. Graceful ornamentation was welcome as long as it did not detract from the purpose or cost too much.

The same principle applied to clothes. To maintain distinctions, what people could wear was controlled by sumptuary laws; these were not enforced in England but they were in New England. The Puritans tended to dress plainly and simply, both because they did not wish to waste money or time on clothes and because they liked to do so. Black carried certain overtones of dignity and formality; it became standard for many kinds of 'best clothes', such as the suits worn on Sundays. Often they enlivened it with a scarlet waistcoat. On weekdays Puritan men wore suits of various grades of broadcloth and women dresses of long-lasting materials. The most common choice of colour for men was russet, which ranged from orange to brown in shade. The colour range was much softer than our own, reflecting the use of vegetable rather than chemical dyes. With the exception of indigo for blue, the trees, flowers and plants of New England produced the dyes for brown, crimson, violet, purple and yellow. Sassafras, yellow root and barberry root, for example, gave the New Englanders dyes for various shades of yellow.

Manifest display of any kind tended to be eschewed by the Puritans of all social ranks, although a gentleman like Arthur Goodwin could be painted by Van Dyck in a plain but well-cut suit which would not have disgraced a Cavalier lord. Women often wore a linen cap or 'coif' on their heads, even at home, and an apron over their gown and petticoat. The Puritans disapproved of all jewelry and wore no wedding rings. In their best clothes men might wear ruffs at neck and wrists, or later, wide falling collars or 'bands' and cuffs. Puritan gentlemen carried fine swords and richly embroidered gloves. At first they wore their hair long, like most Elizabethans, but when the fashion changed in Stuart times, partly in reaction to the Court, many of the younger ones adopted short hair as a party badge. Lord Saye and Sele, for example, was close shorn. Some ministers maintained that short hair was more scriptural. But only a few fanatics measured a man's faith by the length of his hair and the smallness of his falling bands. As a song contemporary with the Civil War makes clear, people did not necessarily associate these styles with the Puritans:

> What creature's this? with his short hair,
> His little band, and huge long ears,
> That this new faith has founded?
> The Puritans were never such,
> The Saints themselves had ne'er so much
> Oh such a knave's a Roundhead.

Charles I's eldest son, Prince Henry, exemplified this Puritan preference for plain clothes. Having worn a suit of Welsh frieze for a considerable time and being told that it was too mean for him, he answered that he was not ashamed of his country cloth and wished it would last for ever. The sober and restrained suits of the Puritans may have passed through many transformations since the seventeenth century. But it is no accident that for many decades the American and British businessman have tended to wear dark or plain suits, white shirts and short hair. The instinct to revert to plain clothes is deep within us. The quest for simplicity in life style and in art is a sure symptom of that enduring Puritan legacy. The seeds go back to Luther and beyond. 'O sancta simplicitas! – O holy simplicity' said John Huss at the martyr's stake.

*   *   *

'Consider what nation it is whereof you are, and whereof you are governors', wrote Milton to the Lords and Commons of England in his plea for the liberty of unlicensed printing in 1644 – 'a nation not slow and dull, but of quick, ingenious and piercing spirit, acute to invent, subtle and sinewy to discourse, not beneath the reach of any point the highest that human capacity can soar to'. In the intellectual awakening of the English nation the Puritans gave considerable leadership to their fellow-countrymen. In the rise of modern science, for example, they showed themselves to be more conscious, articulate and vigorous than most Englishmen. Milton had visited Galileo in Florence, and he cited him as a notable victim of the Roman Catholic censor's tyranny.

The Englishman's interest in science and technology may have stemmed from their intelligent, practical and inventive nature, but it was stifled by an insular conservatism which has also characterized that nation for much of its history. The English would not easily abandon their familiar authorities: Aristotle in natural philosophy, Galen in medicine and Ptolemy in astronomy. The Renaissance spirit, personified in this respect by Leonardo da Vinci, only gradually permeated intellectual life in England, turning science from an amateur hobby of gentlemen into the serious pursuit of natural truth. Because of their insistence that the universe is law-abiding, Puritan preachers and writers powerfully led the way. In *An Apology on the Declaration of the Power and Providence of God in the Government of the World* (1627), George Hakewill argued for the 'moderns' as against the 'ancients' by asserting that scientific observation was more important than traditional authority. Man had a duty to study the universe and discover its laws. Like all good education this would serve to restore the human mind to its original vigour before it was vitiated by the Fall. Hakewill's book inspired a Latin poem from Milton championing the 'moderns' in promoting scientific enquiry.

Modern science looks back upon Francis Bacon, the son of an intensely Puritan mother, as one of its founding fathers. His concept of progress – collecting facts and building them into a body of knowledge in order to improve the human lot on earth – stood entirely within the Puritan tradition. Bacon called attention to industry, such as glass-making, dyeing, gunpowder milling, paper-making and agriculture, as worthy of scientific assistance. He pleaded for a renewal of 'the commerce of the mind with things'; man's empire over nature depends wholly on the technological arts and upon science. 'For we cannot command nature except by obeying her.' Like Hakewill, Bacon also believed that by scientific study we could recover our pristine mental powers in the golden age before the Fall.

As in the case of marriage, the Puritans saw two ends in science. First, it allowed men to study divine providence in nature and therefore to grow in the understanding and love of God. Secondly, it served a socially useful end. Bacon defined the latter as 'the relief of man's estate', by which he meant 'to subdue and overcome the necessities and miseries of humanity' and 'to endow the conditions and life of man with new powers and works'. For men enter into learning for many reasons – through curiosity, to adorn their minds, 'most times for lucre and profession' – but seldom 'to give a true account of their gift of reason for the benefit and use of men'.

Almost all the early Baconians, such as Sir John Eliot, came from the ranks of the Puritans and supported Parliament in the Civil War. After its conclusion a group of Baconian scholars, the nucleus of the later Royal Society, received appointments at Oxford University. These scientists, who valued 'no knowledge but as it has a tendency to use', attracted thither men who became famous later, such as Christopher Wren, Thomas Sprat, Robert Boyle and John Locke. Clarendon became Chancellor of the University after the Restoration and admitted then that under the Commonwealth the colleges 'yielded a harvest of extraordinary good and sound knowledge in all parts of learning'.

The Puritan impetus given to science culminated in the genius of Isaac Newton, who was born two months after the battle of Edgehill. 'In one person,' wrote Albert Einstein, 'he combined the experimenter, the theorist, the mechanic and, not least, the artist in exposition.' Newton's discoveries of natural law, notably the laws of motion, are the most striking expression of the first end of science in the Puritan mind. Had he lived several decades earlier he might have been a Puritan himself; as it was he exhibited the growing influence of reason in his refusal to accept the divinity of Christ. Moreover, his own work forwarded the tendency of the age towards Deism by depicting the universe as a law-abiding and self-regulating clockwork machine set in motion by a First Cause. God became thus remote, inhabiting an immeasurably distant realm beyond the vast heavens which were being further revealed by the reflecting telescope that Newton invented.

The works of Newton soon found favour at Harvard, for the

American Puritans had already made some substantial contributions to science. Governor John Winthrop of Connecticut was chosen a Fellow of the Royal Society at the first regular election in 1663. That year he had brought to New England a telescope more than a yard long which he later presented to Harvard. In fact the Bostonian merchant Thomas Brattle used it to observe the elliptical orbit of the comet of 1680, and his data contributed to Newton's mathematical formulation of the law of gravity.

Although Winthrop studied alchemy, physics, chemistry, astronomy and botany, his interests focused upon the practical uses of knowledge. Before emigrating to America he devised a windmill which used horizontal rather than vertical sails, allowing it to be built closer to the ground. He set up salt pans and iron works in New England, and prospected for lead and other minerals. In 1657, while still Governor, he began to practice as a physician, travelling many miles to visit patients. Like so many of the Puritans, he approached the Renaissance ideal of 'the universal man', combining public activity with learning directed towards useful ends.

Of the nine American members of the Royal Society elected before 1740, only one did not come from New England. The lawyer Paul Dudley prepared papers for the Royal Society on the habits of whales, New England earthquakes, the preparation of maple syrup and a variety of other such topics. Cotton Mather, elected a Fellow in 1713, argued in *The Christian Philosopher* that science was an incentive to religion. The beauty of well-ordered nature, known to man by reason, manifests God's benevolence. Mather safeguarded the traditional Puritan emphasis upon God's freedom to intervene by special providences in his world. But the main drift of his thought heralded the beginning of the Enlightment in America. The themes of man's reason and cosmic order would be expounded further by Franklin, Paine and Jefferson, and again by Emerson and Thoreau. For all his full-blown verbosity and second-hand erudition, Cotton Mather remained in the line of descent of his Puritan father and grandfather. 'God casts the line of election in the loins of godly parents', as one Puritan preacher had said, more in hope than conviction. Mather held true to his inheritance by holding firmly to the social end of science. In 1727 an epidemic of smallpox struck Boston. Mather had heard about inoculation, both from an African slave and from reading an article in the Transactions of the Royal Society about Turkish medical practice. His courage in advocating it despite opposition – someone even threw a bomb into his study window – won the day. Of the fifteen in every hundred who died (there were some 6000 cases) only two had been inoculated.

Nor should the impetus towards the social sciences given by the Puritans be forgotten. The republican James Harrington, who had once served Queen Elizabeth of Bohemia, hoped to base a science of politics on the study of history. In a far more systematic way than Machiavelli, he thought it possible to discover laws about how human beings behaved in the mass. As Harrington saw a relation between changes in political power and shifts in the ownership of property, he may be justly claimed as a forerunner of Karl Marx. The mainstream Puritans, however, studied society in order to improve it. Sir William Petty, who became chief physician to Cromwell's army in Ireland in 1652 and afterwards as Surveyor-General took stock of the forfeited estates there, invented for us the science of statistics. But not until the day of Florence Nightingale (a President of the Royal Statistical Society) did anyone actually use systematically collected facts to engineer social reform.

Not least for this reason, most of the creative ideas of the Puritans about changing society proved stillborn. Yet they were astonishingly inventive and far-sighted. The seeds of the modern concept of the socially responsible state lie in the Puritan mind. In the case of Hugh Peter, to take but one example, the experience of the new beginning in America had clearly stimulated him to question all kinds of assumptions in England. His fertile mind teemed with social reforms and projects: a national legal service, the abolition of church patronage and purchase for army commissions, a national bank, the reduction of most taxes to one income tax, a licensing tax on coaches, a programme of canal building, a system of state insurance for merchants travelling abroad, unrestricted immigration, public orphanages and county courts. With considerable foresight he suggested that in order to reduce the risk of fire in London its old timber buildings should be pulled down and the water supply improved. He also advocated that imprisonment for debt should be replaced by a method of deduction from earnings.

Many pages in science have been turned since the days of the Puritans. Yet the essence of the enterprise owes much to their pioneering spirit. First, there is the work of posing questions to nature and seeking answers in order to understand how the universe actually works. The Puritan in the scientist still finds insistent signs of order. The quest for the neat, symmetrical, and elegant has proved to be an excellent guide to modern scientists. 'Everything should be made as simple as possible', said Einstein, 'but not more simple.' The search for simplicity which characterized the Puritans in everyday life if not in their latter-day theology, seems to have its counterpart in the very structures of the universe, at least as we perceive it. All the forces of nature work together to maintain its simplicity while at the same time banishing deadly perfection. Secondly, when we discover laws we also master them for use. The continuing Puritan spirit in the scientist will constantly remind him of the social and human end of knowledge: that it must be used for 'the relief of man's estate' and not the destruction of his earthly home.

*   *   *

Apart from the Puritan in us today, as husband or wife, artist or craftsman, scientist or manager, the values which the Puritan drew together and refined influence us in many other ways. There is a Puritan in the schoolteacher and in the historian, to name but two callings which they helped to transform. But many of the leading Puritan individuals in these pages – Hampden, Winthrop, Waller and Cromwell – were magistrates or governors of people by vocation. They pioneered a unique sense of destiny for the English-speaking people. Bradford and Winthrop carried that conviction with them to America. They saw it as their task to create a new nation, a visible kingdom of Christ, which would draw the persecuted godly people from the jaws of Antichrist in Europe. This Puritan conviction of a manifest destiny, albeit cast in more secular language, has survived remarkably well in the American political rhetoric. 'Our spirit is greater; our laws are wiser; our religion is superior', declared John Adams with patriotic fervour.

Although the Puritan gentry and ministers were far from democrats, church members under their rule certainly enjoyed more democracy in New England than their cousins back home. The congregational system allowed them plenty of say in the affairs of the church. God's elect could also choose their own deputies, and through them their own magistrates and governors. Although Winthrop might insist that once elected his authority came from God the very action of election pointed to the inescapable truth that power resided in the people. The government had a covenant with the people, with rights and duties balanced equally on either side. In fact Winthrop gave way gracefully whenever the people or their representatives flexed their muscles and demanded more participation, though as a true conservative he never initiated change. In addition, regardless of church membership, all townsmen had the right to assemble together, make local decisions and choose selectmen to carry them out, like the Athenians centuries before them. Perhaps the Renaissance learning of the Puritan pioneers may have inspired this remarkable experiment in democracy, which has justly lasted until this day in all of New England except for Rhode Island. It only seems to work, it may be added, when towns remain no larger in population than ancient Athens, which probably did not exceed about 30,000 inhabitants. Beyond that limit town meetings become too large to be effective.

Apart from democracy, the system of checks and balances built into the Constitution of the United States reflected the Puritan awareness that the 'children of Adam' are fallible, be they never so highly placed. Home, family and church continued to be schools of character, producing individuals with a strong enough sense of personal morality and civic responsibility to make constitutional democracy a workable system. Without an educated, moral, tolerant and fair-minded people it could not work. The commitment to making it work, despite all the odds, is a distinctively Puritan contribution to American life.

The Puritan sense of destiny, of being 'one nation under God', surfaces from time to time. Thomas Jefferson's Latin motto on the reverse side of a one-dollar bill bids Americans to see their nation as the beginning of that 'new order of the ages' for which man born of the Renaissance and Reformation had so ardently hoped. The second inaugural address of President Abraham Lincoln rang with the Puritan themes of God's providential judgement and grace as seen in human events. When President Eisenhower reminded Americans that the nation was based upon a deeply felt religious faith common to Protestant, Catholic or Jew, Baxter would have applauded. When President Carter exhorted the Israeli Knesset to strive for peace as if everything depended on man and pray for it as if everything depended on God, he spoke in the language of the Puritan pulpit. Perhaps the most eloquent statement of the Puritan yearning in the American heart in recent times came in Ronald Reagan's acceptance speech in 1980 to the Republican convention:

My view of government places trust not in one person of one party, but in those values that transcend persons and parties.

The trust is where it belongs – in the people. The responsibility to live up to that trust is where it belongs, in their elected leaders.

That kind of relationship, between the people and their elected leaders, is a special kind of compact: an agreement among themselves to build a community and abide by its laws.

Three-hundred and sixty years ago, in 1620, a group of families dared to cross a mighty ocean to build a future for themselves in a new world. When they arrived in Plymouth, Massachusetts, they formed what they called a 'compact': an agreement among themselves to build a community and abide by its laws.

The single act – the voluntary binding together of free people to live under the law – set the pattern for what was to come.

A century and a half later, the descendants of those people pledged their lives, their fortunes and their sacred honor to found this nation. Some forfeited their fortunes and their lives: none sacrificed honor.

Fourscore and seven years later, Abraham Lincoln called upon the people of all America to renew their dedication and their commitment to a government of, for and by the people.

Isn't it once again time to renew our compact of freedom; to pledge to each other all that is best in our lives; all that gives meaning to them – for the sake of this, our beloved and blessed land?

Together, let us make this a new beginning. Let us make a commitment to care for the needy; to teach our children the values and the virtues handed down to us by our families; to have the courage to defend those values and the willingness to sacrifice for them.

Let us pledge to restore, in our time, the American spirit of voluntary service, of cooperation, of private and community initiative; a spirit that flows like a deep and mighty river through the history of our nation.

In his conclusion the future President of the United States could ask 'Can we doubt that only a divine providence placed this land, this island of freedom, here as a refuge for all those people in the world who yearn to breathe freely?'

When one considers such words from American presidents down the centuries, they seem to be direct appeals to the hidden Puritan legacy of spirit in the nation. Surely the Puritans have stood godfather to America.

The Puritan founding fathers, both magistrates and ministers, formed some powerful ideas about America which their distant sons and daughters still hold in their unconscious minds today. They saw America through the eyes of a creative imagination fed deeply upon the Bible. In this common vision they fused the landscape of New England with that of the Holy Land. The wanderings of the Israelites seemed to mirror their own story. But they could not leave their desert behind them when they entered a land of milk and honey. The very wilderness itself – the endless tracts of green forest, snowy mountains and barren waste – had to be transformed by man's work into the Promised Land that God had assigned to them. The westwards movement of the frontier could be fused in such a mind with the spreading light of the gospel. By making the land in obedience to God's command and in community with his fellows, man would receive a blessing for himself and his family. The Puritans held together the values of society and individual in creative tension. The American enterprise today, which calls for equal dedication to the goal of corporate or national self-fulfilment and to the individual pursuit of happiness, reflects that balance.

Nor may it be fanciful to trace the origins of the prevailing American world view to the Puritans. They saw human existence as a grimly serious, deeply dramatic conflict between good and evil with heaven and hell as their end. Although the latter may have lost their immediacy the struggle between good and evil is still the backcloth of American foreign policy. The Second World War could only be interpreted in those terms, and more so in hindsight. For we looked upon the face of evil itself when they opened the gates of Belsen, Buchenwald and Dachau.

Nowadays the division between the Communist bloc and the Western nations is often interpreted in similar moral terms. It is certainly a remarkable parallel to the Protestant-Catholic divide in the Puritan age. Stalin and his successors can be portrayed as secular substitutes for the pope; the Kremlin supplants the Vatican as the fount of all evil; Communism rivals Catholicism as a hated and feared ideology. It is not for an historian to evaluate such a transfer of the Puritan world view, except to say that it needs very thorough scrutiny. The battle lines of good and evil run down every human heart and vein all societies: they do not follow national frontiers.

To hold together and give direction to a society which aspires to goodness, comprised of individuals equal in the sight of God and each with a piece of political power symbolized by the vote, calls for a high degree of leadership at all levels. The Puritan governors and magistrates in New England not only provided that leadership, but they handed down the Christian basis for it as a legacy to their successors. In the last century children in Massachusetts still had to learn by heart Winthrop's speech to the Court of Assistants after the 'troublesome business' at Hingham in 1645, in which a local group had challenged the executive on the appointment of militia officers. Winthrop stood trial before his peers for his part, but he turned his humiliation to good account. After his acquittal and vindication he took the opportunity to speak his mind on the relation between authority and liberty in a Christian society. Having been called by the people to this office, Winthrop told the crowded meeting-house, magistrates have their authority from God. There is a covenant between magistrate and people, with obligations on both sides. Magistrates, being human, are bound to err and fall short in skill or ability, but if they fall short in integrity they must answer for it.

As for liberty, Winthrop distinguished between the natural, civil or federal kinds. As our natures are corrupt men avail themselves of the former liberty to do evil as well as good. It is the great enemy of truth and peace, the wild beast that the ordinances of God exist to restrain and subdue. The other kind of liberty, which Winthrop also called 'moral', is relevant to the covenant between God and man in the moral law and the political covenants and constitutions among men themselves. This liberty is the proper end and object of government and cannot exist without it. Such a liberty is worth the sacrifice of your life. It is maintained and exercised by a form of subjection to authority. It is the liberty of the Christian. 'If you stand for your natural corrupt liberties,' concluded Winthrop, 'and will do what is good in your own eyes, you will not endure the least weight of authority, but will murmur, and oppose, and be always striving to shake off that yoke; but if you will be satisfied to enjoy such civil and lawful liberties, such as Christ allows you, then will you quietly and cheerfully submit unto that authority which is set over you, in all the administrations of it, for your good.'

This speech explains how the relatively small number of Puritan gentlemen, elected year by year to be the civil rulers of New England, justified their authority. Stripped of its religious allusions and couched in more secular terms, the reasoning behind the speech would serve as the charter for modern government in America. We may look upon the people as the sovereign authority rather than God, but the difference is relatively slight. For the Puritans came to believe that God calls men to high office through the medium of the people, not by hereditary or apostolic succession. Once in office, however, they must be given freedom, trust and support to do as they judge right. Providing, that is, they do not trespass upon the civil rights of the people or reveal fundamental lack of integrity. The American Constitution, which gives far more power to its elected leader than the prime minister enjoys in England, for example, is a legacy of this frame of mind. Thus the office of President of the United States stands in direct linear descent from the Governor of Massachusetts Bay, the first leader of the four United Colonies.

'What is the chief end of man?' 'Man's chief end is to glorify God and to enjoy him for ever.' This famous question-and-answer opens the Shorter Catechism, compiled by the Puritan divines at the Westminster Assembly in 1647 and used widely since then by Presbyterians, Independents or Congregationalists and Baptists alike. The words capture the essence of Puritanism. The Puritan sought to remember God as his 'chief end' in all that he did, thought or said. William Ames, a great Puritan preacher and theologian, once defined the subject of 'divinity' as 'the doctrine of living to God'. That holy science applied daily, hourly, to a man's concerns: work, marriage, recreation, worship, church, society, music, science, clothes, art and the nation. Each day began and ended with calm, searching and devout personal and family prayer. Each task was done to the glory of God. Each event in life was studied in order to disclose God's mind. Every relationship, business or personal, could be related to spiritual principles. Hours free from work were spent gladly in the study of the Scriptures, attending public worship, 'godly converse' with friends or in activities known not to be displeasing to God. In short, the 'great business of godliness' dominated the Puritan's life. It fitted him with zeal which shone from his face, inspired his words and remodelled his life. Neighbours *saw* on earth lives that were not earthly, lives which moved like a company of pilgrims through a moral and spiritual continent of awesome landscape and breathtaking promise.

To live as a Puritan required constant self-scrutiny. In secular terms a legacy of this attitude may perhaps be seen in the tendency of many Americans to be constantly analysing themselves and their motives. The psychiatrist or psycho-analyst may have replaced the Puritan preacher as the 'physician of the soul' but the process is much the same. It would be a mistake to label such secular self-scrutiny as merely self-centredness, alias selfishness, ignoring its religious origins. At its best it is a concern for authenticity. It may also be a quest for God, all that is true and good in one's own heart and experience.

By so living their lives the godly made themselves different from the majority of English folk, and they attracted the inevitable reaction. From envy or malice, they were lampooned with all the invective which the rich language of Shakespeare could supply. The name 'Puritan' stuck. Insulted or stung by the implied rebuke to their own manner of life, and often by the English plain-speaking of the Puritans, the critics and enemies of the Puritans played upon the outward badges of their social difference. With the noble exception of Shakespeare the playwrights laboured to create the stock stereotype of the Puritan man or woman, an image that survives to this day. As the Puritans knew well, there were hypocrites among them who aped their ways in order to pursue self-seeking ends. Moreover, as Puritanism spread among the lower middle-classes it did attract people who wanted to wear a Puritan uniform of sober clothes, short hair-style, nasal intonation, a Sabbath expression on their face and frequent glances up to the heavens to accompany copious references to the Bible. But Puritanism is not to be understood either by its failures or such externals. At best, it saw Luther's vision of the lay Christian life realized in a visible and English form of sanctity.

Neither Luther nor the English Puritans saw themselves as preaching or practising anything other than 'mere Christianity'. Just as the Reformation and the English Puritan movement drew heavily upon the storehouse of Christianity, so they also contributed to it. The Christian today cannot help but be affected by the God-centredness of the Puritan tradition. The Puritans wrestled with the intractabilities of the Scriptures more vigorously than we do, and they came off with a blessing denied to us. In the Anglican or Episcopalian churches as well as among Presbyterians and Baptists, Methodists and Congregationalists, the Puritan hymns of Milton, Baxter, Bunyan and others in their long tradition are still sung. Within the family of churches who still draw upon the genius of Luther for their insights into the essence of Christianity the example of the Puritans in England and America can never die.

Milton came to hold that even one believer could form a true church. Today there are many people who cannot with conscience subscribe to any one church or even confine themselves to

Christianity or Judaism as a whole. For them religion has become a private matter. They stand at the end of the historic process which has led more and more emphasis to be put on the individual. They do not go much to church. Yet the Puritan within them still reaches out for God. They are still committed to faith, hope and love – love, as always, 'the greatest thing in the world'.

It fell to John Milton to write the epitaph of the Puritans in history. In 'Samson Agonistes', published in 1671 in the same volume as 'Paradise Regained', he told the story of God's Hebrew servant Samson. He couched the drama in the form of a Greek tragedy: a perfect symbol of the union of Reformation and Renaissance in the Puritan mind. Samson, 'eyeless in Gaza' like the old and blind poet himself, has overcome more Philistines at the moment of death than in his lifetime. The poet in Milton perceives the relevance of that image to what was happening to the Puritans in the English-speaking world. So he can bring spiritual comfort to his Puritan readers in the concluding words of the Chorus:

> All is best, though we often doubt
> What the unsearchable dispose
> Of Highest Wisdom brings about,
> And ever best found in the close . . .
> Oft He seems to hide his face,
> But unexpectedly returns . . .
> His servants He, with new acquist
> Of true experience from this great event,
> With peace and consolation hath dismissed,
> And calm of mind, all passion spent.

Suggestions for further reading

In a single volume it is clearly impossible for the author to explore all the various ramifications of Puritan thought and practice. In recent years the subject of the Puritans has attracted much interest from historians on both sides of the Atlantic. This bibliography is a guide to that growing literature, designed to help the reader who wishes to go deeper into any particular aspect touched upon in this book.

BIOGRAPHIES

Considering the extent of the literature, there are relatively few readable and accurate biographies of leading Puritan lay men and women and even fewer autobiographical writings or journals.

Cromwell has attracted more biographers than any other Puritan. Antonia Fraser, *Cromwell Our Chief of Men* (London, 1973) is the latest and largest for some time. The religious aspects are well covered in Robert Paul, *The Lord Protector: Religion and Politics in the Life of Oliver Cromwell* (London, 1955); it should be supplemented by Christopher Hill, *God's Englishman: Oliver Cromwell and the English Revolution* (London and New York, 1970).

John Adair, *John Hampden: The Patriot, 1594–1643* (London, 1976) and his *Roundhead General: A Biography of Sir William Waller* (London, 1969) give more information about two very characteristic Puritans. Other recent biographies include: H. Hulme, *The Life of Sir John Eliot* (New York, 1957); Violet A. Rowe, *Sir Henry Vane, the Younger* (London, 1970); R.E.L. Strider, *Robert Greville, Lord Brooke* (Harvard UP, 1958) W.H. Lamont, *Marginal Prynne* (London, 1963) and E.W. Kirby, *William Prynne* (Yale UP, 1973); and Patricia Crawford, *Denzil Holles* (London, 1980). Ruth Spalding's *The Improbable Puritan: A Life of Bulstrode Whitelocke, 1605–1675* (London, 1975) is so called because Cromwell's ambassador to Sweden loved music, dancing and the stage. The democratic John Lilburne is admired in Pauline Gregg, *Free-Born John: A Biography of John Lilburne* (London, 1961). Lucy Hutchinson's portrait of her husband, *Memoirs of the Life of Colonel Hutchinson* (London, 1965 ed.) remains a delight to read.

D.M. Meads has edited the diary of Margaret, Lady Hoby, 1599–1605 (London, 1930). Lady Anne Clifford is the subject of a biography: Martin Holmes, *Proud Northern Lady* (Chichester: Phillimore, 1976).

The journals of Puritans, e.g. those of Margaret Hoby and John Winthrop, should be read in conjunction with Owen C. Watkins, *The*

Puritan Experience, (London, 1972) a study of over 200 Puritan spiritual autobiographies written before 1725, ranging from 'orthodox Puritans' to 'vulgar prophets', Ranters and Quakers. These works paved the way for the early novels and fictitious autobiographies, such as Daniel Defoe's *Robinson Crusoe*.

As yet Bradford lacks a biographer, but his journal makes incomparable reading. The best edition is Samuel E. Morison, *Of Plymouth Plantation, 1620–1647, by William Bradford, Sometime Governor* (New York, 1952).

Edward Morgan's *The Puritan Dilemma: The Story of John Winthrop* (Boston, 1958) is a readable introduction. Winthrop's *Journal* (sometimes called *The History of New England from 1630 to 1649*) is best read in James Savage's edition (1853, reprinted New York, 1972). The Mass. Hist. Soc. edition of the *Winthrop Papers* (5 vols.) contains the *Journal* and letters. R. Winthrop, *Life and Letters of John Winthrop* (Boston, 1864) gives the main letters in full up to 1630. For the family history, see Richard J. Dunn, *Puritans and Yankees: The Winthrop Dynasty of New England, 1630–1717* (Princeton, 1962). Robert C. Black's *The Younger John Winthrop* (Columbia, 1966) does justice to this most interesting man; Alice Morse Earle's life of his mother, *Margaret Winthrop* (London, 1895) has some charming touches.

For the history of Sir Richard Saltonstall and his family, see R. Moody, ed., 'The Saltonstall Papers 1607–1815' (*Mass. Hist. Soc.*, 1980).

Lawrence Shaw Mayo's *John Endecott: A Biography* (Cambridge, Mass. 1936) needs revision but it covers the ground. *The Winslows of "Careswell"*, (Plymouth, Mass. 1975) by Quentin Coons and Cynthia Hagar Krusell, includes a short life of Governor Edward Winslow and his family. Morison's *Builders of the Bay Colony* (1930) contains biographical essays which did much to stimulate a new interest in the Puritans.

THE ELIZABETHAN PURITAN MOVEMENT

The early Reformation on England is well-covered by A.G. Dickens, *The English Reformation* (London, 1964). H.C. Porter, *Reformation and Reaction in Tudor Cambridge* (Cambridge, UP, 1958) is an illuminating case-study. Claire Cross, *Church and People, 1450–1660* and H.G. Alexander, *Religion in England, 1558–1662* are both strongly recommended. The story of the Johnson family is well told by Barbara Winchester, *Tudor Family Portrait* (London, 1955) but the scholar should consult her edition of the voluminous correspondence (London Ph.D., 1953). G.A. Williamson's abridged edition of Foxe's *Book of Martyrs* (London, 1965) is the best one for any reader intrepid enough to tackle this work.

M.M. Knappen's *Tudor Puritanism* (Chicago, 1939) is outstanding on

Puritan thought but Patrick Collinson's *The Elizabethan Puritan Movement* (London and Berkeley, Calif., 1967) is the fullest and best history of events. Specific aspects are dealt with by Mark Curtis, *Oxford and Cambridge in Transition, 1558–1642* (London, 1959); Patrick McGrath, *Papists and Puritans under Elizabeth I* (London, 1967); Horton Davies, *Worship and Theology in England from Cranmer to Hooker, 1534–1603* (Princeton, 1970); R.A. Merchant, *The Puritans and the Church Courts in the Diocese of York, 1560–1642* (London, 1960); P. Seaver, *The Puritan Lectureships* (OUP, 1970); R.T. Kendall, *Calvin and English Calvinism to 1640* (OUP, 1979); W.A. Clebsch, *England's Early Protestants* (Yale, 1954). J.F. Mozley, *John Foxe and His Book* (London, 1940) and William Haller, *Foxe's Book of Martyrs and the Elect Nation* (London, 1963) do justice between them to the Puritans' favourite work after the Bible.

Primary sources are to be found in H.C. Porter, *Puritanism in Tudor England* (London, 1971) and Leonard Trinterud, *Elizabethan Puritanism* (New York, 1971).

For the tradition which gave rise to voyage of the *Mayflower*, see B.R. White, *The English Separatist Tradition from the Marian Martyrs to the Pilgrim Fathers*, (London, 1971); H. Davies, *The English Free Churches* (Oxford, 1963); H. Davies, *The Worship of the English Puritans* (Dacre, 1948) and W.K. Jordan, *The Development of Religious Tolerance in England*, 4 vols (London, 1932–40).

For Puritan activity in Parliament Sir John Neale's *Elizabeth and Her Parliaments*, 2 vols (London, 1953, 1957) is invaluable. Neale also discusses Puritanism in *Essays in Elizabethan History* (London, 1958).

For the influence of the Puritan preacher see W. Haller, *The Rise of Puritanism* (New York, 1938), Irvonwy Morgan's *The Godly Preachers of the Elizabethan Church* (London, 1965). A.F. Scott Pearson, *Thomas Cartwright and Elizabethan Puritanism* (London, 1925) now needs revision. W.S.J. Knox's *Walter Travers: Paragon of Elizabethan Puritanism* (London, 1962) is the study of an Elizabethan presbyterian leader. Peter Lewis has edited an excellent selection from the great Puritan preachers, on such topics as preaching, worship and the pastoral care in *The Genius of Puritanism* (Haywards Heath, Sussex, Carey Publications, 1979). The effects of such teachers are assessed by Richard L. Greaves, *Society and Religion in Elizabethan England* (University of Minnesota Press, 1981), a very large work based upon an analysis of some 500 religious books, mostly by clerics.

THE PURITAN REVOLUTION IN ENGLAND

Lawrence Stone, *The Causes of the English Revolution, 1529–1642* (London, 1972) is an excellent introduction to the debate about the origins of the

Civil War. For the war itself, Richard Ollard's *This War Without an Enemy* (London, 1977) which takes its title from Waller's letter quoted above on p. 191, is a most readable short history. Clive Holmes, *The Eastern Association in the English Civil War* (Cambridge, 1974) is a specialized study of much interest to historians of the Puritans. Brian Manning, ed., *Politics, Religion and the English Civil War* (London, 1973) explores the relationship between religion and politics, while the political transformation of the New Model Army in 1647 is delineated in Mark A. Kishlansky, *The Rise of the New Model Army* (CUP, 1980). Ivan Roots surveys the Interregnum period in *The Great Rebellion, 1642–1660* (London and New York, 1966). Since George Yule's *The Independents in the English Civil War* (Cambridge, 1958) there has been a lively debate, mainly in periodicals, about the meanings of the political terms 'Independent' and 'Presbyterian'. Both Christopher Hill's *The Century of Revolution, 1603–1714* (London, 2nd ed. 1980) and Conrad Russell's *The Crisis of Parliaments, 1509–1660* (London, 1971) are valuable general histories.

In a general spiritual and intellectual history, William Haller's, *Liberty and Reformation in the Puritan Revolution* (New York, 1955) describes how the Puritan revolution triumphed at the cost of the disintegration of Puritanism itself. For the sects see: Christopher Hill, *The World Turned Upside Down: Radical Ideas during the English Revolution* (London, 1972); *The Century of Revolution 1603–1714* (London, 2nd ed. 1980) and *Puritanism and Revolution* (London, 1958); A.S.P. Woodhouse, *Puritanism and Liberty: Being the Army Debates (1647–49) from the Clarke Manuscripts* (London, 1938); Michael Walzer, *The Revolution of the Saints: A Study of the Origins of Radical Politics* (Cambridge, Mass., 1965 and London, 1966).

G.E. Aylmer's edition of Leveller writings, *The Levellers in the English Revolution* (London, 1975) contains the best short history and a good critical bibliography. B. Capp, *The Fifth Monarchy Men* (London, 1972) is a well-documented study of a politically dangerous millenarian sect. For the Quakers, see H. Barbour, *The Quakers in Puritan England* (Yale, 1964).

Among the biographical studies of ministers, I. Morgan, *Prince Charles' Puritan Chaplain* (London, 1957) examines the life of John Preston. See also M.M. Knappen's edition of the journals of Richard Rogers and Samuel Ward in *Two Elizabethan Puritan Diaries* (London, 1933 and Gloucester, Mass., 1966); E.C. Walker, *William Dell, Master Puritan* (Cambridge,. 1970) and P. Toon, *God's Statesman: The Life and Work of John Owen* (Grand Rapids, Mich., 1973). For the significance of Hugh Peter (or Peters) in both countries, see Raymond P. Stearns, *The Strenuous Puritan: Hugh Peters 1598–1660* (Urbana, Ill., 1954). Baxter is well served by Geoffrey E. Nuttall, *Richard Baxter* (London, 1965) and Richard Schlatter, *Richard Baxter and Puritan Politics* (New Brunswick, 1957). The life of a country Puritan cleric is well illustrated by *The Diary of*

Ralph Josselin, 1616–1683, ed. E. Hockliffe (Camden Soc. 1908). See also A. Macfarlane, *The Family Life of Ralph Josselin* (Cambridge, 1970).

For the Restoration settlement, see R.S. Barker, *The Making of the Restoration Settlement* (Dacre, 1951); G.F. Nuttall and W.O. Chadwick, ed., *From Uniformity to Unity* (London, 1962).

The Puritan contribution to the Restoration is discussed by George R. Abernathy, *The English Presbyterian and the Stuart Restoration 1648–1663* (Philadelphia, 1965). For the history of Puritanism after that event, see Gerald R. Cragg, *From Puritanism to the Age of Reason* (Cambridge, 1950) and *Puritanism in the Period of the Great Persecution 1660–1688* (Cambridge, 1957).

NEW ENGLAND

The wider context of the Puritan settlement in New England is conveyed by A.P. Newton, *The Colonizing Activities of the English Puritans* (New Haven, 1914) and Carl Bridenbaugh, *No Peace Beyond the Line: The English in the Caribbean 1624–1690* (Oxford UP, 1972). For a comparison of the different values and experience of English colonists in New England and Virginia, see T.H. Breen, *Puritans and Adventurers: Change and Persistence in Early America* (New York and Oxford UP, 1980).

George Langdon, *Pilgrim Colony: A History of New Plymouth, 1620–1691* (New Haven, 1966) is the best short history of the Pilgrim enterprise. Francis Dillon, *The Pilgrims* (New York, 1975 and London, 1973, first called *A Place for Habitation: The Pilgrim Fathers and their Quest*) and Kate Caffrey's *The Mayflower* (London and New York, 1975) are both readable. Among the older books George F. Willison, *Saints and Strangers* (New York, 1945) is exceptionally lively.

The formative years of the Massachusetts Bay Colony await a reappraisal by a contemporary historian. John Truslow Adams, *The Founding of New England* and Robert Wall, *Massachusetts Bay: The Crucial Decade, 1640–1650* (New Haven, 1972) fill the gap to some extent. For sources, see Alexander Young, *Chronicles of the First Planters of the Colony of Massachusetts Bay from 1623 to 1636* (1846, reprinted Baltimore, 1975); Edmund S. Morgan, *The Founding of Massachusetts Bay: Historians and their Sources* (Indianapolis, 1964).

For more general collections of sources the following are recommended: Perry Miller and Thomas H. Johnson, *The Puritans* (New York, 1938); P. Miller, *The American Puritans* (Anchor Books, 1956). A. Vaughan, *The Puritan Tradition in America, 1620–1730* (New York, 1972) offers a useful guide in his introduction to the historiography of American Puritans and has edited an excellent selection of documents. Both books have extensive bibliographies.

Francis J. Bremer, *The Puritan Experiment: New England Society from Bradford to Edwards* (London and New York, 1977) gives an introductory outline and a detailed bibliography. Perry Miller sets out the dominant religious character of the colony in *Orthodoxy in Massachusetts 1630–1650* (Harvard UP, 1953). The people who upset the applecart in the early decades have received much attention. Ola Winslow ably describes Roger Williams the man in *Master Roger Williams: A Biography* (New York, 1951), while Edmund Morgan concentrates more on his thought in *Roger Williams: The Church and the State* (New York, 1967). Emery Battis draws upon disciplines other than history in her examination of *Saints and Sectaries: Anne Hutchinson and the Antinomian Controversy in Massachusetts Bay Colony* (Chapel Hill, 1962).

Edmund Morgan, *Visible Saints: The History of a Puritan Idea* (New York, 1963) traces the New England insistence upon experience of regeneration for church membership from its English roots until its first stage of modification in the Half-Way Covenant. Other studies in Puritan doctrine include G.F. Nuttall, *The Holy Spirit in Puritan Faith and Experience* (Oxford, 1947); E.B. Holifield, *The Covenant Sealed* (New Haven, 1974), a study of Puritan sacramental theology; James S. McGee, *The Godly Man in Stuart England* (New Haven, 1976), a study of Anglicans and Puritans in relation to the 'two tables' of the Ten Commandments; Norman Pettit, *The Heart Prepared: Grace and Conversion in Puritan Spiritual Life* (New Haven, 1966); Robert G. Pope, *The Half-Way Covenant: Church Membership in Puritan New England* (Princeton, 1969).

The New England pulpit and the ministry have received much recent attention. David Hall has studied the relationship between ministers and congregations in *The Faithful Shepherd: A History of the New England Ministry in the Seventeenth Century* (Chapel Hill, 1972). See also Babette Levy, *Preaching in the First Half-Century of New England History* (Hartford, 1945); E. Elliot, *Power and Pulpit in Puritan New England* (Princeton, 1975). L. Ziff has edited three sermons of John Cotton, with a good introduction, in *John Cotton on the Churches of New England* (Cambridge, Mass. 1968).

Good published examples of the journals kept by Puritan ministers for spiritual purposes: Thomas Shephard (ed. M. McGiffert, under the title of *God's Plot*, University of Mass. Press, 1972); Cotton Mather (Mass. Hist. Soc., 2 vols 1957) and Samuel Sewall (Mass. Hist. Soc., *Coll.*, 5th Series, Vols v–vii).

Darrett B. Rutman, *American Puritanism: Faith and Practice* (Philadelphia, 1970) explores Puritan orthodoxy. A. Simpson, *Puritanism in Old and New England* (London, 1955 and Chicago, 1961) narrates the struggle of the Puritans to preserve their authority in society. The definitive work on the sectarian challenge is William McLoughlen, *New England Dissent 1630–1833: The Baptists and the Separation of Church and State* (Cambridge, Mass., 1971). The impact of the Quakers in one state is well described by Carl Bridenbaugh, *Fat Mutton and Liberty of Conscience: Society in Rhode Island 1636–1690*.

PURITAN INTELLECTUAL LIFE

Spiritually and intellectually the Puritans drew upon *both* the Reformation (Luther, Calvin and the Bible) and the Renaissance (classical learning, Christian humanism and the emergence of natural science). Perry Miller's *The New England Mind: The Seventeenth Century* (New York, 1939) highlights the Renaissance contribution amidst medieval and Reformation elements in Puritan thought. See also his essays in *Errand into the Wilderness* (Cambridge, Mass., 1956) and *Nature's Nation* (Cambridge, Mass., 1967). Later scholars have suggested that Miller read his comprehensive and static theological system into the New England mind; he over-emphasized the uniqueness of New England thought by making too much of the originality of influential English theologians such as William Ames and William Perkins. Morison's *The Puritan Pronaos* (1936; reprinted as *The Intellectual Life of Colonial New England*, 1956) is an earlier study in the theology and philosophy of the Puritans, especially the educational and social implications. Norman Fiering in *Moral Philosophy at Seventeenth Century Harvard: A Discipline in Transition* (University of N. Carolina, 1981) traces a quiet revolution in education as the ethical centre shifted from God to man.

Charles H. George and Katherine George, *The Protestant Mind of the English Reformation, 1570–1640* (Princeton, 1961) emphasizes the common intellectual heritage of the English Protestants in the Church of England, while John F. New, *Anglicans and Puritan: The Basis of Their Opposition, 1558–1640* (Stanford, Calif., 1964) stresses the differences between Anglicans and Puritans.

Christopher Hill has contributed *Intellectual Origins of the English Revolution* (Oxford, 1965) and *Some Intellectual Consequences of the English Revolution* (London, 1980). His *Antichrist in Seventeenth Century England* (Oxford, 1971) explores one of the dominant Puritan ideas.

Science in New England is well surveyed by Raymond P. Stearns, *Science in the British Colonies of America* (Urbana, Ill., 1970). A useful introduction to medical science is Otto Beall and Richard Shyrock, *Cotton Mather: First Significant Figure in American Medicine* (Baltimore, 1954).

Puritan political thought is discussed in Edmund S. Morgan, ed., *Puritan Political Ideas, 1558–1794* (Indianapolis, 1965) and T.H. Breen, *The Character of the Good Ruler: A Study of Puritan Political Ideas in New England 1630–1730* (New Haven, 1970). There is a good selection of articles in American historical periodicals on democracy and the franchise in New England, see bibliography in Bremer, *op. cit.* Radical political views are well discussed in Perez Zagorin, *A History of Political Thought in the English Revolution* (London, 1954); Joseph Frank, *The Levellers: A History of the Writing of Three Seventeenth Century Democrats* (Cambridge, Mass., 1955) and Leo F. Solt, *Saints in Arms: Puritanism and Democracy in Cromwell's Army* (Stanford, UP, 1959), who shows how authoritarian were the Army chaplains who dominated the movement. C.H. George looked at the Puritan view of history in *Puritanism as History and Historiography* (*Past and Present*, No. 41, 1968). See also C.A. Patrides, *The Phoenix and the Ladder: The Rise and Decline of the Christian View of History* (Berkeley, Calif., 1964); Peter Gay, *A Loss of Mastery: Puritan Historians in Colonial America* (Los Angeles, 1966).

PURITAN FAMILY AND COMMUNITY LIFE

Edmund S. Morgan, *The Puritan Family: Religion and Domestic Relations in Seventeenth Century New England* (New York, 1944, 1966 ed.) is outstanding. See also John Demos, *A Little Commonwealth: Family Life in Plymouth Colony* (New York, 1976) and Levin Shucking, *The Puritan Family: A Social Study from the Literary Sources* (London, 1969). Also relevant is James T. Johnson, *A Society Ordained by God: English Puritan Marriage Doctrine in the First Half of the Seventeenth Century* (Nashville, Tenn., 1970) and Roger Thompson, *Women in Stuart England and America: A Comparative Study* (London, 1974). More light on family life can be found in S. Fleming, *Children and Puritanism, 1620–1843* (Yale, 1933) and A.M. Earle, *Child-life in Colonial Days* (London, 1899). C.W. Bardsley, *Curiosities of Puritan Nomenclature* (London, 1888) touches upon a fascinating topic. A.M. Earle's *Sabbath in Puritan New England* (New York, 1900) describes Sundays that were far from joyless. David E. Stannard's, *The Puritan Way of Death: A Study in Religion, Culture and Social Change* (New York, 1977) is an account of changing attitudes to death as reflected in such externals as tombstones.

Communities are studied in Summer C. Powell, *Puritan Village: The Formation of a New England Town* (Middletown, Conn., 1963); Philip Greven, Jr, *Four Generations: Population, Land, and Family in Colonial Andover, Massachusetts* (Ithaca, N.Y., 1970); Kenneth A. Lockridge, *A New England Town: The First Hundred Years* (New York, 1970); and Michael Zuckerman, *Peaceable Kingdoms: New England Towns in the Eighteenth Century* (New York, 1970). Darrett B. Rutman, in *Winthrop's Boston: Portrait of a Puritan Town, 1630–1648* (University of North Carolina, 1965) argues that New England's leading city actually evolved in its first two decades in a way very different from the intention of its founders.

PURITANS AND THE ARTS

Percy Scholes surveys *The Puritans and Music in England and New England* (London, 1934). E.N.S. Thompson, *The Controversy Between the Puritans and the Stage* (New York, 1966) covers the general story, but Margot Heinemann argues convincingly in *Puritanism and Theatre: Thomas*

Middleton and Opposition Drama Under the Early Stuarts (Cambridge, 1980) that early seventeenth-century Parliamentary Puritanism must not be seen as united in opposition to the theatre. J.F. Parker, 'The Development of Fine Arts under the Puritans' (*Royal Hist. Soc. Trans.*, 1891). Dickran Tasjian and Ann Tasjian, *Memorials for Children of Change: The Art of Early New England Stonecarving* (Middlestown, Conn., 1973) explores a striking form of New England art.

As for English Puritan literature W.R. Parker, *Milton: A Biography* (Oxford, 1968) and the much shorter book by David Daiches, *Milton* (London, 1957) are both commended. Monica Furlong, *Puritan's Progress* (London, 1975) is a most readable introduction to John Bunyan, but other good biographies include those by R. Sharrock (London, 1954) and Ola E. Winslow (New York, 1961).

American Puritan literature is discussed by Kenneth B. Murdock, *Literature and Theology in Colonial New England* (Cambridge, Mass., 1949) and Sacvan Bercovitch, ed., *The American Puritan Imagination: Essays in Revaluation* (New York, 1974). Specific poets are examined in Elizabeth White, *Anne Bradstreet: 'The Tenth Muse'*. (New York, 1971) and Richard Crowder, *No Featherbed to Heaven: A Biography of Michael Wrigglesworth*, (East Lansing, 1962). Bercovitch's *The Puritan Origins of the American Self* (Princeton, 1976) looks at the continuing influence of Puritan ideas about America. In American literature these ideas first fused together into myth in Cotton Mather's biography of John Winthrop, to which Bercovitch devotes more than half his book.

American Puritan architecture is discussed by M.C. Donnelly, *The New England Meeting Houses of the Seventeenth Century* (Middleton, Conn., 1968) E.W. Sinnott, *Meeting House and Church in Early New England* (New York, 1969); M.S. Briggs, *The Homes of the Pilgrim Fathers in England and America* (Oxford UP, 1932).

PURITANISM AND SOCIETY

The social, religious, economic and political causes of the Puritan emigration to America are covered by Carl Bridenbaugh, *Vexed and Troubled Englishmen: 1590–1642* (London and New York, 1968); Allen French, *Charles I and the Puritan Upheaval: A Study of the Causes of the Great Migration* (London, 1955); Basil Willey, *The Seventeenth Century Background* (London, 1934); J.T. Cliffe, *The Yorkshire Gentry from the Reformation to the Civil War* (London, 1969); Wallace Notestein, *The English People on the Eve of Colonization* (New York, 1954); George Kitson Clark, *The English Inheritance*, (London, 1950).

The outstanding work in this field is Christopher Hill's *Society and Puritanism in Pre-Revolutionary England* (London, 1964), a discussion of the social and economic factors which encouraged the rise of Puritanism in England.

On Puritanism and capitalism M. Weber, *The Protestant Ethic* (English translation, London and New York, 1930) and R.H. Tawney, *Religion and the Rise of Capitalism* (London, 1926, Pelican ed. 1937 and New York 1947) should be read in conjunction with K. Samuelsson, *Religion and Economic Action* (English translation, London, 1961) and C. Hill's essay in *Essays in Economic and Social History of Tudor and Stuart England*, ed. F.J. Fisher (Cambridge, 1961). B. Bailyn's *The New England Merchants in the Seventeenth Century* (Harvard UP, 1955) is a subtle account of the intellectual and social context of commercial activity in early Massachusetts.

M. James, *Social Problems and Policy During the Puritan Revolution, 1640–1660* (London, 1930) is a guide to what the Puritans attempted when in power. See also W. Schenck, *The Concern for Social Justice in the Puritan Revolution* (London, 1948).

The foundations of Puritan social, economic and political thought are ably explored in Stephen Foster, *Their Solitary Way: The Puritan Social Ethic is the First Century of Settlement in New England* (New Haven and London, 1971). A documentary history of one area where the Puritans are much misunderstood is E. Powers, *Crime and Punishment in Early Massachusetts 1620–1692* (Boston, 1966). Kai T. Erikson, *Wayward Puritans: A Study in the Sociology of Deviance* (New York, 1966) covers the response to certain social problems.

The relation of Puritanism to the enduring folk religion of England is touched upon in Keith Thomas, *Religion and the Decline of Magic* (London and New York, 1971). The relative failure of the Puritan attempt to reform English national customs and attitudes is ably studied in K.E. Wrightson, 'The Puritan Reformation of Manners with special reference to the counties of Lancashire and Essex 1640–1660', (Cambridge Univ. Ph.D. thesis, 1973). See also R.C. Richardson, *Puritanism in North-West England* (Manchester, 1972).

On witchcraft, a subject which has had an exaggerated significance in the image of New England Puritanism, see Marion Starkey, *The Devil in Massachusetts* (New York, 1949); Chadwick Hansen, *Witchcraft at Salem* (New York, 1969); Paul Boyer and Stephan Nissenbaum, *Salem Possessed: The Social Origins of Witchcraft* (Cambridge, Mass., 1974); George L. Kittredge, *Witchcraft in Old and New England* (Harvard UP, 1929). To keep Salem truly in perspective read C. Larner, *Enemies of God: The Witch Craze in Scotland* (London, 1982).

PURITANISM AND EDUCATION

For the English Renaissance background, see J. Simon, *Education and Society in Tudor England* (Cambridge, 1966), which has an extensive bibliography, and Fritz Caspari, *Humanism and the Social Order in Tudor England* (Chicago, 1954). L.B. Wright's *Middle-Class Culture in Elizabet-*

han England (Chapel Hill, 1935) traces the dissemination of learning and the burgeoning of a popular culture based upon the Renaissance, Reformation and English tradition among urban merchants and trades-folk.

Richard L. Greaves, *The Puritan Revolution and Educational Thought* (Rutgers, 1969) explores among other topics the Puritans' contribution to the founding of new universities and their antipathy to the legal profession. W. Jordan, in *Philanthropy in England, 1480–1660* (New York, 1959) points that by 1660 there was a school for every 4,400 of population, and few boys lived more than 12 miles from a grammar school. W.A.L. Vincent, *The State and School Education 1640–1660* (London, 1950) charts this progress.

The enthusiasm of Puritans in America for education comes across in Lawrence Cremin, *American Education: The Colonial Experience, 1607–1783* (New York, 1970); James Axtell, *The School Upon a Hill: Education and Society in Colonial New England* (New Haven, 1974); Samuel Eliot Morison, *Harvard in the Seventeenth Century*, 2 vols (Boston, 1936); and Richard Warch, *School of the Prophets: Yale College, 1701–1740* (New Haven, 1973).

PURITANS AND OTHER NATIONS

Puritan attitudes to European nations are described by Marvin A. Breslow, *A Mirror of England: English Puritan Views of Foreign Nations 1618–1640* (Cambridge, Mass., 1970).

The relations of Puritans with Indians has become a popular topic. Alden T. Vaughan, *New England Frontier: Puritans and Indians 1620–1675* (Boston, 2nd ed. 1980) argues that the Puritans followed a remarkably humane, considerate and just policy in their dealings with the Indians, but Francis Jennings, *The Invasion of America: Indians, Colonialism and the Cant of Conquest* (University of North Carolina Press, 1975) takes the contrary view. See also C.M. Segal and D.C. Stinebach, *Puritans, Indians and Manifest Destiny* (Putnam, 1977). Karen O. Kupperman, *Settling with the Indians: The Meeting of English and Indian Cultures in America 1580–1640* (London, 1980) widens the discussion to include the colonies along the entire coast of North America and places it firmly in the context of English national attitudes and characteristics. Peter N. Carroll, *Puritanism and the Wilderness: The Intellectual Significance of the New England Frontier 1629–1700* (New York, 1965) looks at the general impact of the environment, including the sea voyage, on the Puritans.

Puritan missionary efforts are specifically dealt with in William Kellaway, *The New England Company: 1649–1776* (London, 1961) and Ola Winslow, *John Eliot: Apostle to the Indians* (Boston, 1968).

The various conflicts are described in H.M. Sylvester, *Indian Wars of*

New England (Boston, 1910, Vol. 1). The most important of them is narrated and analysed in Douglas Leach, *Flintlock and Tomahawk: New England in King Philip's War* (New York, 1966). Mary Rowlandson's account of her Indian captivity in 1675 is to be found in R. Van Der Beers, *Held Captive by Indians* (Univ. of Tennessee Press, 1973).

The Puritans were not racists: they thought the Indians were white men whose skins were darkened by the weather or skin dyes. They accepted imported African slaves but on a small scale. Then the Puritan conscience in New England helped to trigger off the anti-slavery movement. Lorenzo Greene, *The Negro in Colonial New England, 1620–1776* (New York, 1942) and Winthrop D. Jordan, *White Over Black: American Attitudes Toward the Negro 1550–1812* (Chapel Hill, N.C., 1968) should be read in conjunction with Bernard Rosenthal, 'Puritan Conscience and New England Slavery', *New England Quarterly*, 1973 and Robert C. Twombly and Robert H. Moore, 'Black Puritan: The Negro in Seventeenth Century Massachusetts', *William and Mary Quarterly* (1967).

Index

adultery, 256
Allen, Edward, 80–1
Allerton, Isaac, 19
Anabaptists, 46
Arminius, Jacobus, 171

Bacon, Francis, 274–5
Bancroft, Richard, 89
Barnes, Robert, 63–4
Baxter, Richard, 193, 209, 219–20, 253, 254, 266
Biddle, John, 263
Bilney, Thomas, 60, 61–2
Birch, John, 197, 200
Blackstone, Reverend William, 16–17
Boston, 17, 20
Bradford, Governor William, 18, 19, 117–26 passim
Brent, Sir Nicholas, 152, 153
Brewster, William, 116–17
Brooke, Lord, 184–7, 213, 215
Brown, Richard, 107
Brownists, 18, 20, 109, 116, 118
Bucer, Martin, 65, 90
Bunyan, John, 216
Burleigh, Captain, 5

Cabot, John, 34–5
Calvin, John, 54–6
Cambridge Agreement, 139
Carlstadt, Andreas, 45–6
Carr, James, 197
Carver, John, 120, 125
Cave, Sir Anthony, 66, 70, 71, 73–4
Chaderton, Dr Laurence, 90, 91, 92
Charles I, 153–4, 208
Charles II, 232

Charlestown, 16, 17, 20
Cheynell, Francis, 215, 219
Chillingworth, William, 215
Christmas celebrations, 226–8
Church of England, 89–90
Civil War, English, 177–8, 180–206
Clap, Captain John, 164–5
Colet, John, 24, 25–6, 28–9, 35–7, 38, 73
Columbus, Christopher, 34, 115
Commonwealth, 207–38
congregationalism, 52, 116
Cotton, John, 19, 164, 166, 172, 175, 178, 239, 241–3
Crashaw, William, 111–16
Croke, Sir George, 155–6
Cromwell, Oliver, 134, 143, 159–61, 178, 195, 202, 203, 204–5, 209, 218, 219, 230–1
Cromwell, Thomas, 30, 62, 63

Dale, Sir Thomas, 116
Daubeney, Oliver, 105, 106
Davenport, James, 263–4
Diggers, 215–16
Donne, John, 269
Dowsing, William, 270
Drake, Sir Francis, 110
Dudney, Thomas, 2, 12, 17, 20, 139, 164
Durston, Hannah, 261–2
Dyer, Mary, 244

Edgehill, Battle of, 182
Eiliot, John, 248
Eliot, Sir John, 146–8
Elizabeth I, 84–9 passim

Emerson, Ralph Waldo, 263
Endecott, Captain, 10, 11, 18–19, 166–7, 237, 240
English, character of, 98–101
Erasmus, Desiderius, 24–33 *passim*, 38–9, 49, 50, 53, 58, 60, 87, 90
Essex, Earl of, 181, 183, 187, 188, 193–4, 197

Fairfax, Sir Thomas, 204, 205
Fifth Monarchy Men, 216
Fox, George, 217–18
Foxe, John, 57–8, 76
freedom (*see also* individualism), 49–50
Frobisher, Martin, 108
Fuller, Dr, 19

Gardiner, Stephen, 75, 76, 77
Garrett, Richard, 21
Gilbert, Sir Humphrey, 108–9
Goodwin, Arthur, 189
Grand Remonstrance (1641), 158–9
Grenville, Sir Bevil, 161, 192
Grindal, Edmund, 87, 88

Hakluyt, Richard, 106–7, 109, 110
Hampden, John, 141, 142, 143, 148, 150, 152, 153, 154–8, 182–3, 187–9, 209, 271
Harley, Sir Robert, 210
Harrington, James, 277
Harvard University, 248–9
Haverhill (Massachusetts Bay), 259–62
Hawkins, Captain John, 107
Henry VIII, 30–1, 62–3
Higginson, Francis, 3, 8
Hoby, Lady Margaret, 93–7
Holles, Denzil, 220
Hopton, Lord, 190–1, 192, 197, 198, 200, 206
Humphrey, John, 2
Hunter, William, 79–80
Hutchinson, Anne, 171, 174, 175
Hythlodaye, Raphael, 34

Independents, 196, 208, 211, 212
Indians, 122–5, 261–2
individualism (*see also* freedom), 26, 27, 32, 213–14
Ingram, David, 107, 108
Ireton, Henry, 207, 209

Johnson, Isaac, 2, 16, 17, 138
Johnson, John, 66–74 *passim*
Johnson, Otwell, 69, 71, 72, 73
justification by faith, 42–4

Latimer, Hugh, 60–1, 61–2, 63, 83
Laud, Archbishop William, 152–3, 157
Levellers, 215
Lilly, William, 35–6, 37, 38
Locke, John, 235
Lollards, 58–9
Luther, Martin, 39–53, 59–60, 62–3, 64, 71

Machiavelli, Niccolo, 29–30
marriage, 57–9, 224–5, 251–9, 268–9
Martyr, Peter, 65, 87
Mary, Queen, 75–6
Mather, Cotton, 276
Mather, Increase, 238, 239, 247, 269
Mayflower, 1, 120–1
Melanchton, Philip, 49, 61, 62–3
Milborne, Captain Peter, 4, 6, 7, 11
Milton, John, 36, 198, 212–14, 250, 257–8, 270, 274, 285
More, Sir Thomas, 33–4, 37–8, 62, 63, 73
Muggletonians, 217

Nayler, James, 217–18
New Model Army, 204–6, 207, 209, 215
Newton, Sir Isaac, 275

Parker, Archbishop Matthew, 85–7 88
Peirce, Captain William, 10, 175
Penn, William, 245–6

Pepys, Samuel, 232, 236
Pericles, 27–8
Perkins, William, 96–7
Peter, Hugh, 170, 173, 178, 228, 229, 237–8, 251–2, 254, 255, 256–7, 263, 268, 277
Pilgrim Fathers, 116–26
plague, 71, 72
predestination, 49–50, 97
Presbyterians, 207–9, 211, 218–19, 220, 232
Puritans, Puritanism, 97–104, 235–6; attitude to science, 274–8; attitude to the Arts, 270–1; attitude to Christmas, 225–6; attitudes to love and marriage, 225, 250–9, 268–9; clothes, 225–6; decline in New England, 246–50; influence on America, 278–81; names, 216; preaching, 91–3; weddings, 225; work ethic, 265–8
Pynchon, William, 17, 243–4

Quakers, 217–18, 244–6

Raleigh, Sir Walter, 109
Reagan, Ronald, 279–80
Reformation (*see also* Calvin; Luther), 51–2, 53, 55, 65
Renaissance, 26–33, 35, 39
Restoration of Monarchy (1660), 232
Ridley, Bishop, 82
Robinson, John, 116, 117, 118, 119, 120
Rogers, Richard, 93
Royal Society, 276
Rump Parliament, 231

sacramental theology, 53–4
St Paul's school, 35–7
Salem, 10–11, 12
Saltonstall, Nathaniel, 260
Saltonstall, Sir Richard, 2, 22–3, 91, 139, 164, 240–1
Sandys, Sir Edwin, 87–8, 119
Saunders, Edward, 75

Saunders, Laurence, 69–70, 74, 75–9
science, 274–8
Seekers, 167–8
Shakespeare, William, 101–2
Ship Money tax, 154–8
Smith, Henry, 91
Smith, John, 110–11, 119, 120–1
stake, death at the, 81–3
Standish, Captain Miles, 120
Stapleton, Sir Philip, 208
sweating sickness, 72–3

Thacher, Anthony, 168–9
Thomkins, Thomas, 80
Trevor, Sir Thomas, 154–5
Twide, Richard, 107
Tyndale, William, 64

Unitarians, 262–3

Vane, Sir Henry, 170–1, 173, 174, 195, 196, 199, 200, 208, 222, 236, 244
Vinci, Leonardo da, 31–3
Virginia Company, 110–11

Waller, Lady Anne, 193–4
Waller, Sir William, 141, 142, 144, 145–6, 149–50, 160–1, 180, 184, 189–204 *passim*, 207, 208–9, 210–11, 214, 220–1, 222–4, 230–1, 233–4, 271
Walsingham, Sir Francis, 108
Ward, Nathaniel, 176–7, 259
Warr, Lord de la, 111, 115–16
Warwick, Earl of, 149
wedding days (*see also* marriage), 224–5
Wentworth, Sir Thomas, 157
Wesley, John, 264
Westminster Assembly, 211–13
Westminster Confession, 211
Wharton, Nehemiah, 180–1
Whitaker, Alexander, 116
Whitgift, John, 89
Williams, Roger, 167

Winslow, Edward, 19, 120
Winthrop, Henry, 12, 13
Winthrop, John, 1–23, 127–40,
  163–76 *passim*, 225, 239–40, 276,
  278–9, 282

work ethic, Puritan, 265–8
Worms, Diet of, 45
Wycliffe, John, 58, 60

Zwingli, Ulrich, 52–4